# Empire's
Reading Hardt and Negri
# New Clothes

# Empire's
Reading Hardt and Negri
# New Clothes

Edited by
Paul A. Passavant and Jodi Dean

Routledge
New York and London

Published in 2004 by
Routledge
29 West 35th Street
New York, NY 10001
www.routledge-ny.com

Published in Great Britain by
Routledge
11 New Fetter Lane
London EC4P 4EE
www.routledge.co.uk

10 9 8 7 6 5 4 3 2 1

Library of Congress Cataloging-in-Publication Data

Empire's new clothes: reading Hardt and Negri / edited by Paul A. Passavant and Jodi Dean
    p. cm.
Includes bibliographical references and index.
    ISBN: 0-415-93554-7 (hardback : alk. paper) — ISBN 0-415-93555-5 (pbk. : alk. paper)
    1. Empire. 2. Imperialism. 3. Political science. I. Passavant, Paul A. (Paul Andrew) II.
    Dean, Jodi, 1962-
        JC359.E458 2003
        325'.32—dc21                                                      2003006590

# Contents

# Acknowledgments

We would like to thank our contributors for their efforts to meet an accelerated timeline for this volume. We would also like to thank the editorial and production staff at Routledge for their fine work. We have received excellent research assistance from Matthew Simpson. Ernesto Laclau's chapter, "Can Immanence Explain Social Struggles?," originally appeared in the journal *Diacritics* 31:4 (2001), © The Johns Hopkins University Press. It is reprinted with permission of The Johns Hopkins University Press. Parts of Malcolm Bull's chapter, "Smooth Politics," appeared in "Hate is the new Love," London Review of Books, vol. 23 n. 2, 25 Jan 2001, pp. 23–4. Thomas Dumm's interview of Michael Hardt, "Sovereignty, Multitudes, Absolute Democracy," originally appeared in the online journal *Theory and Event* 4.3 (2000). A shorter version of "Representation and the Event" also appeared originally in *Theory and Event* 5.1 (2002). We have published here the longer version that was written in October of 2001 for *Theory and Event*'s symposium on September 11. Aside from a few minor editorial changes, it appears here as it was initially written in order to capture that particular moment. We would like to thank the editors of *Theory and Event* for their permission to republish these pieces here, and we would like to acknowledge Michael Hardt's generosity in this regard as well. Finally, Paul A. Passavant would like to thank Hobart and William Smith Colleges for a Faculty Development grant that facilitated this work.

# Postmodern Republicanism

## Paul A. Passavant

> *This book was begun well after the end of the Persian Gulf War and com-*
> *pleted well before the beginning of the war in Kosovo. The reader should*
> *thus situate the argument at the midpoint between those two signal events*
> *in the construction of Empire.*
>
> —Michael Hardt and Antonio Negri, *Empire*

This collection of critical responses to *Empire* was first discussed in conversations emerging from panels organized on *Empire* and on law and globalization at the Law and Society Association Annual Meetings held in Budapest, Hungary, in July of 2001, and at the Critical Legal Conference held at the University of Kent in Canterbury, Great Britain, in early September 2001 (where Antonio Negri took questions via video hookup from Italy). Hence the formation of this collection on *Empire* crossed the event of September 11.

This volume was sent to the publisher between two other events. On the one hand, the French foreign minister, Dominique de Villepin, drew unprecedented applause before the United Nations Security Council on February 14, 2003, when he stated, against the warmongering of the United States, that the "use of force" against Iraq as part of the U.S. "war on terror" was "not justified at this time." The foreign minister argued: "[i]n the temple of the United Nations, we are the guardians of an ideal, the guardians of a conscience. This onerous responsibility and immense honor . . . must lead us to give priority to disarmament through peace."[1] For the *New York Times* and its report on a statement issued by the fifteen heads of state of the European Union and their commitment to the United Nations as the center of the international order, it appeared that most European leaders differed from their American counterparts through a commitment to "a form of world government" and an "international civil service bureaucracy" with headquarters at the United Nations.[2]

On the other hand, on February 15 and 16, 2003, millions in cities worldwide, including New York City where the United Nations is located, protested the United States rush to war. The size of these demonstrations—the largest since the Vietnam War—forced coverage from even the sycophantic *New York Times*. Reflecting on the weekend's events, the *Times* reported that now there may be *two* superpowers in the world—the U.S. and world opinion, as evidenced by the massive show of democratic strength by the people who took to the streets.[3]

Much like the book *Empire*, this book of responses is forged within a context of exceptional global events. Things are now different, we are told incessantly by inescapable talking heads on media. And while we are told that this new timescape began ticking on September 11, many of our contributors share with Hardt and Negri a perception that September 11 merely crystallized conditions and developments that had existed previously. But what are these developments? Are we witnessing the development of Empire—a form of global sovereignty and legality—as it is called into being to address the twin threats to global peace posed by Saddam Hussein and George W. Bush, as would appear from the *New York Times* reportage on the European Union described above? Are we witnessing the birth of the *multitude*—a global biopolitical subject of absolute democracy—in the bodies mobilized onto the streets through global networks of communication to oppose the United States as the imperial police, also described above? Or are we witnessing not the *imperial* power of global sovereignty but the repetition of a more familiar *imperialist* power that the United States is attempting to claim for its own national interests in word, through its 2002 National Security policy, and in deed, through unilateral military action, as some of our contributors suggest?[4] The future is virtually multiple.

Michael Hardt's and Antonio Negri's remarkable book *Empire* is academia's version of a blockbuster. Not long after it was first published, it was described as the kind of intellectual event that "comes along only once every decade or so . . . the Next Big Idea."[5] Conversation about the book was said to be "everywhere" academics meet. Then came September 11. Those publications that had not yet reviewed the book stumbled over each other to do so now. Many of these reviews linked *Empire* to the events of September 11.[6] And some linked *Empire* to the protests against global capital and proceeded to associate both with terrorism.[7] No earlier publications by Hardt or Negri had become the kind of event *Empire* had. Conditions in the world have clearly changed in such a way that *Empire* could be perceived as relevant to it, even if some perceived it to be relevantly dangerous.

*Empire* is a book about globalization. In the story that Hardt and Negri tell, there are two main characters—Empire and the multitude. Empire is the form of sovereignty that exists under conditions of globalization. Hardt and Negri respond to the debate over whether global capitalism has caused sovereignty to decline by arguing that while the nation-state's sovereignty is indeed waning, this does not mean that sovereignty per se is in decline. Rather, sovereignty has been rescaled from the level of the nation-state to the level of the global. Of course, state institutions continue to exist. But now, when governments intervene to keep the peace, their police forces—whether we are talking about Seattle, Washington, in the United States or Genoa, Italy—act in the name of Empire in much the same way that U.S. judges act in the name of the American people and thereby materialize a national imaginary with their juridical actions whether their court is located in the first Circuit or the Ninth. The difference is that "America" is a national identity that is articulated to a given territory, while Empire, since it is global, is *deterritorialized*. There is a consistent juridical logic that the actions of police in Seattle share with the police in Genoa, and this is the logic of the imperial imperatives of Empire. Thus Hardt and Negri use jurisprudence as an index of changes in the present global order, and the result is an original contribution to debates over the fate of sovereignty in a globalized world.[8]

The second main character in *Empire* is the multitude. Hardt and Negri see the coming of Empire and the imperial world as good news in the same way that Karl Marx saw capitalism as good news. Both the imperial world and capitalism are oppressive forms of power that are parasitic upon our labor power, but the very conditions that define Empire will enable the possibility of its overthrow and the self-organization of democracy. The constituent power that will constitute this new world of absolute democracy is the multitude. As capital organizes itself globally to take advantage of a global labor pool and coordinates this activity through global communication networks, it gradually crosses the barriers between one nation and another or between home and factory. By developing increasingly hybrid and mobile subjects to serve its needs, the imperial world paves the way for a democracy that will no longer be limited by exclusionary national boundaries but will become truly global. Indeed, as the protests organized against global capital and a global war on terror illustrate, the very communication networks that elude national control and facilitate the control of global capital's various appendages can also facilitate the

self-organization of democratic action at a global level by a new political subject, the multitude.[9]

Against the background of thirty years of radical theory, we can see
another major contribution *Empire* makes. Since the events of 1968, much
radical academic theory has made its most significant contributions at the level
of micropolitics. Post-1968 radical theory took as its target the Marxism of the
Frankfurt School. This branch of Marxism posited a dominant ideology to
explain why the masses do not rise up against their oppressors—they suffer
from false consciousness and mistake oppression for freedom.[10] Much of the
post-1968 work took as its goal to disprove the notion that the masses suffer
from false consciousness by examining local acts of resistance that illustrate
how the masses have not swallowed the dominant ideology hook, line, and
sinker but instead act far more tactically and self consciously than the armchair
critical theorists assumed.[11] Cultural Studies in particular made important contributions by refusing to assume that a mass audience imbibed the intentions
of a capitalist producer through its consumption of a specific cultural artifact.
Instead, Cultural Studies researched how audiences used the materials their
culture provided them.

The notion of the "masses" slowly died as this research demonstrated the
multiple forms of identity that agents negotiate in their day-to-day life and how
resistance is often enacted by tactical appropriations of a specific mode of identification under specific conditions.[12] When attention went beyond momentary,
site-specific resistance, it focused on the new social movements—social movements that broke with the traditional labor-versus-capital assumptions about
oppression and resistance. These movements coalesced around identities that
the labor-capital dichotomy failed to address—such as race, gender, sexuality—
or issues such as peace or the environment.[13] A totalizing account of oppression or resistance became immediately suspect in academic circles, and along
the way the very notion of an emancipatory revolution got lost or was con-
signed to the dustbin of "totalizing theory." In light of the "Republican
Revolution" of 1994 in the United States and Nike's use of the Beatle's song of
the same name in its advertising, it appears that only "revolution" could be spo-
ken in public discourse. Today, revolution on a global scale against capital and
on behalf of labor has reentered academic discourse with the publication of
Hardt's and Negri's *Empire*, and this is an important contribution Hardt's and
Negri's *Empire* makes.

The remainder of this introduction will assess the distinctiveness of
Hardt's and Negri's approach to politics through a comparison with Hannah
Arendt. After describing their respective approaches to politics—how Arendt
emphasizes the necessity of separating politics from economic concerns, while
Hardt and Negri begin their political analyses upon the terrain of economic

production—we will then proceed to develop Hardt's and Negri's evaluation of emancipatory possibilities in the postmodern world by contrasting their normative vision with Arendt's. This comparison is productive in light of their similar descriptions of historical changes but the dramatically different consequences for politics that they draw from this shared empirical terrain. In particular, we will focus on their divergent perspectives on economy, labor, and place as bases for a politics of freedom and absolute democracy.

## Boundaries and Arendtian Politics

Arendt describes three different activities of life: labor, work, and action. Labor is an activity that focuses on the survival of the species and the biological processes of the human body. Work is human artifice that bestows a measure of permanence in the flux of life through the making of things. It is action, however, that is a truly human activity.

Action is coeval and coequal to speech, occurs in public before the eyes of all, and is necessarily performed with others. Action is political and it seeks to transcend the endless, repetitive cycles of nature—it seeks, that is, to produce an act that will leave a trace of our existence to be remembered by future generations. Action, with its potential for adding something new to the world that will be remembered after our death, gives us a measure of immortality in the otherwise endless flux of birth and death, eating and defecating, genesis and decomposition. This is what makes humanity distinct from nature, from animals—this possibility of transcendence and immortality through the memories of later generations who retell the stories in which we figured.

Action, and hence politics, can be contrasted with religion. Religion and good acts can only be corrupted by occurring in public (when giving a gift, let not thy left hand know what thy right hand doeth).[14] Also, unlike the concern for immortality through honorable or great acts that live on in the memory of one's fellow citizens and future generations, immortality, for the religious, occurs with one's God after death. Or as U.S. Supreme Court Justice Antonin Scalia puts it, for the religious, "death is no big deal."[15]

Arendt is critical of the hostility of religion to public practices and this lack of concern for posterity's memory of one's acts. For Arendt, without the possibility of "transcendence into a potential earthly immortality, no politics, strictly speaking, no common world and no public realm, is possible."[16] This earthly transcendence occurs in the stories that others tell of one's actions. Hence one who seeks fame must be willing to risk disclosure—actions must occur before others in common space.[17] Glory, Arendt writes, "is possible only in the public realm."[18] Political action is therefore "boundless." It is boundless because of human interrelatedness. The consequences of one's action and one's speech are unpredictable because the individual does not control the act. Indeed, the political significance of the act lies in the discourse that reiterates it: "Action reveals itself fully only to the storyteller . . . who indeed always knows better what it was all about than the participants. . . . Even though stories are inevitable results of action, it is not the actor but the storyteller who perceives and 'makes' the story."[19] Political action therefore requires the presence of others.

Politics also requires the constitution of distinct spaces for Arendt—a *polis* and a public realm. Violence, the legal architecture of this *polis*, and the walls around the city are all prepolitical. But these boundaries are the conditions of possibility for political action insofar as they secure a space within which one may act politically, insofar as they constitute a commons.[20]

According to Arendt, these boundaries also separate the public from the private realm. In the private realm, we reproduce our natural lives. The private realm, the *oikos* (home), is where we take care of our necessities, and only once one has mastered the necessities of biological life can one become free to join with equals in the common pursuit of greatness. Otherwise one is still considered a slave—a slave to necessity. Securing the necessities of life is a condition of possibility for free political action in the public realm.

To enter public life requires courage, Arendt argues, because one must not be preoccupied with one's own life and survival, which are private concerns. One must be ready to risk one's life for politics, since politics is never for the sake of life.[21] Labor, that which is concerned merely with life's necessities, does not distinguish our truly human capabilities. Labor is what humans share with animals.

In the modern world, Arendt argues, this firm boundary between public and private has broken down. With the rise of the nation-state, we have witnessed the rise of the social, a making public of properly private concerns. In the modern world, the nation-state has taken responsibility for helping to secure life's necessities, for instance, through the social-welfare state. Thus politics has come to concern itself with that which is necessary for the reproduction of life.

Of course, such an outcome is unfortunate in Arendt's eyes. For Arendt, political economy is a contradiction in terms (as the economy was properly located in the *oikos*). Now society is organized as one superfamily, and politics is reduced to a nationwide administration of housekeeping.[22] Moreover, a successful economy requires unity, which in turn requires command and relations of inequality. Thus the politicization of the economy means that household unity has become socialized, laying the material conditions for making predictable statements regarding political and economic behavior (the behavioral sciences) but also diminishing the possibility for free political action to bring something new into the world. A society where one's primary purpose in life is to be a consumer, for Arendt, is a society that has witnessed the death of politics. Indeed, it is a society that has perhaps forgotten what it means truly to be human.

## Boundaries and Postmodern Republicanism

Hardt's and Negri's postmodern republicanism also describes how the boundaries between public and private no longer make sense. In contrast to Arendt, for whom the maintenance of boundaries, such as the distinction between public and private, is vital for the preservation of politics and freedom, Hardt and Negri celebrate the demise of boundaries as leading to emancipatory possibilities. I consider three areas where this occurs in Hardt's and Negri's thought. These three areas are changes in geography, changes in the organization of economic production, and changes in labor.

First, regarding geographic changes, Hardt and Negri argue that the public spaces of the modern world have disappeared. Boundaries, such as those between inside and outside, have eroded. Thus, instead of the firm divisions of public and private upon which Arendtian politics is based, we have witnessed the privatization of public space through the rise of shopping malls and gated communities (183–188). Rather than bemoaning the loss of a bygone era, Hardt and Negri argue that postmodern republicanism must rethink politics without an outside and invent a purely immanent and immediate politics; it must create a new ontology.[23]

Second, Hardt and Negri describe how changes in economic production from Fordism to a post-Fordist model of economic organization eviscerate boundaries between home and factory or nation and nation. Fordism organized industrial production within the factory and relied on a large-scale workforce. The interests of labor were represented by unions, and the state sought to mediate between the interests of labor and the interests of capital. The "social state" was born, "which took into account more widely and deeply the life cycles of populations, ordering their production and reproduction within a scheme of collective bargaining fixed by a stable monetary regime" (244). In exchange for a disciplined workforce, labor received adequate wages and social-welfare benefits from the social-welfare or "New Deal" state.

Today, we live under conditions of post-Fordism. Production is decentered and dispersed transnationally. Capital has extended "wage liberation" to peasants previously outside capitalist markets by siting factories in the "Third World," for example. It also makes use of a mobile workforce such as Mexican farm workers in California, or Palestinian and Pakistani engineers in the Middle East oil industry, or Filipino domestic workers in Hong Kong, or New

York financiers in London. With "informatization," new communications networks enable the coordination of deterritorialized production, increases in production efficiencies, and a new organization of the workforce. That is, workgroups are now more cooperatively organized, and the division between home and factory has broken down with telecommuting. Through communicative capitalism—capitalism that travels through communicative networks and catches on like a virus so that nothing can remain outside of it and indeed even communication about its problems winds up extending and deepening its hold—discipline has extended beyond the walls of the factory. We are both mommy or daddy *and* accounts manager *simultaneously* when we telecommute. New subjectivities are being formed that are hybrid, mobile, and that experience a real subsumption within the capitalist order.

This new organization of capital and the labor force, however, has also produced the material conditions of possibility for global communism. Deterritorializing capital has outrun the state's efforts to code or dam its streaming effects; or as Hardt and Negri put it: "corporations now rule the earth" (306).[24] The conditions of production have produced the conditions for revolution, as the incorporation of peasants as wage laborers produces "new desire for liberation" (252, emphasis removed). Hybrid, mobile, cooperating labor can cease to be a disciplined national workforce and can become the multitude.

Third, the change in economic regimes has also produced changes in labor. Indeed, new subjectivities are born on the terrain of production. Hardt and Negri argue that our laboring bodies create all value, value that is immeasurable. Therefore production takes center stage in their analyses, the production of social being (28). This production is described by Hardt and Negri as *biopolitical.*

Biopolitics is a term Hardt and Negri borrow from Michel Foucault. Biopolitics concerns not a way of life (which would be the question of politics for Arendt) but biological life itself—our body as a species, biological processes, and the supervision of a "population." Forms of power that arose in the seventeenth century, according to Foucault, sought to take charge of life. Forms of knowledge that facilitated this shift in the organization of power include the rise of public health, demography, and eugenics. In this way, the life and health of the population became a central political preoccupation. But when mass life is a constant political question, mass death is a constant political possibility.[25]

Production is biopolitical for Hardt and Negri. As members of a species, we reproduce. But economic production is also biopolitical. Labor produces affect and desire. This is illustrated by the way nurses relieve anxiety or make patients happy as part of the medical care they provide their patients. Consider as well the way in which commodities incite desire in us. Moreover, we *produce* our lives as social beings. Rather than relying on a stark contrast between the natural as that which is unchanging and given and the social as variable and artificially constructed, Hardt's and Negri's analyses reject such a division. On the one hand, "nature" adapts to environmental changes just as social identities do. On the other hand, in our "social" nature we are *desiring* machines. According to Hardt and Negri, "there are no fixed and necessary boundaries between the human and the animal, the human and the machine, the male and the female." Rather, they urge the "recognition that nature itself is an artificial terrain open to ever new mutations, mixtures, and hybridizations. . . ." A new social being requires a differently embodied existence. In this light, Hardt and Negri diagnose hopeful possibility in the changes in our bodily culture: "Today's corporeal mutations constitute an anthropological exodus and represent an extraordinarily important, but still quite ambiguous, element of the configuration of republicanism 'against' imperial civilization" (215). For Hardt and Negri, then, instead of a divide between the natural and the social, it is better to say that life is creative. Production produces new forms of life and incites new desires, creating new beings—new assemblages of desire in new machines.

The changes in the economy that highlight service, the affective labor of the helping professions, and the heightened importance of the entertainment industry mean that the products of those who labor in these industries include feelings of "well-being, satisfaction, excitement, or passion." These industries specialize in the "creation and manipulation of affect." This affective labor is labor in a bodily mode and it also produces "social networks, community, biopower" (293). Together with "informatization," conditions have been produced enabling a new, hybrid, and desiring social being that is capable of global communism, of acting as a joyful, constituent power. This new mode of being, what Hardt and Negri call the multitude, is a biopolitical form of life that exists purely on the plane of immanence and it constitutes the ontological basis for absolute democracy, for life that exceeds any attempt to represent or measure its value—legally, nationally, or financially.

## Assessing Economy

While Hardt and Negri share Arendt's descriptions of what we may call, to continue borrowing Foucault's term, the rise of *biopolitics*, their normative conclusions for contemporary political life following from this insight differ dramatically. For Arendt, economics implies relations of command and inequality in order to impose a functionally useful unity, represented traditionally by the head of household.[26] Therefore, the escape of economics from the *oikos* and the state of national housekeeping that has been caused by the rise of the social contaminates politics, which is based in a condition of plurality and upon relations among equals. For Hardt and Negri, this analysis is time-bound to the social-welfare state. The power of the state to mediate conflict between labor and capital and to represent the interests of all as a unified identity transcending any particular interests is the cause of the unity that Arendt links with the rise of the social. Thus Hardt and Negri associate the repressive unity due to the power of command with state sovereignty and the disciplinary institutions of civil society that mediate social conflict rather than relations of economy per se (328–330). For Hardt and Negri, the transcendent power of sovereignty represses difference and coerces unity.

## Assessing Labor

Arendt is highly critical of deriving politics from labor. Labor concerns the cycles of nature. Labor is the toil that is necessary for biological life to continue; it produces goods that life must consume. The products of labor are therefore spent almost immediately after their production. Hence, despite the urgency of this production for survival, labor is ultimately futile in Arendt's estimation.

Labor ends only in death; because none of its products last, it fails to transcend nature's metabolism. Labor never produces anything other than life, and thus Arendt disdains the celebration of labor insofar as labor does not allow humans to distinguish themselves from the flux of the natural world. The dominance of consumer society, therefore, is the dominance of a society that has succumbed to the cycle of life and fails to produce anything durable. This society is organized merely to meet appetites. For Arendt, the heightened productivity that automation enables only makes matters worse in that the rhythm of machines will amplify the rhythms of nature.[27] In our capacity as laborers or consumers of the products of labor, we are no better than animals.[28]

Hardt and Negri assess labor differently for at least three reasons. First, as productive excess, as life, labor's value is "beyond measure." Since labor is beyond measure, attempts to calculate and thereby capture labor or life's value—whether through financial, legal, or national means—are doomed to failure and injustice, negating aspects of labor's value. Labor is an expression of desire, an expression of the vitality of life in a productive context, the creation of new values (356–359).

Second, labor provides the ontological basis for global democracy, for the birth to presence of the multitude. Labor is transnational. With informatization, labor is increasingly hybrid and mobile. Furthermore, one of the changes in the organization of labor is that it has become more cooperative for the purposes of problem-solving. Arendt would reject this mode of interaction as "cooperation" because the division of labor is based on the fact that two individuals can put their labor power together and behave toward each other as though they were one. For Arendt, this oneness is the opposite of cooperation, particularly political cooperation which emerges out of human plurality and difference, since it promotes a unity of the species that implies that all its members are the same and interchangeable.[29] Hardt and Negri, however, argue that work is no longer organized according to Taylorist tenets—immaterial labor, for instance, focuses on symbolic manipulation and problem-solving. Immaterial labor is a form of work that has changed to become more cooperative (291–294). This cooperation, then, along with the mobility and hybridity of labor, can become the ontological basis for global communism.

Third, the fact that labor is productive of life does not characterize a lack of value, for Hardt and Negri, but rather indicates its excessive value. We can gesture towards this value by considering briefly the vitalism of Gilles Deleuze. For Deleuze there is a kind of unity to Being. In *Difference and Repetition*, Deleuze writes: a "single voice raises up the clamour of being."[30] Here Deleuze expresses the commonality, the multiplicity, and the singularity of Being. Being is multiple multiplicities. We are not one but an assortment of qualities we share with divergent others, like an infinite dispersal of family resemblances. We are members of an infinite number of sets of attributes. A clamor expresses this multiplicity—*multiple* voices are raised in a clamor. Being is common, and this also is expressed by a clamor—this multiplicity is joined together in *common* through this clamour. Finally, a being is completely singular. One blade of grass differs from another infinitely, as one blade of grass differs from me infinitely. A *single* voice. . . .

Toward the end of his life, Deleuze sought to express this sense of life. Immanence, he wrote, "is not related to Some Thing as a unity superior to all things or to a Subject as an act that brings about a synthesis of things: it is only when immanence is no longer immanent to anything other than itself that we can speak about a plane of immanence."[31] This is why singularity is not the same thing as the "individual." Whenever immanence is interpreted as immanence *to* something, say, the individual, this formulation reintroduces transcendence, here with the individual who reintroduces a falsely transcendent unity. An individual cannot contain the plane of immanence.

"What is immanence? A life . . ." And no one, according to Deleuze, has described a life better than Charles Dickens. Dickens describes a contemptible man who lies dying. Everyone around who cares for him bustles about to save him:

[I]n his deepest coma, this wicked man himself senses something soft and sweet penetrating him. But to the degree that he comes back to life, his saviors grow colder, and he becomes once again mean and crude. Between his life and his death, there is a moment that is only *a* life playing with death. The life of the individual gives way to an impersonal and yet singular life that releases a pure event. . . . It is a haecceity no longer of individuation but of singularization: a life of pure immanence, neutral, beyond good and evil, for it was only the subject that incarnated it in the midst of things that made it good or bad. The life of such individuality fades away in favor of the singular life immanent to a man who no longer has a name, though he can be mistaken for no other. A singular essence, a life . . .[32]

Somewhere between life and death in this example, this particular man ceased to be and instead became impersonal life, the cherished, vital power we share with all. This life can also be perceived in small children, Deleuze notes. Infants and small children all resemble one another. And although they hardly have any individuality, they have singularities: "a smile, a gesture, a funny face." In small children, one can perceive "an immanent life that is pure power and even bliss."[33] This is the beauty, the power of life beyond measure: *a* life . . .

## Assessing Place

Arendt recognizes that action, that is, speech or communication, since it requires the presence of others, is potentially boundless. One acts in concert with others in a web of previously existing acts and words of others and in so doing enters the "boundlessness of human interrelatedness." Action, then, cuts across all boundaries and forces open all limitations upon human affairs. But rather than celebrating this fact of the boundlessness of speech—the productivity of action—and seeking to extend it, she reminds us that fences and laws are necessary to make the *polis*. Boundaries make possible political existence even if the actions that issue forth from this place extend beyond it.[34]

According to Arendt, politics can occur only once a definite place has been constituted. Political action requires a structure to have been built where subsequent actions can take place. Action requires city walls and laws to secure the space from which action can occur. Action, in the Arendtian sense, and speech are coterminous because the lack of speech indicates the lack of a subject, the lack of an actor. The *polis*, its language, and other cultural materials for signification—including those with whom one can engage in discourse and who will remember the events of this day and reiterate these memories and the discursive structures of the *polis* (the discursive structures which in turn will enable future generations to become actors)—are necessary conditions of possibility for political action.[35]

Hardt and Negri describe proliferating networks of communication as constructing Empire but as also constituting the conditions of possibility for the formation of the multitude and absolute democracy. The multitude contests Empire on its own level of generality as another deterritorializing power of non-place, as a counterglobalization (206–207). It is a concrete universal, a common species (362). The multitude is absolute democracy, an "absolute and equal inclusion of the entire immanent social plane."[36] The multitude, therefore, is not a particular people—a people is a *representation* of a plane of singularities that represses and excludes difference, while forcefully imposing a false unity upon this plane. Representation—as a nation, people, or other specific social identity—is necessarily alienating by re-presenting to one who one is or what one desires from the outside. The multitude—like Empire—is inclusive and deterritorializing.

Therefore, like Arendt, Hardt and Negri recognize the boundlessness of networks of communication and how this interrelatedness is deterritorializing. But while Arendt argues that boundaries and limits are necessary to constitute political space and the possibility for political action, Hardt and Negri celebrate the existential fact of an infinite web of interrelatedness as the condition of possibility for absolute democracy, for the formation of the multitude. The multitude is antagonistic to any constitutional state, since constitutions limit democracy. It is also antagonistic, as we have just seen, to the limits of any specific place or community, since the city walls would institutionalize a relation of inequality between insider and outsider—again compromising the absoluteness of democracy.

## Political Events

We can further illustrate this contrast on territories and deterritorialization between Arendt and Hardt and Negri and its potential implications for global democracy with reference to the French foreign minister Villepin's speech. Foreign Minister Villepin describes an "onerous responsibility" and "immense honor" that obliges disarmament through peace. In the "temple of the United Nations, we are the guardians of an ideal, the guardians of a conscience."[37] The foreign minister, before the eyes and ears of others, has given a courageous speech in which for peace he is standing up to an imperialist power with awesome military strength. This is a risk, but to do less would be to default on our obligations to future generations. The French foreign minister guards an imagined future that will have happened, a future to come, perhaps, of global democracy. We are responsible to future generations who will have remembered this event, for this future of global democracy, of human rights, of peace. These ideals demand that we decide how to act conscientiously for their realization. In the eyes of our posterity—our future—we will have been honored in these risky decisions we take today, perhaps. The felt presence of this future constitutes our conscience in these matters. The French foreign minister, then, is an actor in a story about shared global responsibility for democracy, human rights, peace, and opposition to militaristic imperialism despite the odds. The possibility of this story is that to which we owe responsibility.

If we bring an Arendtian perspective to bear on this event, we would note first that it brought something new into the world. The unprecedented applause that arose from the gallery after his speech indicated that another world politics beyond national self-interest and imperialist militarism—one based on peace and international law—was in the process of becoming actual. The French foreign minister's action issued from a specific place—the United Nations. It was done before the eyes of others. It was a courageous act. He made use of the materials this institution gives him—a story about the horrors of war and genocide, a story represented pictorially in Pablo Picasso's artwork that Ambassador John Negroponte and Secretary of State Colin Powell shrouded, hopefully more out of shame than mendacity.[38] It is a story about the dangers of aggressive militarism; the preference for international law over war as a method for settling disputes; and a commitment to human rights made in several public declarations. The foreign minister is seeking to recall the community that declared itself committed to these rights, a community that does not exist outside of such calls and responses, that comes to exist through the performance of such speech acts. This commitment, then, may come to be a governing force in world politics in a way that is completely new in response to this call. For this act to occur, the foreign minister must use linguistic conventions that we can understand while he simultaneously reiterates their existence as conventions so that they are not lost to their posterity. He is a recognizably political actor in a story the contours of which are controlled now largely by the readers of this book, among others. The reason for this, according to Arendt, is that we act with others who are also capable of action, hence the outcome of our interventions in the web of human interaction is unpredictable at the moment of the event.

For Hardt and Negri, however, the fact that political action must issue from an established place is precisely the problem. The foreign minister's speech sets forth the place of its enunciation—he is speaking in the "temple of the United Nations." The foreign minister purchases significance for his speech from the authority of the United Nations, an authority he himself helps to sacralize. The authority of his voice comes, therefore, from the fact that he is authorized by the constituted power of the United Nations as an institution. His speech takes for granted the authority of the United Nations and seeks to use it against the United States and Great Britain.

When one's speech issues forth from a definite place, it must claim this place as its own in order to gain standing as a speaker. Despite the fact that one may speak against war and in favor of human rights, despite the fact that one may offer or grant hospitality in a given place, to do any of these acts requires one to stand upon grounds previously constituted by power. This, in turn, requires one to ignore, even if temporarily, the diversity of claims that might be made upon a place; the fact that it is haunted by the others who have been warned or eradicated from this place to make it "yours"—even if you are offering it in a gesture of hospitality to nurture or provide sustenance to yet another.[39]

While international law is a method for dealing with disputes that is preferable to war, to lend authority to international law occludes the acts of repression and exclusion that lie beneath it. Even putting to one side the question of the way that the U.N. Security Council has been constituted by a sort of victor's law, the constituent elements in international law are nations.[40] Within a legal system whose primary subjects remain nation-states, indigenous peoples, for example, are placed in a system institutionalized upon grounds that continue to negate their existence.[41] During the nineteenth century, John Stuart Mill argued that the treatment of colonized barbarians did not violate international law since barbarians were not nations.[42] Nationalism is a form of representation that enacts exclusions and repressions of the multiplicity of cultures that have inhabited even "old" nations like France.

Thus Hardt's and Negri's analyses suggest that there may be a hidden authoritarianism that lies within Arendtian republicanism. This republican politics is based upon defending the constituted forms of power congealed within the grounds upon which the subject gains standing as a speaker.[43] The power that authorizes speech is not questioned but reiterated and relied upon in the political act. Hardt and Negri wish to challenge all constituted power since it necessarily represses, excludes, and alienates the power that belongs to the multitude—constituent power. According to Hardt and Negri, the latter form of power—constituent power—is coextensive with democracy. Therefore absolute democracy requires that constituent power remain "alien to the law."[44]

## Specters of Machiavelli

Niccolò Machiavelli concludes *The Prince* by wondering whether the "times are propitious to honour a new prince, and whether the circumstances existed here which would make it possible for a prudent and capable man to introduce a new order."[45] What would this new order become, and who is Machiavelli trying to convince? Machiavelli, Antonio Gramsci notes, does not engage in "disquisitions and pedantic classifications," as another political scientist might have, but begins through tracing "the qualities, characteristic traits, duties, necessities of a concrete person . . . [to] excite the artistic fantasy of those he wants to convince and give a more concrete form to political passions." Machiavelli's epilogue to *The Prince*, Gramsci argues, "is not something extrinsic, 'stuck on,' from outside, rhetorical, but must be understood as a necessary part of the work, and, moreover, as that part which sheds a true light over the whole work and makes it seem like a 'political manifesto.'" Through this symbol of a leader, "Machiavelli makes himself the people, merges himself with the people." These are not the "people in a 'general' sense, but . . . the people whom Machiavelli has convinced with the preceding tract."[46] Through this entire practice—analysis, artistry, exhortation, reading, interpellation—this people may come to arrive as Machiavelli, however tentatively, expresses their popular consciousness. Who is this new people? We know now that the concept of a national people and the Italian national people have been summoned by Machiavelli's political act.

Who, Gramsci wonders, will be Italy's modern prince? It cannot be a real person but, rather, it must be a "complex element of society in which the cementing of a collective will, recognized and partially asserted in action, has already begun." The modern prince will have to devote himself significantly to the question of "world outlook," creating the basis for the development of a collective will directed towards the "realisation of a higher and total form of modern civilization." Gramsci conceives this ideological perspective as a kind of "public spirit." Does such a thing exist? Can it be developed? Were public spirit to emerge, it would presuppose some form of continuity, whether with the past or with the future, that is, it would presuppose that "every act is a stage in a complex process which has already begun and which will continue." We would feel solidarity with the very old; we would feel solidarity with the babies for whom we are responsible. For Gramsci, if it can be said that "public spirit" infuses our practices, we would need "time and again to fight against distortions of it and deviations from it." The party spirit, Gramsci argues, is a fundamental element of this public spirit and must be sustained in order to defend this public spirit. The party will take on the role of the Prince in modern times and aim to found "a new type of State."[47] Thus, for Gramsci, history provides an equivalent to Machiavelli's Prince in "the political party: the first cell containing the germs of collective will which are striving to become universal and total."[48]

Today we are told that global capital has made national sovereignty an anachronism and that it no longer makes sense to speak in terms of public and private.[49] How are we to make sense of our present? Gramsci reminds us that Machiavelli was "not merely a scientist; he is a partisan, with mighty passions, an active politician, who wants to create new relations of forces and because of this, cannot help concerning himself with 'what should be.'" The active politician, for Gramsci, is a creator or an awakener, but he doesn't create out of nothing. According to Gramsci, he "bases himself on effective reality ," but not something static—rather, a "relationship of forces in continuous movement and change of equilibrium." In this way:

> To apply the will to the creation of a new balance of the really existing and operating forces, basing oneself on that particular force which one considers progressive, giving it the means to triumph, is still to move within the sphere of effective reality, but in order to dominate and overcome it (or to contribute to this). "What should be" is therefore concrete, and it is moreover the only realistic and historicist interpretation of reality; it is the only active history and philosophy, the only politics.[50]

Hence our analysis of the present, of what "exists," is also, immediately, political. So many things are determined that we bear the "onerous responsibility and immense honor" of deciding which of the futures that are determined is progressive and of trying to summon it into existence, like Machiavelli, like Gramsci, even if the consequences of events crossing the limits of the present are unpredictable. As they were for Machiavelli. As they were for Gramsci.

In some ways, Hardt and Negri have been writing the same book now for over ten years, singly or collectively, with restless repetition. Is this output perhaps animated by the tortured spirit of Machiavelli or the imprisoned Gramsci as they trace the outlines of their hopes for republicanism, for revolution, for democracy? Like Machiavelli's Prince or Gramsci's Party, Hardt and Negri assert rights and hope that the multitude will take shape in these claims on the multitude's behalf—the right to global citizenship, the right to a social wage, and the right to reappropriation. Just as Machiavelli made himself the people, so do Hardt and Negri make themselves the multitude in these demands that conclude *Empire*, hoping to will into existence those who will have been convinced by the book. The analysis must be at the same time a manifesto.

It is telling, then, that the world has changed in such a way that *Empire* has become the event that it has, that people can see their world through these imperial eyes. And the denunciations that followed September 11 also speak to an important change—to denounce, one must concede the existence of that which you would seek to ban. Events today allow us to see the virtual existence of multiple futures. Will the United Nations act as a hinge that swings government out towards Empire? Will democracy stop a war that is said to be unstoppable? Will the actions of the United States lead to a future of nationally inspired military imperialism—a future even Hardt himself can sense and fear?[51] All of these futures are determined and exist, virtually. All are becoming in these events. In sum, will the conditions of the world be as propitious to a book on the multitude as they were to a book on Empire?

## Acknowledgments

I wish to acknowledge the comments of Jodi Dean on an earlier version of this introduction as well as conversations and arguments about *Empire* I have had with her in the months leading up to these conferences and in the time since—their influence pervades this essay. I have also benefited from numerous discussions of these subjects with Peter Fitzpatrick.

## Notes

1. "French Minister Delivers Appeal for More Time," *New York Times*, February 15, 2003, A11.

2. Richard Bernstein, "Nations Seek World Order Centered on U.N., not U.S.," *New York Times*, February 19, 2003, A16.

3. Patrick Tyler, "A New Power in the Streets: A Message to Bush Not to Rush to War," *New York Times*, February 17, 2003, A1.

4. In this volume, see Kevin Dunn, "Africa's Ambiguous Relation to Empire and *Empire*"; Mark Laffey and Jutta Weldes, "Representing the International: Sovereignty after Modernity?"; Peter Fitzpatrick, "The Immanence of *Empire*."

5. Emily Eakin, "What Is the Next Big Idea? The Buzz Is Growing," *New York Times*, July 7, 2001, B7.

6. Malcolm Bull, "You Can't Build a New Society with a Stanley Knife," *London Review of Books*, October 4, 2001, 3.

7. Peter Beinart, "Sidelines," *New Republic*, September 24, 2001, 8.

8. Michael Hardt and Antonio Negri, *Empire* (Cambridge, MA: Harvard University Press, 2000), 9. Subsequent references to *Empire* will be made parenthetically within the text.

9. Farah Stockman, "Opposition over Iraq Takes Rise via the Net," *Boston Globe*, October 14, 2002, p. A1. Jodi Dean's "The Networked Empire: Communicative Capitalism and the Hope for Politics," this volume, investigates this "flip" from technologies of control to technologies of liberation.

10. Max Horkheimer and Theodor Adorno, "The Culture Industry: Enlightenment as Mass Deception," in *Dialectic of Enlightenment*, trans. John Cumming (New York: Continuum, 1991).

11. Michel de Certeau, *The Practice of Everyday Life*, trans. Steven Rendall (Berkeley, CA: University of California Press, 1984).

12. John Fiske, "British Cultural Studies and Television," in *Channels of Discourse, Reassembled*, ed. Robert Allen (Chapel Hill, NC: University of North Carolina Press, 1992), 284–326; Dick Hebdige, *Subculture: The Meaning of Style* (New York: Methuen, 1979).

13. Alberto Melucci, *Nomads of the Present: Social Movements and Individual Needs in Contemporary Society*, ed. John Keane and Paul Mier (Philadelphia: Temple University Press, 1989); Jean Cohen, "Strategy or Identity: New Theoretical Paradigms and Contemporary Social Movements," *Social Research* 52 (1985): 663–716; Claus Offe, "New Social Movements: Challenging the Boundaries of Institutional Politics," *Social Research* 52 (1985): 817–868; Alain Touraine, "An Introduction to the Study of Social Movements," *Social Research* 52 (1985): 749–787.

14. Hannah Arendt, *The Human Condition* (Chicago: University of Chicago Press, 1998), 74.

15. Antonin Scalia, "God's Justice and Ours," *First Things* 123 (May 2002): 19. Thanks to Pierre Passavant for this reference.

16. Arendt, *Human Condition*, 55.

17. For a discussion of the appreciation of fame among the framers of the U.S. Constitution, see Douglass Adair, *Fame and the Founding Fathers*, ed. H. Trevor Colbourn (New York: W. W. Norton, 1974); Garry Wills, *Explaining America: The Federalist* (New York: Penguin Books, 1981), 83–84.

18. Arendt, *Human Condition*, 180.

19. Ibid., 192

20. Ibid., 194–195.

21. Ibid., 36–37.

22. Ibid., 28–29.

23. With this emphasis on ontology and the need for politics to recognize a new ontology, Hardt's and Negri's work converges with the emerging work of a number of other philosophers; see Alain Badiou, *Ethics: An Essay on the Understanding of Evil*, trans. Peter Hallward (New York: Verso, 2001); Giorgio Agamben, *Homo Sacer: Sovereign Power and Bare Life*, trans. Daniel Heller-Roazen (Minneapolis: University of Minnesota Press, 1998); Jean-Luc Nancy, *Being Singular Plural*, trans. Robert D. Richardson and Anne E. O'Byrne (Stanford, CA: Stanford University Press, 2000).

24. See also Gilles Deleuze and Felix Guattari, *Anti-Oedipus: Capitalism and Schizophrenia*, trans. Robert Hurley et al. (Minneapolis: University of Minnesota Press, 1983); Paul Patton, *Deleuze and the Political* (New York: Routledge, 2000).

25. Michel Foucault, *The History of Sexuality: An Introduction*, vol. 1, trans. Robert Hurley (New York: Vintage, 1990), 133–159.

26. Arendt, *Human Condition*, 31, 39–40.

27. Ibid., 87–135

28. For Alain Badiou also, mere life is beneath good and evil and it is what we humans share with animals. For Badiou, to become distinctively human or a subject, one must distinguish oneself from one's existence as a member of a biological species. See Badiou, *Ethics*, 12–13, 41, and passim.

29. Arendt, *Human Condition*, 123.

30. Gilles Deleuze, *Difference and Repetition*, trans. Paul Patton (New York: Columbia University Press, 1994), 35.

31. Gilles Deleuze, "Immanence: A Life," in *Pure Immanence: Essays on A Life*, trans. Anne Boyman (New York: Zone Books, 2001), 27. For a discussion of the question of positing something as immanent to something else in *Empire*, see Peter Fitzpatrick, "The Immanence of *Empire*," in this volume.

32. Deleuze, "Immanence: A Life," 28–29. Deleuze is drawing from Charles Dickens, *Our Mutual Friend*, (New York: Oxford University Press, 1989).

33. Deleuze, "Immanence: A Life," 28–30. For a discussion, see Giorgio Agamben, "Absolute Immanence," in *Potentialities: Collected Essays in Philosophy*, trans. Daniel Heller-Roazen (Stanford, CA: Stanford University Press, 1999): 220–239.

34. Arendt, 191–192.

35. Ibid., 194–195, 178.

36. Michael Hardt and Antonio Negri, *Labor of Dionysus: a Critique of the State Form* (Minneapolis: University of Minnesota Press, 1994), 290.

37. "French Foreign Minister Delivers Appeal for More Time," *New York Times*, February 15, 2003, A11.

38. Maureen Dowd, "Powell without Picasso," *New York Times*, February 5, 2003, A27.

39. On the complex and haunted etymological roots to territory, see William Connolly, *The Ethos of Pluralization* (Minneapolis: University of Minnesota Press, 1995), xxi–xxii. On the problematic of hospitality, see Jacques Derrida, *Of Hospitality*, trans. Rachel Bowlby (Stanford, CA: Stanford University Press, 2000); Jacques Derrida, "Hostipitality," in Jacques Derrida, *Acts of Religion*, ed. Gil Anidjar (New York: Routledge, 2002). On the hauntedness of a given territorialization, see Paul A. Passavant, *No Escape: Freedom of Speech and the Paradox of Rights* (New York: New York University Press, 2002), chap. 4. On the way that a given deterritorialization results in a coinciding reterritorialization, see Kam Shapiro, "The Myth of the Multitude," in this volume.

40. Ruth Buchanan and Sundhya Pahuja, "Legal Imperialism: *Empire's* Invisible Hand?" in this volume.

41. Colin Perrin, "Approaching Anxiety: The Insistence of the Postcolonial in the Declaration on the Rights of Indigenous Peoples," in *Laws of the Postcolonial*, eds. Eve Darian-Smith and Peter Fitzpatrick (Ann Arbor, MI: University of Michigan Press, 1999), 19–38; on the colonial origins of international law, see Antony Anghie, "Francisco de Vitoria and the Colonial Origins of International Law," in ibid., 89–107.

42. Passavant, *No Escape*, 103–105.

43. For an extended discussion of this question, see Passavant, *No Escape*.

44. Antonio Negri, *Insurgencies*, trans. Maurizia Bascagli (Minneapolis: University of Minnesota Press, 1999), 1, quoting Georges Burdeau, *Traité de sciences politiques*, vol. 4 (Paris: Librairie Générale de Droit et de Jurisprudence, 1983).

45. Niccolò Machiavelli, *The Prince*, trans. George Bull (New York: Penguin Books, 1981), 133–134.

46. Antonio Gramsci, *The Modern Prince*, trans. Louis Marks (New York: International Publishers, 1987), 135–136. Gramsci's remarks on Machiavelli are made in the context of a critique of Georges Sorel's notion of "myth." For a discussion of Sorellian myth in relation to *Empire*, see Kam Shapiro, "The Myth of the Multitude," in this volume. See also Louis Althusser, *Machiavelli and Us*, trans. Gregory Elliot (New York: Verso, 1999). I am indebted to Jodi Dean for the latter reference.

47. Gramsci, *Modern Prince*, 139, 145–146.

48. Ibid., 137.

49. On the "public" and contemporary politics under conditions of communicative capitalism, see also Jodi Dean, *Publicity's Secret* (Ithaca, NY: Cornell University Press, 2002).

50. Gramsci, *Modern Prince*, 163.

51. Michael Hardt, "Comment and Analysis: A Trap Set for Protesters," *The Guardian*, February 21, 2003, p. 19. Thanks to Ernesto Laclau for bringing this source to my attention.

# 1

## Can Immanence Explain
## Social Struggles?

### Ernesto Laclau

In a recent interview,[1] Jacques Rancière opposes his notion of "people" (*peuple*)[2] to the category of "multitude" as presented by the authors of *Empire*. As is well known, Rancière differentiates between *police* and *politics*, the first being the logic of counting and assigning the population to differential places, and the second, the subversion of that differentiating logic through the constitution of an egalitarian discourse which puts into question established identities. The "people" is the specific subject of politics and presupposes a sharp division in the social body that cannot be led back to any kind of immanent unity. *Empire*, on the contrary, makes immanence its central category and the ultimate ground of the multitude's unity.

It is worthwhile describing the main lines of Rancière's critique because they provide a good starting point for what we have to say about the book on which we are commenting. The immanentism of Hardt and Negri would be linked, according to Rancière, to their Nietzschean/Deleuzian ethics of affirmation, which does away with any reactive or negative dimension. *Empire* would belong, in that respect, to the whole tradition of modern political philosophy, which is profoundly metapolitical: "the kernel of metapolitics is to lead back the precarious artifices of the political scene to the truth of an immanent power which organizes beings in a community and identifies the true community with the grasped and sensible operation of this truth."[3] From Hardt's and Negri's rejection of any inherent negativity in political subjects it follows that the power inherent in the multitude has to be a disruptive power, "lodged in all state of domination as its ultimate content, a content destined to destroy all barriers. 'Multitudes' have to be a content whose continent is Empire."[4] Disruptive forces operating through a purely immanent movement are what Marxist theory called 'productive forces' and there would be, according to Rancière, a strict homology between the place of productive forces and that in which multitudes, as described in *Empire*, act. Rancière points out that productive forces should not necessarily be understood in any narrow productivist sense: there has been a constant widening of the concept from the strict economism of classical Marxism to the recent attempts to introduce in it the ensemble of scientific and intellectual abilities, passing through the Leninist attempt to supplement via political intervention a role that productive forces refused to fulfill.

I think that Rancière has rightly stressed what I see as the main source of several weaknesses of *Empire*, including a central one: that within its theoretical framework, politics becomes unthinkable. So I will start from a discussion of its notion of immanence and move later to various other theoretical and political aspects of the book.

Let us start with the authors' discussion of the origins of European modernity. While the usual insistence is on the secularization process, that process would be: "in our view . . . only a symptom of the primary event of modernity: the affirmation of the powers of *this* world, the discovery of the plane of immanence. 'Omne eus habet aliquod esse proprium'—every entity has a singular essence. Duns Scotus' affirmation subverts the medieval conception of being as an object of analogical and thus dualistic predication—a being with one foot in this world and one in a transcendental realm."[5] Duns Scotus's insistence on the singularity of being would have started an assertion of immanence that the authors describe as a process whose representative names would have been Nicholas of Cusa, Pico della Mirandola, and Bovillus—other names quoted are Bacon and Occam—and whose point of arrival is Spinoza: "By the time we arrive at Spinoza, in fact, the horizon of immanence and the horizon of the democratic political order coincide completely. The plane of immanence is the one on which the powers of singularity are realized and the one on which the truth of the new humanity is determined historically, technically and politically. For this very fact, because there cannot be any external mediation, the singular is presented as the multitude."[6] The revolution, however, ran into trouble. It had its Thermidor. The Thirty Years War was the outcome, and the need for peace led to the defeat of the forces of progress and the instauration of absolutism.

The first striking thing that one finds in this analysis is that it gives us a truncated narrative. For the assertion of a radical immanentism does not start, as Hardt and Negri seem to believe, at the time of Duns Scotus but much earlier, during the Carolingian Renaissance—more precisely, in Scotus Erigena's *De Divisione Naturae*. And in its initial formulations it had nothing to do with secularism, for it was an answer to strictly theological difficulties. The attempt to go back to those origins does not obey a purely erudite scruple; on the contrary, to clarify the context of theological alternatives of which immanentism was only one has direct relevance to the political issues that we are discussing today. The original theological question—which occupied the mind, among others, of no less a thinker than Saint Augustine—was how to make compatible the worldly existence of evil with divine omnipotence. If God is responsible for evil, he cannot be absolute Goodness; if he is not responsible for evil, he is not Almighty. Immanentism in its first formulations is an answer to this question. According to Erigena, evil does not really exist, for things we call evil are necessary stages that God has to pass through in order to reach his divine perfection. But this is obviously impossible without God being, somehow, internal to the world.

From that point onward, immanentism had a long career in Western thought. It is very much present in Northern mysticism and in some of the authors discussed in *Empire*, such as Nicholas of Cusa and Spinoza, and it is going to find its highest point in Hegel and Marx. Hegel's cunning of reason closely follows the argument that Erigena formulated one thousand years before. As the *Philosophy of History* asserts, universal history is not the terrain of happiness. And the Marxian version is scarcely different: society had to supersede primitive communism and pass through the whole hell of class division to develop the productive forces of humanity, and it is only at the end of the process, in a fully developed communism, that the rationality of all this suffering become visible.[7]

What are, however, really important in reference to these theological debates are the other existing alternatives in case the immanentist route *is not followed*. For in that case evil is not the appearance of a rationality underlying and explaining it, but a brute and irreducible fact. As the chasm separating good and evil is strictly constitutive and there is no ground reducing to its immanent development the totality of what exists, there is an element of negativity that cannot be eliminated either through dialectical mediation or through Nietzschean assertiveness. We are not very far here from the alternatives referred to by Rancière in his interview. (Let us observe that, strictly speaking, the category of *excess* is not incompatible with the notion of a nondialectical negativity that we are proposing. It is only if we try to combine excess with immanence that the nonpolitical turn that we will presently discuss is unavoidable.)

In the same way that, with modernity, immanence ceased to be a theological concept and become fully secularized, the religious notion of evil becomes, with the modern turn, the kernel of what we can call "social antagonism." What the latter retains from the former is the notion of a radical disjuncture—radical in the sense that it cannot be reabsorbed by any deeper objectivity that would reduce the terms of the antagonism to moments of its own internal movement, for example, the development of productive forces or any other form of immanence. Now, I would contend that it is only by accepting such a notion of antagonism—and its corollary, which is radical social division—that we are confronted with forms of social action that can truly be called *political.* Why so? To show this I will consider an early text by Marx that I have discussed fully elsewhere.[8] In it, Marx opposes a purely human revolution to a merely political one. The differential feature is that in the former a *universal* subject emerges in and for itself. In the words of Marx: "By proclaiming the *dissolution of the hitherto world order* the proletariat merely states the *secret of its own existence,* for it *is in fact* the dissolution of that world order." To put it in terms close to Hardt and Negri: the universality of the proletariat fully depends on its *immanence* within an objective social order that is entirely the product of capitalism—which is, in turn, a moment in the universal development of the productive forces. But precisely because of that reason, the universality of the revolutionary subject entails the end of politics—that is, the beginning of the withering away of the State and the transition (according to the Saint-Simonian motto adopted by Marxism) from the government of men to the administration of things.

As for the second revolution—the political one—its distinctive feature is, for Marx, an essential asymmetry: that between the universality of the task and the particularism of the agent carrying it out. Marx describes this asymmetry in nonequivocal terms: a certain regime is felt as universal oppression, and that allows the particular social force able to lead the struggle against it to present itself as universal liberator—universalizing, thus, its particular objectives. Here we find the real theoretical watershed in contemporary discussions: *either* we assert the possibility of a universality that is not politically constructed and mediated *or* we assert that all universality is precarious and depends on a historical construction out of heterogeneous elements. Hardt and Negri accept the first alternative without hesitation. If, conversely, we accept the second, we are on the threshold of the Gramscian conception of hegemony. (Gramsci is another for whom—understandably given their premises—Hardt and Negri show little sympathy.)

It is interesting to see the consequences that *Empire* draws from its approach to immanence. There is an actual historical subject of what they conceive as the realization of a full immanence: it is what they call the "multitude." The full realization of the multitude's immanence would be the elimination of all transcendence. This can be accepted only, of course, if the postulate of the homogeneity and unity of the multitude as an historical agent is not put into question—a matter to which we will return shortly. But some of the results of this strict opposition between immanence and transcendence can be quickly detected. Let us take their way of dealing with the question of sovereignty. For them, modern political sovereignty—well anchored in the counterrevolutionary trend of the second modernity—is reduced to the attempt at constructing a transcendent political apparatus:

> Sovereignty is thus defined both by *transcendence* and by *representation*, two concepts that the humanist has posed as contradictory. On the one hand, the transcendence of the sovereign is founded not on an external theological support but only on the immanent logic of human relations. On the other hand, the representation that functions to legitimate this sovereign power also alienates it completely from the multitude of subjects. . . . Here [in Bodin and Hobbes] the concept of modern sovereignty is born in its state of transcendental purity. The contract of association is intrinsic to and inseparable from the contract of subjugation.[9]

So sovereignty was an essentially repressive device trying to prevent the democratic upsurge of an unspecified multitude. What a beautiful fabula! For as anybody acquainted with the modern theory of sovereignty knows, its practical implementation entailed a far more complicated process than the story proposed by Hardt and Negri. In the first place, the multitude they are speaking about is a purely fanciful construction. What we had in early modernity was an estamental society, profoundly fragmented, which did not move at all in the direction of constructing a unified political subject capable of establishing an alternative social order. Royal sovereignty was established fighting on a double front: against the universalistic powers—the Church and the Empire—and against local feudal powers. And many newly emerging social sectors—bourgeois, especially—were the social base that made possible the emergence of royal sovereignty. That the transference of control of many social spheres to the new social states is at the root of the new forms of biopower is incontestable, but the alternative to that process was not autonomous power of any hypothetical multitude but the continuation of feudal fragmentation. It is more: it was only when this process of centralization had advanced beyond a certain point that something resembling a unitary multitude could emerge through the transference of sovereignty from the king to the people.

This leads us to the second aspect of Hardt's and Negri's dichotomy: the question of representation. What are the conditions for the elimination of any form of representation? Obviously, the elimination of any kind of asymmetry between actual political subjects and the community as a whole. If the *volonté générale* is the will of a subject whose limits coincide with those of the community, there is no need for any relation of representation but neither for the continuation of politics as a relevant activity. That is why, as we mentioned earlier, the emergence of a universal class heralded, for Marxism, the withering away of the State. But if we have an internally divided society, the will of the community as a whole has to be *politically* constructed out of a primary—constitutive—diversity. In that case, the *volonté générale* requires representation as its primary terrain of emergence. This means that any "multitude" is constructed through political action—which presupposes antagonism and hegemony.

The reason why Hardt and Negri do not even pose themselves this question is that for them the unity of the multitude results from the spontaneous aggregation of a plurality of actions that do not need to be articulated between themselves. In their words: "If these points were to constitute something like a new cycle of struggles, it would be a cycle defined not by the communicative extension of the struggles but rather by their singular emergence, by the intensity that characterizes them one by one. In short, this new phase is defined by the fact that these struggles do not link horizontally, but each one leaps vertically, directly to the virtual center of Empire"(58).

One cannot avoid finding it a little difficult to understand how an entity that has no boundaries—"The concept of Empire is characterized fundamentally by a lack of boundaries: Empire's rule has no limits"(xix)—can still have a virtual center, but let it pass. What we are told, anyway, is: 1) that a set of unconnected struggles tend, by some kind of *coincidentia oppositorum*, to converge in their assault on a supposed center; 2) that in spite of their diversity, without any kind of political intervention, they will tend to aggregate with each other; and 3) that they could never have aims that are incompatible with each other. It does not take long to realize that these are highly unrealistic assumptions, to put it mildly. They clash with the most elementary evidence of the international scene, which shows us a proliferation of social actors fighting each other for a variety of religious, ethnic, or racial reasons. And the assumption that imperialism is over ("*The United States does not and indeed no nation-state can today, form the center of an imperialist project.* No nation will be world leader in the way modern European nations were") does not fare any better, as anybody looking at what is going on in the world after September 11 can easily realize (xiv; emphasis in original). What is totally lacking in *Empire* is a theory of *articulation*, without which politics is unthinkable.

This gap in the argument is particularly visible if we consider the way in which *Empire* deals with the distinction strategy/tactics. For our authors the distinction collapses, but it is clear that the autonomous vertical struggles belong to the sphere of tactics rather than to strategic calculation. I want to be very precise on this point of my critique because I also think—although for reasons different from those of Hardt and Negri—that the distinction between strategy and tactics, as inherited from the socialist tradition, cannot be accepted any longer. For classical socialism there was a clear differentiation between both and a strict subordination of tactics to strategy. Now, a basic assumption in this vision was that the class identity of the strategic actors remained unchanged throughout the political process. For Kautsky, the strict working-class identity of the socialist actors was a basic dogma. For Lenin, class alliances did not transform the identities of the intervening forces ("to strike together and to march separated"). And for Trotsky, the whole strategy of the permanent revolution makes sense only if the taking up of democratic tasks by the working class does not contaminate the aims and nature of the latter.

It is precisely this assumption, in my view, that has to be put into question. For the present proliferation of a plurality of identities and points of rupture makes the subjects of political action essentially unstable and thus makes impossible a strategic calculation that covers long historical periods. This does not mean that the notion of strategy becomes entirely obsolete, but it does definitely mean that the strategies have to be short-term ones and that the various tactics become more autonomous. What is clear, however, is that this situation gives an increasing centrality to the moment of political articulation—the moment, precisely, which is entirely absent from Hardt's and Negri's analysis as a result of their conception of struggles *spontaneously* converging in their assault on a systemic center.

There is another feature of Hardt's and Negri's multitude that requires consideration: their inherent nomadism, that they explicitly link to the Deleuzian rhizomic movements. What is proper of the multitude is being-against: "One element we can put our finger on at the most basic and elementary level is *the will to be against*. In general, the will to be against does not seem to require much explanation. Disobedience to authority is one of the most natural and healthy acts. To us, it seems completely obvious that those who are exploited will resist and—given the necessary conditions—rebel" (210; emphasis in original). Today, however, the very ubiquity of Empire—which is no longer an *external* enemy—would make it difficult to identify those to whom the multitude is against. The only solution would be to be against everything, in every place. The main pattern of this new kind of struggle is desertion:

> Whereas in the disciplinary era *sabotage* was the fundamental notion of resistance, in the era of imperial control in may be *desertion*. Whereas being-against in modernity often meant a direct and/or dialectical opposition of forces, in postmodernity being-against might well be most effective in an oblique or diagonal stance. Battles against the Empire might be won through substraction and defection. This desertion does not have a place; it is the evacuation of the places of power. (212; emphasis in original)

This desertion takes the form of nomadic migrations—economic, intellectual, and political exodus creates an essential mobility that is the new pattern of class struggle. Mobility would have been the privileged terrain of republicanism since early modern times (the examples quoted are the Socians of the Renaissance, the religious transatlantic migrations of the seventeenth century, the International Workers of the World agitation in the United States in the

1910s, and the European autonomists of the 1970s). These nomadic actors are the new barbarians. The concept of migration can however be expanded: it is a question not only of physical, literal migrations but also of figural ones—the transformation of bodies can also be considered as an *anthropological exodus*:

> We certainly do need to change our bodies and ourselves, and in perhaps a much more radical way than the cyberpunk authors imagine. In our contemporary world, the now common aesthetic mutations of the body such as piercing and tattoos, punk fashion and its various imitations, are all initial indications of this corporeal transformation, but in the end they do not hold a candle to the kind of radical mutation needed here. The will to be against really needs a body that is completely incapable of submitting to command. It needs a body that is incapable of adapting to family life, to factory discipline, to the regulations of traditional sex life, and so forth. (216)

From this perspective the proletarians of the nineteenth century could be seen as nomads, for although they did not displace themselves geographically, "their creativity and productivity define corporeal and ontological migrations" (217).

What are the difficulties with this rather triumphalist vision? There are several. In the first place, the assertion that "the will to be against does not seem to require much explanation" is mere wishful thinking. Here the alternative is clear: either resistance to oppression is some kind of natural and automatic mechanism that will spontaneously operate whatever the circumstances, or it is a complex social construction that has conditions of possibility external to itself. For me the second is the correct answer. The ability and the will to resist are not a gift from heaven but require a set of subjective transformations that are only the product of the struggles themselves *and that can fail to take place*. What is missing in *Empire* is any coherent theory of political subjectivity—psychoanalysis, for instance, is entirely absent. Largely because of that reason, the whole notion of being-against does not resist the slightest examination. It is easy to see the role that it plays in the economy of Hardt's and Negri's argumentation: if one is "against" without defining an enemy, the idea that struggles against Empire should take place everywhere finds its justification (and, a fortiori, we have the guarantee that vertical struggles would coalesce around a single target without any need for their horizontal articulation). Unfortunately social struggles do not follow this simplistic pattern. All struggle is the struggle of concrete social actors for particular objectives, and nothing guarantees that these objectives will not clash with each other. Now, I would agree that no overall historical transformation is possible unless the particularism of the struggles is superseded and a wider "collective will" is constituted. But this requires the implementation of what in our work we have called the *logic of equivalence*, which involves acts of political articulation—precisely the horizontal linking that Hardt and Negri put aside. The "being-against" is, once more, a clear indicator of the antipolitical bias of *Empire.*

Finally, the notion of "anthropological exodus" is hardly more than an abusive metaphor. The role attributed to migration is already extremely problematic. It is true that the authors recognize that misery and exploitation could be determinant of the will of people to move across frontiers, but this element of negativity is immediately subordinated to an affirmative will to migrate that ultimately creates the possibility of an emancipatory subject. Needless to say, this martial conception of the migratory process does not correspond to any reality: reasons for various groups to migrate are very different and are not unified around any anti-Empire crusade. But when we are told that the rebellion against family life or the development of proletarian capacities in the nineteenth century has also to be conceived as a migratory act, the notion of migration loses all specificity: any kind of historical change—for better or worse—would be conceived as migration. A good metaphor is the one that, through analogy, reveals a hitherto concealed aspect of reality—but that hardly happens in the present case.

It is towards the end of their book that the authors address, to some extent, the question that we have been posing throughout this note: that of political articulation. Let us quote them:

> How can the actions of the multitude become political? How can the multitude organize and concentrate its energies against the repression and incessant territorial segmentations of Empire? The only response that we can give to these questions is that the action of the multitude becomes political primarily when it begins to confront directly and with an adequate consciousness the central repressive operations of Empire. It is a matter of recognizing and engaging the imperial initiatives and not allowing them continually to reestablish order; it is a matter of crossing and breaking down the limits and segmentations that are imposed on the new collective labor power; it is a matter of gathering together these experiences of resistance and wielding them in concert against the nerve centers of imperial command. (399)

How, however, is this "gathering together [of] these experiences of resistance and wielding them in concert" going to operate? Hardt and Negri assert that about the specific and concrete forms of this political articulation they can say nothing. They, however, formulate a "political program for the global multitude" that is organized around three demands: the demand for global citizenship (so that the mobility of the working force under the present capitalist conditions is recognized and that groups of the population such as the *sans papiers* have access to full citizenship); the right to a social wage (so that an income is guaranteed to everybody); the right to reappropriation (so that the means of production are socially owned).

I can only say that I do not disagree with any of these demands—although it is clear that they do not amount to a full-fledged political program—but what sounds strange, after a whole analysis centered on the need to strike everywhere from a position of total confrontation with the present imperial system, is that these three political aims are formulated in a language of *demands* and *rights*. Because both demands and rights have to be *recognized*, and the instance from whom that recognition is requested *cannot be* in a relation of total exteriority vis-à-vis the social claims. Each of the three demands, in order to be implemented, requires strategic considerations concerning changes in the structure of the State, autonomization of certain spheres, political alliances and incorporation to the historical arena of previously excluded social sectors. That is, we are in the terrain of what Gramsci called "war of position." But this political game is strictly incompatible with the notion of a plurality of unconnected vertical struggles, all targeting—through some unspecified mechanism—an assumed virtual center of the Empire. Perhaps the ultimate incoherence of the book we are commenting on is that it proposes fragments of a perfectly acceptable political program, while its conditions of implementation are denied by the central theoretical and strategic categories on which its analysis is based. Multitudes are never spontaneously multitudinarious; they can become so only through political action.

## Notes

1. "Peuple ou multitude: question d'Eric Alliez à Jacques Rancière," *Multitudes* 9, May–June 2002, 95–100.

2. Jacques Rancière, *La Mésentente* (Paris: Galilée, 1995).

3. "Peuple ou multitude," 96.

4. Ibid., 97.

5. Ibid., 71.

6. Ibid., 73.

7. I have discussed these matters in more detail in my essay "Beyond Emancipation," in E. Laclau, *Emancipation(s)* (London: Verso, 1996), 1–19.

8. In my essay "Identity and Hegemony: The Role of Universality in the Constitution of Political Logics," in J. Butler, E. Laclau and S. Žižek, *Contingency, Hegemony, Universality. Contemporary Dialogues on the Left* (London: Verso, 2000), 44–89. The text by Marx to which I am referring is "Contribution to the Critique of Hegel's Philosophy of Law, Introduction," in K. Marx and F. Engels, *Collected Works*, vol. 3 (London, Lawrence and Wishart, 1975), 186–187.

9. Michael Hardt and Antonio Negri, *Empire*, (Cambridge, MA: Harvard University Press, 2000) 84. emphasis in original. Subsequent references to *Empire* are given parenthetically in the text.

# 2

# The Immanence of *Empire*

## Peter Fitzpatrick

*O God, I could be bounded in a nutshell, and count myself a king of infinite space, were it not that I have bad dreams.*

—*Hamlet* II, ii

## Introduction

An intensity of opposition to a book can be more revealing of inadequacy in the reader than in the author. Caution on this score should be heightened when the objection is a simple one. With some wariness, then, the objection to Hardt's and Negri's *Empire* pursued here is that its founding ontology of liberation is ultimately at one with the very *imperium* it is so resolutely directed against.[1] In this work and in others, Hardt and Negri would identify liberation with a "constituent power" of pure immanence, an uncontainable power, infinitely protean and continually creative.[2] This power is contrasted to a "constituted power" that is always set in a constricting transcendence. Yet Hardt and Negri would also endow the illimitable constituent power with quiddity and measure. They would populate their "common framework," their "global theory," with entities to which constituent power is immanent.[3] And as their guiding spirits, Deleuze and Guattari, would succinctly counsel: "whenever immanence is interpreted as immanent *to* Something, we can be sure that this Something reintroduces the transcendent."[4]

31

The thrust, or in the Deleuzian idiom, the movement of that transcendence is distinctly imperial. This movement, in something of a constituent mode, is searching and responsive but in a constituted mode it also and ultimately appropriates and reduces—and thence, as we shall see, creates or recreates disasters. To take a core example, considered soon in some necessary detail, Hardt and Negri advance "the multitude" as the ubiquitous force of liberation, as itself indistinguishable from their ontology of pure, pervasive immanence. Aptly, then, such a multitude is illimitably including and expansive. It accommodates, even if vaguely, all the poor and all those exploited by capital. Yet this same multitude is a contained "subject" that assumes a coherence through its domination by a type of vanguard labor. Furthermore, our authors can themselves encompass the multitude and articulate its primal "demands" as a small collection of "rights" (400–407). Their journey out was, after all, undertaken with the incurious intention of a secure return.

Still, this is a large and wonderfully rich volume that says many things in many different ways, and caution remains advisable. With that in mind and with some regard for an enfolding irony, what will be attempted in this chapter is an immanent critique. The chapter will not, then, be concerned—or at least not directly concerned—with the surpassing position from which the authors can discern, even prescribe for, a world entire. It will not inquire into how something as uncontainable and infinitely protean as constituent power or the multitude can be known without the utter dissipation of the knower. And even the chapter's dissent from the deific claims of immanentism will be muted in its extracting and adapting from *Empire* a more plausible picture of current imperialism.

## Constituting Immanence

It would befit the materiality that Hardt and Negri would bestow on pure immanence to begin where they do—with its supposed historical emergence. This is an origin found in the (European) Renaissance, where "humanity," or the "world," or "society" came to know itself immanently—that is, without resort to a transcendent reference beyond it (See 76–77). What happens next, however, is that this discovery and the "emancipation" from the transcendent is blocked by, of all things, Eurocentrism, along with related constraining forces of modernity. The resulting scene is unsettled. With modernity comes a formative crisis: "a crisis that is born of the uninterrupted conflict between the immanent, constructive, creative forces and the transcendent power aimed at restoring order" (76). That crisis was held in check through an excessive ordering and containment, and this constraint, it seems, constituted an "inside" the "outside" of which was "constructed from within" (184–185). Now, in present time, with global empire and postmodernism, "there is no more outside," or less abruptly: "In the passage from modern to postmodern and from imperialism to Empire there is progressively less distinction between inside and outside" (181–187).[5] The resulting or pending unified reality does not invoke a transcendent reference but is purely immanent and "purely positive," a situated "universality" (354). As we will soon see, Hardt and Negri are not constant in perceiving this as a realized reality, but there is one constant consequence of the denial of an outside which seems to trigger the mainspring of their whole thesis.

"In this new historical formation it is . . . no longer possible to identify a sign, a subject, a value, or a practice that is 'outside'" (385). The momentous corollary is that, with such a self-encompassing, there cannot now be an explicitly ordered or even mediated containment of "the liberated singularities and the revolutionary constitution of the multitude," the multitude being that force impelling the original upsurge in the Renaissance having now become "the plural multitude of productive, creative subjectivities of globalization," "a multitude *within* Empire and *against* Empire" (60, 61, 83; emphasis in original) That multitude and that Empire will be encountered more revealingly in the next two sections, but first we need to look more closely at the quality that Hardt and Negri would ascribe to this immanence in the world.

That quality is brought into operative being through constituent power. Such power is an "originating productivity"; it "constitutes everything"; and appropriately enough, it is free in the sense of being quite unconstrained—"absolute and unlimited," "beyond measure," and expansive, "always open," and flowing, completely revolutionary.[6] In all of this constituent power continually opposes constituted power, a power that takes such forms as law, sovereignty, and the constitution of a state.

In its equation with constituent power, the immanence of Hardt and Negri fits aptly that advanced by one of their main sources, Deleuze and Guattari, for whom immanence is characterized by "openness" and "movement of the infinite [that] does not refer to spatiotemporal coordinates"; it is akin to "chaos," "formless, unlimited, absolute"; it "escapes every transcendence of the subject as well as the object"; or, in Agamben's terms, it "is precisely what can never be attributed to a subject, being instead the matrix of infinite-desubjectification."[7] Aptly still, this immanence opposes any delimited fixity—"law, limit, castration. . . ."[8] Yet no matter how "relentless" the struggle against a constraining transcendence, transcendence is for Deleuze and Guattari unavoidable.[9] Hardt and Negri would only go so far as to see resort to transcendence as "a constant threat," and they would attribute instantiation and palpability to immanence itself and to constituent power (165). So we are told that immanence is "tied only," but tied nonetheless, "to regimes of possibility that con-

stitute its formation and development"; we are told that it can be an "apparatus" or that its "horizon" can coincide with "the democratic political order";
and we are told that it can assume an active subjectivity.[10] Constituent power
itself is a "process" and a "procedure"; it is "material"; it "configures" as "common actions" and is "constituted in ontological mechanisms or apparatuses."[11]
Hence there is a certain disaffection for Deleuze and Guattari, who:

> seem to be able to conceive positively only the tendencies toward continuous
> movement and absolute flows, and thus in their thought . . . the creative ele-
> ments and the radical ontology of the production of the social remain insubstan-
> tial and impotent. Deleuze and Guattari discover the productivity of social
> reproduction (creative production, production of values, social relations, affects,
> becomings), but manage to articulate it only superficially and ephemerally, as a
> chaotic, indeterminate horizon marked by the ungraspable event. (28)

And Deleuze's notion of revolutionary possibility is found to be "pallid" in the
contrast with their "material and explosive . . . solution" (368).

This dissonance between the two sets of authors may at first seem strange,
because the founding inspiration of both comes from Spinoza. That, however,
could suggest a like dissonance in the source. Deleuze's and Guattari's immanence provides "a ground from which idols have been cleared," and appropriately, what takes their place is the simulacrum of the sole and surpassing god,
an illimitable god, one of infinite possibility.[12] The Spinoza who would accommodate this deity is "the infinite becoming-philosopher," the one who would
show, or ever seek to show, "the possibility of the impossible."[13] Hardt's and
Negri's Spinoza is closer to another version of the one god. This is a god of
nature and of nature's laws, a god of perfected order wherein things can only
ever be as they are. Such a god would conform to Hardt's and Negri's endowing absolute immanence on a "natural order," or on "democratic political
order," or on "society."[14] And the Spinoza who would accommodate this situation is, as Nancy has it, "the first thinker of the *world*."[15]

How, then, would Spinoza unite this disparate deity? And how, in particular, can there be a coming of the illimitable into the world, "our world?"[16] These
questions will be approached here through the impelling concern of Spinoza's
*Ethics*: how we can know God as the whole and know ourselves in relation to
that.[17] Indeed, and more pointedly, Spinoza's argument and his ability to
advance it depend on the proposition that "the human mind has an adequate
knowledge of the eternal and infinite essence of God."[18] We may start, then,
with "certain and determinate" or finite "modes," being modes of "the attributes of God," since it is "the modes of thinking" that make up "the essence of
man" and that constitute "the being of the human mind."[19] In turn, "the

essence of the mind consists in knowledge . . . which involves the knowledge of God," and without that knowledge, mind itself "can neither exist nor be conceived," yet that mind is not commensurate with God and can perceive "another thing" only "partially, that is, inadequately."[20] It is this intimate and constituent link between mind and God, and the hiatus between the two, which I now wish to hone.

Spinoza's famed monism would render God as a singular, entirely self-generated "substance" that is "absolutely infinite" and has an infinity of attributes, "each of which expresses eternal and infinite essence."[21] The "necessity" of this "divine nature" determines everything, and everything that exists is within this nature.[22] Mind, however, is far from being intimidated by this necessity. Although created within a nature having an infinity of attributes, each of which is eternally expressive, and itself being able to perceive only partially and inadequately, mind can still somehow encompass that nature, speak definitively of it, and know it to be one. This surpassing feat is achieved in an attribution of an all-encompassing completeness and "absolute perfection" to this deific substance, its denial of anything "external" to it, and then by holding it within a confining elaboration of the quality of this perfection, a quality that by way of its "extension" can include the knowing mind as integral to its substance.[23]

Matters become less resolved, however, when Spinoza takes some account of how, from within the finite, there can be a knowledge of the infinite, including God's infinity of attributes. Arguably, the human mind can know something of the two attributes of God through which it is integrated into the whole, the attributes of thought and extension. What of the other attributes of God which do not "extend" to "man" and "the human mind?" Spinoza's "view, then, is that we know that there are attributes other than these, but that we do not know what they are. This view has puzzled scholars. . . ."[24] What should be just as puzzling is that the human mind can know that God does not have certain specific attributes even though it does not know what the attributes of God are, apart from the known two, and even though God has an infinity of attributes.[25] As finitely positioned, the limited quality of mind could relate only to that which is infinitely beyond yet affects it in ways that are ultimately unknowing and expectant. The God related to in such ways is knowable only as illimitable and formless. Yet this is the same surpassing God of determinate order from whom Spinoza would derive all else in a procedure indistinguishable from "the old philosophical [and theological] idea of emanation": "a process whereby the various grades of reality were imagined to flow from a single, primal source, which the monotheists identified as God."[26]

The irresolution of Spinoza's deity may mute surprise at Hardt's and Negri's rejection of a Spinoza whom they also find foundational, a Spinoza for whom "the search for an outside seems to run aground and [to] propose merely phantasms of mysticism, negative intuitions of the absolute" (186). They would put their faith, for such it is, in an ostensibly positive derivation from Spinoza, that of the multitude.

## The Multitude of the Multitude

In *The Savage Anomaly*, Negri had adroitly rendered Spinoza's God and the political philosophy accompanying it in ways compatible with "the multitude" found now in *Empire*—compatible with its "absolute democratic power," with democracy's being "the absolute form of government" through which "all of society, the entire multitude, rules," and compatible, in a sense above all, with the complete coinciding of "the horizon of immanence and the horizon of the democratic political order."[27] This immanence is, or corresponds to, an ontology, one "that resides in the creative and productive practices of the multitude."[28] So endowed, the multitude inherits from Spinoza's God the deific competence of self-constitution.[29] And the same multitude manifests also the divergent dimensions of that deity. There is, for one, a dimension of continuous production and destruction, of illimitable possibility—something "unrepresentable."[30] Yet there is also another dimension that is actual, finite, conducive to "institutionality," and capable of becoming an "order."[31] Such a duality runs unresolved through Hardt's and Negri's proliferous account of the multitude.

Seeking first the dimension of actuality, we find that it is somewhat obscured by a wide casting of the conceptual net. The multitude extends to all those who are poor—"the foundation of the multitude"—and to those who feel forced to migrate; but the most sustained "founding" emphasis is given to a new category of labor, one that "includes all those whose labor is directly or indirectly exploited by and subjected to capitalist norms of production and reproduction" (18, 56). Some refinement is brought to bear on these considerable categories in order to identify the postmodern multitude. In an earlier work, Hardt and Negri found that "in the developments we discern in contemporary society, productive labor tends to propose completely immanent social dimensions of meaning, independent of any coercion to cooperate that could be posed outside labor itself," and those developments they perceive in terms of "the increasingly immaterial dimensions of labor."[32] By the time *Empire* comes on the scene, matters have firmed up considerably:

> At a certain point in capitalist development, which Marx only glimpsed as the future, the powers of labor are infused by the powers of science, communication,

and language. General intellect is a collective, social intelligence created by accumulated knowledges, techniques, and know-how. The value of labor is thus realized by a new universal and concrete labor force through the appropriate and free
usage of the new productive forces. What Marx saw as the future is our era. This
radical transformation of labor power and the incorporation of science, communication, and language into productive force have redefined the entire phenome-
nology of labor and the entire world horizon of production. (364)

More pointedly: "Our claim . . . is that immaterial labor has become predominant, not in quantitative but in qualitative terms. The various material forms
of labor are bathed in the light of immaterial labor and thereby transformed."[33]
This radiance emanates from "a tendency for all forms of production to be
informationalized, immaterialized."[34] Thus is the chasmic and hugely exploita-
tive international division of labor overcome.[35] Even if we grant that scenario, it
should be recalled that it is not only all of labor that is quite suffused by one of
its rarefied forms, but the multitude cohering in this way also and somehow
incorporates all those who are poor or who want to migrate. The multitude,
then, is an appropriative machine of enormous range, if not efficacy.

Putting immaterial labor in a defining vanguard in this way does insinu-
ate into the multitude the aura of its other dimension. In that dimension, the
multitude becomes illimitable and "open," a multitude that does not "tend to
become a totality but, rather, a set of singularities, an open multiplicity."[36] It
would be understandable, then, if the multitude remained ill-defined and even
resisted any "constituted" signification—the multitude as "unrepresentable."[37]
When it comes to the ending of *Empire*, however—to that siren place still calling for some resolution—Hardt and Negri transform this vacuity into an
abstraction yet to be made palpable.[38] That is convenient because it is also the
case that "our theorizing of the multitude" in *Empire* and beyond "has
remained abstract."[39] And Hardt has confirmed that "it is still not at all evident
how to understand the multitude in social and sociological terms. This appears
to us now as the most significant shortcoming of our book. After a theory of
Empire, we now need to write a theory of the multitude."[40] Yet the "theory of
Empire" itself, as we shall soon see, was reliant on "a theory of the multitude"
in something like the first place, that first place being not only a self-generated
ontology founding the whole work called *Empire* but also the "real productive
force of our social world" (62). When that force extends in this illimitable
dimension of the multitude, only to return as appropriative in the dimension
of actuality, then the multitude itself is constituted in an imperial movement,
one inherently manifested in the exemplary elevation of immaterial labor.

*Empire* produces another resolution for the multitude resonant with the imperial, something not unlike social evolution. By way of this resolution, the multitude can be actual but still take on something of a dimension beyond by being as yet to come. So, even though the multitude is repeatedly affirmed as "a subject," "a temporal subject," it is a "properly political subject" only in its being projected toward a liberatory "telos."[41] Or we learn that the multitude "produces the chromosomes of its future organization," or that the "multitude of subjects" has still to construct the "institutionality" of its perfect democracy: the multitude awaits "the construction, or rather the insurgence, of a powerful organization," this being "the only event we are still awaiting."[42]

Yet, even with its operative being still to come, the actuality, the existent presence, of the multitude is still affirmed at the work's end and nowhere more strikingly than in Hardt's and Negri's authorial ability—no matter how illimitable the multitude, no matter how ontologically encompassing, and no matter how diverse it may be or how enormous its range—to bound the multitude and articulate its primal "demands" as a small collection of "rights" (400–407).

There is yet another and hardly less striking delimiting of the illimitable multitude, and that comes from its relation to Empire. For Hardt and Negri, the multitude makes Empire. It is this multitude that provides an "ontological basis" alternative to current hegemonies, one that endows Empire, filling what Hardt and Negri see as a void at its heart; and so, along with a revived revolutionary rhetoric of smashing and exploding whatever gets in its way, the multitude's liberatory assertions repeatedly provide a reactive Empire with content.[43] Yet a constant theme of *Empire* is a relation between the multitude and global empire that seems dialectical, although we are decidedly and immanently not to see it as such (47). The dynamic is one in which the multitude and Empire are each constituted and impelled by the other as its contrary. This dynamic is not just directed from the multitude to the global empire. Despite repeated assertions that Empire emanates solely from the multitude, that it is "a mere apparatus of capture that lives only off the vitality of the multitude," Hardt and Negri also have the multitude emanating from Empire (62). Hence it is the multitude that, as the force of "counterglobalization," has to be posed "at an equally global level," a multitude whose "global conditions . . . follow in part from our conception of Empire itself."[44] Just as "the new disciplinary regime" that goes with Empire "constructs the tendency toward a global market of labor power, it constructs also the possibility of its antithesis" (252–253). It is, furthermore, this "new disciplinary order" which effects a convergence of the "various struggles" against it into "an objective unity" (261). The puzzle, then, is how the multitude can be ontologically and solely prime whilst constituently depending on Empire.

## Emanations of the Multitude

That difficulty is heightened by Hardt's and Negri's placing themselves not just within the multitude but within Empire itself.[45] Such an immanent positioning is, however, quite concordant with their finding in Empire the same divergent dimensions as those just extracted from their account of the multitude—that is, the divide between a located actuality and what is illimitably beyond, or yet to come.

Hardt's and Negri's account of Empire is not overburdened by much detail. It is barely distinguishable from standard versions of globalization. So, along with the general run of globalizers, they discern certain quasi-universal yet somehow realized or realizable conditions, such as the "simple fact" of an enveloping "world order," the pervasion of the market and of technologies of communication, and a political terminus in which "government and politics come to be completely integrated into the system of transnational command" (3, 307). The order that is a "simple fact" is one that is "transnational, world-wide, total."[46] Taking an instantiation that for Negri corresponds with Empire itself, there is a roundly realized "global market," a "new order," a "unity," the existence of which "only the insane can deny."[47]

What this "total," ordered existence could be is not entirely clear. There do, after all, still remain "potential sites for expanding markets," and even Empire itself is sometimes described as "the coming Empire" (271, 384). Not only does the requisite order seem to be rather less than total, it is also somewhat dissipated. The world market is associated with a "space of uncoded and deterritorialized flows"; along with it "a myriad of differences appears"; and it "attacks nothing more violently than fixed boundaries" (150, 332–333). Yet there is also some coding and bounding. So "one important element" in the "paradigm shift" to global empire "was the fact that the world market as a structure of hierarchy and command became more important and decisive" (251). What is more: "The global politics of difference established by the world market is defined not by free play and equality, but by the imposition of new hierarchies, or really by a constant process of hierarchization" (154). Vertiginously by now, this seemingly concentrated power can itself somehow be also diffuse: the differences emanating from the world market "do not play freely across a smooth global space, but rather are regimented in global networks of power consisting of highly differentiated and mobile structures" (151). In short, what we have here is the same alternation as that found with the multitude, an alternation between a realized actuality and a formless, illimitable quality beyond. Accompanying that alternation of the two is a neo-evolutionary "coming" in between them.

That same outcome attends something that should be another emanation of the multitude, given the multitude's ontological primacy, but it is a something that is at times seen by Hardt and Negri as foundationally prior. This is a "biopolitical ontology"—subsisting in "simplicity," "the immediate actor of biopolitical production and reproduction" being the multitude (65, 355, 413). The biopolitical element operates also within Empire, making of it "a biopolitical reality" and engaging generally in a "biopolitical production of world order."[48] Again, we are spared encumbering detail and, yet again, a familiar alternation emerges. The realm of the biopolitical is nothing less than "life" and a fusion of life's "economic, political, and cultural" dimensions (56). Unsurprisingly, its is a constituent force, ever reaching out to the possible.[49] But "the machine of biopolitical command" that constructs Empire and Empire's "source of . . . normativity" is "a globalized biopolitical machine"; and this machine is a constituted power, its "birth" being found in "the realization of modern sovereignty" (31, 40, 60, 89). Constituent power itself is materially "realized on the biopolitical terrain" (358). The combining ability of the biopolitical joins together not only the constituent and the constituted but also "the natural and the artificial, needs and machines, desires and the collective organization of the economic and the social," and in all this it assumes a neo-evolutionary impetus with its "power of generation" and with its own "becomings" (355, 388–389).

What that repeated configuration of alternations and becomings reveals is an imperial formation. Somewhat in the spirit of Deleuze and Guattari, Hardt and Negri find that the imperialism of postmodern Empire differs from previous imperialisms precisely in its "immanent" quality, its breaking away from a predominant fixity of transcendent and constituted power, and its implanting of a constituent power whereby everything is now brought within: "The internalisation of the 'outside' seems to us the fundamental characteristic of the becoming of imperial globalization."[50] For Hardt and Negri, this quality of an encompassing within must be realized and emplaced materially, even if in "the world finally outside measure" (355). The fusion, finally, of the "outside" with the "inside" has to assume an operative efficacy that is either accomplished in actuality or is being augmented in its becoming. How can that fusion be effected in a way that avoids, as Hardt and Negri so want to avoid, the mysticism of Spinoza or Deleuze's and Guattari's lack of grasp and substance (28, 186)?

With the multitude, as we saw, this was done quite simply by endowing the multitude with reality as a subject, and that included being the subject of quite particular rights, or by endowing it with reality as a surpassing and exemplary vanguard of labor. Even as becoming, the multitude is something already and distinctly "there." In its various realizations and becomings, then, the multitude corresponds to that "Something" that we saw Deleuze and Guattari pinpointing like this: "whenever immanence is interpreted as immanent *to* Something, we can be sure that this Something reintroduces the transcendent."[51] With Empire, however, Hardt and Negri would want to saturate it with a "virtuality" that, although seeking "to be real," leaves the contents of Empire ever labile and dependent on a transformative "realm beyond measure," a realm powered by "constituent labor" (359). A shortcut through this maneuver would be to say that Empire, through its being constituted by the multitude, joins it in transcendence. But, as we saw, Hardt and Negri also accord some primacy to Empire and make the multitude partly contingent on it. To deal with this attribution of some independence or autonomy, it could be sufficient to say that the equation of Empire with such of its real and particular contents as the market elevates a transcendent, much like the apotheosis of the multitude's vanguard of labor or the affirmation of its subjectivity. It would, however, advance my analysis to make things a little more difficult by trying to show that the transcendence of Empire comes from the original, the ontological, claim to pure immanence.

The issue of difference can orient this effort. What for Hardt and Negri markedly distinguishes postmodern Empire from modern imperialism is Empire's universal inclusiveness and its being thus "blind to . . . differences" (198). Yet, when any claim to the universal and the all-inclusive is instantiated and thence made particular, there results inevitably a difference from what is thereby excluded. Hardt and Negri do recognize hierarchies of difference within Empire, something we saw when looking at the market and something we will see further when dealing with emanations of Empire in the next section. These differences, however, are for Hardt and Negri managed, evanescent differences, quite unlike the differences created by a previous imperialism, by a "colonial power [that] sought to fix pure, separate identities," such as identities based on racism (199).

It can hardly be denied that imperialism now differs in the terms of its inclusion and exclusion from the type of imperialism against which Hardt and Negri would so starkly set it, but the similarities are what is significant here. The claim to or on the inclusively universal that both imperialisms share imports a differential that is inexorable and chasmic, even if its manifestations do vary. When, in terms of the claim to it, the absolutely universal enters a finite world and becomes particularly emplaced, those outside that place must be absolutely apart from it, must be of a different order of existence. The more operatively encompassing the emplaced universality, the more "in" common its commonality may be, then the more emphatic is the inevitable difference. So Žižek can remark that, with the increasing homogenization of the explicitly political, there is an emphasis on difference and a masking of the political by way of other terms such as the ethnic.[52] Since both the asserted reach of the universal and the ensuing difference are absolute, there can be no settledness and no stability of "identity" between the excluded and the included. But the emplaced, the achieved universal entails also the demand for some settled and comprehensible consistency. Hence, and for example, social evolution mythically reconciles exclusion and inclusion. For imperialism at the present time, the burden of consistency tends to be carried by the exemplar. With this exemplar, the universal can be concentrated in and exemplified by the particular, by particular people, and these not only supremely manifest the universal but also have a prerogative hold on it. From this exorbitant position, the exemplar can persist in sameness yet bring to itself, in a ravening extraversion, what is ever beyond it.

It would help confirm this analysis if, when looked at in a little more detail, the distinction Hardt and Negri draw between their postmodern Empire and other imperialisms becomes less sharp. From the way Hardt and Negri describe it, the imperialism they are setting against Empire is the so-called second imperialism originating in the nineteenth century. It could be seen as Empire's immediate predecessor, and the contrast they draw is one between the state-focused fixity of its colonizations and the flexibility and decentered quality of Empire's power (200, 384). The contrast is at best overdrawn. It ignores forms of indirect and localized power-sharing through which the second imperialism conducted much of its rule. It ignores the "informal" colonizations of, for example, parts of South America. It ignores that exaltation of the comity of imperial states which came to combine them, as well as their mutual involvement as carriers of "civilization." And it ignores the seeming similarities between the Empire of Hardt and Negri and other dispersed or decentered modern imperialisms, such as "the bright empire," "the empire of trade," "the empire of liberty," to use the catch-cries of the time, pursued by Britain and France in the seventeenth and eighteenth centuries. This disparity of imperial manifestations is explicit also in their resort to the Roman Empire, usually evoked by them for its responsive inclusiveness and its diversity (20, 163, 166). This aspect of Rome's *imperium* is sometimes put summarily by others as its "horizontal dimension," something characteristically contrasted with its "vertical" dimension, also advanced by Hardt and Negri—contrasted, that is, with a centralized control that not only remains unparalleled to this day but was itself a condition for the existence and persistence of the horizontal dimension.[53]

I will now illustrate and extend this critique by looking at emanations of Empire and then at a specific historical origin of the modern multitude Hardt and Negri would derive from some of these.

## Emanations of Empire

Hardt once remarked that "proposing an antagonism" between constituted and constituent power "brings to mind Spinoza's warning '*non opposita sed diversa*,' 'not opposed but different.'"[54] And Negri has wondered, inconclusively, whether we must "accept the juridical paradox that constitutive [that is, constituent] power can be defined only by constituted power," or whether there is some other way for us all "to come forward" as a constituent power.[55] It could be said that *Empire* was poised to sharpen that paradox of the juridical. Negri's *Insurgencies* treats law as the paradigm of a constituted power quite opposed to a constituent power that is apart from and resists being reduced to law.[56] In apparent contrast, *Labor of Dionysus* by Hardt and Negri sets its overall "orientation" towards a notion of the "juridical" and of "law" that is decidedly constituent.[57]

*Empire*, as the major work following on these two, might be expected to engage with, even combine, these two conceptions of law. It might, further, be expected to relate Negri's juridical paradox productively to his speculation about an alternative way of being as a constituent power, relate it perhaps even to the multitude. The stakes would seem to be considerable. If constituent power and its commensurate immanence depend upon constituted power for a "defined" existence, the constituent is definitively immanent to a delimited "Something" and, as Deleuze and Guattari would have it, the transcendent is "reintroduced."[58] Expectation, then, is heightened when Hardt and Negri open *Empire* with the assertions that: "The problematic of Empire is determined in the first place by one simple fact: that there is a world order. This order is expressed as a juridical formation" (3). They proceed for several more pages in making out a claim that the "constitution" of Empire is to be understood "in juridical terms" (3). What supposedly emerges is "a new paradigm," "a new notion of global order" that is wearyingly old and disordered (4, 13).

Their focus fixes first on the United Nations "as the culmination of this entire constitutive process," a process in which an "international order" forms as a prelude to "a new notion of *global* order" (4; emphasis in original). More particularly, "the notion of right defined by the U.N. Charter . . . points toward a new positive source of juridical production, effective on a global scale—a new center of normative production that can play a sovereign juridical role" (4). In short, it is with the United Nations that "the juridical concept of Empire began to take shape" (6). Kelsen is then, aptly enough, called in aid to evidence "a sort of juridical positivism" which "dominates the formation of a new juridical ordering" (15). Such a "juridical positivism can emphasize the necessity for a strong power to exist at the center of the normative process." (16). Yet, despite the professed centrality of this initiating concern with "juridical positivism," the rest of the book barely touches on the norms and forms needed to give it any operative existence. Something like this existence is evoked in wordy miasma: "imperial right . . . seems" to require "a machine that creates a continuous call for authority"; or what we may be "witnessing is a process of the material constitution of the new planetary order, the consolidation of its administrative machine"; or, drawing a comparison with Polybius and his "model" of government, they find that "postmodern imperial monarchy involves rule of the unity of the world market" (14, 19, 334). There are also rare sightings of something more tangible: "The U.N. organizations, along with the great multi- and transnational finance and trade agencies (the IMF, the World Bank, the GATT, and so forth), all become relevant in the perspective of the supranational juridical constitution" (31; see also 334).

Hardt and Negri also locate a juridical power within their Empire that is seemingly the antithesis of order, one set not in its "positive" norms and forms but in "a state of exception." Empire is ruled in "a permanent state of emergency and exception," and what "is born, in the name of the exceptionality of the intervention, [is] a form of right that is really a *right of the police*" (17, 18; emphasis in original). "From the juridical perspective," then, "when the new notion of right emerges in the context of globalization and presents itself as capable of treating the universal planetary sphere as a single, systemic set, it must assume an immediate prerequisite (acting in a state of exception) and an adequate, plastic, and constitutive technology (the techniques of the police)" (26). The unconstrained exception, or the power to rule by exception, "as Carl Schmitt has taught us," can exist and be sustained only in relation to some constraining, ordering norm to which it is exceptional.[59] The constraining norm, in turn, could be seen as constituted by the power of exception, a power beyond the norm yet connecting to it—also something Schmitt "has taught us."[60]

Decisive positing of the norm always entails its becoming exceptional or other to what it had been. But in this scheme the exception, to repeat, itself constituently depends on the posited norm. Indeed some such positedness is necessary for the "the juridical power to rule over the exception," as Hardt and Negri would want it to do (17). Yet in Empire's dissipated dimensions, there can be no concentrated force, no "positive" cohering to this power. It can at best "accord . . . to a model of postmodern right and postmodern law, through mobile, fluid, and localized procedures" (354). In all, however, these scattered fragments about law accord with its disparate dimensions, with its being determinately enduring yet indeterminately protean. Although these dimensions oppose each other, if is to "rule," law has to combine them, has to accommodate constancy and change in its creating enforceable relations between us.

Even though modern law can now be seen bringing together "in" itself disparate dimensions of Empire, that law is not self-endowed with either content or operative force. It could be expected that the occasional resort by Hardt and Negri to sovereignty as a motor of Empire would go at least some way towards providing that content and force. The feat performed by sovereignty classically was the combining of being unconstrained with being determinate. Hardt and Negri once saw sovereignty as determinate, as a constituted power, and as quite antithetical to constituent power.[61] Empire, however, is "a new form of sovereignty," and it would seem to be a formless form (ix). With the completeness of Empire, it may just be recalled, it is "no longer possible to identify a sign, a subject, a value, or a practice that is 'outside,'" and likewise, now with its sovereignty, "there is no longer an outside that can bound the place of sovereignty" (189, 385). "Liberty," with its irrepressible frontier, "is made sovereign" (169). This plenitudinous sovereignty goes beyond a fixedly constituted "modern sovereignty" in that "its space is always open," as befits the decentered ubiquitous nature of global empire, an Empire whose "rule has no limit" (xiv, 167, 251). In such dissipated and illimitable terms, there can be no concentrated force or distinctive emplacement, and we would be left, presumably, with a "postmodern law" operating "through mobile, fluid, and localized procedures" (354).

Yet, in an alternation which must be excessively familiar by now, Hardt and Negri also wish to have a more palpably placed and cohering sovereignty. This same "sovereignty has taken a new form, composed of a series of national and supranational organisms," although these are "united under a single logic of rule" that could conceivably be constituent (xii). The singular logic, however, fails to emerge and what would seem to be these organisms remain diffuse except when they "all become relevant in the perspective of the supranational juridical constitution" (31). All of which sovereign concern returns us to the juridical, to a juridical that would accommodate "in" itself the constituted and the constituent.

In modernity, the paradigm location of the juridical has been the nation or the nation-state, a location necessarily matching the constituted and constituent dimensions of the juridical. As far as *Empire* is concerned, nation is quite surpassed by global empire. It is the emanation denied. Doubtless some would think that if there were a mode of academic assertion as wearisome as the apparently interminable elevations of the global, of which Hardt's and Negri's is not untypical, it would have to be the counter that the so-called global is simply more of the same. Sameness here subsists in the global being simply a concentration or a configuration of the powers of dominant nations. The elevation of the global would pointedly distinguish it not only as something going beyond nation but also as thriving in nation's deliquescence. There is, however, an alternative to the opposition between the global rampant and the reduction of the global to the powers of nations.

The contention between the global and the national is impelled by a false opposition between them. It takes place in terms of a straitened "territorial" idea of the nation. The modern nation is not just the particular nation of "blood and soil." It is also nation as universally, and it can be imperially, inclined beyond its territorially bounded plot. Nation is a making operatively possible of the impossible combination of these two dimensions. As for the monotonous assertions, in which Hardt and Negri join, of its now failing before the force of globalization and such, the nation of modern nationalism has always endured in and as its very failures (52, 336). It was particular but could not be only or autonomously that. It was universal but could never be universal enough. The universal could only be realized in some particular and was thence unable to be universal. Yet a pure, contained particularity was not possible either, a stasis immune to the infinity of relation beyond it. Since the range of that necessary relation could never be predetermined, the particular evokes and depends upon the universal. This mutual appetency of the universal and the particular within the modern nation does not configure only in the singular nation. It configures also in a variety of densities and forms once known as the comity of nations, or as the great powers, or as the community of nations, but these days usually depicted as international and global, or as a "coalition."

For something relegated, nation has a strikingly insistent presence throughout *Empire*. Hardt and Negri do recognize the nation as "a complete figure of sovereignty," but as such it is for them a repository of set, constituted power.[62] And they do offer an abundance of standard synopses about "the decline of the nation-state" or, more robustly, about being "liberated" from it, or about its "burial" (52, 151, 336). There ensues one world in which old national divisions have been subordinated in "the new world order" or in which they have quite disappeared, and this includes the disappearance of that "Third World . . . constructed by the colonialism and imperialism of nation-states."[63] Like what passes for theories of globalization, the nation here is very much the contained creature of blood and soil, "founded" as it is "on a biological continuity of blood relations, a spatial continuity of territory, and linguistic commonality" (95). In seeking the juridical power of Empire, Hardt and Negri find that it cannot be emplaced in the "juridico-economic structure" of nation, since "the declining effectiveness of this structure can be traced clearly through the evolution of a whole series of global juridico-economic bodies, such as GATT, the World Trade Organization, the World Bank, and the IMF," all of which go to make up a "supranational juridical scaffolding [that] supersedes the effectiveness of national juridical structures" (336).

Yet these same bodies are all controlled and their dictates enforced by congruities of dominant nations.[64] And it is on a national basis that those bodies and those nations operate a "global" gift economy combining "aid," debt, trade, and investment, an economy incorporating the market identified by Hardt and Negri with Empire. What is more, the division and hierarchy generated by that very market, as well as the scope for its expansion, are recognized by them in national terms. They recognize, for example, that the huge preponderance of trade and financial transfers remains concentrated within or under the control of a very few counties (297, 309). They recognize that these countries "are bound together in a series of organisms—the G7, the Paris and London Clubs, Davos, and so forth" (309–310). Indeed, "where would imperial capital be if big [national] government were not big enough to wield the power of life and death over the entire global multitude?"—and this is a form of government they see as strengthening.⁶⁵ In the result, we have a nationally based division in which it seems the Third World has not disappeared after all, for "underdeveloped" countries "remain subordinate in the global system" where they find themselves incapable of implementing countervailing strategies: "The most subordinated regions . . . are effectively excluded from capital flows and new technologies," things preeminently identified with Empire (283, 286, 288).

Conceiving of Empire as a national extraversion and not as something that qualitatively and simply goes beyond nation can illuminate the one specific history Hardt and Negri offer of Empire and of the multitude, and that is a history of the United States. They present this history in two tranches, only patchily connected, one being the part of the United States in the current globalized empire, and the other being the origin of Empire and the multitude in the "American" revolution. Hardt and Negri would add to the long list of claims to American exceptionalism and identify a momentous peculiarity of the United States which could be taken as resolving the persistent irresolution in *Empire* between realized actuality and what is illimitably beyond it. I will now argue that the peculiarity is not such and that the situation it would address can be rendered in those terms of nation just outlined.

The operative ambivalence of nation becomes explicitly concentrated in the large attention that Hardt and Negri pay to the United States. Repeatedly, we are told such things as: "at the narrow pinnacle of the pyramid" of what they call the global constitution "there is one superpower, the United States, that holds hegemony over the global use of force"; that it is the United States which comes "to serve the role of guaranteeing and adding juridical efficacy to . . . [the] complex process of the formation of new supranational right"; and that "the United States certainly occupies a privileged position in the global segmentations and hierarchies of Empire" (180, 309, 384). What is more, Hardt and Negri perceive the United States occupying a preeminent place in the control and coordination of capital, and it is for them the case that the United States occupies a considerable position in the "organisms," transnational and supposedly supranational, which Hardt and Negri see binding together "a group of nation-states" dominating the economy of Empire (247). Indeed, their picture of the "global constitution" has at its "first and highest tier of unified global command" the United States at the "pinnacle" and a predominant "group of nation-states" just below (247–248).

Yet toward the end of the book, the Empire so "constituted" is revealed as "not American and the United States is not its center. The fundamental principle of Empire as we have described it throughout this book is that its power has no actual and localizable terrain or center" (384). All of which may seem to be a striking confirmation of the dimensions of nation outlined earlier—its being particularly placed yet universally extraverted, determinate and the indeterminable—and so what we may be observing with the United States is not the decline, much less the demise, of nation but rather its fullest realization so far.

Hardt and Negri would add historical depth to this linking of a determinate entity to an insistent extraversion by finding that "the contemporary idea of Empire," along with its constituent connection to the multitude, is "born through the global expansion of the internal U.S. constitutional project," a project carrying the new order of the American revolution (82). This project they conceive, with reassuring exactitude, as definitively emerging "in the first phase of the Constitution, between the presidencies of Thomas Jefferson and Andrew Jackson, [when] the open space of the frontier become the conceptual terrain of republican democracy" (168) In this so-called first phase of the Constitution, "a new principle of sovereignty is affirmed, different from the European one: liberty is made sovereign and sovereignty is defined as radically democratic within an open and continuous process of expansion. The frontier is a frontier of liberty" (169). Such an "immanent concept of sovereignty is inclusive, not exclusive," it is "a power entirely within society," and with its constant burgeoning "the entire sovereign body is continually reformed" (164, 166). "This new idea of power" is an instantiation of and "grounded on the multitude's power to construct its own political institutions and constitute society" (165; see also 161, 163–164). The pivotal notion in all this is the frontier: "The conception of frontier and the idea and practice of an open space of democracy were in fact woven together with an equally open and dynamic concept of people, multitude, and *gens*" (170).

*Empire* is at one with Negri's exaltation of the "American revolutionary experience" in *Insurgencies*.[66] Here we find the invention of constituent power explicitly—a power democratic and revolutionary, expansively open and immense with possibility, "a completely new space" with freedom "as its frontier."[67] This is the milieu of "a new man," or in *Empire* of "a new people," a "republican people," whose virtue is formed in the very pursuit of the frontier.[68] Yet the pioneers who provide Hardt and Negri with some "ontological

facticity" were neither uniformly noted for virtue at their outset nor conspicu-
ously elevated by their quest.[69] There is, of course, a standard scenario, one
definitively advanced by Frederick Jackson Turner, that an achieved good soon
came of all this when the "lawless" frontier was rid of "that line of scum that
the waves of advancing civilization bore before them."[70] But what Turner wel-
comes as the pacifying "organs of authority" are for Hardt and Negri the carriers of a constituted power that supervenes and suppresses the burgeoning
constituent frontier. Yet with the United States, for Hardt and Negri, the frontier still persists, continuously going beyond that which would contain it
within constituted power. It is difficult to be more precise about this mix of
constituent and constituted forces, because Hardt and Negri provide only varied and vague accounts of how and where constituted power becomes effective.[71] Some uncertainty on this score may well be inevitable given the
openness, the illimitable freedom of the space into which the frontier ever
opens, and the now-uncontainable efficacy of that opening-out within society
itself.

Yet, again, Hardt and Negri would also have us remember that the very
point of this situating of constituent power is to accord it a materiality, an
immanent actuality. So we should also remember that they do spot an exact
and actual origin of constituent power in that frontier-forming "first phase of
the Constitution, between the presidencies of Thomas Jefferson and Andrew
Jackson" (168). What is distinctive of this period is the intensified settler expansion westward. What is also distinctive is what Negri calls "the progressive
impulse."[72] Put another way, this was an "acquisitive world" where a "civilized"
reasoning reassuringly revealed "voracity [to be] a virtue."[73] This is the selfsame
virtue as that infusing Hardt's and Negri's irrepressible frontier with its formation of "a new man" or "a new people." What ensues is an "Empire of
Innocence," as the irrepressible Patricia Nelson Limerick would put it—innocent because its relentless and acquisitive expansion took place in a "space"
that was ever open, "a completely new space," a wilderness awaiting its taming
telos, a space befitting the quest for freedom from an "Old World colonialism."[74] Opposition to such a completeness of virtue and to such a manifestness
of destiny, such as the resistances of indigenous peoples, was met, understandably enough, with "injured innocence."[75] "Occasionally," says Limerick,
"continuities in American history almost bowl one over."[76]

Righting ourselves temporarily, we can gauge the completeness of identity
between Hardt's and Negri's frontier and the Empire of Innocence by returning with an apt expansiveness to Frederick Jackson Turner, the inventor of the
frontier (or at least the dramaturgical elevating of this frontier over others) as
"the distinguishing feature of American life."[77] Here one finds a rhetoric and a
mythos of the frontier indistinguishable from Hardt's and Negri's. As Turner

lofts it, the frontier promotes democracy; "movement has been its dominant fact"; it is ever "developing," a place of "free land" and "incessant expansion"; and this "fluidity" inherent to the "expansive character of American life" is itself "incessant" and "continually agitating."[78]

Turner would differ tellingly, however, from Hardt and Negri in one respect. Despite the scant attention he devotes to indigenous peoples, Turner does see the frontier as an "Indian frontier," see that frontier as constituted by the "Indian question," a question posed at "the meeting point between savagery and civilization."[79] True, Hardt and Negri do acknowledge that their "first phase of American Constitutional history . . . already hides ingenuously a brutal form of subordination . . ."; they concede that the "North American terrain can be imagined as empty only by wilfully ignoring the existence of the Native Americans"; and they confirm that indigenous peoples had to be treated as "excluded from the terrain to open its spaces and make expansion possible. If they had been recognized, there would have been no real frontier on the continent and no open spaces to fill" (169–170). It is a little difficult, however, to attribute this deluded imagination, willful ignorance, and lack of recognition simply to the settlers in their imperial innocence. After all, as Francis Jennings tells us, "the first objective of American empire was rule over Indian peoples and their lands."[80] Rather, the ignorance and so on are characteristic more of subsequent subscribers to the Turneresque myth of a fantastic frontier opening onto a nothingness of unburdened possibility and absolute freedom—the eidolon of constituent power.[81]

The antithesis of this deracinated history can be found in a subversive sharing of Hardt's and Negri's affection for Nietzsche, especially in their calling on him to support the force of the freely constituent (359). There is also a Nietzsche, however, for whom "freedom is measured . . . by the resistance which has to be overcome, by the effort it costs to stay *aloft*."[82] Such freedom is an affective "superiority over him who must obey"; it entails a readiness "to sacrifice men to one's cause" and, when "viewed more closely" in the setting of liberalism, it is a "war *for* liberal institutions."[83] And this is the freedom advanced by Hardt's and Negri's new republican people. It is a freedom specifically constituted in the sacrifice of indigenous peoples. This sacrifice was given formed, constitutional effect in the so-called Indian cases in the Supreme Court, cases set in that very "first phase of the Constitution" that is so seminal for Hardt and Negri. These cases decided that the "momentous" national settlement depended upon an explicitly counterrevolutionary and explicitly antidemocratic exclusion and sacrificing of Indian peoples, and in so doing they created the racial ur-Constitution of the United States.[84]

Even before Hardt's and Negri's "first phase of the Constitution," the empire of liberty (borrowing the phrase in this setting from Jefferson) already excluded slaves, and the republican franchise for long after that phase would not extend beyond propertied, white, adult males. Indeed, a revisionist historiography, one that has some regard for detail, would show that an unexceptional "American" variety of empire had existed long before this "first phase of the Constitution."[85] The very effort to reconcile being a republic with being an empire confirmed a standard racially and nationally constituted character of both.[86] The solution to this conundrum, usually identified with Jefferson, was that, in the expanding imperial mode, new states could be acquired but that, in the republican mode, they had to be admitted to the Union on the basis of equality with other states. A republican federalism could hardly countenance anything else. Lands could be acquired initially as "territories" under the temporary control of the federal government, but they would eventually have to be accorded the status of states and then be able to enter the fold.[87]

That scheme never applied to Indian peoples and, as an "ignoble history" ground on, they were subjected in regimes that came to resemble those of the second imperialism generally.[88] Even if this exception is brushed aside, the Jeffersonian resolving of the demands of empire and republic was much strained in the latter half of the nineteenth century, when the expansion of empire was inhibited because such an expansion threatened to include peoples perceived as racially different from the citizens of the United States, peoples whose entry into the Union as states was anathema. In the aftermath of the Spanish-American War, this already precarious resolution was destroyed.

The coup de grâce was administered by the Supreme Court in the "Insular Cases," cases that remain good law—to abuse the legal phrase.[89] This was a collection of cases, variously grouped, decided in the late nineteenth and early twentieth centuries, almost all of which concerned the colonies the United States acquired in the war with Spain. The basic issue throughout these cases was whether the conquered territories were part of the United States. The particular call for decision varied widely. It could be a question of whether customs duty was to be levied on imports from the territories. Or it could be the question whether the colonized population enjoyed certain constitutional rights. The outcomes also varied, but the constant was that the colonized themselves were held to be qualitatively different from the citizens of the United States and could not be admitted to that select company. Such people would be "utterly unfit for American citizenship," and they were incapable of assuming "the rights which peculiarly belong to the citizens of the United States."[90] In thence embracing an unabashed colonialism, in departing from "the present system of republican government," the Supreme Court felt that its colonized charges were nonetheless protected by "certain principles of natural justice inherent in the Anglo-Saxon character which need no expression in constitutions or statutes. . . ."[91]

In sum, it is a challenge to see, with Hardt and Negri, how the United States can be distinguished from "Europe in the eighteenth and nineteenth centuries" where "the construction of an absolute racial difference is the essential ground for the conception of a homogeneous national identity," nor how the United States may be exempted from their more general observation that "the modern conception of the people is in fact a product of the nation-state."[92] With this outcome of the specific history of their origins, Empire and the multitude join their other manifestations as transcendent, constituted entities extending appropriatively in the name of the constituent, making all immanent to them—a classic imperial combination. There is no awakening here.

## Acknowledgments

The thought of many is thoroughly immanent to this chapter, but two contributions are especially significant. Paul Passavant commented extensively and incisively on the first draft, and Sundhya Pahuja enlivened work on the last one just when it was becoming wearisome.

## Notes

1. Michael Hardt and Antonio Negri, *Empire* (Cambridge, MA: Harvard University Press, 2000). Subsequent references to *Empire* are given parenthetically in the text.

2. This and the constituted power touched on next in the text will be considered more extensively in the following section of this chapter. For a seminal account, see Antonio Negri, *Insurgencies: Constituent Power and the Modern State*, trans. Maurizia Boscagli (Minneapolis: University of Minnesota Press, 1999), chap. 1.

3. For "common framework" and "global theory," see Michael Hardt and Antonio Negri, "Adventures of the Multitude: Response of the Authors," *Rethinking Marxism* 13 (2001): 236–43, 236. See also Hardt and Negri, *Empire*, 302–303, 350, 358–359.

4. Gilles Deleuze and Félix Guattari, *What Is Philosophy?* trans. Hugh Tomlinson and Graham Burchill (London: Verso, 1994), 45.

5. The former quote is a heading but accurately captures more prolix renditions.

6. *Empire*, 74, 358; Negri, *Insurgencies*, 11, 16, 23–24, 29; Michael Hardt and Antonio Negri, *Labor of Dionysus: A Critique of the State Form* (Minneapolis: University of Minnesota Press, 1994), 294.

7. Deleuze and Guattari, *Philosophy*, 35–38, 41–42; Gilles Deleuze, "Immanence: A Life," trans. Nick Millett, *Theory, Culture & Society* 14 (1997): 3–7, 4. Giorgio Agamben, *Potentialities: Collected Essays in Philosophy*, (Stanford, CA: Stanford University Press, 1999), 232–233. Could these invocations of the infinite be effecting some closure in thought, perhaps through a mixing of infinity as ever-variant possibility with infinity as producing the inevitable recurrence of the existent?

8. Michel Foucault, "Preface," in Gilles Deleuze and Félix Guattari, *Anti-Oedipus: Capitalism and Schizophrenia*, trans. Robert Hurley, Mark Seem, and Helen R. Lane (Minneapolis: University of Minnesota Press, 1983), xiii.

9. Deleuze and Guattari, *Philosophy*, 51, 59.

10. *Empire*, 73, 373–374. The point about subjectivity is illustrated in my next section on the multitude.

11. *Empire*, 358; Hardt and Negri, *Dionysus*, 287; Negri, *Insurgencies*, 24. Perhaps it should be emphasized that Hardt and Negri are not situating their immanence and constituent power in what could be called Deleuze's and Guattari's particular planes of immanence—in varied determinations of the absolute plane of immanence; see Deleuze and Guattari, *Philosophy*, 39–40, 50, 57–58; cf. Hardt and Negri, *Dionysus*, 287.

12. Deleuze and Guattari, *Philosophy*, 43, for the quotation.

13. Ibid., 60.

14. See, e.g., *Empire*, 73. On "society," cf. Claude Lefort, *The Political Forms of Modern Society:*

*Bureaucracy, Democracy, Totalitarianism* (Cambridge, UK: Polity Press, 1986), 201, 203; David Frisby and Derek Sayer, *Society* (London: Tavistock, 1986), 121.

15. Jean-Luc Nancy, *The Sense of the World*, trans. Jeffrey S. Librett (Minneapolis: University of Minnesota Press, 1997), 54, emphasis in original.

16. The phrase is from *Empire*, 92.

17. Spinoza, *Ethics*, trans. and ed. G. H. R. Parkinson (Oxford: Oxford University Press, 2000). The help I derived from this most engaging and thoughtful of editions was generously supplemented by the insights of its editor in commenting on my fledgling efforts.

18. Ibid., 154, being Part 1, Proposition 47.

19. Ibid., 97, 122–123 being Part 1, Proposition 24, Corollary, and Part 2, Proposition 11, Demonstration.

20. Ibid., 123 and 252, being Part 2, Proposition 11, Corollary, and Part 4, Proposition 37, Demonstration.

21. Ibid., 82 and 86, being Part 1, Proposition 11, and Part 1, Proposition 15.

22. Ibid., 93, being Part 1, Proposition 18, Demonstration.

23. Ibid., e.g., at 84, 91–92, 103–105 and 115, being Part 1, Proposition 11, Scholium, and Part 1, Proposition 17, Scholium, and Part 1, Proposition 33, Scholium 2, and Part 2, Proposition 2.

24. G. H. R. Parkinson, "Editor's Introduction" to ibid., at 18.

25. Ibid., 91, being Part 1, Proposition 17, Scholium.

26. Karen Armstrong, *A History of God: The 4,000-Year Quest of Judaism, Christianity and Islam* (New York: Ballantine Books, 1993), 312, 402.

27. Antonio Negri, *The Savage Anomaly: The Power of Spinoza's Metaphysics and Politics*, trans. Michael Hardt (Minneapolis: University of Minnesota Press, 1991); Hardt and Negri, *Empire*, 73, 185, 344.

28. *Empire*, 47, see also 202.

29. E.g., ibid., 373. See also Negri, *Savage*, 195.

30. *Empire*, 164, 368, 373; Hardt and Negri, *Dionysus*, 295, 307.

31. *Empire*, 66, 161, 165; Hardt and Negri, *Dionysus*, 312.

32. Hardt and Negri, *Dionysus*, 309.

33. Hardt and Negri, "Adventures," 240.

34. Ibid.

35. For some recognition of this divide see Hardt and Negri, *Empire*, 422–423, note 17. I am grateful to Sundhya Pahuja for referring me to the Hardt and Negri note.

36. Negri, *Insurgencies*, 14, 30.

37. For "unrepresentable," see, again, Hardt and Negri, *Dionysus*, 295, 307.

38. The constitutive task of the multitude in become political "remains rather abstract"; Hardt and Negri, *Empire*, 399.

39. Hardt and Negri, "Adventures," 242.

40. In Michael Hardt and Thomas Dumm, "Sovereignty, Multitudes, Absolute Democracy: A Discussion between Michael Hardt and Thomas Dumm about Hardt's and Negri's Empire (Harvard University Press, 2000)," *Theory & Event* 4. (2000); and also in this volume.

41. *Empire*, 64, 395; Negri, *Insurgencies*, 30.

42. Hardt and Negri, *Empire*, 410; Hardt and Negri, *Dionysus*, 19.

43. See, for example, 140, 249, 256, 265, 363, 368.

44. *Empire*, 206–207; Hardt and Negri, "Adventures," 238.

45. E.g., Hardt and Negri, "Adventures," 237. .

46. The work of Negri's relied on here is a tract displayed at XI Festa dei Comunista, held in August 2001 at Spoleto. It is called "L'Agonia dello Stato Nazione: L''Impero', stadio supremo dell-imperialismo," 1. I am greatly indebted to Bill Magnuson for a translation.

47. Ibid., 1. See also *Empire*, 317.

48. *Empire*, 31; and Hardt and Negri, "Rethinking," 242.

49. *Empire*, 56, 387–388; Hardt and Negri, "Rethinking," 242.

50. Deleuze and Guattari, *Anti-Oedipus*, 222–240; Hardt and Negri, "Rethinking," 241.

51. Deleuze and Guattari, *Philosophy*, 45.

52. *Start the Week*, BBC Radio 4, May 27, 2002.

53. *Empire*, 317; Michael Mann, *The Sources of Social Power: Volume I: A History of Power from the Beginning to A.D. 1760* (Cambridge, UK: Cambridge University Press, 1986), chap. 9.

54. Michael Hardt, "Translator's Foreword: The Anatomy of Power," in Negri, *Savage*, xiii. More exactly, the difference Hardt mentions is between *potestas* and *potentia* in Spinoza's usage; ibid., xi–xii.

55. Antonio Negri interviewing Deleuze in Gilles Deleuze, *Negotiations. 1972–1990*, trans. Martin Joughin (New York: Columbia University Press, 1995), 173. See also Hardt and Negri, *Dionysus*, 21–22.

56. Negri, *Insurgencies*, chap. 1.

57. Hardt and Negri, *Dionysus*, 4, 7. Negri does refer to "constituent power" as a "juridical concept" in Negri, *Insurgencies*, 1, 5.

58. Deleuze and Guattari, *Philosophy*, 45.

59. *Empire*, 16, for this quote about Schmitt.

60. Carl Schmitt, *Political Theology: Four Chapters on the Concept of Sovereignty*, trans. George Schwab (Cambridge, MA: MIT Press, 1985). See also Hardt and Negri, *Dionysus*, 20.

61. E.g., Hardt and Negri, *Dionysus*, 285, 312; Negri, *Insurgencies*, 21. An offstage exception is their aptly seeing Benjamin's "divine violence [as] constituent power"; Hardt and Negri, *Dionysus*, 294. For Benjamin, such violence "may be called sovereign violence"; Walter Benjamin, "Critique of Violence," in *One-Way Street and Other Writings*, trans. Edmund Jephcott and Kingsley Shorter (London: Verso, 1979), 154.

62. Ibid., 101; Negri, *Insurgencies*, 3, 25.

63. *Empire*, 363; Hardt and Negri, *Dionysis*, 297.

64. For the most compelling of case studies, see Sundhya Pahuja, "Technologies of Empire: IMF Conditionality and the Reinscription of the North South Divide," *Leiden Journal of International Law* 13 (2000): 749–812.

65. *Empire*, 349; Hardt and Negri, *Dionysis*, 242–243; cf. Bobbitt's "Market-State," in Philip Bobbitt, *The Shield of Achilles: War, Peace and the Course of History* (London: Allen Lane/Penguin Press, 2002) at, e.g., 912—a promising notion but one derived from a tendentious argument.

66. Negri, *Insurgencies*, especially at 141–155.

67. Ibid., 151, 154.

68. Ibid., 147; *Empire*, 170.

69. Negri, *Insurgencies*, 148 for the phrase.

70. Frederick J. Turner, "The Significance of the Frontier in American History," *Annual Report of the American Historical Association for the Year 1893* (1893): 223.

71. See, e.g., Negri, *Insurgencies*, 157–161, 175, 185; Hardt and Negri, *Empire*, 165, 172.

72. Negri, *Insurgencies*, 176.

73. Patricia Nelson Limerick, *The Legacy of Conquest: The Unbroken Past of the American West* (New York: W. W. Norton, 1987), 182, dealing with the 1830s, a time immediately following the period of Hardt's and Negri's "first phase of the Constitution."

74. Ibid., chap. 1 in general and 48 in particular; Negri, *Insurgencies*, 151.

75. Limerick, *Legacy*, 48.

76. Ibid.; cf. generally Patricia Nelson Limerick, *Something in the Soil: Legacies and Reckonings in the New West* (New York: W.W. Norton) chap. II-C.

77. Turner, "Frontier," 199.

78. Ibid., 199–200, 204, 221, 227.

79. Ibid., 200, 206, 210.

80. Francis Jennings, *The Creation of America: Through Revolution to Empire* (Cambridge, UK: Cambridge University Press, 2001), 16.

81. Cf. Limerick, *Something in the Soil*, chap. I-B.

82. Friedrich Nietzsche, "Twilight of the Idols," in *Twilight of the Idols and the Anti-Christ*, trans. R. J. Hollingdale (Harmondsworth, UK: Penguin, 1968), 92, emphasis in original.

83. Friedrich Nietzsche, *Beyond Good and Evil*, trans. R. J. Hollingdale (Harmondsworth, UK: Penguin, 1973), 30, emphasis in original.

84. See Chief Justice Marshall in *Fletcher v. Peck* (1810) 10 U.S. (6 Cranch), 87, 142. The most significant case of this kind is *Johnson v. M'Intosh* (1823) 21 U.S. (8 Wheat.) 543. For the point about national settlement generally and for the terms of the sacrifice, see Peter Fitzpatrick, *Modernism and the Grounds of Law* (Cambridge, UK: Cambridge University Press, 2001), 164–175.

85. See Christopher Tomlins, "The Legal Cartography of Colonization, the Legal Polyphony of Settlement: English Intrusions on the American Mainland in the Seventeenth Century" *Law & Social Inquiry*, 26 (2001) 315–372; Jennings, *Creation of America*; James G. Wilson, *The Imperial Republic: A Structural History of American Constitutionalism from the Colonial Era to the Beginning of the*

*Twentieth Century* (Aldershot, UK: Ashgate, 2002). Jennings, at 6, would describe this historical strand not so much as revisionist but as "neglected" when contrasted to those "dominant" sanguine accounts of the origins and progress of freedom and such.

86. See generally Wilson, *Imperial Republic*, chap. 1.

87. A. H. Leibowitz, *Defining Status: A Comprehensive Analysis of United States Territorial Relations* (Dordrecht, Netherlands: Martinus Nijhoff, 1989), 6, 8–16.

88. Petra T. Shattuck and Jill Norgren, *Partial Justice: Federal Indian Law in a Liberal Constitutional System* (Providence, RI and Oxford, UK: Berg, 1991), chap. 2 and 3.

89. Efrén Rivera Ramos, "The Legal Construction of American Colonialism: The Insular Cases (1901–1922)," *Revista Jurídica Universidad de Puerto Rico* 65 (1996): 225–328, for an invaluable account and analysis of these cases on which my engagement here relies considerably.

90. *Downes v. Bidwell* (1901) 182 U.S. 244, 311, 324.

91. *Downes v. Bidwell*, 231.

92. *Empire*, 102, 103, the latter quote being emphasized in the original.

# 3

# On Divine Markets and the Problem of Justice: *Empire* as Theodicy

## Bill Maurer

*Divine violence, which is the sign and the seal but never the means of sacred execution, may be called sovereign violence.*

—Walter Benjamin, 1921.

## Thinking Empire

Is *Empire* useful because it is "good to eat?" That is, would its consumption and absorption result in theoretical growth? Or is *Empire* useful because it is "good to think?"[1] That is, is it homologous to other practical and theoretical interventions in contemporary social fields? Lévi-Strauss had argued that the logical relations differentiating totemic creatures from one another could be seen as similar to the system of social differences constituting a society.[2] The resemblance between these two sets of logical relationships dispelled the totemic illusion by revealing it to be something in the structure of all human thought. That resemblance, then, was not strictly speaking an analogy but a structural homology, a concordance of structure, function, and functional interrelationships among constituent parts of the animal kingdom, human society, and the mind. Lévi-Strauss claimed to find homologies in customs, beliefs, and practices that reacted "dialectically among themselves in such a way that we cannot hope to understand one of them without first evaluating, through their respective relations of opposition and correlation, *institutions, representations, and situations.*"[3] Anthropology, as a mode of knowledge, was simply to assert the homology of structure evident in that dialectic, integrating "essence and form" and reflecting "a more necessary integration: that between method and reality."[4]

The analogy I am drawing between Michael Hardt's and Antonio Negri's *Empire* and the phenomenon of totemism is not necessarily apt, however, since the critical work of *Empire* would itself preclude its own incorporation via simple consumption, "eating" *Empire* for critical practical and theoretical projects. The book, after all, seeks to theorize other means of transformation besides those suggested by incorporation as a dialectical means to growth. "Eating" is far too linear for the project *Empire* sets out. Indeed, the sort of (theoretical, corporeal, social) development occasioned by *Empire* would, like the structuralist theory put forward in *Totemism*, defer the possibility of the analogy between *Empire* and totemism in favor of homology.

A principle of lateral homology occupies much of the book and provides it with theoretical momentum: the two sides of the body of the contemporary global political order correspond in terms of structure, function, and organization. Empire and counterempire or "multitude" are each and everywhere diffuse and dispersed yet linked by multiple and overdetermined points of contact and/or homological correspondence, as two rhizomatic assemblages immanent to each other at every point and every level of scale, simultaneous laterality and unity.

This principle of lateral homology is both analytically fertile and analytically limiting, since it lies in the way of conceptualizing alternative theoretical, corporeal, and social morphologies. Such homology, after all, is not universal in the existent biological phyla. Just as there are not only trees but also rhizomes, so too there are not only chordates like fish (which exhibit lateral symmetry) but also echinoderms like sea stars (which exhibit radial pentamerous symmetry). The move from tree to rhizome is not necessarily a total break with preexisting modes of conceptualizing global capitalism. Other phylic imaginaries could well reveal deeply rooted—or densely lateralized—assumptions about causality, power, and the social. As Katherine Gibson and Julie Graham have demonstrated, the very languages used to describe and analyze phenomena like "global capitalism" themselves presume the existence and, indeed, transcendent dominance of those phenomena.[5] Is *Empire* the new language we are looking for or as equally unsatisfactory as the ones heretofore at our disposal?

This chapter argues that the book has been compelling not because of its theoretical innovation but because it is itself homologous to certain tactical interventions in a number of social fields. The chapter builds its case through a consideration of recent interventions in contemporary money and finance and probes a double homology. The first part of the homology is the relation between Empire and the multitude, as articulated in the book *Empire*. The second is the relation between the book's lateral homologous form and contemporary money and finance. This double homology calls for a reappreciation of Lévi-Strauss's insistence on the integration of essence and form and an opening up of the relation between method and reality—indeed, a reunifying of method and reality occasioned as much by *Empire* as by the conditions it names. *Empire* articulates a theoretical perspective infused with the principle of lateral homology and immanence at a moment when certain elements in contemporary money and finance—which form the hidden background to the world condition the book purports to describe—themselves are also animated by the same principles. Like a totemic animal whose relations to other animals are homologous to human social relations, *Empire* is good to think. Indeed, it expresses a certain limit of thought and language that hinders the appreciation of alternative forms of knowing and expressing because it compels itself by its own demonstrations.[6]

## Divine Justice

The double homology with which I am concerned becomes clearer when considering both *Empire* and finance capital as a joint exercise in theodicy. From the Greek for God and justice (θεος + δικη), theodicy concerns the question of God's goodness in the face of the evident evils of the world. Are such evils themselves the product of divine will? Are they deviations from divine purpose? If the former, how can God be considered truly good? If the latter, how can God be considered truly omnipotent? Such questions exercised theologians and philosophers in both of the "two modernities" outlined by Hardt and Negri.[7] Those of the dominant modern tradition emphasized God's transcendence; those of the countertradition, in which Hardt and Negri place themselves, emphasized God's immanence. Augustine and Spinoza illustrate the essential contrast, and Hardt's and Negri's reformulation of Augustine tracks Spinoza's quite closely.

The Neoplatonic conception of the universe as a great chain of being unified the highest plane of divine intellect with the lowliest plane of degraded matter, a many-leveled universe itself embodying the Oneness of God.[8] Augustine accepted the limitless fullness of the universe but separated God from it, turning the One into two, a transcendent, uncreated God and a created universe dependent on God's divine power:

> Ex plenitudine quippe bonitatis tuae creatura tua subsistit, ut bonum, quod tibi nihil prodesset, nec de te aequale tibi esset, tamen quia ex te fieri potuit, non deesset.

> For of the fullness of Thy goodness, doth Thy creature subsist, that so a good, which could no ways profit Thee, nor was of Thee (lest so it should be equal to Thee), might yet be since it could be made of Thee.[9]

This doubling reflects his conception of the Heavenly City and the Earthly City, the former a state of ultimate perfection and the latter the degraded condition of humankind. Evil in Augustine's theodicy is not an intrinsic quality of beings in the Earthly City, for God does not create evil things. Rather, it results from the privation of good, from beings acting outside of their divinely ordained place in the cosmic hierarchy. Augustine accepts the principle of plenitude but, in making it separate from God and without its own independent principle or power of generation, simultaneously invests it with mutability and contingency.

In Spinoza's *Ethics*, we find a particular reformulation of Augustine's Christian-inflected Neoplatonism. Spinoza, like Augustine, separates God from cosmos. They have ontologically separate existences and essences.[10] At the same time, however, God is internal to cosmos:

> All things which are, are in God, and must be conceived through God, therefore God is the cause of those things which are in him. This is our first point.
> Further, besides God there can be no substance, that is nothing in itself external to God. This is our second point. God, therefore, is the indwelling and not the transient cause of all things.[11]

Similarly, as Hardt and Negri have argued elsewhere in passages that prefigure the political thrust of *Empire*, Spinoza's separation yet infolding of divine and worldly causes allows for a dual conception of power, as *potestas* (Power) and as *potentia* (power). The former maps onto God and Empire, the authorized power of the sovereign; the latter maps onto the creation and the multitude, the immanent capability or potentiality of life itself.[12]

*Empire* is theodicy that rotates around the shift from "plenitude" to "multitude" and a reconfiguration of power as always dual (as *potestas* and as *potentia*). At the heart of the old Neoplatonist cosmology and reflected in the quotation from Augustine above, plenitude referred to the fullness of the universe and of God's intellect. In *Empire*, multitude refers to the irrepressible and manifold powers of human and nonhuman agents whose attributes and actions compel and challenge new kinds of sovereign power. Ultimately and intimately, Power (*potestas*) is separate from power (*potentia*) yet internal to it, and vice versa, yet they are not self-identical, any more than God is to creation.

Furthermore, for Spinoza, as for Hardt and Negri, there is an important revolutionary element in the immanence of sovereign power. As they write, "the horizon of immanence and the horizon of democratic political order coincide completely":

> The plane of immanence is the one on which the powers of singularity are realized and the one on which the truth of the new humanity is determined histori-

cally, technically, and politically. For this very fact, because there cannot be any external mediation, the singular is presented as the multitude.[13]

Continuing in the Spinozist revision of Augustine, Hardt and Negri develop the potential power of the multitude as political agent via the contrast between the City of God and the Earthly City. In Empire, "corruption" rules as the "negation" of life and generation. Like evil for Augustine, yet transposed from the multitude's Earth to Empire's Heaven, "Corruption . . . is not an ontological motor but simply the *lack* of ontological foundation of the biopolitical practices of being" (389; emphasis added). Corruption is not a prime cause but rather the privation of the good. It presents to the multitude "a smoke screen." Imperial power exercises command "in this putrid cloud, in the absence of light and truth" (389). The Earthly City is thus defined by life itself, its irrepressible biopolitical constitution. Empire is the privation of true life, even as it channels and grows a corrupted life. Nevertheless, ultimately the Earthly City will sunder itself "from any belonging or subjection to a city of God which has lost all honor and legitimacy." It will do so "by the power of its own destiny" via the "endless paths" of the "movements of the multitude."[14]

The theoretical motion of *Empire* is to travel through Neoplatonism to the Augustinian theodicy that defined evil as the privation of good but transposing that lack onto Heaven, and then to follow Spinoza's absorption of Augustine with the crucial return of the divine immanence into the worldy cosmopolitical order. Spinoza's insistence on immanence—returning God into the muck of the Earthly City—had led to his being variously labeled pantheist, monist, or atheist. Hardt and Negri sidestep the theological import of Spinoza by insisting that, in their vision, the "multitude . . . resides on the imperial surfaces where there is no God the Father and no transcendence. Instead there is our immanent labor" (396). Labor is the divine principle of the multitude.

Immanent to multitude itself, however, there are two abstractions. The first abstraction involves the transposition from God to labor. It hinges on the abstraction of "labor" itself, bringing all productive human activity under a single sign and conjuring a sameness that is possessed of an unchanging essence such that all human activity can be brought into that sameness. Labor is the universal equivalent. This is the work of capitalism.

The second abstraction involves a principle in the shift from plenitude to multitude. For Augustine, the cosmos, as God's creation that is separate from God, has no independent power. Evil, which may seem to the unlearned to be an independent power of creation separate from God's will, is merely the lack of good, and therefore has no aseity or independent existence. Spinoza, by making Creator and creation immanent to one another, recuperates that aspect of Neoplatonism jettisoned by Augustine but also disperses and multiplies the sources of being. This is the essential shift from plenitude to multitude. That shift, however, homologically related to the abstraction of "labor," keeps constant the problem of aseity: plenitude and multitude each leave unquestioned the -tude that is itself the grammatical marker of the abstract state of being.

This -tude turns a temporary and descriptive quality that demands a subject to qualify (e.g., altus, high) into an unchanging, atemporal essence that is a subject in its own right (altitudo, height). It is the question of the divine ordination of such unchanging essences that makes multitudo—the state of being many—another exercise in theodicy, divine justice, even as it is put forward as a principle of democratic biopolitical plurality. The postulate of abstract labor and principle of -tude place Empire firmly within an analytical project that seeks to identify abstractions in the world whose independent existence from their analytical enlistment goes without saying. And yet the practical unfolding of Empire and multitude would itself obviate such enlistment, as each is always immanent to the other, demanding that the aseity of analytical tool and object be at once infolded into the integration of method and reality of which Lévi-Strauss had reminded us. To paraphrase the anthropologist Roy Wagner, it is not so much a matter of Empire's objects (Empire and multitude) being inadequate to the book's tasks as it is of the book's own analytical apparatus being completely swallowed by the potency of the objects it defines.[15]

## Marking to Market

The multitude, for Hardt and Negri, is not only the locus of democratic plurality. By way of a utopianism that saps it of its real strength, it is the locus of the capitalist market. In his exegesis of Spinoza, Negri had argued that early Dutch capitalism was linked ideologically to the Neoplatonic emphasis on immanence and the internal potentia of creation. The ideology of the market, like the Neoplatonic universe, produced "extraordinary effects that [were] constitutionally effective."[16] Spinoza, Negri maintained, pushed Neoplatonism "to the limit, toward a philosophy of surfaces" and to a "revolutionary materialism."[17] Spinoza's thought thus did not underwrite the bourgeois market so much as it pushed it to its limit. As Negri argued:

> If the metaphysical utopia was a transcription of the ideology of the market, the ethical disutopia is the proposal of the rupture of the market, here transposed and projected in the material and practical dimension of a philosophy of the future. . . . Either one can submit to the crisis of the market or one can live its crisis, going beyond it through the constitutive tension. The disutopia is the discovery of a real and future revolutionary horizon.[18]

In *Empire*, Empire is the metaphysical utopia. The capitalist world market—which "has always run counter to any division between inside and outside"—presents itself as "a model for understanding imperial sovereignty" (190). According to Negri, Spinoza's thought, in and through its production in relation to the capitalist world market, presents an ethical disutopia that partakes of the power of the multitude but has not (yet) extended beyond the revolutionary horizon to rupture the market itself. Rather, it traces the limit of that horizon as it asymptotically approaches it. For Negri, Spinoza's thought is marked to the market, identified through a relation to it, and fundamentally marked by the market, identified by the stamp of it.[19] It is nearly but not yet beyond the market.

In this formulation, the productive disutopia of the multitude possesses a homological relation to the utopia of the capitalist market. This homology, in turn, demonstrates a sort of metahomology between the abstractions of *Empire* and the abstractions of the capitalist market. For example, there is a metahomology between the function of abstract labor in the theoretical project of *Empire* and the function of abstract labor in the practical project of capital. Rather than turn to labor, however, here I consider aspects of contemporary money and finance that themselves exemplify the method of Hardt's and Negri's work. They also exemplify the reality *Empire* stands for—as a book that has been taken up in widely divergent quarters—and names—as a guide that names the features of an unfolding landscape of which it is a part. That reality is in the nature of theodicy. God is immanent to the design, and a transcendental abstract justice is found to reside in and be marked to the divine market. Again, this shows that *Empire* may be good to think, because it points up the unity of analytical object and analytical apparatus. But it is not necessarily good to eat, to be taken in or taken on as descriptive of an independent empirical reality, because it does not linger over the necessity of reflecting on the tools of critique and the failure of knowledge produced by those tools. Such a reflection has the potential to point up the practical as well as theoretical limits of *Empire*'s laterality, a laterality found in other quarters as well, which obviates alternative imaginaries of the contemporary moment.

Contemporary adherents to Islamic banking and finance often invoke a particular *hadith*, or story from the life of the Prophet, to differentiate between financial interest and *riba*, the form of financial increase that is forbidden in Islam.[20] Generally, interest was simply understood to be the English translation of *riba*. Often, especially in the early to middle twentieth century, Islamic economic theorists would argue that *riba* referred to excessive interest, or usury. The full blossoming of Islamic banking and finance in the 1980s and 1990s was accompanied by a vast expansion of theorizing and practical activity around financial techniques to allow observant Muslims to adhere as closely as possible to scriptural injunctions about money and economic exchange. It is in this context that the following *hadith* has become significant:

> Abu Sa'id reported: Bilal (Allah be pleased with him) came with [dates of] fine quality. . . . Allah's Messenger (may peace be upon him) said to him: "From where you have brought them?" Bilal said: "We had inferior quality . . . dates and I exchanged two *sa's* of inferior quality with one *sa'* of fine quality as food for Allah's Apostle (may peace be upon him)," whereupon Allah's Messenger (may peace be upon him) said: "Woe! It is in fact usury; therefore, don't do that. But when you intend to buy dates of superior quality, sell [those of] the inferior quality in a separate bargain and then [buy those of] the superior quality."[21]

Contemporary economists interested in exploring the convergence between modern economic theory and classical Islamic texts use the Bilal *hadith* to argue that prohibition against *riba* was intended by God to prevent injustice by ensuring equality in market transactions. Barter and trade, of course, make equal transactions difficult, since they always involve comparisons of unlike goods and services. Money as a universal equivalent is supposed to mitigate the valuation anomalies introduced by barter. Hence in the Bilal *hadith*, adhering to the prohibition of *riba* requires that the ratio of barter trade equal the ratio of market prices. As contemporary economist Mahmoud El-Gamal argues, we have in this *hadith* a specification for the conditions for Pareto efficiency in the market.[22] Bilal should have marked his poor dates to the market by selling them for the highest price he could get. Then, he should have purchased high quality dates with the money thus obtained at the lowest price he could find. In so doing, he would have brought into alignment traders' desires with market mechanisms. This is what the Prophet demanded of him. And this confirms the market itself, the mechanism for equating utilities with prices, as at one with divine plan.

Others in Islamic banking take very different routes through Islamic jurisprudence to find a unity between the form of money and the shape of divine order. Hence, an Islamic economist influenced strongly by Neoplatonism writes:

> Money in Islam is seen as a highly significant carrier of values that span real market exchange, justice, security, growth and organization [and] also the realm of mankind's medium that links existence between this world and the Hereafter. . . . Thus, money in Islam is the carrier *par excellence* of all the attributes of *Shari'ah* (Islamic Law). Besides, for those who are ready to accept *Shari'ah* as the be all and end all of existence in the universe, money as such a social contravention [*sic*] then becomes the carrier of cosmic meaning and purpose.[23]

As immanent to the money form and divine knowledge itself, the epistemology of Islamic economics presents itself here as "identical with the unifying knowledge-centered circular causation and continuity model of unified reality."[24]

Both Pareto optimality and Neoplatonism come together in contemporary Islamic financial practice. The most mundane example of marking-to-market and the divine unity of knowledge can perhaps be found in contemporary Islamic mortgage alternatives in the United States, currently offered by several Islamic financial services companies and underwritten by the U.S. federal mortgage underwriter, Freddic Mac.[25] Instead of interest-based mortgage financing, one model for an Islamic mortgage alternative is based on an equity partnership. A house buyer enters into a partnership with a financial institution in which each pays a percentage of the cost of a house and serves as co-owner. If the financial institution pays 80 percent and the buyer pays 20 percent, the buyer will then buy back the financial institution's share over a predetermined term (e.g. thirty years). In accordance with divine law, there are no interest payments. Instead, each month, the financial institution calculates the market *rental* value of the house and charges the buyer a percentage of the rental value based on the institution's current share of the ownership of the house. In the first month, then, the financial institution would receive 80 percent of the rental market value of the property. Its share of this value decreases with each payment made by the buyer, who, in effect, is paying rent to the institution and to him- or herself until the point of the full transfer of ownership from institution to buyer.

This process is utterly dependent on the marking-to-market of the rental value of the house on a month-to-month basis, exactly as the Prophet had instructed Bilal for the minute-to-minute transactions at the date market. The market here is the motor of justice, for the market obviates the inequalities inherent in *riba*. The assumption, of course, is that markets are free and fair. More importantly, markets are efficient: the value of any given commodity in a market is equivalent to its price at any given time. As Louis Bachelier wrote at the turn of the twentieth century, "At a given instance, the market believes in neither a rise nor a fall of true prices. . . . Clearly the price considered most likely by the market is the current true price: if the market judged otherwise, it would quote not this price, but another price higher or lower."[26] As final arbiter of price and judgment, the market is in the transcendent space of God and in the minute details of everyday transactions; closed and complete yet open and indeterminate.[27]

The understanding of money, market, and knowledge as all immanent to one another and to divine will should not be taken to characterize Islamic banking alone. It is also common across contemporary capitalist economic formations. The multitude's disutopia, as it were, contains within itself the mark of *Empire*'s theodicy. God and market are translations and transpositions of one another, just as, for Freud, the gods and demons are each other's doubles.[28]

Consider the United States Senate Committee on Finance hearings on tax evasion in the spring of 2002. Seeking to address growing concerns about the use of offshore money havens among corporations and individuals, the Committee on Finance solicited testimony not only from academic and regulator "experts" but also from convicted tax evaders themselves. Striking in their testimony is the manner in which God is both cause and consequence of their actions.

Daniel Bullock, now in prison in Atwater, California, began by asserting that he was "a spiritual man—a leader in my church and community," but then "the enemy of all that is good had crept into my heart and slipped a tentacle around my soul."[29] In his act of contrition before the committee, he proclaimed:

> It's too late for me to learn other than the hard way. It is not too late for our materialistic society. As Paul wrote to Timothy 2,000 years ago: "People who want to get rich fall into temptation and a trap and into many foolish and harmful desires that plunge men into ruin and destruction" (1 Timothy 5:19). Please act now to help keep other citizens from ruin and destruction.[30]

Robert Spears, also convicted of tax evasion, believed that the federal income tax was unconstitutional and followed "anti-tax gurus and Pied Pipers [who] send their 'patriotic' calls to ears ready to hear how to get our country back. They appeal to our patriotism, desire for more freedom and privacy, and love of God to encourage us to join in their crusade."[31] He related that his "journey began in spring of 1993 shortly after I retired. I had formed a foundation for the purpose of teaching our Christian heritage and the Constitution."[32] That foundation served as a money-laundering structure hiding his assets from the Internal Revenue Service. His wife, in her own testimony, extolled the role of religious transformation in atoning for one's sins: "Our world can change but first it must change within you."[33] Another testifier at the hearings, Kelly Stone, got involved in tax evasion through her church:

> In November of 1994 I received a phone call from my sister. She had heard from one of her church friends about a Tax and Insurance Seminar being held at an Insurance Agency in Billings, Montana. The man running this Seminar was supposedly a Christian man with solid morals and an uncanny knowledge of American History.[34]

In each testimonial, the desire to evade federal income taxes is connected with a vision of divinely ordained American patriotism. Taxes, the lifeblood of the state, are seen to suck off the God-fearing and to pervert or corrupt the national body. At least in the beginning, setting up complicated tax evasion structures is an act of fealty to God and country. Later, reconciliation with the taxman comes about through renewed faith in God, a "true" faith that sees state law, however unjust, as nevertheless legitimate. The road to change after the act of contrition involves the legislative process rather than tax vigilantism, as one of the convicted tax evaders argued in his statement, before he concluded: "May God bless America."[35]

## Nomological Machines

The immanence and homology between Empire and multitude are good to think because they themselves are homologous to phenomena such as the finding of God in finance and money. In the examples discussed above, God is cause and consequence of both markets and tax avoidance. Other examples could be used to make much the same claim.[36] It is worth remarking, too, that the technique of marking-to-market was central to the accounting scandals that took place in the early 2000s. Those scandals, which began with the Enron Corporation and the Arthur Andersen accounting and consulting firm, involved marking debt equities and options contracts to market and essentially recording future value "today." They also involved complicated offshore corporate architectures, making use of tax havens in the Caribbean and the Channel Islands. As early as 1993, the business press picked up on the potential risks of mark-to-market accounting at Enron and expressed worries about the embrace of the practice by other corporate giants such as Coca-Cola.[37]

Of interest here is the particular temporality of mark-to-market accounting. As a reporter for *Forbes* noted, there is nothing inherently "wrong" with mark-to-market accounting, but only so long as "nothing major happens to impair the value of the contracts" being valued today at tomorrow's price.[38] That statement echoes a classic pronouncement of John Maynard Keynes, who maintained that the chief illusion governing the stability of the market as an entity "lies in assuming that the existing state of affairs will continue indefinitely."[39] It is in effect a religious chronology, infinitely extendable into a future horizon, asymptotically approaching but never quite reaching the End Times.

Yet marking-to-market also fixes that chronology in the immediate moment, in the calculative event among traders and prices, concretizing as law (the law of supply and demand, the law of marginal utilities) the divine violence of God's sovereignty and in effect deferring endlessly the sign and seal of divine justice. The belief that the future will be like the present both projects the present forward infinitely and operates in the shadow of apocalyptic or millennial time. The theodicy here is true to the term's original Greek, where δικη signified not only justice and penalty but also struggle, discord, conflict, and injustice as well.[40] God's discord is the movement of the market. At the same time, under the principle of immanence, the market is the horizon of democracy through the abstractions of the capitalist machine, "living its crisis," as Negri stated,[41] to move it to the plane of a revolutionary new humanity.

My argument, in short, is that if Hardt and Negri are correct about the homology between Empire and multitude, then so too are Islamic bankers and tax evaders who live in the crisis of market theodicy. My argument is also that the homology between *Empire* and these other social phenomena demands attention to the tools of the analytical enterprise.[42] It is not simply that *Empire* performatively constitutes what it names. It is also that *Empire* and these phenomena operate in terms of an ontological complicity, forming what philosopher of science Nancy Cartwright terms a nomological machine: "a fixed (enough) arrangement of components, or factors, with stable (enough) capacities that in the right sort of stable (enough) environment will, with repeated operation, give rise to the kind of regular behaviour that we represent in our scientific laws."[43] Or, I would add, our critical analytical apparatus. This is why *Empire* is good to think. Like marking-to-market, *Empire*'s modality of knowledge production contains two opposed positions that can be variously characterized as transcendence and immanence, completeness and indeterminacy, closed being and unfolding becoming, *potestas* and *potentia*. As Peter Fitzpatrick has argued in another context, these two positions "correspond . . . to the characteristic attempts in modernity to account for society,"[44] which produces the "illusion . . . that the institution of the social can account for itself."[45]

## Echinodermata

In this sociotheological sense, it is not particularly a problem, then, that *Empire* declares itself with the voice of prophetic oracle. Prophecy is in the nature of its nomological machine. It is more of a problem that the book, like the interventions in money and finance discussed above, is so preoccupied with lateral homology. The totality presumed in *Empire* is troubling,[46] but I am more interested ultimately in the interrelated theodicy and morphology.

Christian myth has incorporated one echinoderm into its own nomological machine, organized through a series of supposed homological correspondences between the animal and the body of Jesus. The sand dollar's five holes are said to correspond to the wounds of Jesus (four nail holes, one side wound). The five "bones" inside are said to be five doves of peace; and the patterns on either side of the animal are held to be a poinsettia flower, the star of Bethlehem, or an Easter lily. Fitting rather nicely into eschatological traditions within Christianity, the creature thus has become, for some, an object of reflection and meditation on the unity of creation and the wonder of the incarnate God-man.[47] The God-man in itself suggests the problems of adequation that have preoccupied monetary theorists since the Greeks, again homologically: How can the substance of flesh (Jesus-as-man) approximate the divine essence of the Word (Jesus-as-God); how can any physical substance (gold, paper) approximate the transcendence of value ("money")? The problem of adequation here is also a problem of language and meaning, sense and reference.[48]

At the same time, however, while sand dollars seem at first glance to exhibit a basic five-part homological pattern, what distinguishes sand dollars from some other echinoderms is their irregularity and deviation from strict pentamery and, indeed, from strict homology. The petal patterns on either side of the animal often do not correspond to one another. The leftmost petals may differ in length from the rightmost ones. One of the five may be smaller than the other petals and also of a different size and shape from the corresponding petal on the other side of the creature.[49] The sand dollar's systematicity for Christian eschatology thus is belied by its own radical morphological underdetermination. Furthermore, sand dollars, like more systematically pentamerous echinoderms like starfish and sea urchins, are internally relatively morphologically undifferentiated. There is no circulatory system, no respiratory system; and no nervous system but rather a distributed patchwork of nerve cells. There is, however, a water-vascular system unique to the phyla that pumps seawater into and out of the creature and in the process achieves the functions filled by such "systems" in other animals while providing a means of locomotion via hydraulic tube feet. In short, the echinoderm has no "universal cover of law" governing it.[50] This may account for its uncanny regenerative capabilities: a whole organism can regrow itself entire from almost any tiny part.

*Empire* ruptures one version of totality through the Spinozist reformulation of immanence, and this is a welcome move for critical analyses of the contemporary moment. It forecloses both global triumphalism and metaphors of global or capitalist totality by excavating the potentiality of the multitude. At the same time, however, the Spinozist theodicy puts in place of totality a radically limited lateral homology. This prevents *Empire* from coming to terms with both nonlaterality and radical overdetermination by particular sites at least in some moments (e.g., the United States—but not always, or everywhere, and not as hegemon in the classic sense but as nonetheless powerful, both as *potestas* and *potentia*). It also prevents *Empire* from even beginning to approach sites of nonimmanence or radically different homological relation other than through its tropes of envelopment, incorporation, or unity.[51] In addition, opening to the possibility of other morphologies like that embodied by echinoderms also means accepting a principle of underdetermination. As a theodicy, the work of *Empire* and its homologies is to attempt to fix a cover of law for the morphology of the contemporary moment, obviating divine justice even as the book depends on it. This is why, while good to think, *Empire* is ultimately not good to eat.[52]

Off the seafloor, far from the echinoderm, and in a properly "social" space, I cannot necessarily imagine what such sites of nonimmanence or different homological relation might be. But that lack of imagination is precisely the failure of knowledge with which *Empire* leaves us, because it leaves us soundly within the modern imagination of the social, configured paradoxically yet productively as both closed and indeterminate, when perhaps what we need most is some antisocial, even echinodermatic, theorizing.[53]

## Acknowledgments

I would like to thank Tom Boellstorff, Thomas J. Douglas (with apologies for the penultimate note), Susan Greenhalgh, Diane Nelson, Charles Piot, and the editors of this volume for comments and criticisms of earlier versions of this chapter. I am also grateful for fruitful conversations with Stefan Helmreich, Liisa Malkki, and Hugh Raffles as this chapter was taking shape, as well as published and unpublished writings shared by Hirokazu Miyazaki and Annelise Riles that spurred my thinking. I thank all the Islamic finance professionals interviewed over the course of my research for their candor, insight, and good humor. Research on financial alternatives has been supported by the National Science Foundation, Law and Social Science program (SES-9818258), and the Russell Sage Foundation. The opinions expressed here are my own and do not reflect those of any other agency; all errors and inconsistencies are my responsibility alone.

## Notes

1. Claude Lévi-Strauss, *Totemism* (Boston: Beacon Press, 1963), 89.
2. Ibid., 79.
3. Ibid., 91, original emphasis.
4. Ibid.
5. J. K. Gibson-Graham, *The End of Capitalism (As We Knew It): A Feminist Critique of Political Economy* (Oxford: Blackwell, 1996). J. K. Gibson-Graham is the pen name of Katherine Gibson and Julie Graham, who have been conducting research on noncapitalist economic formations and querying the very tendency to define them in terms of a negative relation to capitalism.
6. In that, it is much like the category of the social and modern sociological knowledges, to which I return at the end of this chapter. Roy Wagner writes, of one such knowledge, anthropology: "To the extent that it may *compel* knowledge, rather than merely explain or interpret it . . . the science of the human is compelled by its own demonstrations. The science of humanity's capabilities and limitations is after all carried out by human beings, who become their own self-demonstration in the act of carrying it forth." Wagner, *An Anthropology of the Subject: Holographic Worldview in New Guinea and Its Meaning and Significance for the World of Anthropology* (Berkeley, CA: University of California Press, 2001), 6.
7. Michael Hardt and Antonio Negri, *Empire* (Cambridge, MA: Harvard University Press, 2000), 69–92. Subsequent references to *Empire* are given parenthetically in the text.
8. See, generally, Arthur O. Lovejoy, *The Great Chain of Being* (Cambridge, MA: Harvard University Press, 1936).
9. The Latin is from *S. Aurelii Augustini confessiones: ad fidem Codicum Lipsiensium et editionum antiquiorum recognitas*, ed. Herm. Bruder (Leipzig: Tauchnitz, 1837), XIII, 2. The English is from *The Confessions of St. Augustine*, ed. Ernest Rhys (London: J. M. Dent and Sons, 1946), XIII, 2.
10. Benedict de Spinoza, *Ethics*, in R. H. M. Elwes, trans. and ed., *The Chief Works of Benedict de Spinoza* (New York: Dover Publications, 1951), I, Prop. XVII.

11. Spinoza, *Ethics*, I, Prop. XVIII, references omitted.

12. See Michael Hardt, "Translator's Forward: The Anatomy of Power," in *The Savage Anomaly: The Power of Spinoza's Metaphysics and Politics*, by Antonio Negri (Minneapolis: University of Minnesota Press, 1991), xi–xvi; Antonio Negri, *The Savage Anomaly*.

13. *Empire*, 73. See also Negri, *Savage Anomaly*, and Negri, "*Reliqua desideratur*: A Conjecture for a Definition of the Concept of Democracy in the Final Spinoza." In *The New Spinoza*. ed. Warren Montag and Ted Stolze (Minneapolis: University of Minnesota Press, 1997), 218–246.

14. *Empire*, 396, 397, emphasis removed; see also 206–208.

15. Wagner writes: "it is not so much a matter of anthropology's pragmatic exemplars being inadequate to its tasks as it is of the discipline being completely swallowed by their potency"; Wagner, *An Anthropology of the Subject*, 7.

16. Negri, *Savage Anomaly*, 18.

17. Ibid., 19, 20.

18. Ibid., 176.

19. By stamp, I refer to Nietzsche's assault on metaphysics using the numismatic metaphor of the χαρακτήρας or *charaktēr*, the die used to produce the obverse impression on a coin. He wrote: "truths are . . . metaphors worn out and without sensuous power; coins which have lost their impressions and now matter only as metal, no longer as coins"; Nietzsche, as quoted by Marc Shell, *The Economy of Literature* (Baltimore, MD: Johns Hopkins University Press, 1978), 154.

20. On Islamic banking and the prohibition of *riba*, see, for example, M. Umer Chapra, *Towards a Just Monetary System* (Leicester, UK: The Islamic Foundation, 1992); Timur Kuran, "The Genesis of Islamic Economics: A Chapter in the Politics of Muslim Identity," *Social Research* 64 (1997): 301–337; Bill Maurer, "Engineering an Islamic Future: Speculations on Islamic Financial Alternatives," *Anthropology Today* 17 (2001): 8–11; and Bill Maurer, "Anthropological and Accounting Knowledge in Islamic Banking and Finance: Rethinking Critical Accounts," *Journal of the Royal Anthropological Institute* 8, 4 (2002): 645–667.

21. Quoted and translated in Muhammad Akram Khan, *The Economic Teachings of the Prophet Muhammad* (Delhi: Noor Publishing House, 1992), 153–154; some punctuation removed to modernize the text.

22. Mahmoud El-Gamal, "An Economic Explication of the Prohibition of *riba* in Classical Islamic Jurisprudence," in *Proceedings of the Third Harvard University Forum on Islamic Finance* (Cambridge, MA: Center for Middle Eastern Studies, Harvard University, 2000), 31–44.

23. Masudul Alam Choudhury, *Money in Islam: A Study in Islamic Political Economy* (London: Routledge, 1997), xv.

24. Ibid., xvi.

25. See, e.g., Freddie Mac Press Release, "Freddie Mac Investing in Islamic 'Mortgages' from American Finance House—Lariba," March 28, 2001; and "Freddie Mac, Standard Federal Bank Announce New Islamic Home Financing Initiative for Michigan Families," August 10, 2001; copies in possession of the author.

26. Louis Bachelier, "Théorie de la spéculation," *Annales de l'Ecole Normale Supérieure*, 3rd ser., 17 (1900): 26.

27. A note of the ethnographic kind: in interviews, at moments when I expect Islamic finance professionals to say "God," they say "market," and vice versa. In an interview conducted in the summer of 2002, one professional stated that "the technique of marking to market" is what makes Islamic finance truly "unique."

28. Sigmund Freud, "The 'Uncanny,'" in *The Standard Edition of the Complete Psychological Works*, trans. James Strachey et al. (London, 1955), vol. 17, 217–256; originally published 1919.

29. Statement of Daniel Bullock, 1. All references to the Senate committee testimony are from: United States Senate Committee on Finance, "Hearings: Schemes, Scams and Cons, Part II: The IRS Strikes Back." April 11, 2002. Available at http://finance.senate.gov/sitepages/hearing041102.htm, accessed April 12, 2002. The statements of each witness who gave testimony are paginated independently.

30. Ibid., 6.

31. Statement of Robert Spears, 1.

32. Ibid.

33. Statement of Mary Elaine Spears, 3.

34. Statement of Kelly Stone, 1.

35. Statement of Robert Spears, 2–3.

36. For the example of derivatives trading, see Bill Maurer, "Repressed Futures: Financial Derivatives' Theological Unconsciousness," *Economy and Society* 31 (2002): 15–36.

37. See Toni Mack, "Hidden risks," *Forbes* 151; 11 (May 24, 1993): 54–56; and Ronald Fink, "Off again, On again: The FASB Says that Equity Accounting for Unconsolidated Subsidiaries May Not Reflect Reality," *CFO Magazine*, July 1, 1997.

38. Mack, "Hidden Risks," 54.

39. John Maynard Keynes, *The General Theory of Employment, Interest, and Money* (New York: Harcourt, Brace and Co., 1964; originally published 1935), 152.

40. Jacques Derrida, "Force of Law: The 'Mystical Foundation of Authority,'" in *Deconstruction and the Possibility of Justice*, ed. by Drucilla Cornell, Michael Rosenfeld, and David Gray Carlson (New York: Routledge, 1992), 6.

41. Negri, *Savage Anomaly*, 176.

42. I am indebted to conversations with and unpublished manuscripts by Annelise Riles for my thinking about analytical tools.

43. Nancy Cartwright, *The Dappled World: A Study of the Boundaries of Science* (Cambridge, UK: Cambridge University Press, 1999), 50.

44. Peter Fitzpatrick, "Bare Sovereignty: *Homo Sacer* and the Insistence of Law," *Theory and Event* 5 (2001), 24. I would like to thank Paul Passavant for pointing me toward this essay.

45. Ibid., quoting Claude Lefort, *The Political Forms of Modern Society: Bureaucracy, Democracy, Totalitarianism* (Cambridge, UK: Polity Press, 1986), 184. See also Wagner, *An Anthropology of the Subject*.

46. E.g., Gibson-Graham, *End of Capitalism*.

47. The sand dollar myth is widespread and has been taken up by hundreds of Florida tourist traps selling shell wares.

48. Marc Shell has written eloquently on this topic in *Art and Money* (Chicago: University of Chicago Press, 1995).

49. See A. M. Kerr and J. Kim, "Bi-penta-bi-decaradial Symmetry: A Review of Evolutionary and Developmental Trends in Holothuroidea (Echinodermata)," *Journal of Experimental Zoology (Molecular and Developmental Evolution)* 285 (1999): 93–103; J. M. Lawrence, C. M. Pomory, J. Sonnenholzner, and C.-M. Chao, "Bilateral Symmetry of the Petals in Mellita tenuis, Encope microp-ora, and Arachnoides placenta (Echinodermata: Clypeasteroida)" *Invertebrate Biology* 117 (1998): 94–100; S. V. Rozhnov, "The Left-Right Asymmetry in Echinoderms," in R. Mooi and M. Telford, eds., *Proceedings of the 9th International Echinoderm Conference, San Francisco, 5–9 August 1996* (Rotterdam: Balkema, 1998), 73–78.

50. The phrase is Cartwright's (*Dappled World*, 6), in relation to science, not starfish.

51. This point is closely allied to Gibson-Graham's criticism (*End of Capitalism*, 126) that Negri only ever allows noncapitalist relations to enter the discussion as subject to "invasion." In their gloss on Negri, such relations may be "recalcitrant but [ultimately] incapable of retaliation."

52. Sea urchins and sea cucumbers, of course, are delicious.

53. See Fitzpatrick, "Bare Sovereignty." The idea of an antisocial theory is derived from the work of authors such as Michel Callon, Bruno Latour, Alain Pottage, and especially Marilyn Strathern. See, for example, the special issue of the journal, *Economy and Society* 31; 2 (2002) on Callon; Alain Pottage, "Persons and Things: an Ethnographic Analogy," *Economy and Society* 30 (2001): 112–138; and Marilyn Strathern, *Property, Substance, and Effect* (London: Althone Press, 1999).

4

Law

# Legal Imperialism:
# *Empire*'s Invisible Hand?

## Ruth Buchanan and Sundhya Pahuja

Since its publication only three years ago, *Empire* has spawned a remarkable amount of commentary and debate, including a number of responses and elaborations from the authors.[1] Indeed, one is tempted to suggest that *Empire* has been so successful in encapsulating current conditions of social and intellectual production that it has failed to escape them, and that it too has become just another "commodity undergoing metamorphosis in our globalized, networked, academic market."[2] But, whether because there is no outside to Empire or because, as Spivak has suggested, "the mainstream has never run clean, perhaps never can,"[3] there is no way to write about *Empire* without becoming somehow implicated in its reproduction and amplification. We can, however, seek to engage in a "constructive, rather than disabling complicity"[4] with our sources, which here include not only Hardt's and Negri's *Empire* but also that more decidedly mainstream publication, the World Bank's annual *World Development Report.*

Hence, as critical scholars interested in the legal aspects of international economic institutions, our concern in this chapter is to determine whether *Empire* provides us with any new tools with which to advance or refine our analysis and critique. More specifically, given *Empire*'s self-professed juridical orientation,[5] we ask whether the text helps us to understand the role that law plays in the current global order. So, in our reading of *Empire*, we investigate the legal contours of the ostensibly new imperialism whose arrival it heralds.

In particular, we ask what insights it might provide for an engagement with what must by implication be a central institution of Empire, the World Bank (336). In this chapter, we juxtapose *Empire* with a text that has played an important role in the constitution of the current order of legal imperialism, the World Bank's flagship annual publication, the *World Development Report.* Here we will focus on the two most recent such reports. This exercise in concurrent reading suggests that instead of helping us to understand the legal mechanisms by which the World Bank and other multilateral economic institutions have constructed, and construct in an ongoing way, the current, putatively "empirial" global order, Hardt and Negri conceal those mechanisms by adopting an essentially unidirectional and positivist conception of the relationship between law, states, and markets.[6]

This conception of law produces three effects. The first is that, somewhat ironically for a book that purports in some senses to be a work of jurisprudence, there is no account in *Empire* of the constitutive role of law, in relation either to the social or to the market. Rather, despite the purported immanence of Empire,[7] in Hardt's and Negri's account the constitution of the world market appears ontologically prior to law; that is, it is the market that produces the laws of Empire. The role that law itself plays in the constitution of global markets as well as of the subjects who operate within them is missing from their analysis. The second effect of adopting this one-way conception of law and states is to produce a misreading of the rise of international law as evidence of a decline in national sovereignty (and national law), whereas in our argument, international law is not distinct from nation, but rather an extraversion of the nation itself. Because of this misreading, Hardt and Negri mistakenly ascribe to Empire modes of governance that are better understood as practices or modes of national sovereignty itself.[8] The third and related effect of this positivist conception of law is that *Empire* fails to recognize the way in which the concept of "the rule of law" itself operates as a sustaining narrative both for nations and for the international system of multilateral institutions. As we illustrate by reference to the World Bank, interventions undertaken by international economic institutions are frequently legitimated by reference to the "rule of law."[9] Indeed, it would not be going too far to assert that the normative framework of the current world order is increasingly framed in terms of this indeterminate yet presumptively universal concept. We argue that *Empire* reproduces (and hence reinforces) rather than dismantles this pervasive myth.

We begin by considering what Hardt and Negri mean by Empire, drawing out what we perceive to be three key characteristics attributable to it. We then foreshadow the two main problems that we argue arise from this characterization of the current world order: the disempowering naturalization of the market, and the mistaken assertion of the decline of the nation and its corollary, modern sovereignty. We then show how these two problems arise largely through Hardt's and Negri's limited conception of law. We illustrate this connection by considering recent developments at the World Bank alongside the characterization of law in *Empire*. Specifically, we argue that while at first glance, World Bank practices do appear to resonate with "empirial" modes of power, looking closely at the role that law plays in those practices shows us that they are ultimately more reliant on what one might characterize as modern sovereignty than the postmodern version that Hardt and Negri argue is the mode of Empire. In particular, we show why Hardt's and Negri's conception of law and, in particular, the three key limitations identified above, lead them both to underplay the continuing significance of the nation state, and to overlook the constitutive role that multilateral legal and economic institutions play in relation to the production of the world market. Their misreading of law, we argue, leads them to a misdiagnosis of our current condition.

## Reading Empire

What do Hardt and Negri mean by Empire? First, they tell us repeatedly that Empire is something new. They claim that Empire is a new form of legal imperialism, one that is not "a weak echo of modern imperialisms but a fundamentally new form of rule" (146). In their view, Empire heralds a paradigmatic shift, a break with the past precipitated by the crisis of postmodernity and the dismantling of the welfare state.

Second, Empire is decentered and deterritorializing insofar as it "establishes no territorial center of power and does not rely on fixed boundaries or barriers. It is a decentered and deterritorializing apparatus of rule that progressively incorporates the entire global realm within its open expanding frontiers" (xii) The postmodern form of sovereignty in Empire is said to have surpassed the modern form that inhered in territorial nation states: "Government and politics come to be completely integrated into the system of transnational command" (307). The boundaries of nation-states are constantly transgressed and effaced in the context of Empire, their "declining sovereignty . . . and their increasing inability to regulate economic and cultural exchanges is in fact one of the primary symptoms of the coming of Empire" (xii).

Third, the concept of Empire emphasizes totality, both of its territorial reach and of its capacity to incorporate all human activity into its scope. "First and foremost then, the concept of Empire posits a regime that effectively encompasses the spatial totality, or really that rules over the entire 'civilized' world. No territorial boundaries limit its reign" (xiv). It is effectively global and is sometimes even referred to as analogous to the more familiar term, "globalization" (8–9)[16] One of its key instantiations is in the "global market." Because it is all-encompassing, Empire can be resisted only "in toto":

> We believe that toward the end of challenging and resisting Empire and its world market, it is necessary to pose any alternative at an equally global level. Any proposition of a particular community in isolation, defined in racial, religious, or regional terms, "delinked" from Empire, shielded from its powers by fixed boundaries, is destined to end up as a kind of ghetto. Empire cannot be resisted by a project aimed at a limited, local autonomy. (206)

Mirroring and supporting this assertion is the depiction of the world market as "fully realized," meaning that everything is included within its sphere:

> It is useful to remember here . . . that the capitalist market is one machine that has always run counter to any division between inside and outside. It is thwarted by barriers and exclusions; it thrives instead by including always more within its sphere. . . . In its ideal form there is no outside to the world market: the entire globe is its domain. We might thus use the form of the world market as a model for understanding imperial sovereignty. (190)

In contrast to the striated space of modern imperialism, then, the world market of Empire operates in a smooth space of uncoded and deterritorialized flows (333). This "smooth" space is, we discover, postmodern in its logic (151): "The ideology of the world market has always been the antifoundational and anti-essentialist discourse par excellence. Circulation, mobility, diversity and mixture are its very conditions of possibility" (150). It thrives on the hybrid and fragmentary subjectivities (that is, all of us) produced by the postmodern sovereignty of Empire. Within this postmodern space, "every difference is a new [marketing] opportunity" (152), and there is a place for everyone in the global shopping mall.[17]

In our view, this conception of global capitalist forms poses two main difficulties in trying to understand current juridico-economic configurations. First, Hardt's and Negri's insistence that Empire is "decentered and deterritorializing," cutting across and rendering obsolete the "territorial" idea of nation, conceals more than it reveals about our current condition. To insist that the arena of determinations is now exclusively "transnational" is to misrecognize the extent to which the international realm presumes the existence of a community of territorially bounded nation-states governed along certain Western lines and the extent to which international law is in fact a *mode* of national sovereignty itself, that is, a mode of its practice rather than an indication of its decline.

Second, Hardt's and Negri's approach naturalizes the market and elides the fact that markets do not exist without law, a point that even the World Bank itself seems now to have learned. Emphasizing the realized existence of a common (global) subjectivity in relation to Empire draws our attention away from the ways in which the ongoing processes of incorporating people (and subjectivities) into the global market must actively be facilitated by multilateral institutions such as the World Bank and by international economic law. Ironically, this represents a failure to recognize the constitutive role of what are said to be the "constitutional" institutions of Empire. In this, Hardt and Negri repeat the common mistake of "naturalizing" the functioning of the world market, rendering it more rather than less powerful.[12]

In the next section, we turn to two recent publications of the World Bank. Our purpose in reading these texts in relation to *Empire* is twofold. We seek to elaborate further on the difficulties surrounding the focus on "deterritorialization" and "totality" introduced above and to demonstrate how they are based upon and in turn perpetuate a static and positivist conception of law. Our examination of current World Bank discourse illustrates as well some salient features of an emergent international legal imperialism that remain largely unexplored in Hardt's and Negri's account.

## Reading the *World Development Reports* against *Empire*

The texts of the World Bank are useful to read alongside Hardt's and Negri's account of Empire because of the central and constitutive role the bank performs in the current world order. The bank's powerful role in the ongoing production of interstate hierarchies in the global economy ought to have located it at the center of Hardt's and Negri's analysis. Not only is it a powerful generator of ideas about economic development, but its lending practices—which include conditionality—are important instruments for both disseminating and enforcing the ideas it generates. The *World Development Report* plays a considerable role in securing the bank's preeminent position in the arena of "development." For example, Bonnie Campbell, writing about the 1997 development report, observes:

> The publication of this Report and the most recent writings of the leading members of the team which produced it underline the fact that the World Bank now occupies, among the multi- and bi-lateral institutions, the central place as a producer of new normative frameworks in social and political spheres. Together, they seem to suggest that these norms reflect a world consensus on institutional procedures and arrangements which will best ensure continuing economic devel-

opment. These norms then become the "rules of the game" which are put forward as having universal validity.[13]

Indeed, the bank has often been criticized for its role in maintaining the architecture of imperialism. Notwithstanding its important functions as a juridical and economic regulator, the World Bank is rarely mentioned specifically in *Empire*. And although Hardt and Negri have subsequently stated that international economic organizations such as the World Bank are key to Empire,[14] we think that this omission is a telling one. This is particularly so because while on some levels the bank does seem to have taken an "empirial" turn, upon closer examination, we would argue that the bank's regulatory practices both are more reliant on a modern notion of sovereignty than a postmodern one (as Hardt and Negri characterize it) and demonstrate that even the bank understands that the ongoing production of the global market is reliant upon the institutional and legal frameworks produced by nation-states.

Some recent developments at the World Bank, however, do appear homologous to Hardt's and Negri's account of the coming of Empire. In recent years, the bank's publications suggest that it has significantly altered its conceptual frameworks, seemingly responding to those who would criticize it for maintaining and perpetuating the hierarchies of past imperialisms. It would appear that, correspondingly, its practices and policy prescriptions for developing countries have changed.[15] This shift seems to be roughly synchronous with the advent of Empire and on some levels does exhibit certain tendencies resonant with Hardt's and Negri's conception of the shift from modern to postmodern imperialisms.[16] This ostensible change of position is particularly well reflected in its two most recent *World Development Reports*.[17]

The recent shift in the World Bank's approach to development policy has sometimes been described in a shorthand form as the replacement of the "Washington consensus" with a "post-Washington consensus."[18] We would hesitate to describe what has emerged from critiques of the Washington consensus as a new consensus; however, we would certainly agree that there have been important changes in bank perceptions and prescriptions. While some questioning of various tenets of the Washington consensus was visible in the early 1990s, the Asian currency crisis in 1997 prompted a more widespread and public rethinking. One consequence of that process was seen in the preparation of the *World Development Report 2001: Attacking Poverty* (WDR 2001). Ravi Kanbur, the lead author of the report, was selected by then–chief economist Joseph Stiglitz for his willingness to rethink previous orthodoxies. Kanbur engaged in an unprecedented amount of consultation outside the bank's usual policy circles and widely circulated a controversial draft report. Indeed, the controversy led to his resignation and a limited retreat from the positions taken in the draft. This controversy notwithstanding, the shift we are tracing is not confined to the 2001 *World Development Report* and the bank's subsequent recoil from the report's "softer" approach.[19] It is arguable that elements of this shift are still clearly visible in the *World Development Report 2002: Building Institutions for Markets* (WDR 2002).

The "Washington consensus" is a term that became a kind of shorthand for a package of policies including tight fiscal and monetary policies, freer trade and capital flows, privatization, deregulation, and openness to foreign direct investment. These policies were urged on developing countries by the World Bank and the International Monetary Fund (IMF) and often imposed through conditionality clauses in lending arrangements. Many if not all of these policies were directed towards integrating developing countries into global markets for finance, investment, and goods and services. It was a set of policies that prioritized the operations of the (global) market over the interventions of the state. Within the debates framed by the Washington consensus, state and market were understood as opposing rather than complementary institutions.[20]

The Washington consensus and the key institutions identified with it such as the bank came under criticism as the severe impacts of the policies became clearer.[21] Many commentators have elaborated on specific problems with the prescriptions.[22] In short, by the mid-1990s, the Washington Consensus had lost some of its earlier unassailability both within and outside the bank.

The "Post-Washington consensus" has been used to describe the more recent policy prescriptions emanating from the bank, although, as remarked upon above, we are less than certain that any "consensus" as such has emerged, both because many elements of the new orientation are conflicting and because there are many continuities with the old. Nevertheless, there are three important differences that we wish to highlight here. In relation to the first two of these shifts, we find instructive homologies with Hardt's and Negri's account of the coming of Empire. A close examination of the third difference in bank practice, which reflects evolving understandings of the relationship between state, law, and markets, however, suggests the opposite. In contrast to Hardt and Negri, the bank has become more attentive to the role played by law and state-based legal institutions in the success of market-based reforms. This third shift in bank practice provides evidence in support of the continued significance of modern modes of sovereignty and weighs against accepting the paradigm shift to the postmodern sovereignty depicted in *Empire*.

The first shift in bank practice is an increased awareness of the institutional embeddedness of economics and the corresponding need to promote "good governance" to ensure the effectiveness of reform. With this awareness comes an implicit recognition that transformations will be more effective where local policy-makers and communities have greater "ownership" over them.[23] For example, the WDR 2001 relies heavily on what the bank calls "participatory poverty assessments," as collected in the three-volume study, *Voices of the Poor*.[24] These stories about poverty, as told by "the poor" themselves, were collected and cataloged by the bank and are woven through the report, providing a legitimating narrative for the bank's prescriptions. The second point of difference is the use of the notion of "social capital." The notion is used in the WDR 2001 both as a mechanism for quantifying degrees of social exclusion and as an antidote to its worst effects. Social capital invokes the elusive fabric of communities, families, cultures, and networks, the very things that critics had admonished the bank for overlooking in its previous conceptions of human well-being.

Some have argued that these two shifts herald the advent of a new inclusiveness in relation to bank practice and represent a movement towards greater autonomy for the groups subject to bank intervention. We would suggest, however, that rather than drawing power away from the bank, these shifts intensify and extend its regulatory scope. It is at this point that our analysis resonates with that of Hardt and Negri. The new emphasis on "social capital," for example, means that the opportunities for conditionality are now expanded. The bank can legitimately extend its gaze to the broad range of matters included within that amorphous concept, such as family relations, domestic work, community networks, and subsistence-oriented agricultural co-ops. Social capital becomes, in the hands of the bank, a vehicle with which to integrate "poor people" (those without financial capital) into global markets more rapidly. In similarly tentacular fashion, the move towards "participatory" poverty assessments seeks to incorporate the work of researchers and activists working with local communities and nongovernmental organizations (NGOs) into the bank's own assessments. While some have seen this as a laudably more democratic approach, we would argue that, considered in the context of the bank's increasingly explicit efforts to position itself as a knowledge-producing institution, it becomes potentially insidious. As the bank reaches out to embrace its former critics, fewer avenues are open for the production and dissemination of knowledge outside the expanded framework of the bank. In this respect, the bank's expansionist tendency appears similar to Empire's characteristic reliance on network power as described by Hardt and Negri:

> This democratic expansive tendency implicit in the notion of network power must be distinguished from other, purely expansionist and imperialist forms of expansion. The fundamental difference is that the expansiveness of the immanent concept of sovereignty is inclusive, not exclusive. In other words, when it expands, this new sovereignty does not annex or destroy the other powers it faces, but on the contrary opens itself to them, including them in the network. (166)

These striking parallels notwithstanding, our analysis of the third shift in bank practice reveals a dimension that Hardt and Negri have not explored. This shift can be seen most clearly in WDR 2002.[25] In that report, there is a marked retreat from the earlier Washington consensus position that cast states and markets in opposition to each other. While that earlier view advocated that states needed to "get out of the way" by privatizing and deregulating industry and reducing regulatory barriers to trade and investment in order to allow markets to do their work, in the most recent report, attention has been refocused on the significance of national institutions and infrastructure, including legal institutions. Well-functioning institutions and an effective legal system are now recognized as the necessary prerequisites for efficient markets. This is somewhat ironic given the strength with which the contrasting view was held and the degree to which many were convinced of its truth, including apparently, Hardt and Negri. In our argument, the modern nation was never in abeyance, although it was under attack. Rather, the bank and others influenced by the Washington Consensus held a particular understanding of the state's relationship to the market that turned out, in its most ideological forms, simply to be wrong.

Indeed, during the ascendancy of the Washington consensus a series of interventions was made in the South informed by the theory that states and markets work in opposition to each other. "Markets" were opened as the states themselves were stripped back by the collective efforts of investors, international economic organisations, and creditor states. But it was rapidly seen that the "world market" cannot function, even on its own terms, without the infrastructure, both tangible and intangible, that the state creates. A key aspect of this "infrastructure" is law and, in particular, law as derived from and produced by nations, either in its internal (such as domestic laws and regulations) or external forms (such as international law and the law of multinational institutions). In other words, the market depends on modern sovereignty and its corollary, the mutually sustaining relationship between law and nation. The value of tracing the ostensible "return" of the bank to the state is that it provides us with a useful heuristic through which we can understand why Hardt's and Negri's diagnosis of our current condition—of being within Empire and subject to its postmodern sovereignty—fails precisely because it misses that circular relationship and, in turn, the market's reliance on it.

## Locating Nation (and Law) in *Empire*

We begin by returning to a consideration of Empire as "decentered and deterritorializing," cutting across and rendering obsolete the "territorial" idea of nation. The deterritorializing effects of Empire seem to operate along two dimensions: the economic and the juridical:

The nation was not only a cultural formation, a feeling of belonging, and a shared heritage, but also and perhaps primarily, a juridico-economic structure. The declining effectiveness of this structure can be traced clearly through the evolution of a whole series of global juridico-economic bodies, such as the GATT, the World Trade Organization, the World Bank, and the IMF. The globalization of production and circulation, supported by this supranational juridical scaffolding, supercedes the effectiveness of national juridical structures. (334)

Empire is instantiated in its avatars: the world market and the world constitution. What is missing in *Empire*'s account of each, however, is an adequate account of the functioning of law.

## World Market

The first point is simple, but important. Hardt's and Negri's understanding of the world market pays insufficient attention to the extent to which the world market relies on states and, in particular, the state's regulatory and lawmaking capacities to function. They say that:

As the world market today is realized ever more completely, it tends to deconstruct the boundaries of the nation-state. In a previous period, nation-states were the primary actors in the modern imperialist organization of global production and exchange, but to the world market, they appear increasingly as mere obstacles. (150)

This worldview would seem not dissimilar to the neoliberal economic perspective we witnessed in the Washington consensus in which states and markets were cast in opposition to one another. However, as we have already suggested, even the World Bank has realized that the "world market" cannot function without the infrastructure that the state creates and maintains. And a key element of that infrastructure is law. That this is a significant shift from earlier understandings at the bank about markets, states, and law cannot be overemphasized.[26]

For instance, WDR 2002 is overtly directed at strengthening state institutions, which it believes are necessary to the functioning of markets. Instructively, most of the exemplars of such institutions are legal:

Effective institutions can make the difference in the success of market reforms. Without land-titling institutions that ensure property rights, poor people are unable to use valuable assets for investment and income growth. Without strong judicial institutions that enforce contracts, entrepreneurs find many business activities too risky. Without effective corporate governance institutions that check managers' behavior, firms waste the resources of stakeholders.[27]

We can read here both a retreat from the old view that the state hindered the functioning of markets and the emergence of a new regulatory norm, "good governance." Implicit in the Bank's revised approach is the understanding that the state, through its lawmaking function, becomes the site of the legal instantiation and governance of the market:

> Many of the institutions that support markets are publicly provided. The ability of the state to provide these institutions is therefore an important determinant of how well individuals behave in markets and how well markets function. Successful provision of such institutions is often referred to as good governance.[28]

Put another way, the bank appears to have realized that what had been touted as "deregulation" must actually mean "reregulation."

Suggesting that the market somehow regulates the terrain of the globe in a way that sweeps away nation and, by implication, national law, as Hardt and Negri do, is to misunderstand the nature of the relationship between law and the world market, even as it is now read by the World Bank. Perhaps not unexpectedly, though, the bank's insight has not carried through to its logical conclusion. That conclusion would be the destabilization of what could be called the myth of regulatory normalcy that inheres in so much international economic law, particularly international trade law.[29] According to this myth there is an imagined legal order that is neutral and, further, functions as a "natural" complement to the market. In the WDR 2002, this understanding emerges repeatedly. For example, in one illustrative box entitled "What are Institutions?" institutions are described as the "rules, enforcement mechanisms and organizations" that, in this instance, support market transactions. They are described further as "the rules . . . by which agents interact" and are contrasted with "policies" or "social norms."[30] These "rules," which are effectively coextensive with law, are assumed to be neutral, and even though the substantive content of this regulatory background may vary, it is through the perpetuation of that myth, the idea that there is a regulatory "baseline" from which all markets depart, that the politics of substantive normative choices are erased.[31]

Indeed, the bank's new approach participates in reinforcing the myth by universalizing a particular set of (mostly Anglo-American) legal norms and institutions. It does this through determining that markets require "baseline" legal institutions for their operations such as certain kinds of contract laws and intellectual property legislation, independent courts and judiciary, and certain types of enforcement mechanisms.

Rather more surprisingly, in *Empire,* the myth is also left intact. This is because suggesting that the market somehow regulates the terrain of the globe in a way that sweeps away nation and, by implication, national law implies that the capitalist market has an existence that is universally productive and simultaneously both autonomous and immanent. According to Hardt and Negri, there is no outside to the capitalist market, and all social subjects are necessarily constituted within its rhizomatic and fluid embrace. The significance of the concurrent ubiquity and diversity of legal institutions making up markets around the globe, however, seems to drop out of their analysis. This want of consideration has significant effects, despite the frequent invocations of the constitutional role that *Empire* grants to international economic institutions in regulating the global market. It is to these incantations we now turn.

## World Constitution

Although Hardt and Negri are not explicit about the role of specific international institutions in Empire, collectively they are identified as forming part of the (new) imperial constitution, which has gained ascendancy over national law and constitutions. Through its contemporary transformation of supranational law, the imperial process of constitution tends either directly or indirectly to penetrate and reconfigure the domestic law of the nation-states, and thus supranational law powerfully overdetermines domestic law (17).

*Empire* scarcely refers to international economic organizations per se, drawing the most detailed evidence for this point from discussions of the United Nations and its related institutions. In more recent writings it has nonetheless become clear that Hardt and Negri meant to include the World Bank, the IMF, and the World Trade Organization within the ambit of an imperial constitutional construct.[32] They argue that relations between states are now constitutionalized in a novel way because of the international organizations: "The networks of agreements and association, the channels of mediation and conflict resolution, and the coordination of the various dynamics of states are all institutionalized within Empire" (182). This new order is to be distinguished from imperialism, in which nation-states were the cornerstone. Imperialism represented "an extension of the sovereignty of the European nation-states beyond their own boundaries" (xii). and the maintenance of a hierarchy of territorial boundaries between centre and periphery, self and other. In contrast to this, Empire is "*decentered* and *deterritorializing*" (xii; emphasis in original). Nation-states have been superseded as important sites of production or juridical formation: "The distinct national colors of the imperialist map of the world have merged and blended in the imperial global rainbow" (xiii).

For us, this conception of an internalized constitutional order of supranational organizations begs a key question in relation to what might be called the "laws of *Empire*":[33] What is the place of nation and national laws in this supranational constitution? In arguing that the juridical sovereignty of the nation is superseded by a supranational one in which the international organizations play a significant part,[34] Hardt and Negri are overlooking the way in which any "supranational" order is a relational concept in which the elements of the whole are still decidedly national. Such an order implicitly accepts the idea of international law and, in so doing, Empire assumes the very nation-state it would ostensibly transcend. Nation is the pivot between domestic and international law. International law encapsulates the vexed relationship between the universalist orientation of nation[35] and sovereignty as nation's juridical assertion. International law relies on the paradox of the legitimacy of national sovereignty in general to answer instances in which it must be limited in the particular. In other words, the public international lawyer can have no argument with the foundational nature of sovereignty in the international system because it is only through the exercise of sovereignty that sovereignty can be limited. That is, international law is created through sovereign acts, either through state practice and *opinio juris* in the formation of custom, or through entering into international agreements, and these acts lead to international law, which, in turn, is the only legitimate limitation on sovereignty itself.[36]

Much of international human rights law, for example, is a classic embodiment of a universalist orientation and its ambivalent relationship with the concept of the nation-state.[37] Human rights law generally makes a universal assertion directed at checking the excesses of nationalism.[38] It is hostile toward nation-states using the veil of sovereignty to avoid these universal obligations to their own citizens or people within their territory. Yet it also relies upon the claim to authenticity of international law and the invocation of the "community" of nation-states as constituted by it to act as the structure within which to promote these rights or censure breaches of them. Hence when we consider the form of legal ordering on which the supranational constitution of Empire must depend, we can see that Empire and nation are intimately intertwined.[39] Far from operating as an "imperial global rainbow," the postmodern sovereignty of Empire must function inside the same terrain, a field of clearly delineated nation-states, as modern sovereignty.

Indeed, it would seem that Hardt and Negri themselves implicitly accept the idea of the inevitability of international law, regarding it to be both problem (i.e., constitutive of and constituted by Empire's juridical dimension) and solution. As Slavoj Žižek has observed, the prescriptions that Hardt and Negri come up with are framed precisely in the liberal terms of human rights:

The authors propose to focus our political struggle on three global rights: the rights to global citizenship, a minimal income and the reappropriation of new means of production. It is a paradox that Hardt and Negri, the poets of mobility, variety, hybridization and so on, call for three demands formulated in the terminology of universal human rights. The problem with these demands is that they fluctuate between formal emptiness and impossible radicalization.[40]

This implicit reliance on international law and the assertion that it has superseded nation fail to take account of the way in which international law (and especially human rights law) operates precisely as the most potent instance of nation's universal claim. This in turn effaces the insight that certain national forms of social organization become naturalized and, through concepts such as cosmopolitanism (the sustaining spirit of international law), their particularity becomes elevated as "an exemplar of the universal."[41] It is in this way that some nations become more exemplary than others.

One manifestation of this is evident in the conceptualization of "governance" contained in the WDR 2002 and the investiture in the state of "good governance" as its main responsibility. "Governance," it is said, is "epitomized by predictable, open and enlightened policy making; a bureaucracy imbued with a professional ethos; an executive arm of government accountable for its actions; a strong civil society participating in public affairs; and all behaving under the rule of law."[42] Yet, as we have observed above, this purportedly generalized conception of governance clearly refers to a specific set of principles and institutions. From this perspective, we can see that implicit in the bank's conception is the understanding that the state, through its lawmaking function, becomes the site of the legal instantiation and governance of the market: "Many of the institutions that support markets are publicly provided. The ability of the state to provide these institutions is therefore an important determinant of how well individuals behave in markets and how well markets function. Successful provision of such institutions is often referred to as good governance."[43]

In conflating government per se with "good governance," the bank provides an example of the way in which certain state forms with specific sociopolitical characteristics become exemplary through their ostensible neutrality. That is, recalling the myth of "regulatory normalcy" referred to above, the market-state (with its attendant legal and political features) is rendered equivalent to "state" *tout court.* That such a displacement is possible at all is a telling instance of the way in which the modes of international institutions and international law itself are reliant on both the form of the modern nation-state and the inherently universal orientation of the same, a duality that, we would suggest, the conception of international law in *Empire* misses.

## The Rule of Law as a Sustaining Myth

In their insistence on the deterritorializing effects of the postmodern sovereignty characteristic of Empire, Hardt and Negri miss something essential about the mutually sustaining configuration of nation-sovereignty-law. They miss the way that law functions as an unacknowledged transcendent in both the national and the international realms. This understanding of the paradoxical position of modern law also provides an explanation for the durability of the myth of the "rule of law." According to this myth, law is viewed as already constituted and determined outside the messy and contingent processes of history, nationalism, or imperialism. The myth presents a positivist conception of law in which law is viewed as essentially—rather than contingently—a good thing.

We see the potency of the rule-of-law myth reflected both in the texts of the World Bank and in *Empire*. While the World Bank is explicitly instrumentalist in its embrace of the "rule of law" as a means to the end of expanding the reach and effectiveness of world markets, Hardt and Negri implicitly view law as subordinate to the world market they claim is already realized. The World Bank has turned its attention to the national, Hardt and Negri to the global juridical realm, yet the myth leads each mistakenly to conflate a particular national model of regulation with a universalized legal framework.

The constituent elements of the rule-of-law story—legal objectivity, the conflation of law and justice, the rationality of law as a check to the excesses of humanity—are all present in the extraordinary beginning of chapter 6 of WDR 2002:

> The *Gongyan Commentary* to the *Spring and Autumn Annals*, a fourth century B.C. text on law in China, illustrates a problem that all societies face. Analyzing a son's responsibility when the state has unjustly executed his father, the text concludes that without a public institution to settle disputes between private parties and between public and private parties, the only recourse open to those who seek justice is revenge. But revenge can spark an endless cycle of violence, as first one side and then the other retaliates. In many countries, disputes over land and other assets have led to increased violence. The uprising led by Thomas Meuntzer in 16th century Germany and the current debate in Zimbabwe are but two examples. Adjudication of a dispute by a court of law offers an alternative, one where facts are carefully assayed and self-defense and other considerations that may excuse or explain the conduct are reviewed. In short, courts are the way to resolve disputes justly. Justice forms the basis of a lasting social order. The legal and judicial system must therefore provide a method for determining the truth and justice of the actions of private agents and of the state. (117)

Just as this awkward parable is deeply imbued with a sense of law as essentially (rather than contingently) a good thing, the universalist discourse of international human rights on which Hardt and Negri implicitly rely in their concluding prescriptions for the liberation of the multitude is similarly sustained in and through rule-of-law mythology.

A further indication that Hardt and Negri have not been able to free themselves from the centrifugal logic of nation-sovereignty-law is found in their apparent location of the source of the "postmodern" sovereignty of Empire in the particular logic of the U.S. Constitution:

> We want to highlight its [the U.S. Constitution's] originality. Against the modern European conceptions of sovereignty, which consigned political power to a transcendent realm and thus estranged and alienated the sources of power from society, here the concept of sovereignty refers to a power entirely within society. Politics is not opposed to but integrates and completes society. (164)

In this they are arguing that the particular idea of power or logic of rule in the U.S. Constitution has, in a sense, detached itself from that Constitution per se and expanded to encompass the whole globe. The key feature of that logic of rule would appear to be a movement from an ontology of transcendence to one based on immanence. Rather than the desires of the multitude being mediated by the institutions of transcendence, such as the Church or the Hobbesian ideal of the state, a constitution based on immanence no longer requires mediation as it biopolitically produces desires among the multitude. Where the former sought to invoke a people out of the multitude (creating nations and citizens), the later, through the vast communications apparatus it wields, produces a people that "looks like" a multitude.[44]

This line of argument reveals the Foucauldian concept of (bio)power that runs throughout *Empire*: that it has no outside and is produced from within, in and through practices of resistance. In Hardt's and Negri's words:

> In line with the Protestant ethic, one might say that only the productive power of the multitude demonstrates the existence of God and the presence of divinity on Earth. Power is not something which lords over us, but something we make. The American Declaration of Independence celebrates this new idea of power in the clearest terms. The emancipation of humanity from every transcendent power is grounded on the multitude's power to construct its own political institutions and constitute society. (165)

In the explicit investiture of power in the people and a breaking away from the divine, Hardt and Negri are claiming that a shift occurred in which the systems of mediation between people and power were no longer seen as a conceptual necessity. That is, U.S. constitutionalism made immanent the system of rule. In their account, the incipience of the multitude in U.S. constitutionalism, combined with the end of imperialism, created the conditions in which Empire was able to cohere. When confronted with these two conclusions, capitalism, which they argue was hitherto reliant on both a transcendent political ontology and a territorial outside, suddenly morphed into a new form which no longer relies on this "dialectic of inside and outside, that can operate immanently, and that no longer needs transcendence to protect it from the desires of the multitude."[45]

Again, this is strangely resonant with the rule-of-law discourse expounded by the World Bank in its WDR 2002:

> Political institutions help determine limits on the arbitrary exercise of power by politicians and bureaucrats. They do so by delineating property rights between the state and the private sector and providing for their *enforcement*. A historical example of this can be found in the changes in political institutions in 17th century England, which placed limits on the power of the Crown to expropriate property and so contributed to the security of private property.[46]

And further:

> In formal democracies, which constitute a growing share of the world's countries, political institutions include the electoral rules that lay out the procedures by which governments are elected and replaced. They also include the constitutional rules that determine the division of power between the executive and legislative branches of government—and the limits on the power of each.[47]

In identifying the U.S. Constitution as the particular model for their conception of the paradigm shift from a transcendent to an immanent conception of sovereignty announced by Empire, Hardt and Negri are uncannily reflecting the process of elevating to the universal *the same* particular national instantiation as the World Bank.

Not only that, but as we have suggested, instead of the production of a plane of immanence and a corollary possibility for revolution, what we witness now (in the discourse of the World Bank and in the U.S. constitution) is an implicit reliance on the transcendence of law. Following Fitzpatrick, we have been arguing that the internal contradiction of modern law is that it must bring together the universal and the particular, and yet that internal paradox does not seem to pull it apart. As Fitzpatrick shows, what sustains these contradictions and, indeed, explains the rule-of-law myth's enduring power, is the transcendent referent it finds in the modern nation.[71] What this means is that in the story of law's legitimacy, when it needs to, nation precedes law, but the reverse is also true—when it needs to legitimate the state, law comes before nation: "But for courts to be effective, rulers must follow the law, too. The judicial system must also provide checks and balances on arbitrary state action. Forcing rulers to follow the law is a problem as old as government itself" (118).

Nation occupies the same kind of space as law—that is, it contains the same antinomies of the universal and the particular—in the nation of "blood and soil" versus the nation's claims to universality.[49] It is not surprising to us, then, that in denying the continued significance of the nation and of modern sovereignty, Hardt and Negri have also failed to recognize the necessary cohering function performed by law.[50]

## Conclusion

To the extent that we too are interested in gaining a better understanding of the contours of our current global order, we are sympathetic to Hardt's and Negri's undertaking in *Empire*. Like them, we want to find the tools most useful for analyzing the ways in which current global inequalities are created and maintained. And like them, we are interested in how these analyses might be useful in locating and building upon effective practices of resistance and strategies for change. But, we fear that in their rush to herald the arrival of a postmodern sovereignty, Hardt and Negri have missed paying close attention to some of the most salient constitutive practices of imperialisms (both new and old), including, most pointedly for us, the enduring framework of the modern nation-state and its sustaining myth of the rule of law.

In reading *Empire* against the two recent World Bank annual *World Development Reports*, we found intriguing similarities but an ultimately more revealing divergence. At the outset of this project, we had wondered whether discursive shifts at the bank might coincide with the emergence of the new paradigm heralded by Hardt and Negri. Indeed, the bank's efforts to become more inclusive and responsive to its critics do seem to parallel Hardt's and Negri's view of the logic of the world market in incorporating those things which might previously have challenged it. However, we are not convinced that the "new" discourse of the bank and other international economic organizations, the so-called post-Washington consensus, provides any evidence of the arrival of the kind of "postmodern sovereignty" that Hardt and Negri proclaim. Rather, we observed that an important foundation of the discernible shifts in bank discourse is its rediscovery of the significance of the "nation," that is, nationally bounded legal and institutional frameworks, for the success of market-based reforms. This is in contradiction to Hardt's and Negri's account of the "decentered and deterritorialized" nature of Empire, its totalizing tendencies, and the obsolescence of the modern nation-state.

Indeed, while some commentators have pointed to the admittedly under-developed concept of the multitude as the void at the heart of *Empire*,[1] we have come to the conclusion that Empire itself is also a hollow concept. In their invocations of Empire as a new global juridico-economic formation that displaces the nation-state, Hardt and Negri do not explain how the purportedly constitutional international institutions might work in concert with other bodies (such as corporations) actually to produce Empire. Instead, they rely on incantation, assuming that we will fill in the blanks for ourselves. We argue that inattention to the details of the ongoing practices of international economic institutions such as the World Bank in enabling the continued expansion of market-based legal reforms produces in *Empire* a significant blind spot. In that blind spot is the mutually constitutive relationship of nation-sovereignty-law.

Without trying to understand the potency of the myth of the rule of law, its relationship to nation, and in turn to international law, Hardt and Negri are themselves ultimately unable to escape the logic that binds those concepts together like a Möbius strip. As a consequence, Hardt and Negri have failed to convince us that we might already have found ourselves beyond this circular juggernaut of nation-sovereignty-law, and in "the passage of sovereignty toward the plane of immanence," as they claim (332). As *Empire* fails to grasp the critical role of law in constituting the current imperial order, it misses the opportunity to identify what might be truly new or different about *this* imperialism.

## Acknowledgments

Many people have assisted in the long gestation of the ideas presented in this paper. We are grateful in particular to Paul Passavant for his careful and generous reading of several drafts. Peter Fitzpatrick also kindly read and commented on more than one version, and Peter Rush and Jodi Dean also read and commented on earlier drafts. Many thanks are also owed to Sean Robertson and Robert Russo for able assistance with research, editing, and footnoting.

## Notes

1. On its publication, the book was widely reviewed, in publications such as *Theory and Event* 4.4 (2000). This volume is a case in point. See also the "dossier" on *Empire* in *Rethinking Marxism* 13; 3/4 (2001); Gopal Balakrishnan, "Hardt And Negri's Empire," *New Left Review* 5 (2000): 142–148; Ronaldo Munck, "Michael Hardt and Antonio Negri's *Empire*," *Cultural Logic* 3, no. 1 (2000).

2. Mahmut Mutman, "On Empire," *Rethinking Marxism* 13; 3/4 (2001): 43.

3. Gayatri Spivak, *A Critique Of Postcolonial Reason: Toward a History of a Vanishing Present* (Cambridge, MA: Harvard University Press, 1999), 2.

4. Ibid., 2. See also Ruth Buchanan and Sundhya Pahuja, "Collaboration, Cosmopolitanism, Complicity," *Nordic Journal of International Law* 71 (2002): 297–324.

5. Michael Hardt and Antonio Negri, *Empire* (Cambridge, MA: Harvard University Press, 2000), 3. Subsequent references to *Empire* are given parenthetically in the text.

6. As this essay was nearing completion, we encountered a parallel critique of the limits of positivist conceptions of law embedded within the writing of "constructivist" international relations scholars. See Jutta Brunee and Steven Toope, "International Law and Constructivism: Elements of an Interactional Theory of International Law," *Columbia Journal of Transnational Law* 39 (2000–2001): 18–74. While the subject matter of our respective critiques is different, there are many points of resonance between our approach and that of Brunee and Toope.

7. See Peter Fitzpatrick, "The Immanence of *Empire*," in this volume.

8. We thank Paul Passavant for suggesting that we formulate the point in this manner.

9. On this point generally, see Yves Dezalay and Bryant Garth, "Legitimating the New Legal Orthodoxy," in *Global Prescriptions: The Production, Exportation, and Importation of a New Legal Orthodoxy* (Ann Arbor, MI: University of Michigan, 2002), 306–334.

10. For example, "In constitutional terms, the processes of globalization are no longer merely a fact but also a source of juridical definitions that tends to project a single supranational figure of political power."

11. Timothy S. Murphy, "Ontology, Deconstruction and Empire," *Rethinking Marxism* 13; 3/4 (2001): 21.

12. J. K. Gibson-Graham, "The Economy, Stupid! Industrial Policy Discourse and the Body Economic," and "Querying Globalization," in *The End of Capitalism (As We Knew It): A Feminist Critique of Political Economy* (Cambridge, MA: Blackwell, 1996), 92–119 and 120–147.

13. Bonnie Campbell, "New Rules of the Game: The World Bank's Role in the Construction of New Normative Frameworks for States, Markets, and Social Exclusion," *Canadian Journal of Development Studies* 21; 1 (2000): 10.

14. Michael Hardt and Antonio Negri, "Globalization and Democracy," *Adelaide University Online Symposium: Globalization Conference*, July 17, 2001, on file with author.

15. See Campbell; "New Rules" actually identifies a shift evident in the *World Development Report 1997: The State in a Changing World*. While we will not engage here in a lengthy debate over the timing of the shift, what is significant is that in the last decade the bank has moved decisively away from its earlier position in favor of a minimalist state toward a significantly more robust model.

16. Or at least the first phase of its coming. It is difficult to pin down whether Hardt and Negri think Empire is upon us or whether it is yet to come.

17. World Bank, *World Development Report 2001: Attacking Poverty* (New York: Oxford University Press, 2001) (hereinafter cited as WDR 2001); and World Bank, *World Development Report 2002: Building Institutions in Developing Markets* (New York: Oxford University Press, 2002) (hereinafter cited as WDR 2002).

18. For a useful synopsis of the critiques, see Massimo Florio, "Economists, Privatization in Russia and the Waning of the 'Washington Consensus,'" *Review of International Political Economy* 9; 2 (2002): 374.

19. Robert Hunter Wade, "US Hegemony and the World Bank: The Fight over People and Ideas," *Review of International Political Economy* 9 (2002): 215.

20. Ben Fine, "Neither the Washington nor the Post-Washington Consensus: An Introduction," in *Development Policy in the Twenty-First Century: Beyond the Post-Washington Consensus*, ed. Ben Fine, Costas Lapavitasas, and Jonathan Pincus (London: Routledge, 2001).

21. Florio, "Economists," 24.

22. Joseph Stiglitz, the recently departed chief economist of the Bank who was a critic of the Washington consensus (WC), pointed to three key indicators of its "failure": 1) the unhappy experience of most postcommunist countries in too rapidly embracing market reforms without adequate institutional infrastructure; 2) the growing evidence that WC reforms were producing "dual economies" in which inequality was increasing and the poorest segments of society were excluded from the benefits of reform; and 3) the counter-factual of the East Asian miracle, which was accomplished through key departures from WC prescriptions.

23. Joseph Stiglitz, "Scan Globally, Reinvent Locally: Knowledge Infrastructure and the Localization of Knowledge," *Keynote Address, First Global Development Network Conference, December 1999, Bonn, Germany*, December 5–8, 1999, available at http://www.gdnet.org/subpages/events_gdn99_speeches.html: "If a global knowledge based institution wants a country to learn a 'truth' about development, then it should help the local knowledge institutes and policy makers . . . to make it a 'local social discovery.'"

24. Deepa Narayan-Parker et al., *Voices of the Poor* (Oxford: Oxford University Press, 2000).

25. WDR 2002.

26. Anne Orford and Jennifer Beard, "Making the State Safe for the Market: The World Bank's World Development Report 1997," *Melbourne University Law Review* 22 (1998): 196.

27. *WDR 2002*, Foreword by President Wolfensohn, iii.

28. Ibid., 99.

29. Daniel Tarullo, "Logic, Myth, and the International Economic Order," *Harvard International Law Journal* 26; 2 (1985): 533.

30. WDR 2002, 6.

31. See Sundhya Pahuja, "Trading Spaces: Locating Sites for Challenge within International Trade Law," *Australian Feminist Law Journal* 14 (2000): 38.

32. See Hardt and Negri, "Globalization and Democracy": "Our contemporary Empire is indeed monarchical. . . . The supranational institutions, such as the WTO, the World Bank and the IMF also at times exercise a monarchical rule over global affairs." "Consider, for example, the functioning of the supranational economic institutions, such as the World Bank, the IMF and the WTO. To a large extent, the conditionality required by these institutions takes out of the hands of nation states decisions over economic and social policy. . . . It is clear that these supranational economic institutions do not and cannot represent the people, except in the most distant and abstract sense. . . . It is no accident in our view, in other words, that these institutions are so isolated from popular representation. They function precisely to the extent that they are excluded from mechanisms of popular representation."

33. Peter Fitzpatrick, "Laws of Empire," *International Journal for the Semiotics of Law* 15 (2002): 253.

34. Hardt and Negri, "Globalization and Democracy," 29.

35. Peter Fitzpatrick, *Modernism and the Grounds of Law* (Cambridge, UK: Cambridge University Press, 2001), 120–125.

36. See, for example, Pahuja, "Trading Spaces," 53.

37. On this point, see Fitzpatrick, *Modernism*, 120.

38. An archetypal example of such a right is the right to free speech. For a detailed examination of this right and its cosmopolitan pedigree, see R. Delgado and J. Stefancic, "Cosmopolitanism Inside Out: International Norms and the Struggle for Civil Rights and Local Justice," *Connecticut Law Review* 27 (1995): 773.

39. See Buchanan and Pahuja, "Collaboration."

40. Slavoj Žižek, "Have Michael Hardt and Antonio Negri Rewritten the *Communist Manifesto* for the Twenty-First Century?" *Rethinking Marxism* 13; 3/4 (2001): 192.

41. Fitzpatrick, *Modernism*, 20; also Buchanan and Pahuja, "Collaboration."

42. World Bank, *Governance: The World Bank's Experience* (Washington, D.C.: World Bank 1994) as cited in WDR 2002 at 203.

43. Ibid., 99.

44. For a more detailed investigation of the relationship between mass media, mass culture, and biopower, see Imre Szeman, "Plundering the Empire: Globalization, Mediation, and Cultural Studies," *Rethinking Marxism* 13; 3/4 (2001): 181, 185.

45. Szeman, "Plundering," 181.

46. WDR 2002, 100, emphasis in original.

47. Ibid., 100.

48. Fitzpatrick, *Modernism*, 129–136.

49. Hardt and Negri, *Empire*, 118.

50. Law can, as it must, deny its transcendent role only by locating itself in the nation—which lays claim to both blood and place. The modern conception of sovereignty, then, is the pivot point on which both national and international law rests—where law and nation meet in their circular self-constitution.

51. See Peter Fitzpatrick, "The Immanence of *Empire*," in this volume.

# 5

# From Empire's Law to the Multitude's Rights: Law, Representation, Revolution

## Paul A. Passavant

Michael Hardt and Antonio Negri argue in *Empire* that the fact that global capital has undermined the sovereignty of nation-states does not mean that sovereignty no longer operates. Rather, sovereignty has become displaced from the nation-state to the global level. "Empire" describes this new mode of global sovereignty. When the police act to protect this global order, whether in Vancouver, Seattle, Washington, D.C., or Genoa, they act on behalf of Empire.

By using juridical forms as indices of social developments in order to diagnose our contemporary historical moment and by contributing to current thinking about sovereignty and the state under conditions of postmodernity, Hardt and Negri seem to have helped bring law once again to the center of debates over social change. What I find, however, is that Hardt and Negri actually tell a story of law's increasing irrelevance, as law has become increasingly inadequate to hybrid and networked postmodern life. Postmodern law and state abstract themselves from their former role of mediating social conflict and seek to avoid it instead. The now-unmediated confrontation of social forces can become Empire's soft underbelly, thereby giving the current situation revolutionary potential.

In this chapter, I argue that Hardt's and Negri's refusal of representation and, more specifically, of law as a mechanism of representation is a problem if we are to confront the challenges posed by global capital, global militarism, and the biopolitical impulse to genocide. In *Empire* and *The Labor of Dionysus*, in addition to other works, Hardt and Negri describe the passage to the postmodern age as a separation of state and society. The multitude, the biopolitical force for revolution, is born in the networks of control society and communicative capitalism—within, that is, the space of the "social." The multitude is thus the presence of absolute democracy beyond the state, and all attempts to represent it via forms of sovereignty do violence to it and thwart the passage to democracy. Or, as Antonio Negri puts it, the "question is not to limit constituent power, but to make it unlimited."[1] I argue that the strict separation, between law on one side and society on the other that Hardt and Negri present as the passage to postmodernity overlooks the mutual imbrication of state and society and the mutually constitutive relation of law and society. I reconsider the American Revolution, a privileged instance of constituent power for Hardt and Negri, to illustrate how the mutual imbrication of law and society, the latter figured here nationally, resulted in the American Revolutionaries making use of law in order to create a constituent act, thereby disturbing the strict separation of constituent and constituted power upon which Hardt and Negri insist.

This mutually imbricated and constitutive relation between law or the state and society, however, continues to haunt *Empire* despite the separation Hardt and Negri try to effect for the sake of the multitude's self-identity as a political subject of absolute democracy. By describing a strict separation of law or the state and society, Hardt and Negri neglect the inescapability and indeed the revolutionary potential of law. Although they fail to analyze the mutually constitutive relation between law and the multitude, the multitude's birth to presence as a political force for democracy and justice is paradoxically produced at the nodal point of the revolutionary rights Hardt and Negri claim in the name of the multitude.

## The Decline of Representation and the Significance of Separation

Hardt's and Negri's jurisprudence is organized around the opposition of constituent power to constituted power. As Negri describes, to "speak of constituent power is to speak of democracy" (I, 1). Or, as Hardt states, constituent power (*potentia*) is the "other" to the constituted Power (*potestas*) of the state: constituent power is "a radically distinct , sustainable, and irrecuperable alternative for the organization of society" (TF, xi). Constituent power, as democratic, collective, immediate, and joyously desiring, stands opposed to constituted power, where the latter is a centralizing, "mediating, transcendental force of command" (TF, xiii). Constituent power, as the "revolution itself," refuses to be fully integrated in a hierarchical legal system and it "always remains alien to the law" (I, 1–2). Our productive nature exceeds measure, and so constituted power cannot do our nature justice. Constitutions limit democracy, and are therefore the enemy of constituent power, as the latter is absolute democracy, according to Hardt and Negri. Despite the many attempts of the Western legal tradition to tame constituent power in a constitutional system or theory, constituent power, properly understood, resists being constitutionalized.

Hardt's and Negri's defense of constituent power against constituted power rests in part on a critique of representation. Representation absorbs, tames, controls, and segments constituent power. The multitude is the revolutionary subject of constituent power. It is a plane of singularities, an expression of multiplicity. Representation, however, functions to serve sovereign, constituted power. This is particularly clear in Hardt's and Negri's treatment of nations and nationalism. For Hardt and Negri, every "nation must make the multitude into a people" (E, 103). The people, in contrast to the multitude, has one will. As a national representation of the multitude, the identity of a people mediates multiplicity and singularity by producing homogeneity internally and by "excluding what remains outside" this representation. Internal differences are eclipsed through "the representation of the whole population by a hegemonic group, race, or class." The nation is the "antidote" to the forces of revolution and placates the crisis of sovereignty by reappropriating constituent power for sovereign purposes through representation. Hence, what appears to be revolutionary and liberatory—popular sovereignty—in fact turns out to be nothing other than another "turn of the screw" through the "totalizing representation" of the nation (E, 102–105).

Hardt and Negri present modernity as a dialectic of crises for sovereignty and then the recuperation of sovereignty through the containment of an earlier act of resistance. The modern period begins with the Renaissance, illustrating the power of immanence against transcendence. But this revolution in turn provokes a counterrevolution that neutralizes the revolutionary power of immanence by playing on the "anxiety and fear of the masses" to "deploy a new transcendent power of command and authority" as a way to "reduce the uncertainty of life and increase security" (E, 75). Modern sovereignty, that unified, transcendent form of constituted power, functions through representation by transferring "every autonomous power of the multitude to a sovereign power that stands above it and rules it" (E, 84). Representation, by mediating diverse interests, displaces the singular wills of the multitude by re-presenting them as a single, "general" will that transcends any particulars. Representation, for Hardt and Negri, legitimates sovereign power and "alienates it completely from the multitude of subjects" (E, 84). The machine of sovereignty consumes the multitude and produces an ordered totality in its place.

Under contemporary conditions of globalized capital, the dialectic of modern sovereignty has come to an end. From a socioeconomic point of view, imperial practices have become flattened upon a singular plane with the real subsumption of labor into the capitalist machine. From a juridical point of view, however, there has been a growing separation between law and the state, on the one hand, and the social, on the other. Under the conditions of Empire, law and the state have increasingly abstracted themselves from social conflict, according to Hardt and Negri. Without the mediation of the modern state, social forces confront each other directly, and various acts of resistance strike immediately at the heart of Empire. In other words, Hardt and Negri join an apparently growing trend on the left that looks skeptically at law and the state as useful sites for the pursuit of justice as they place their hopes for justice in an escape from law in the sphere of the social.[2] According to Hardt and Negri, we see evidence of this growing separation in three different places: the plane of practical politics, the plane of postmodern juridical theory, and in the withering of civil society.

On the plane of practical politics, Hardt and Negri argue that the state has played an active role in abstracting itself from political conflict in part through its neoliberal economic policies. The state has eviscerated antitrust protections, weakened the position of labor, and deregulated and privatized industry. Rather than mediating the separate interests of labor and capital in the national interest, as it once might have during the welfare-state period of the twentieth century, the neo-liberal state turns a blind eye to union-busting and then meets those labor strikes that do occur with force and replacement workers rather than negotiations, as President Reagan did in the Professional Air Traffic Controllers' Organization (PATCO) strike (LD, 240).

On the plane of jurisprudence, Hardt and Negri propose viewing John Rawls's theory of justice not as a throwback to an anachronistic liberal state but, in light of developments on the plane of practical politics, as anticipating the postmodern liberal state. In light of the real subsumption of labor within capital, Rawls's theory is functionally adequate to the present state form (LD, 224). Now that the capitalist economy is "freed" from an economic model based on production, juridical theory "no longer has to pose labor as the material source of normative production" (LD, 226). Rawls's theory of justice works homologously, as it neglects production (economic production, production of norms) and focuses instead on distribution (LD, 223). Postmodern legal theory hence presents itself as a critique of foundationalism—of the foundation of social valorization in the category of labor and the foundation of the formal constitution in the material constitution of society. Postmodern constitutionalism focuses not on production, then, but on the circulation of norms and rights throughout the juridical system, as normative discourse is raised to a level of total abstraction (LD, 227).

Rawls's theory of justice insulates itself from the material constitution of society by presenting a "simulation of social reality" that is "emptied of all social contents." Although the theory alludes to plurality, it "only accepts an abstract unitary subject." According to Hardt and Negri, this "postmodern unity is not created by mediating or even coercing a multiplicity to order, but rather by abstracting from a field of differences to free the system and thus pose a generic unity" (LD, 233). Postmodern liberal legal theory promotes an "overlapping consensus" not by engaging, reconciling, or mediating differences, but by an "abstraction of the juridical system from the social field" (LD, 235). It seeks a procedure to *avoid* rather than to *resolve* social conflicts. Its procedure is to exclude social conflict from the juridical system to maintain an empty and abstract unity and order. The juridical system, in this theory, abstracts itself from the social field much as the neoliberal state has on the plane of practical politics.

Developments in civil society correspond to the way that, in practical politics and juridical theory law and the state have become abstracted from the social field so that they cease to mediate social conflict in order to represent differences at a higher plane of transcendent unity. Across the spectrum, politicians, activists, and theorists decry the decline of civil society. Hardt and Negri agree that the institutions of civil society are withering, but rather than perceiving this as a problem, they see the decline of civil society as presenting revolutionary opportunities.

The institutions of civil society, as illustrated in the work of G. W. F. Hegel, take what is foreign to the capitalist system, such as "savage" or "untamed" labor, and subjugate and transform concrete labor into abstract labor. Differences and particularities are negated and subsumed in the universal, as particular needs and interests are related to those of others and are made to contribute to the satisfaction of all. Trade unions, among other institutions of civil society, "structurally orient the particular interests of workers toward the universal interests of society." This is a process of formal subsumption, as labor is at this point external to the capitalist system, but it must be passed through the mediating institutions of civil society so that which is alien to the system can become incorporated within it (CS, 25).

Hardt and Negri relate the period of civil society's greatest strength to Michel Foucault's historical work on different power formations, arguing that the organizations of civil society are disciplinary institutions. As Hardt puts it, the "institutional labor union . . . is viewed not so much as a passage for the expression of worker interests to be represented in the plurality of rule but rather as a means to mediate and recuperate the antagonisms born of capitalist production and capitalist social relations—thus creating a worker subjectivity that is recuperable within and will actually support the order of the capitalist State." The function of civil society's institutions, then, is to "'educate' the citizens, creating within them the universal desires that are in line with the State"

(CS, 27). Foucault's critical descriptions of disciplinarity are cause for Hegelian celebration, as discipline, seen from another perspective, is educational.[3]

The demise of the institutions of civil society correspond, according to Hardt and Negri, to a shift from disciplinary society to societies of control (E, 22–23, 318–332). Hardt and Negri draw from Gilles Deleuze's analyses in which he argues that the walls of the disciplinary institutions Foucault analyzed are everywhere crumbling.[4] Today, social space, rather than being striated by the enclosures of disciplinary society, is smooth. But the fact that the walls have come down on disciplinary institutions does not mean that disciplinary power has ceased to function. Rather, through forms of new media, communications technology, and the heightened use of surveillance, whether through closed-circuit TV, nanny-cams, or rating the creditworthiness of individuals, disciplinary power is no longer enclosed within the walls of institutions but has networked its way across the now-smooth social space to produce control societies. Societies of control, then, represent a shift from the merely formal subsumption of labor to the real subsumption of labor within the capitalist system. Today, labor is a force that is internal to the capitalist system and no longer needs to be tamed, as subjects have internalized the capitalist order and reproduce it through their social practices. For example, capitalist subjects pay for the opportunity to advertise capitalism's products by purchasing clothing with proper and obviously displayed logos while inciting the desires of others to do the same, becoming producers and consumers simultaneously. Subjects are now immediately productive within societies of control.

Civil society no longer serves as a point of mediation between the immanence of capital and the transcendence of state sovereignty (E, 326–328). The institutions of civil society, such as those that facilitated the representation of labor within the state, were "an instance of sovereignty" (E, 329). Today, discipline is exercised immanently, and consensus is produced not politically (i.e., through mediation or through representative institutions) but by economic factors and communicative "ether" (E, 330, 307, 346–347).[5]

The subjectivities produced in societies of control, however, are more mobile and flexible—to suit the changed needs of capitalism—than those produced within earlier disciplinary institutions. But in so doing, technologies of control have produced a "new milieu of maximum plurality and uncontainable singularization—a milieu of the event" that the "new forms of imperial right can at best only partially represent" (E, 25–27). Moreover, this situation privileges the active economic subjects of the producer-consumer over the passive and repressed political subject, a privilege that shifts struggle to the terrain of production and hence could prove Empire's undoing (E, 320–321). Thus, with the decline of labor unions and other representative/disciplinary institutions, new forms of action are needed for these new conditions. Paradoxically, Hardt

and Negri argue to this end against the "common wisdom that the U.S. proletariat is weak because of its low party and union representation with respect to
Europe and elsewhere." Instead, they claim that "we should see it as strong for
precisely those reasons. Working-class power resides not in the representative
institutions but in the antagonism and autonomy of the workers themselves"
(E, 269). The productive cooperation of labor under conditions of postmodern
capitalism "has the potential to be transformed into . . . an absolute democratic
power" (E, 344). Counterintuitively, the lack of working-class organization is an
indicator of not worker weakness but worker *strength*.

According to Hardt and Negri, representation is everywhere in crisis. The
neoliberal state has abstracted itself from mediating social conflict. Postmodern
liberal legal jurisprudence has likewise abstracted law from social conflict, producing an empty and abstract unity through the exclusion of difference. And the
institutions of civil society that once mediated between particular interests—
such as labor and capital—and the state's universality have eroded.

We should not be nostalgic for representational practices, on Hardt's and
Negri's view. The representative institutions of civil society were disciplinary,
taming labor so that it would be functional in a capitalist state, for instance.
Furthermore, Empire: "despite its efforts, finds it impossible to construct a system of right adequate to the new reality of the globalization of social and economic relations" (E, 394). In response, imperial law has abstracted itself from
difference, meaning that social conflict now possesses greater revolutionary
potential in unmediated form. And confronted by a neoliberal state that has
abstracted itself from social conflict and merely simulates political participation, as polling, political action committees (PACs), and other marketing techniques create a spectacle of "democracy," the multitude has exited the political
system through mass refusal and exodus (LD, 272, 295). This crisis of representation is producing the conditions of possibility for revolutionary action.

The major theme to emerge from Hardt's and Negri's analyses of postmodern law and the state is "the theme of separation and autonomy" (LD,
266). As the postmodern juridical formation is highly abstract, it has lost its
capacity for social relevance. Imperial power, according to Hardt and Negri:

> can no longer resolve the conflict of social forces through mediatory schemata
> that displace the terms of conflict. The social conflicts that constitute the political
> confront one another directly, without mediations of any sort. This is the essen-
> tial novelty of the imperial situation. Empire creates a greater potential for revo-
> lution than did the modern regimes of power because it presents us, alongside
> the machine of command, with an alternative: the set of all the exploited and the
> subjugated, a multitude that is directly opposed to Empire, with no mediation
> between them. (E, 393)

Due to the abstraction of the juridical formation and its separation from the social, social forces now confront each other directly. The decline of representation leads to a situation with greater revolutionary potential.

The separation between the juridical formation and society leads to a greater possibility for defeating Empire. It also enables the formation of the multitude on a separate and autonomous basis, uncorrupted by imperial command or by forms of representation, including law as a mechanism of representation. The social and communicative dimensions of living labor enable the construction of a new revolutionary figure, one that necessarily arrives on the terrain of production (E, 205). The multitude's birth to postmodern presence occurs within the networks of the society of control; within, that is, the order of the social that has become disengaged from the state. According to Hardt and Negri, in "the separation between the two autonomies there remains nothing in common" (LD, 310). Now, since the multitude is an "unrepresentable community" (LD, 307) and "alien to the law" (I, 1–2), this separation allows the multitude's formation. The separation provides an "autonomous, independent site where this subject is born" (LD, 310). The multitude can express its constituent power on the proper ontological basis of a plane of immanence and produce absolute democracy completely outside of and opposed to the sovereign power of the state and law (cf. LD, 285). A "community outside sovereignty as a separate and autonomous entity" can be founded to realize a vision of democracy in a horizontal plane on which "social bodies are set loose to destroy the strictures of predetermined social forms and discover their own ends, invent their own constitution" (LD, 308, 289). Constituent power triumphs over constituted power, as the separation of law and the state from society allows a radical alternative to become effective (LD, 308).

## The Special Case of the American Revolution and the U.S. Constitution

The history of modernity, for Hardt and Negri, represents a struggle between the democratic forces of immanence and the transcendent power of sovereignty. The American Revolution and the U.S. Constitution, however, represent something of an exception to this history of modernity. According to Hardt and Negri, the American Revolution represents a "rupture in the genealogy of modern sovereignty" (E, 160).

The Declaration of Independence expresses a democratic revolutionary process for Hardt and Negri. The constituent power of the American Revolution, however, became "absorbed, appropriated by the constitution, transformed into an element of the constitutional machine" (I, 158). The Constitution is a "central axis of political mediation, of filtering, balance, control, and compromise of social interests" (I, 157). The "original constituent fact is confined within the *Declaration of Independence*," and its "might is interpretable only as a power of government. Without the constitution, outside of the constitution, outside of the constitutional machine and of the organism of government, there's no constituent power" (I, 161). The Constitution, as illustrated by Negri's reading of the *Federalist Papers*, absorbs constituent power and its subject through its centralizing powers (I, 167–175). Can the American experience indicate a future beyond the repression of modern sovereignty? It does so on the frontier.

During the first half of the nineteenth century, America's "material constitution" exceeded its "formal constitution," according to Negri, as the "constituent principle and its determination of freedom and originality manage each time to materialize and break through the constitutional wrapping" (I, 177). As he writes, the "American constituent spirit and the American constitution [are] incommensurable and irreconcilable" (I, 181). The "open" spaces of the frontier enable new lines of flight that provide for a displacement of the "ambiguous dialectic we saw developing within the American Constitution that subordinated the immanent principles of the Declaration of Independence to a transcendent order of constitutional self-reflection. Across the great open spaces the constituent tendency wins out over the constitutional decree . . . the initiative of the multitude over the centralization of power" (E, 169). The constituent power of the revolution survives beyond the reach of the constitutional machine on the American frontier. Again, the revolutionary subject exists in its separation from law.

When the "open" space ran out, however, this constituent power was negated, and the United States threatened to be transformed into a "European-style sovereignty" as America's expansive tendencies took the form of imperialism (E, 173). But with the end of the Cold War, the U.S. Constitution's network power and America's expansive tendencies become, on the one hand, institutionalized within Empire, as the United States is called to act in the name of global right; on the other hand, this network power and expansive tendency enable the possibility of the multitude's birth to presence on a global scale.

Of course, the space of the frontier so necessary for the multitude was not vacant. It was inhabited by Native Americans. The "democratic pressure of the multitude to surpass every limit and every control" means, then, that the coming to presence of the multitude occurred on the grounds of the continued repression and destruction of these indigenous peoples (E, 166). These tribes are necessarily outside the multitude's law of development. Yet, as this expansive force realizes itself in the continuous overcoming of limits, the negation of North America's tribes of indigenous peoples becomes constitutive of the

multitude. Those Native Americans who remained on the frontier did not recognize this law of the multitude's development, and this law did not recognize
the Native Americans. Rather, it excluded them (E, 170).

## Imperial Law?

Empire marks a "new notion of right." It represents a new form of authority
and "a new design of the production of norms and legal instruments of coercion" (E, 9). But this new notion of right can only "partially represent the
underlying design of the new constitution of the world order and cannot really
grasp the motor that sets it in motion" (E, 27) due to "a global domination that
is continually more abstract and thus blind to the sense of the apparatuses of
life" (E, 64). That is, the growing abstraction of the postmodern juridical formation and its increasing separation from the social means that it is ever less
capable of representing or relating to the increased mobility and biopolitical
hybridity germinating in the space of the social through the networks of control. In light of juridical abstraction, the separation between law and society,
and the consequential inability of imperial power to resolve or mediate social
conflicts (E, 393), one might wonder who recognizes this new "right of intervention" and how it is legitimated.

On the one hand, Hardt and Negri emphasize that Empire is "called into
being" (E, 15, 181), although the forces that can be presumed to have made this
call—those who acted as if this force already existed—are institutions that Hardt
and Negri include within Empire's pyramid of sovereignty (E, 181, 309–314). On
the other hand, since the abstract apparatus of imperial command has "no
access to the local spaces and the determinate temporal sequences of life where
the administration functions" and "does not manage to put its hands on the singularities and their activity," juridical power is limited in its effectiveness to a
police power operating in a "permanent state of exception"—as a force of last
resort to defend the prerogatives of sovereignty and to keep the "peace." But why
would the world recognize the U.S. exercise of force (or any other exercise of
force, for that matter) as an instance of "global right" on behalf of imperial sovereignty if postmodern law has become so detached from society?

The problem with Hardt's and Negri's juridical analysis is a mirror image
of the problem with Giorgio Agamben's. Agamben describes certain biopolitical zones of "bare life" as places where "law is suspended" in permanent states
of exception. Here, power confronts pure life with no mediation, as law is no
longer distinguishable from factual situations in these moments of sovereign
decisionism.[6] For Hardt and Negri, the sovereign decisions in states of exception retain their juridical character but they exist in a state of separation from
the social. Both Agamben and Hardt and Negri draw from Carl Schmitt's the-

ory of sovereign decisionism. For Schmitt, all law is situational law, because chaos has no law.[7] The sovereign produces a factual situation or social order and guarantees its existence. Only when there is a "normal" situation can a norm define this state of affairs and distinguish it from other possible situations or social orders. A normal situation is therefore a prerequisite for legal validity, and the sovereign is the one who decides whether this normal situation indeed exists. Correspondingly, an "exception" is a situation of extreme peril or danger to the existence of the state. Under such emergency conditions, the state's sovereign will suspend ordinary law to exercise the state's right of self-preservation.[8]

We should recognize, however, that sovereign power and decision-making continue to exist in relation to law during a state of exception. Schmitt describes sovereign power in the state of emergency as follows: "[The sovereign] decides whether there is a state of emergency as well as what must be done to eliminate it. Although he stands outside the normally valid legal system, *he nevertheless belongs to it*, for it is he who must decide whether the constitution needs to be suspended in its entirety."[9] Moreover, Schmitt argues that because "the exception is different from anarchy and chaos, order in the juristic sense still prevails even if it is not of the ordinary kind."[10] Indeed, there must be an underlying rule or principle that guides decision-making even in a state of exception. Sovereignty and sovereign decisions cannot be a case of "anything goes" because that would be chaos, something incompatible with a given state of affairs or decisions made with the purpose of protecting the state's fundamental nature. Decisions will be made in accordance with preserving a particular state of being.

The exercise of sovereign power in a state of exception cannot be described, as Agamben does, as power unmediated by law or as a suspension of law. But neither can this exercise of power be described, as Hardt and Negri do, as still a juridical act but one completely abstracted from a social order. Both of these analyses are two sides of the same coin, one that posits the possibility of an absolute separation between law and society. Such a model of the relationship between law and society maintains, for good or ill, the concept of an abstract or purely formalistic law uncontaminated by social impurities as well as the possibility of a social order (or power) unmediated by law. Hardt and Negri, then, accept Agamben's analytic but reverse its ethical charge, as this social order unmediated by law becomes a space where biopolitical life in the constituent form of the multitude can produce an absolute democracy outside of law. Both Agamben and Hardt and Negri neglect, however, Schmitt's insight that law and its social situation must always exist in relation to each other. If we accept the latter analytic, one in which law and society are mutually imbricated and mutually constitutive, then law and its social subjects will be seen as existing in a mutually articulated relationship until the end of their joint time. Forms of law will imply their social subjects by the modes of being that they enable or make interdict. And a social subject cannot exist without its law to represent it for what it "is" and to distinguish it from other modes of being. Reciprocally, law cannot exist without its subjects who will recognize a given claim as (their) law.[11]

Although Hardt and Negri borrow conceptually from Schmitt in their juridical analysis, I have shown that they neglect a key insight of Schmitt's. This insight, that law and its social situation must exist in relation to each other because only in chaos is there no law, runs against the grain of Hardt's and Negri's revolutionary narrative describing the growing separation of the postmodern juridical formation from society that enables the multitude's birth to presence in an absolute form that has not been alienated by law. Guided by the insight that law and society are related by a mutually imbricated and constitutive relationship, I shall consider the founding of America—Hardt and Negri's exemplary instance of constituent power—as less an exception to modern sovereignty and more an example of it. My treatment of the American Revolution illustrates the theme of nationalist revolution with all of its potentials and dangers—a theme Hardt and Negri take up in *Empire* to discuss how nationalism is a poisoned gift for postcolonial struggles. There is, then, less of an opposition between the American Revolution and the framing of the U.S. Constitution than Hardt and Negri make out—the conditions of possibility for the constitutional moment were immanent in the constituent act of the American Revolution. In other words, if we recognize the mutually imbricated and constitutive relation between law and society, then the relation of strict separation between forms of constituent and constituted power in Hardt's and Negri's narrative cannot be maintained.

Although one may be tempted to pessimistic nihilism or paralysis due to the inescapability of law, this should be resisted. As Foucault argues, the "point is not that everything is bad, but that everything is dangerous." If everything is dangerous, then "we always have something to do."[12] Hence, we should seize on the hope that things can be better and act when we perceive strategic opportunity, since the constituent act of the Revolution was itself forged from the constituted materials of British constitutionalism. With this more nuanced understanding of the relationship between law and society on the one hand and constituted and constituent power on the other, I will then return to *Empire* and, in reading it against its grain, show how Hardt's and Negri's attempt to summon the multitude into existence is itself based on not only the mutually constitutive relation between law and society or the fact that the multitude must take up forms of representation to become politically effective but also an aspiration for law's revolutionary potential.

## Claiming Identity to Claim Rights

The British Americans claimed that their rights under the British constitution were being infringed upon by acts of Parliament in the 1760s and 1770s. If the British government did not recognize these rights in the colonies, then English constitutional history provided the Americans a script to follow and into which the Americans narrated themselves.[13] The script was familiar: British Americans widely consumed the stories of the British struggle during the seventeenth century to recover their Ancient Constitution and constitute themselves properly as English by recovering their free origins against a tyrannical monarchy. Ultimately, the British Americans would invoke and extend this narrative by breaking their ties with the British government in order to preserve their identity as a people to whom freedoms are legitimately entrusted. The rights the British Americans claimed in the period leading up to the American Revolution were "British liberties" or the "rights of Englishmen." By claiming *these* rights, the British Americans were drawing upon British constitutional discourse.[14]

When arguing for their rights, the British Americans used a narrative of a people migrating to a new land, suggesting both connection to the origin of rights and a spatial relation of difference from the government that sought to rule over them. John Adams, in his *Novanglus* letters, frequently referred to "British" or "English" liberties. For Adams, the emigration of the colonists' ancestors both constituted and bridged a gap between England and America. He argued:

> English liberties are but certain rights of nature, reserved to the citizen, by the English constitution, which cleaved to our ancestors, when they crossed the Atlantic, and would have inhered in them, if instead of coming to New England they had gone to Outaheite, or Patagonia, even although they had taken no patent or charter from the king at all. These rights did not adhere to them the less, for their purchasing patents and charters, in which the king expressly stipulates with them, that they and their posterity should forever enjoy all those rights and liberties.[15]

Americans had rights because rights adhered to the bodies of the ancestors of the Americans who then populated North America.

Like Adams, Thomas Jefferson depended on the authority of ancestral heritage and migration to legitimize the rights he claimed on behalf of British America. Jefferson argued in "A Summary View of the Rights of British America" (1774) that America was conquered by their ancestors, who, "before their emigration to America, were free inhabitants of the British dominions in

Europe."[16] Their ancestors were acting just like England's ancestors, the Saxons, who "in like manner left their native wilds and woods in the North of Europe," and took possession of "the Island of Britain," and "established there that system of laws which has so long been the glory and protection of that country." From there, Jefferson argued that Germany never attempted to claim power over England. If they did, however, Britains would "have too firm a feeling of the rights derived to them from their ancestors, to bow down the sovereignty of their state. . . ." Jefferson used the Germanic variant of the Whig view to mark America's similarities and differences from Britain. Because of the freedom-loving nature of this people and its capacity to exercise liberty, it would be ludicrous for England to submit its sovereignty to Germany, and so just as ridiculous for Americans to lay down their forms of self-government before Parliament.[17]

Jefferson believed in the small, independent farmer as the basis for the free republic. Consequently, feudalism was contrary to such republican values. Therefore, in a way, America could realize the values of Anglo-Saxon freedom better than England could, under Jefferson's treatment. That is, the Norman Conquest brought feudalism to England, something that was considered foreign to the laws and values of the "original" Saxons. Migration to America meant that America could possibly realize these values to a more pure extent than England, since "America was not conquered by William the Norman."[18] Therefore, claims by Americans to their rights cannot be divorced from a simultaneous invention of a national identity that, in resting upon the authority of a people's migration, inaugurated racial concerns with purity and corruption, inside and outside, identity and difference.[19] Claiming rights, on this view, is a moment of deterritorialization and reterritorialization of social identities, in contrast to the usual understandings of rights as antithetical to social identity.

## Claiming Rights and Producing a National People: The Declaration of Independence

Not only did the British Americans claim an identity in order to claim rights, as shown in the previous section, but, as I shall demonstrate here, the constant invocation of rights and legal principles called forth a new identity formation— the American nation. This challenges Hannah Arendt's claim that the American Revolution was "unprecedented"—a claim which has received significant scholarly attention.[20] Even Arendt herself, however, is forced to recognize that in fact the founders did cite precedents upon which to base their actions constituting the new nation. The framers were bound back to the ancients not by tradition, according to Arendt, but because they needed "models and precedents." A beginning as such is saved from arbitrariness because it carries its own "principle" within itself. Beginning and principle, Arendt states, are *related* to each other and are coeval. One who begins something, Arendt argues, starts by laying down "the law of action for those who have joined him in order to partake in the enterprise and to bring about its accomplishment." In like fashion, we can say that a nation and its fundamental law are born simultaneously and in relation to each other.

While in the previous section I emphasize how the British Americans used a narrative of ancestry to create an identity justifying their rights, here I highlight how claiming legal rights produces a corresponding form of subjectivity. By citing legal precedent, the framers of America produce a distinctive national people. Hence, although a certain body politic provided the grounds for rights, this people is identified by their rights and is called into being through the law and legal declarations.

The Declaration of Independence is a particularly celebrated instance of a national people called into existence through the act of claiming rights. It is a legal declaration of right addressed to the British people and to the king. This declaration, however, follows a tradition in Atlantic republicanism of making declarations of right, reiterating earlier such declarations made by the British Americans, such as "The Bill of Rights [and] a List of Grievances" of October 27, 1774. This 1774 declaration, in turn, is part of a legal tradition including the 1689 "Declaration of Rights," a legal intervention forming part of the Glorious Revolution in Great Britain.[21] The American declarations exhibited structural similarities to the republican models earlier used in Great Britain, for instance through the use of "whereas clauses" opening the declarations to summarize grievances violative of rights. The Americans also invoked the preceding legal models more directly, using awkward phrasing borrowed from the English Declaration of Rights.

The Americans also cited the preceding British models more directly to make clear the tradition or conventions within which the American interventions ought to be understood, as when the 1774 declaration states: "as Englishmen their ancestors in like cases have usually done, for asserting and vindicating their rights and liberties, DECLARE. . . ."[22] For one and another to understand themselves as enemies, they must share something, whether it be language or, as in this case, certain conventions of claiming rights within a shared legal tradition that allowed the significance of the American declarations to be understood by their addressees.[23]

From one perspective, the Declaration of Independence marks a failure in the American attempt to claim the rights of Englishmen. From another perspective it represents a successful performative speech act. The rhetorical conventions marking relations of identity and difference with Britain facilitate the legal construction of an American counternation out of the cultural resources provided by the discourse of British constitutionalism. The performative utterance of the declaration is enabled by the staging provided by the spatial difference of America in relation to Great Britain, the negotiation of these relations of identity and difference through the narrative of migration, and the discourse of the Ancient Constitution. In order to recognize these ancient rights, the Declaration as a legal action dismembers one population, "British America," and forms an American national body. The declaration breaks and founds.

Jefferson's version of the Declaration of Independence enacts a painful process of cutting and reconstituting. After a series of protests that the declaration lodges against the king, the document turns to the British people:

> Nor have we been wanting in attentions to our British brethren. . . . We have reminded them of the circumstances of our emigration and settlement here . . . we have appealed to their native justice & magnanimity [as well as to] the tyes of our common kindred to disavow these usurpations which [were likely to] interrupt our connection and correspondence. They too have been deaf to the voice of justice and of consanguinity, [and when occasions have been given them . . . of removing from their councils the disturbers of our harmony, they have, by their free election, reestablished them in power. . . . These facts have *given the last stab to agonizing affection; and manly spirit bids us to renounce forever these unfeeling brethren.*] We *must* [*endeavor to forget our former love for them*, and to hold them, as we hold the rest of mankind, enemies in war, in peace friends. We might have been a free & a great people together. . . . Be it so since they will have it. . . . We will climb (the road of happiness and glory) apart from them, and] acquiesce in the necessity which denounces our eternal separation![24]

This portion of Jefferson's declaration indicates that the Revolution involves more than merely throwing off a government. It is also a rejection of a people— a reformation of the body politic through the severance of ties to create a new identity as a new national people. The pain, anticipated by John Dickinson, who wrote: "Torn from the body, to which we are united by religion, liberty, laws, affections, relation, language, and commerce, we must bleed at every vein," is evident in Jefferson's legal text calling forth a new national-legal people.[25]

## Exclusions

After a brief and confusing period of governance under the Articles of Confederation, the Americans redeclare themselves a national people through the Constitution. While sovereignty technically remained lodged in the several states under the Articles, a new form of sovereignty is invented in the Constitution—the sovereignty of the people. This move makes the legal basis for national government and the protection of rights consistent with the nationalist claims used to declare rights in the 1770s. Contrary to Hardt's and Negri's treatment of the American founding as an exemplary act of self-constitution by the multitude, in both the U.S. Constitution and in the declarations leading to the American Revolution, the focus of juridico-political energy is upon the *rights of the people*. Here I elaborate the boundaries used to identify a distinctive American people and the exclusions produced by these boundaries.

In his opening address to the Pennsylvania ratifying convention, James Wilson reviews the traditional theory of sovereignty—that it must exist in some singular place in a given system—in order to explain the proposed Constitution. Citing William Blackstone, Wilson states that in Great Britain sovereignty resides in Parliament. Where does it lie in the new U.S. Constitution? While some might say it resides in the states, Wilson corrects this misapprehension of the new system. Sovereignty under the Constitution "remains and flourishes with the people."[26]

The "people" is now the foundational referent of power and rights in the American system. The Bill of Rights protects *the people*'s liberties—those powers that the people have decided not to delegate to the national government. Echoing the 1774 "Bill of Rights [and] a List of Grievances" which refers to the "people of America" and the "rights of the people," the First Amendment to the Constitution refers to the "right of the people peaceably to assemble. . . ." The Fourth Amendment refers to the "right of the people to be secure in their persons, houses [etc.]. . . ." Thomas Jefferson in a letter refers to the Constitution as an "instrument of security for the rights of the people. . . ."[27] The Constitution secures rights in part by securing a national subject position from which to claim these rights. Neither God nor Philosophy, therefore, is the guarantor of these rights or provides the conditions of justice. This is the function of the people, an entity that is *before the law*, that is both inside and outside this constitution. As I have shown, the people is both legally constituted and a national condition of possibility for rights-claiming in this context.

A national people is being invented through these paradigmatic instances of recognizing rights. This discourse of rights generates the following logic: to claim rights under the U.S. Constitution, one must declare one's self an American. For this claim to be successful, however, one must be recognizably American. How does one identify an "American"? What are the signs? Many of the Euro-American legal arguments against the British give substance to the "people" on whose behalf rights are being claimed. The signs that function to designate who is included in a claim on rights also function at the same time to designate who is excluded from such a claim. Not just anybody is an American, or else the term is meaningless. Consistent with this insight, the Americans distinguished themselves through their rights claims.

While the declaration castigates the king for behavior "totally unworthy the head of a *civilized* nation," it also locates a boundary, distinguishing the American people from other possible peoples. The declaration complains that the British have brought upon the inhabitants of "*our* frontiers, the merciless Indian *savages*. . . ." Here we can see that the Americans use a discourse that categorizes peoples according to the opposition of civilization versus barbarism and savagery in order to differentiate Americans who are claiming their rights from the indigenous peoples who also happen to live on the continent. Similarly, the "Declaration . . . Setting Forth the Causes and Necessity of Taking up Arms" (1775) places the migration of British Americans in the context of America's previous territorial identity as a space filled with inhospitable wilds inhabited by warlike nations of "barbarians."[28] Adams's *Dissertation on the Canon and Feudal Law* effects the transition of deterritorialization and reterritorialization of this space to which the British Americans migrated: remarking upon the civility amongst the common people of America, Adams goes on to recollect how their ancestors labored in "clearing their grounds . . . amidst dangers from wild beasts and savage men."[29] The drive to create a national people inevitably requires exclusions that produce remainders, and here we can see that the process of identifying the American people as a civilized people excludes the indigenous population from the national imaginary, based on the meaning produced within the paradigm of modernity by the racial opposition of the "civilized" and the "savage."

Moreover, although observers frequently note that Jefferson's version of the declaration included a long passage condemning slavery that was edited out by Congress, this effort hardly indicated a racially inclusive vision of the American people in terms of black-white relations. Indeed, this passage betrays Jefferson's greatest fears of race war. He condemns the British for inciting insurrections by slaves against whites: "thus paying off former crimes committed against the *liberties* of one people, with crimes which he urges them to commit against the *lives* of another."[30] Jefferson may have proposed various ways to bring slavery to an end, and his views on whether blacks were subordinate to whites may be complex, but he doubted very deeply that blacks and whites could become submerged in the same national body. Indeed, Jefferson advocated the removal of blacks from America upon emancipation in his *Notes on the State of Virginia*, a position endorsed by Adams and put forward by others. This doubt that blacks and whites could be joined within the same national body becomes manifest in the Declaration, which inscribes several racially distinctive peoples but declares independence and claims rights for only one of these entities. Hence, when the Declaration refers to the "rights of the people" this would appear to be a distinctively bounded social body.[31]

This treatment of the American founding is in contrast to Hardt's and Negri's treatment of it, which uses the United States to exemplify an expansive power of the multitude over the centralizing power of sovereignty. Hardt and Negri are able to maintain the distinction between constituent and constituted power by representing the Declaration of Independence as an expression of constituent power while the Constitution tames constituent power through a centralizing representational logic (I, chap. 4; E, 160, 165). The democratic nature of the American people and their constituent power post-Revolution, in this scheme, are maintained either in the yawning gap between law and society or in the open spaces of the frontier.[32] The discussion of the Declaration above, however, demonstrates the fallacy of presenting the "constituent power" of the Revolutionaries as purely different from constituted power. The Americans made their declaration through a creative appropriation of British legal discourse, which allowed the Americans to claim that their rights were being violated. Indeed, this reiteration of British legal discourse, engrafted onto a new territorial context, enabled their Declaration of Independence to be comprehensible to their British addressees while severing the preexisting relation, thereby allowing the British Americans to reinvent themselves as the American people. In other words, the constituted power of British constitutional discourse enabled a revolutionary act of constituent power to be made present.[33]

The Declaration appears to be a legal moment with great democratic potential. I imagine this is why Hardt and Negri seek to claim it on behalf of the multitude. Similarly, Martin Luther King, Jr., claimed the principles inscribed within the Declaration on behalf of the Civil Rights Movement. In his address, "The American Dream," King refers to the Declaration of Independence's statement that all men are created equal and that they are endowed with the inalienable rights of life, liberty, and the pursuit of happiness. Analyzing this passage, King observes: "One of the first things we notice in this dream is an amazing universalism. It does not say some men, but it says all men. It does not say white men, but it says all men, which includes black men."[34] Immanent to the Declaration is a promise of liberty and equality—a promise that can inspire commitment and that requires continuing good faith efforts to make real, again and again.

Law, like any representational form, is inadequate to the immeasurable qualities of life's flows, as Hardt and Negri also argue. But the gap between law and society is a constitutive indeterminacy enabling at once the possibility of relation and the impossibility of this calculated gesture towards justice finally achieving its ends. While law's indeterminate nature enables sovereign power to misappropriate the declared rights of subjects, it also provides the possibility that newly invented grounds will enable us to redeclare our commitment to the spirit of those rights in a way that is more adequate to justice under differing conditions. Hence, the same gap that allowed the misappropriation of the Declaration of Independence by the Supreme Court in *Dred Scott v. Sandford* (1857) through its white-supremacist American imaginary also allowed a more just appropriation of these rights by those inspired by King's American Dream and his proud maladjustment from such a white-supremacist America.[35] Differing conditions have produced the need, which Hardt and Negri recognize, for these rights to be extended and given new life under contemporary conditions of global capital and global militarism. But the gaps and indeterminacies that will enable the reiteration of these rights under conditions other than those in which Jefferson acted also mean that law can be made unresponsive to the commitments of liberty and equality unless we join the struggle against those who seek legal authorization for the inequalities and violence of global capital and global militarism.

## Representing the Multitude

In the final chapter of *Empire*, entitled "The Multitude against Empire," Hardt and Negri claim that "Imperial power can no longer resolve the conflict of social forces through mediatory schemata that displace the terms of conflict" (E, 393). This is an abridged version of their argument in *Labor of Dionysus*, where they describe a separation of the state from society. They go on to argue that social conflicts now confront each other directly, without mediations of any sort. In this way, Empire creates "a greater potential for revolution than did the modern regimes of power" (E, 393). This, in turn, sets the stage for Hardt and Negri to examine: "how the multitude can become a political subject in the context of Empire" (E, 394).

Hardt and Negri then proceed to hail the multitude in a manner that would constitute the multitude as a political subject. Their rhetoric in this regard is instructive. As their subject headings indicate, they make three major demands on behalf of the multitude. The discourse they appropriate to make these demands is a *legal* discourse—specifically, a discourse of *rights-claiming*. In the name of the multitude, Hardt and Negri claim 1) The Right to Global Citizenship; 2) The Right to a Social Wage; and 3) The Right to Reappropriation.

Clearly, Hardt and Negri hope that the multitude qua politically active subject will become interpellated by these rights. They hope that the multitude will be activated by what these rights represent and will recognize themselves as being represented by these claims. I am not condemning Hardt's and Negri's strategy here. To the contrary, this strategy makes complete sense *despite* the arguments they have made against representation and mediation. Although their arguments are premised on the separation of state from society so that the multitude could begin its presencing under postmodern conditions outside the alienating order of representation, their attempts to call the multitude into being cannot do without the order of representation, as shown by their invocation of rights to constitute a politically viable multitude. As linguistically oriented philosophy from Ferdinand de Saussure to Jacques Derrida has taught us, meaning is constituted in relations of difference, and a space of difference is essential to any act of communication, whether this be the space of difference between pointer and object or between acoustic signifier and conceptual signified. To gain an identity, one must make use of representational forms that are not oneself in order to represent one's identity.

Identity is signified by relations of difference and a social order is signified by its law—something that is in a way other than the social but exists in relation to it. Law is a site where we make manifest our commitments with the hope that they can become re-presented under future circumstances. And when we cite this law, we are performatively representing to ourselves that to which we have committed ourselves—if, that is, we are willing to reauthorize those commitments as a valid law for our existence. Does this appeal inspire in us the self-recognition as the sort of people or "community" that would be committed to such principles? Does this legal call interpellate us? Or does it leave us saying "so what" in response to the call?[36] If the legal commitment will help realize the equal concern and respect that humanity deserves, then perhaps the decision will be yes. If not, then perhaps the decision will be no, as our legal commitments will be otherwise. Law and our commitments to justice thus require constant and insistent decisions (decisions that will be inevitably less than totally adequate) in the space between legal citations.[37] Significantly, then, the multitude's birth to presence occurs in a *legal* moment.

This legal invocation of the multitude, though creating the possibility of a political subject, necessarily makes impossible the total inclusivity Hardt and Negri claim on behalf of the multitude. Either the ontological multitude exists immanently and is inclusive but with no political subjectivity, or it has political subjectivity but is rent by difference.[38] Hardt and Negri cannot have it both ways. By putting forward rights claims as they have done, Hardt and Negri have set the stage for politics, difference, and exclusion, much as the Native Americans were constitutively excluded from the laws of the "multitude's" development on the North American frontier.

What if there *was* a revolution? Inevitably, there would be disagreements over whether there should be rights in addition to or other than those Hardt and Negri claimed for the multitude. In practice, there would be struggles in which the rights claims Hardt and Negri have put forward might be considered antagonistic to other rights that people believe are essential to justice. But even in the unlikely event of total agreement on a total list of multitudinous rights, disagreements would arise whenever rights claims were concretized in specific circumstances. Outcomes of these interpretive battles over what the rights of the multitude oblige in given circumstances would position those interpretations that do not carry the day as not-multitudinous, if not antimultitudinous.

Where there is politics, there is representation, as "we" need to figure out who "we" are and what our commitments mean in particular circumstances, circumstances that will be different from those under which we committed ourselves previously.[39] And where there is representation, there is difference and exclusion, as Hardt and Negri know and fear. Hardt and Negri avoid the problematic of representation in order to save the inclusiveness of the multitude, but they cannot do this without sacrificing the political significance of the multitude. For the multitude to take on political significance, it will become rent by difference and repression. But sacrificing the chaos of anything goes leads to the *possibility* that something (good?) can happen. There will be exclusions and repressions involved in any one move toward justice. Rather than complacency or a false universality, we must make what remains after an (necessarily) incomplete move toward justice the fuel for subsequent moves toward justice, since *total* justice will elude our time.

## Conclusion

In this chapter, I have described how, from a juridical point of view, Hardt and Negri present the formation of a postmodern form of global sovereignty, Empire, that is increasingly separating itself from the socioeconomic plane. The imperial juridical formation that Hardt and Negri elaborate is increasingly unable to mediate social conflict or represent the increasingly complex socioeconomic conditions within societies of control. This growing separation of postmodern law and the state from the domain of the social, however, provides increased opportunity for revolutionary action as the forces of domination are confronted with resistance directly. This separation also enables the possibility that the constituent power of the multitude can create absolute democracy within this space which is freed from constituted power's alienating structures of law or sovereignty.

This revolutionary narrative, however, relies on a strict separation between the categories of law and society, on the one hand, and constituted and constituent power, on the other. By returning to a privileged instance of constituent energies for Hardt and Negri—the American Revolution—I have shown how law and society (the latter figured here nationally) function in a mutually constitutive manner, as the Revolutionaries made claims regarding their identity in order to enable the validity of their rights claims while simultaneously utilizing legal declarations in order to reconstitute their identity as a free and independent national people. Moreover, this example also disrupts an absolute division between constituent and constituted power, as the Americans used the constituted forms of British constitutional discourse and reinflected them under different circumstances in order to produce a constituent act that severed ties with the British government.

When Hardt and Negri describe their legal theory, they argue that the Constitution "should also be understood as a material regime of juridical interpretation and practice that is exercised not only by jurists and judges but also by subjects throughout society" (E, 168). But the weight of their analysis regarding the developing revolutionary conditions posits a strict separation between the juridical and social orders—necessarily so if the multitude's practices are to be "not representational but constituent activity" (E, 413) or if law is treated merely as an alienating parasite upon the productive and constituent nature of the multitude. Yet in their efforts to call the multitude into being under globalized conditions, Hardt and Negri are forced to utilize a legal discourse of rights-claiming. This indicates, despite the narrative development of their arguments, that law is not so easily escaped and that law is not only a repressive form of power but one with constitutive, productive effects as well.

We would do better, I suggest, not to seek an impossible purity in our practices and to come to a more complex appreciation of law's strategic opportunities as well as its dangers—indeed, to recognize the real need to struggle on multiple fronts, including legal fronts, for greater justice and greater democracy. Rights claims and other legal practices can provide nodal points enabling the hegemonization of a social force like the multitude for these purposes.[40] Hegemonizing a force for a specific purpose, however, means excluding that which is contrary to that purpose. The significance of this insight, however, requires theorists of postmodernity to grapple, in a far more nuanced way than yet demonstrated, with the problems of law, the state, politics, and representation for globalization to be met more forcefully by this quest for justice and democracy.

## Acknowledgments

I would like to thank Jodi Dean and Kevin Dunn for reading an earlier draft of this chapter.

## Notes

1. Antonio Negri, *Insurgencies: Constituent Power and the Modern State*, trans. Maurizia Bascagli (Minneapolis: University of Minnesota Press, 1994), 24. Further references to the works of Michael Hardt and Antonio Negri will be made parenthetically within the text. Michael Hardt, "Translator's Forward: The Anatomy of Power," in Antonio Negri, *The Savage Anomaly: The Power of Spinoza's Metaphysics and Politics*, trans. Michael Hardt (Minneapolis: University of Minnesota Press, 1991), is abbreviated as TF. Michael Hardt, "The Withering of Civil Society," in *Deleuze & Guattari: New Mappings in Politics, Philosophy, and Culture*, ed. Eleanor Kauffman and Kevin Jon Heller (Minneapolis: University of Minnesota Press, 1998), is abbreviated as CS. Michael Hardt and Antonio Negri, *Empire* (Cambridge, MA: Harvard University Press, 2000), is abbreviated as E, and Michael Hardt and Antonio Negri, *Labor of Dionysus: A Critique of the State Form* (Minneapolis: University of Minnesota Press, 1994), is abbreviated as LD. Finally, Antonio Negri, *Insurgencies,* is abbreviated as I.

2. For evidence of this trend, see Stanley Fish, *The Trouble with Principle* (Cambridge, MA: Harvard University Press, 1999); *Left Legalism/ Left Critique,* ed. Wendy Brown and Janet Halley (Durham, NC: Duke University Press, 2002); Judith Butler, *Excitable Speech: A Politics of the Performative* (New York: Routledge, 1997). For a strategic critique, see Paul A. Passavant and Jodi Dean, "Laws and Societies," *Constellations* 8 (2001): 376–389; for a descriptive critique, see Paul A. Passavant, "Enchantment, Aesthetics, and the Superficial Powers of Modern Law," *Law & Society Review* 35 (2001): 709–729.

3. Hardt's and Negri's critical assessment of labor unions, describing them more as vehicles for taming laborers and making labor more amenable to the capitalist system, is thus similar to the treatment of unions in Frances Fox Piven and Richard Cloward, *Poor People's Movements: Why They Succeed, How They Fail* (New York: Vintage, 1979), 96–180.

4. Gilles Deleuze, "Control and Becoming," and "Postscript on Control Societies," in *Negotiations: 1972–1990,* trans. Martin Joughin (New York: Columbia University Press, 1995).

5. See also Jodi Dean, "The Networked Empire: Communicative Capitalism and the Hope for Politics," in this volume.

6. Giorgio Agamben, *Homo Sacer: Sovereign Power and Bare Life*, trans. Daniel Heller-Roazen (Minneapolis: University of Minnesota Press, 1998), 170–175.

7. Carl Schmitt, *Political Theology: Four Chapters on the Concept of Sovereignty* (Cambridge, MA: MIT Press, 1985), 13.

8. Ibid., 13, 6, 12. This paragraph and the next draw heavily from Paul A. Passavant, *No Escape: Freedom of Speech and the Paradox of Rights* (New York: New York University Press, 2002), 16–17.

9. Schmitt, *Political Theology,* 7; emphasis added, citation omitted.

10. Ibid., 12.

11. Paul A. Passavant, "Enchantment, Aesthetics, and the Superficial Powers of Modern Law," 721, 724. For a fuller discussion of Agamben, see Peter Fitzpatrick, "Bare Sovereignty: Homo Sacer and the Insistence of Law," *Theory and Event* 5 (2001).

12. Michel Foucault, "On the Genealogy of Ethics: An Overview of Work in Progress," in *The Foucault Reader,* ed. Paul Rabinow (New York: Pantheon, 1984): 343.

13. For a discussion of the American appropriation of this script, see Bernard Bailyn, *The Ideological Origins of the American Revolution* (Cambridge, MA: Harvard University Press, 1967); Gordon Wood, *The Creation of the American Republic 1776–1787* (New York: Norton, 1972); H. Trevor Colbourn, *The Lamp of Experience: Whig History and the Intellectual Origins of the American Revolution* (Chapel Hill, NC: University of North Carolina Press, 1965). Pauline Maier, *American Scripture: Making the Declaration of Independence* (New York: Knopf, 1997), compares the American declarations with their precedents in British constitutional history, particularly the 1689 Declaration of Rights. For a discussion of the persistence of this discourse in early American politics, see Lance Banning, *The Jeffersonian Persuasion: Evolution of a Party Ideology* (Ithaca, NY: Cornell University Press, 1978); and J. G. A. Pocock, *The Machiavellian Moment: Florentine Political Thought and the Atlantic Republican Tradition* (Princeton, NJ: Princeton University Press, 1975).

14. This section and the following two sections draw heavily from research and arguments I have presented in *No Escape,* chap. 1.

15. John Adams, *Novanglus and Massachusettensis* (1774–1775) (Boston: Hews and Goss, 1819), 96–97.

16. Thomas Jefferson, "A Summary View of the Rights of British America" (1774), in *The Complete Jefferson*, ed. Saul Padover (New York: Tudor, 1943).

17. Ibid., 15, 6–7.

18. Ibid., 17. The emigration argument is referred to in the "Declaration of Independence," although it is a longer reference in Jefferson's draft than in the version Congress approved. In the final draft, the reference reads: "We have reminded them of the circumstances of our emigration and settlement here. . . ." "Declaration of Independence," (1776), in *Complete Jefferson*, 33. John Adams saw in England a corruption leading to a decline practically to Roman depths, and thus the migration allowed the possibility that the essence of the British constitution might be saved from corruption in America. Hence, he taunted the British: "if we enjoy, and are entitled to more liberty than the British constitution allows, where is the harm? Or, if we enjoy the British constitution in greater purity and perfection than they do in England, as is really the case, whose fault is this? Not ours." John Adams, *Novanglus and Massachusettensis*, 91.

19. On the question of identity, see William Connolly, *Identity\Difference* (Ithaca, NY: Cornell University Press, 1991).

20. Hannah Arendt, *On Revolution* (New York: Viking Press, 1963); Bonnie Honig, "Declarations of Independence: Arendt and Derrida on the Problem of Founding a Republic," ed. Frederick Dolan and Thomas Dumm, *Rhetorical Republic: Governing Representations in American Politics* (Amherst, MA: University of Massachusetts, 1993).

21. "The Bill of Rights [and] a List of Grievances," in *A Decent Respect to the Opinions of Mankind: Congressional State Papers 1774–1776*, ed. James Hutson (Washington, DC: Library of Congress, 1975); Maier, *American Scripture*, 54–57. For a discussion of the legal discourse of this period in United States history, see Paul A. Passavant, *No Escape*, chap. 1.

22. Maier, *American Scripture*, 54–55; "The Bill of Rights [and] a List of Grievances," in *A Decent Respect to the Opinions of Mankind*, 53.

23. Jacques Derrida similarly argues that Schmitt's friend-enemy antithesis cannot be as absolute as is claimed by Schmitt if one gains political identity through one's relation with the enemy in part because the two enemies must be able to understand their relationship to be what it is for it to have the political consequences Schmitt claims for it; they must share something anterior to the political relationship of friend-enemy (244–252). In fact, Derrida considers the proximity of the relation of the enemy (absolute other) to the relation of the brother (one closest to me who is perhaps part of me) and the play between the two categories of identity, a play born out in the American Declaration of Independence that declares the brother to be an enemy. Jacques Derrida, *Politics of Friendship*, trans. George Collins (New York: Verso, 1997).

24. I have used Maier as my source for the Declaration of Independence (Appendix C). The bracketed portions are parts of Jefferson's version that Congress cut. The parenthetical portion is an insertion by me made necessary by my use of ellipses. I have added capitalization. Pauline Maier, *American Scripture: Making the Declaration of Independence* (New York: Knopf, 1997).

25. John Dickinson, "Letters from a Farmer in Pennsylvania" (1767), in *Empire and Nation*, ed. Forrest McDonald (Englewood Cliffs, NJ: Prentice-Hall, 1962), 18.

26. James Wilson, "James Wilson's Opening Address," (November 24, 1787) *The Debate on the Constitution: Federalist and Anti-Federalist Speeches, Articles, and Letters during the Struggle over Ratification*, Part One (New York: Library of America, 1993), 801–802.

27. Jefferson to Francis Hopkinson, March 13, 1789, *The Portable Jefferson*, ed. Merrill Peterson (New York: Viking, 1975), 436.

28. "Declaration of Independence," cited in *American Scripture*, Appendix C, 239, italics mine; "Declaration . . . Setting Forth the Causes and Necessity of Taking up Arms" (1775), in *A Decent Respect to the Opinions of Mankind*, 91.

29. John Adams, "Dissertation on the Canon and Feudal Law," in *The Works of John Adams*, vol. 3, ed. Charles Francis Adams (Boston: Little & Brown, 1851), 456, 462.

30. "Declaration of Independence," cited in *American Scripture*, Appendix C, Emphases in the original.

31. Jefferson's views on blacks are discussed in Garry Wills, *Inventing America: Jefferson's Declaration of Independence* (Garden City, NY: Doubleday, 1978). On the generality of these views, see Gary Nash, *Race and Revolution* (Madison, WI: Madison House, 1990), 48. St. George Tucker explicitly links his plan to eliminate slavery with Jefferson's in St. George Tucker, "A Dissertation on Slavery: With a Proposal for the Gradual Abolition of It" (1796), in Nash, *Race and Revolution*, 151–158, citing Jefferson at 155. John Adams also described the passages in Jefferson's "Notes on the State of Virginia" on slavery as being worth "Diamonds." See "Adams to Jefferson," May 22, 1785, in *The Adams-Jefferson Letters: The Complete Correspondence between Thomas Jefferson and Abigail and John Adams*, vol. 1, ed. Lester J. Cappon (Chapel Hill, NC: University of North Carolina Press, 1959), 21. The reference to the "rights of the people" is in Maier, *American Scripture*, 237.

32. Cf. Negri, *Insurgencies*, 152, 154, 161 ("the constituent power that continues to live outside the constitution"), 177 ("the 'material constitution' exceeds the formal constitution . . . the constituent principle and its determination of freedom and originality manage each time to materialize and break through the constitutional wrapping"). For a critique of a mutually exclusive conception of law and society, see Paul A. Passavant, "Enchantment, Aesthetics, and the Superficial Powers of Modern Law."

33. For a more extended discussion of the American appropriation of British legal discourse during this period, see Paul A. Passavant, *No Escape*, chap. 1. We might also note that the Declaration claims the independence of a national people, and Hardt and Negri present the concept of the nation or the people as a representational form, hence as a form that takes the place of the multitude. Thus, to the extent that the multitude is constituent power as they understand the notion, representing the Declaration as a constituent act would seem to be problematic on these grounds as well.

34. Martin Luther King, Jr., "The American Dream" (1961), in *A Testament of Hope: The Essential Writings of Martin Luther King, Jr.*, ed. James M. Washington (New York: HarperCollins, 1986), 208.

35. *Dred Scott v. Sandford* 60 U.S. (19 How.) 393 (1857). Indeed, this gap enabled the Justices McLean and Curtis to come to a different, and to my mind superior, legal view in *Dred Scott*. For Martin Luther King, Jr.'s "dream" that the promises of equality inscribed within the Declaration of Independence and indeed the Constitution will become realized, see also King, "I Have a Dream" (1963), and for his proud maladjustment to white supremacist reality, see "The American Dream" (1961), in *A Testament of Hope*. For a discussion of how King sought to use law to inspire a more egalitarian America while seeking to inspire an American imaginary that would authorize *Brown*'s rule of equality as the law of the land, see Paul A. Passavant, *No Escape*, chap. 4.

36. Miles Davis, "So What" (March 2, 1959), *Kind of Blue* (New York: Sony Music Entertainment/ Columbia Legacy, reissued 1997).

37. See, generally, Jacques Derrida, "Force of Law: The 'Mystical Foundation of Authority,'" in *Deconstruction and the Possibility of Justice*, ed. Drucilla Cornell, Michel Rosenfeld, and David Gray Carlson (New York: Routledge, 1992); and Derrida, *Spectres of Marx: The State of the Debt, the Work of Mourning, & the New International* (New York: Routledge, 1994).

38. My thinking about this has been aided by numerous conversations with Jodi Dean. See Paul A. Passavant and Jodi Dean, "Representation and the Event," in this volume.

39. My thinking about representation has been improved by Ernesto Laclau, *Emancipation(s)* (New York: Verso, 1996).

40. For a discussion of "nodal points," see Ernesto Laclau and Chantal Mouffe, *Hegemony and Socialist Strategy: Toward a Radical Democratic Politics* (London: Verso, 1985), 112–113. See also 142, 177, 188–189.

# 6

*Sovereignty*

# Representing the International: Sovereignty after Modernity?

## Mark Laffey and Jutta Weldes

There is widespread confusion about the nature of the contemporary world. Images of the international abound: some old, some new, some competing and incompatible, others intertwined and overlapping. The great narratives of Western modernity, with their constitutive reliance on the rise of the sovereign state in Europe and its gradual spread across the planet's surface, have lost their power. Globalization, itself a deeply contested concept, is only the most prominent sign of our uncertainty—despite capital's efforts to convince us otherwise. Overwhelmed with contradictory information, we literally do not know where we are.

Whatever its precise cause, the continuing crisis of representation, signaled in proliferating efforts to offer a true account of our world, renders political action more difficult, if not impossible. Answering Lenin's "What is to be done?" requires knowledge we simply do not have: if we do not know where we are, how can we know what to do? In the shadow of capitalist triumphalism and environmental crisis, of accelerating militarism and barbarism on a global scale, plotting new maps and writing new scripts is fundamental to the recovery of politics now. In this chapter, we assess Michael Hardt's and Antonio Negri's *Empire* as an ambitious but flawed attempt to end this crisis of representation by offering a new and compelling account of the world in which we live.

Hailed as "a rewriting of *The Communist Manifesto* for our time," *Empire* is explicitly and self-consciously designed as a call to arms.[1] The aim is to identify the enemy, rally the troops, and send them over the top in quest of a better future, or at least better theory. To that end, Hardt and Negri construct a novel vocabulary and use it to produce a sweeping narrative of world politics past and present organized around the transformation of sovereignty from a modern to a postmodern form, which they call Empire. The effort to rearticulate the international as Empire is central to the book's argument and its political project.

In common with many other recent attempts to map world politics, Hardt and Negri write against the background of an increasingly tattered modernist narrative of sovereign territoriality. Modern sovereignty and the territorial state are being overwhelmed and transformed by capitalist globalization. Or so we are told. Beginning with sovereignty and drawing a sharp divide between its modern and postmodern forms, however, produces difficulties for Hardt's and Negri's analysis of Empire and of the place of coercion in our allegedly post-colonial and postimperial world.[2] In particular, it leads to a misleading analysis of the nature and distribution of power, thus rendering effective political action less likely. As a corrective, we offer an alternative representation of the contemporary world, one that makes central the internationalization of the state.

The chapter is organized as follows. First, we sketch the contours of the contemporary crisis of representation in the context of globalization and note the shared dependence of these representations on a conception of the international dominated by the sovereign Westphalian state. Second, we discuss Hardt's and Negri's work as a novel attempt to address this crisis, offering a critical assessment that shows a similar dependence in their account of Empire. Third, we provide an alternative representation of the international grounded in the literature on the internationalization of capital and the state. In conclusion, we argue that conceptualizing the international in our terms is politically more enabling than is Hardt's and Negri's account of the international as Empire.

## Proliferating Representations and the Sovereignty Narrative

For many analysts and policy-makers, particularly in the West, the Cold War provided the central coordinates for mapping and negotiating the world. The implosion of the Soviet Union and the consequent evaporation of the Cold War meant the loss of these coordinates; the sudden irrelevance of the bipolar model of world politics spurred a search for a new one. "Globalization" quickly became "the buzzword of the 1990s"[3]—the new authoritative account of our time and context and a seemingly apt slogan for capturing contemporary trends and transformations—and it shows no sign of retreating with the start of the new millennium. Instead, there is a proliferation of "global babble,"[4] as we are inundated by talk of the global village, global capital, the global economy, global markets, global communication, global threats, the global environment, global consumers, global teens, global civil society, and global governance. Globalization, it seems, is quite literally everywhere.

The pervasiveness of "globalization" rhetoric notwithstanding, no single representation of this supposedly globalized world has emerged or become generally accepted. Instead, representations of globalization and its effects are proliferating as the international is reimagined after the Cold War. Most prominent in the West, and certainly in the Anglo-American context, has been the politically potent neoliberal vision. For its proponents, this offers the only realistic view of globalization because, as John Weeks, Canadian permanent representative to the World Trade Organization (WTO), has said, "globalization is the reality."[5] On this view, technological change is making possible the global spread of production, trade, and finance, which in turn is eroding state sovereignty. For Kenichi Ohmae, an early neoliberal spokesman: "traditional nation-states have become unnatural, even impossible business units in a global economy."[6] Instead, neoliberal representations of the international depict a world "tied together into a single globalized marketplace and village."[7] Civil society is also globalizing, as anarchy among states is "fading away" and state-based identities are replaced with other forms of social and political identity.[8] On this view, widely shared by boosters and critics of neoliberalism, state sovereignty is progressively being overcome or undone by globalization: ours is an increasingly borderless world in which "production is . . . mobile, capital footloose, technology diffuse."[9]

Other representations, in contrast, defend the sovereign-state ideal. Contesting the neoliberal "global village," for instance, is Linda Weiss's expressly "inter-nationalized" economy in which states are adaptable and state power might even be expanding. On this view, "nation-states are penetrated by crossborder networks of trade, finance and production."[10] But this does not mean the end of the sovereign state and its power. States remain central to world politics, albeit with differential capacities to engage with globalization: strong states "with fairly firm control over socio-economic goal setting and robust domestic linkages" can actually "facilitat[e] the changes identified as 'globalization.'"[11] This second type of representation, then, sees globalization not as the end of the state but only as a reworking of the terms and context of state sovereignty.

Both representations of the (allegedly) new international are tied, either positively or negatively, to what we call the sovereignty narrative. This narrative—organized around the assumption that, before the end of the Cold War and the onset of globalization, "the international" was defined by the sovereignty of states—provided the image of the international that, during the Cold

War, was acted on by statespersons, rendered commonsensical in the media, and theorized by scholars of international relations. It begins with a world of sovereign entities called states which are the primary actors in world politics.[12] As a result, "the international" is anarchic, that is, without overarching or centralized rule. The sovereignty narrative thus constructs a world defined by sovereignty, peopled by sovereign (nation-) states, and characterized by anarchy.

In this context, four characteristics conventionally define the state: a territory with well-defined boundaries, a population to be governed, a government to make binding decisions, and sovereignty.[13] Its sovereignty—usually dated, contentiously, from the Treaty of Westphalia in 1648—ultimately depends on its "monopoly of the legitimate use of physical force within a given territory."[14] Within its territory, the state is assumed to have pacified its population, to be the sole source of binding decisions, and to enforce both the pacification and its decision-making authority with legitimate coercive capabilities. Externally, sovereignty means independence from outside interference: states "develop their own strategies, chart their own courses, make their own decisions."[15] Because the state answers "to no higher authority in the international sphere,"[16] the international system is by definition anarchic.

The representations of the international sketched above start from this sovereignty narrative. For each, the world really did, at least until recently, consist of sovereign territorial states. But for some, technologically determined "time/space compression"[17] and the "ascendance of highly mobile, transnational forms of capital"[18] mean that states are being eclipsed. For others, in contrast, the sovereign state persists despite globalization or is indeed responsible for it.[19] In either case, the resulting representations of the contemporary international are significantly influenced by—and the arguments largely couched in terms of—this dominant Western sovereignty narrative. That is, this model has incited a particular discourse in which the nature of our (putatively) new, post–Cold War, globalizing world—what it really looks like, how it is structured, and its fundamental dynamics—is discussed, ad nauseum, in terms of the relations of globalization to the sovereign state.

This sovereignty narrative is flawed in several ways, however, with significant consequences for our representation of the contemporary international. For our purposes, three interconnected problems are particularly important: a debilitating statecentrism, an unsustainable Eurocentrism, and the corresponding failure to grasp important aspects of coercion in world politics. A consequence of these problems, both singly and in combination, has been either an inability to see the internationalization or "rescaling"[20] of the state or, as in the case of Hardt and Negri, a failure adequately to conceptualize it.

The profound statecentrism of the Westphalian model presumes that sovereign territorial boundaries contain and represent a meaningful guide to social relations and processes in the international system. The "territorial trap," that is, assumes that social relations are defined largely in terms of state boundaries.[21] But this is clearly incorrect. Many social processes—such as the internationalization of capital or modernity—and relations—such as those of gender, class, race, or colonialism—transcend state boundaries in complex and significant ways. Arguably, then, the sovereign territorial state is simply the wrong place to begin analysis. Indeed, reflection on the past three hundred or so years—since Westphalia—indicates that the dominant political form has in  any case been the imperial state and empire rather than the sovereign state.[22] Certainly this was true of what is often taken to be the high noon of sovereign territoriality, the post–World War II "Free World" dominated by the United States. Statecentrism, then, misses a lot, and not just in the contemporary globalizing world.

The sovereignty narrative is deeply Eurocentric as well. On this view, the history of modernity, at least as related to world politics, becomes the story of the rise of the sovereign territorial state in Europe and its diffusion to or imposition on the rest of the world.[23] But this is, again, simply inaccurate. It denies the persistent and integral relations between Europe and the non-European world and their joint role in generating the characteristic social forms of modernity, including the state itself. As Fernando Coronil observes, for example: "Since the European conquest of the Americas, the West and its peripheries have been mutually constituted through processes of imperial transculturation and capital accumulation that continue, in different forms, in the present."[24] European and Western imperial and military adventures abroad had massive effects on non-Western social formations; but involvement outside Europe and the West shaped the West as well, and contributed and continues to contribute to the making of the modern state. United States involvement in Vietnam, to provide just one recent example, affected not only the Vietnamese and the rest of South East Asia; it had fundamental effects on the U.S. state, including practices central to the character of its democracy, such as media-military relations, the organization and deployment of U.S. military forces, and the nature of U.S.-led war.[25]

The inadequacy of both the statecentrism and the Eurocentrism of the sovereignty narrative are readily apparent in analysis of state violence.[26] The sovereignty narrative assumes that the modern state recruits military force internally and then projects that force into the international system.[27] But this, again, is profoundly mistaken: force has instead often been organized "internationally," transcending the state's territorial limits. For instance, European states have used foreign military and security manpower. Recruiting local soldiers and police forces from within colonized territories was integral to imperial relations between Europe and non-Europe throughout the period marked by the so-called Westphalian sovereign state, as the British empire in India attests. Similarly, the United States and Soviet Union both constituted proxy military forces abroad during the Cold War. The United States (among many examples) funded regular and irregular proxy forces in South Vietnam and Afghanistan, raised mercenary forces to overthrow the Arbenz regime in Guatemala and undermine the Sandinista regime in Nicaragua, and constituted and deployed the ill-fated Cuban exile force of the Bay of Pigs. More generally, the construction of a transnational coercive apparatus—an "external state"[28] intimately articulated with the "internal state" located on sovereign U.S. territory—was central to the processes of order-making carried forward by the U.S. state and its allies after World War II. The sovereignty narrative obscures the international constitution of state power, a routine practice in the history of imperial relations. Ironically, examining the actual constitution of military force—allegedly the central characteristic of the Westphalian state—leads to a distinctively non-Westphalian understanding of the state and of the international.

Through these problematic assumptions, the sovereignty narrative restricts our representations of the international, highlighting particular issues and channeling debate in certain narrow directions—particularly whether and to what extent globalization is undermining state sovereignty. At the same time, other representations of the international—notably those based on conceptions of hierarchy, empire, and the internationalization of the state—are effectively, if not always logically, precluded. Hierarchy is precluded by the assumption of anarchy, empire by sovereignty, and internationalization—or globalization—is viewed principally as a problem for sovereign territoriality. A telling example of how the sovereignty narrative works to structure contemporary efforts to represent the international is found in the repeated assertion of globalization's novelty. Such a representation makes sense only against the assumption that states were in fact once sovereign in the territorial, Westphalian sense. If we discard that assumption, globalization looks strikingly different. As in most Marxist analyses, for example, we would see a long history of practices and processes of imperialism or, more generally, of the internationalization of capital. Adding a subaltern point of view, globalization would be recognized as only the most recent stage in the long march of European or Western institutions and practices to global dominance, part of a shared history of engagement between the West and the rest.

The assumptions that make up the sovereignty narrative, then, have collectively led analysts up what Darel Paul aptly called the "Westphalian blind alley," seriously limiting our vision of the international. For one thing, defining states as sovereign and as monopolists in the use of legitimate force within their territories precludes, by definitional fiat, "an ontology of overlapping political authorities in a single territory but at distinct scales."²⁹ For another, it precludes taking seriously the complicated relations of power—exceeding simple sovereignty relations—evident in histories of imperial and colonial relations or recognizing the possibility that we are witnessing the formation of a new type of imperial system. And it makes difficult even imagining the internationalization of the state, whether, as discussed by historical materialists, in terms of primarily economic state functions or in terms of the rescaling of the state's coercive practices. The central categories of sovereignty, the state, and anarchy, in short, have prevented us from seeing the imperial and hierarchical character of world politics, not least in practices of coercion. As we will now show, Hardt and Negri recognize some of the limits of the sovereignty narrative's representation. But in other ways, they too remain stuck up a Westphalian blind alley.

## Empire: The World according to Hardt and Negri

We live, Hardt and Negri remind us, in a world of struggles but we lack a common language with which to make sense of them. Part of the explicit purpose behind *Empire* is to fashion a theoretical language—a toolbox—that enables us to reimagine our world and so remake our future: "Our book," Hardt and Negri explain, "seeks to give new names to a series of phenomena that can no longer be conceived adequately using our old categories."³⁰ *Empire* offers a novel representation of the international but one that remains indebted, both positively and negatively, to modern sovereignty. Significantly, it also obscures the very phenomenon it seeks to illuminate—the internationalization of the state.

*Empire*'s thesis is a familiar one: sovereignty is not what it used to be. Under the pressure of capitalist globalization, sovereignty's very nature is being transformed from a modern to a postmodern form. Hardt and Negri call this new global logic and structure of rule "Empire." The "twilight of modern sovereignty" is also the dawn of Empire, a new "*decentered* and *deterritorializing* apparatus of rule that progressively incorporates the entire global realm within its open, expanding frontiers" (xi, xii, 333; emphasis in original). However, the decline of the sovereign territorial state does not mean that sovereignty as such has declined. Emerging in tandem with the global market and global circuits of production, "Empire is the political subject that effectively regulates these global [economic and cultural] exchanges, the sovereign power that governs the world" (xi), Empire encompasses the entire world, extending to the intimate recesses of social life, "the depths of the biopolitical world" (26). There is no longer an "inside" and an "outside," whether defined by the boundaries of the household, the sovereign territorial state, or larger subjects such as the West. Instead, we are witnessing "a process of the material constitution of the new planetary order, the consolidation of its administrative machine, and the production of new hierarchies of command over global space" (19) In our new postcolonial and postimperial world, Empire is the international.[31]

On its face, Hardt's and Negri's representation of the international as Empire takes us a good distance from the sovereignty narrative.[32] First, against accounts of globalization and its consequences that foreground the agency of capital or the state, Hardt and Negri rewrite standard genealogies of modern sovereignty by locating the agency that generates sovereignty in the multitude—their term for what used to be called the proletariat—and rearticulate sovereignty as a capitalist social form.[33] Successive stages in the evolution of capitalism and sovereignty—including globalization as a capitalist strategy—are driven by the antagonism between capital and labor, with labor always the active subject. *Empire*'s genealogy of the international functions as a grand narrative in which history is nothing but a series of struggles between the communism of the multitude and capitalist forces of reaction, initially vested in modern sovereignty and the state and now located in Empire.

Second, Hardt and Negri also challenge the militant Eurocentrism of the sovereignty narrative by foregrounding the integral relationship between sovereignty in Europe and colonial rule. "Modern sovereignty" may have "emanated from Europe," but "it was born and developed in large part through Europe's relationship with its outside, and particularly through its colonial project and the resistance of the colonized. . . ." It follows that "rule within Europe and European rule over the world" are "two coextensive and complementary faces of one development" (70).

Third, they rehabilitate the concept of empire as a tool for the analysis of world politics. One consequence of the sovereignty narrative is that it renders imperial relations exceptional and makes sovereignty the norm to be aspired to. As a result, imperial relations are sidelined theoretically; they are incidental to rather than definitive of "the international." Hardt and Negri challenge this view, conferring theoretical legitimacy onto the notion of empire, and with it the centrality of hierarchy in the international.

A significant contribution of *Empire* is to challenge the either/or terms, derived from the sovereignty narrative, in which much popular and scholarly discussion of the state and globalization still takes place: *either* globalization overwhelms and undermines the state *or* the state persists and globalization only generates for it new opportunities and pressures. In an increasingly common move, Hardt and Negri reject this false choice. The sovereign state and its powers may be undermined by capitalist globalization, but capital still needs the state. The "state-capital dialectic" is conflictual only from the point of view of the individual capitalist: "Without the state, social capital has no means to project and realize its collective interests." State functions remain necessary and under capitalist globalization are "effectively displaced to other levels and domains," local and transnational (307, 308). The international is thus a single "imperial machine" composed of a series of national and supranational organisms united under a single logic of rule (xii). Empire is the subject that ties these various agencies and institutions—the means through which state functions are carried out—together and effectively regulates global processes and relations. In these ways, then, Hardt and Negri help us rethink the character of power and the international.

Despite these achievements, Hardt and Negri remain indebted, both negatively and positively, to the sovereignty narrative. Their negative dependence on the narrative is readily apparent. The emergence of Empire is synonymous with the "decline of the nation-state," with the smoothing of the "striae of national boundaries," and this decline is "structural and irreversible." Empire has no territorial boundaries: "the borders of national sovereignty are sieves," and the "distinction between inside and outside" is disappearing (213, 332, 336). Global space has become smooth, in the sense that the world market has been realized and the overcoded "striations" or borders typical of modern sovereignty and imperialism are no more (xii, xiv, 332–333). Although they note the existence of old and new forms of hierarchy and domination, including class and a global division of labor, Hardt and Negri argue that these are not aligned with state boundaries. The Other against which Empire is defined is, in short, modern territorial sovereignty.

But contrary to Hardt's and Negri's claim, the international is not characterized by "smooth space": borders, while being transformed, remain significant. They are in some instances becoming thinner and in others thicker. European Union borders within the Schengen[34] area, for instance, are being eliminated for some purposes but not for others. Within Schengen, despite the elimination of border controls, the movements of "football hooligans" are being surveilled and policed; at the same time, borders around Schengen are being strengthened to keep out undesirable migrants.[35] Nor is this phenomenon restricted to the overdeveloped states of Western Europe: South Africa's northern borders are also being strengthened, possibly with electric fences of lethal dosage.[36]

Borders are being extended outward as well: policing functions, for instance, are being projected into the territory of foreign states. Extraterritorial policing by the U.S. Drug Enforcement Agency (DEA), the Federal Bureau of Investigation (FBI), and the Bureau of Citizenship and Immigration Services (BCIS) within the Department of Homeland Security entails the insertion of U.S. organizations into many states around the world, while simultaneously diffusing U.S. policing methods. At the same time, borders are being "fattened" or deepened into home territory.[37] In Germany, for instance, workplaces are routinely policed for illegal aliens, employers are responsible for hiring illegal immigrants, and fines are imposed directly on employers. National identification papers allow routine police checks of residency and citizenship status. Through such practices, border policing takes place throughout society.

Finally, as Schengen demonstrates, borders are also being rescaled regionally. Since September 11, for example, the United States has been pressuring the European Union (EU) to construct a common system of policing the joint borders of the "West," leading to the potential creation of a "new northern 'Fortress Europe-U.S.'"[38] Contrary to Hardt and Negri, borders continue to matter, even if not all borders matter equally or in the same way. Beginning with modern sovereignty as the benchmark for measuring change and assuming that borders (for example) are either important or not produces a systematic blindness to the diverse transformations taking place in the international system.

Hardt's and Negri's negative dependence on modern sovereignty is also apparent in their explication of Empire itself. In seeking to clarify what Empire is, they differentiate it from a range of things that it is not. First, Empire is not equivalent to domination of the international system by a set of overdeveloped capitalist nation-states. "What used to be conflict or competition among several imperialist powers," Hardt and Negri argue, "has in important respects been replaced by the idea of a single power that overdetermines them all, structures them in a unitary way, and treats them under one common notion of right that is decidedly postcolonial and postimperialist" (9). Second, Empire is not a quasi-international state: "When the royal prerogatives of modern sovereignty [e.g., taxation, military force and justice] reappear in Empire, they take on a completely different form." Empire is not centralized; rather, it is a "globalized biopolitical machine" through which these functions and prerogatives are carried out by a decentralized array of agencies spread across the globe (39, 40). Third, within Empire—and everything is within Empire—there is no territorial center of power: "our postmodern Empire has no Rome" (317). Fourth, Empire is not imperialist. The old European empires were founded on modern sovereignty: they divided the world up and established borders between their respective territories. In contrast, Empire is imperial, for the simple reason that "its space is always open" (xii–xiii, 166–167). All of these arguments depend negatively on the notion of modern sovereignty and the state found in the sovereignty narrative.

So what do we do about the United States? Despite Hardt's and Negri's repeated claims that Empire is not simply U.S. imperialism updated and redefined for the twenty-first century, even on their own terms the United States is central to their account of this new form of global rule. The United States played a key role in preparing the political forms and terrain of Empire (160). The United States sits atop the imperial pyramid of power: it enjoys hegemony over the global use of force and a central role in global monetary institutions and cultural and biopolitical networks. In addition, U.S. corporations dominate the world economy, and a growing number of states have dollarized their economies, tying their fate to the policies of the U.S. Federal Reserve Bank. Nonetheless, Hardt and Negri insist that Empire is not U.S. imperialism: "This Empire cannot be a U.S. Empire the way the British imperialist project was British or French imperialism French, because it is not based on the sovereignty of the nation-state. This Empire has no center. . . ."[39] The United States appears to hold "the reins" of global military power, finance, and communications, but Hardt and Negri claim—against the evidence—that this is not the case.[40] How do they reconcile these seemingly contradictory positions? In two ultimately unsuccessful ways.

First, they attempt to do so by definitional fiat. Their claim that "This Empire cannot be a U.S. Empire . . . because it is not based on the sovereignty of the nation-state" simply asserts what needs to be demonstrated. They need to but do not show that there really is something fundamentally different about Empire as opposed to imperialism and that this difference hinges on a dramatically transformed relationship between sovereignty and the state.[41] Our analysis of borders reveals change but also continuity, throwing doubt on Hardt's and Negri's position. Second and related, they attempt to ground this claim empirically in the U.S. role in the Gulf War, which they use to argue that: "the U.S. world police acts not in imperialist interests, but in imperial interest. In this sense the Gulf War did indeed, as George Bush claimed, announce the birth of a new world order" (180). On this basis they claim the United States is "a superpower that can act alone but prefers to act in collaboration with others under the umbrella of the United Nations" (309). But this underplays the strategic benefits of UN cover. It ignores the short-lived character of U.S. reliance on the UN, as was evidenced by the British-U.S. "no fly" zones over Iraq, for instance, and by the conduct of the Gulf War itself. And it has been rendered wildly anachronistic by the "War on Terrorism," as the U.S. government sidelines the UN and flouts international law.

Hardt's and Negri's account of the international also betrays a positive reliance on the sovereignty narrative: their entire argument assumes that states really were sovereign before Empire. But this is a dubious assumption. As we noted earlier, the Westphalian image of world politics, while perhaps elegant, was always a "myth"[42] because: "the Westphalian sovereign state model has never been an accurate description of many of the entities that have been regarded as states."[43] Sovereignty in the colonies was never what it was in the metropole, and careful attention to the actual relations of rule through which European empires governed reveals diverse relations not explicable in terms of the simple inside/outside logic of modern sovereignty. During the Cold War, the United States did define itself through an explicit rejection of relations of formal empire, the promotion of decolonization, and the normalization across a range of institutions and practices of the sovereign territorial state as the basic building block of world order. But we should not confuse fantasies of sovereignty—particularly those convenient for imperial rule—with the realities of state power: side by side with the promotion of formal sovereignty, the United States constructed a transnational apparatus for the organization of coercion that enabled U.S. domination of a decolonized periphery as well as a pacified core. It is simply not possible to reconcile the realities of U.S. power with Hardt's and Negri's (largely fictional) depiction of a pre-Empire world of sovereign territorial states.

"One of the most harmful habits in contemporary thought," Foucault argued, is "the analysis of the present as being . . . a present of rupture."[44] The sovereignty narrative is clearly rooted in the sort of presentism that Foucault warned against. Hardt's and Negri's *Empire* too, like the neoliberal globalization discourse, is characterized by "the faddish rush to present the partially new as paradigmatically revolutionary,"[45] albeit in the interest of a quite different politics. This is especially evident in their peculiar treatment of the United States on the one hand as central to Empire but on the other as nonimperialist. In the process, they both illuminate and obscure the place of power in the international. To address the weaknesses of Hardt's and Negri's account—and the contradictory role assigned the United States in particular—while retaining their attention to empire and hierarchy, we turn to an older literature that enables us to represent the international without beginning with sovereignty.

## Taking the Internationalization of the State Seriously

In common with Hardt and Negri, we begin with globalization and the state. Like them, we too reject the claim that globalization and the state stand in opposition to one another. State actors enable globalization, which we understand as the internationalization of capital: the continuing extension of the logic of commodification to ever more social relations and domains, both extensively and intensively, across state boundaries and within them. Markets are created and regulated by diverse actors, including states, but property rights—the core of markets—are ultimately defined and enforced by state agencies. The last thing capital wants is the demise of the state. The policies of deregulation—more precisely, of reregulation—crucial to the internationalization of capital are put into place by state actors, even if state action is not reducible to the individuals and institutions that carry it out but reflects the outcomes of social struggles within particular social formations. With globalization, it is true, the "nature of state intervention has changed considerably" and continues to change.[46] But the integral relation between the state and capital persists.

Our alternative representation of the international thus retains an emphasis on the state, but not as the "static, bounded block" of the sovereignty narrative; as Neil Brenner observes, the state is "at once the *subject* and the *object* of the globalization process."[47] Rather than defining states in terms of sovereignty, and thus as actors, as do both *Empire* and the sovereignty narrative, we regard the state as a structure of rule. The state is the "organizing principles" that give an "underlying structural coherence" to the many and diverse "agencies and institutions of governance."[48] It encompasses "the entire institutional-legal order" and as such is a rather "enduring structure of governance and rule in society." This means it encompasses and is defined by the complex of regulations—whether explicitly codified or not—and practices that govern social relationships and processes.[49] Definitions of property rights, for instance, are central features of the state, as are the rules governing their enforcement. Concrete political agents such as state managers and other state actors are constituted and empowered by the institutions of governance and the principles that underpin them. State action typically refers to these agencies: understood as a set of principles and an institutional-legal order, states as such do not act.[50] This conception of the state, because it does not assume a sovereign, territorial actor, allows us to recognize the multiple forms, levels, and scales of governance and rule that overlap and are intertwined in a complex and internally contradictory internationalizing state. Central to our representation of the international, then, are the principles around which governance and rule are organized.

As a structure of governance and rule, the state is transformed—internationalized—in the context of globalization in ways that favor the interests of transnational capital—and in particular finance capital—over local or industrial capital and democratic publics. Transformation in the state is not restricted to particular states but extends across the international system as a whole, taking in local, national, regional, and international institutions and practices. Robert Cox defines the internationalization of the state in the following terms:

> First, there is a process of interstate consensus formation regarding the needs or requirements of the world economy that takes place within a common ideological

framework (i.e., common criteria of interpretation of economic events and common goals anchored in the idea of an open world economy). Second, participation in the consensus formation is hierarchically structured. Third, the internal structures of states are adjusted so that each can best transform the global consensus into national policy and practice, taking account of the specific kinds of obstacles likely to arise in countries occupying the different hierarchically arranged positions in the world economy.[51]

The internationalization of the state is a multidimensional process, encompassing not only consensus formation and the structural impact of centralized policy formation on national governments but also the reworking of internal state structures and a shift in power away from agencies dealing with domestic issues and toward agencies dealing with transnational ones. At stake in this process, argues Stephen Gill, is the global constitutionalization of the rule of capital, both at the level of the radically reworked nation-state itself and at the level of a proliferating array of international institutions.[52]

Much of this is in fact evident in Hardt's and Negri's analysis of Empire but, as we demonstrated in our discussion of borders, it is too often obscured or misrepresented as a result of their style of presentation, lack of empirical analysis, and continuing reliance on the sovereignty narrative. Similar problems bedevil their discussion of the role of the United States in Empire. Hardt and Negri recognize the United States' privileged position in world politics but also rule out U.S. imperialism by fiat: "our Empire has no Rome," they confidently assert. At the same time, however, they acknowledge the key role played by the United States in promoting the political forms of Empire. They trace this special relation to the peculiar character of the United States and in particular the U.S. Constitution, which, they say, provides the model for the networks that constitute the spaces of Empire. At its heart, *Empire's* representation of the international draws on a familiar version of U.S. exceptionalism.[53] In contrast, we locate the distinctive character of the United States where Marx did, in the absence of a feudal system in North America: the United States is "not so much 'exceptional' as fully bourgeois: the most advanced capitalist society."[54] We can make better sense of the role of the United States in the world if, instead of sovereignty and exceptionalism, we begin with the internationalization of capital and the state.

As David Harvey points out, "globalization as a process has since 1945 been U.S. centered. . . . It simply would not have happened in the way it has without the U.S. operating as both a driving force and a supervisory agent. . . ."[55] Politically, as we noted, the U.S. role entailed the construction after World War II of a "Free World" comprised of formally sovereign states penetrated by a coercive, "external," U.S. state that structured the outer limits of acceptable political action. Economically, it entailed, particularly in Western Europe and Japan, "the induced reproduction of the form of the dominant imperialist power within each national formation and its state."[56] The fundamental analysis of this process, as Leo Panitch reminds us, was carried out by Nicos Poulantzas, who discerned and sought to theorize "the American capacity to manage the radical restructuring of global capitalism in forms that reproduced their imperial dominance."[57]

Drawing on his analysis of relations between U.S. and Western European capital, Poulantzas argued in 1975, while others were lamenting U.S. decline, that U.S. hegemony over the other imperialist metropolises "is not in fact analogous to that of one metropolis over the others. . . ." On the contrary, U.S. hegemony "is achieved by establishing relations of production characteristic of American monopoly capitalism and its domination inside the other metropolises . . ." In other words, U.S.-driven globalization implied the "extended reproduction" within other social formations "of the ideological and political conditions for this development of American imperialism."[58] It was this set of relations that explained the character of the North Atlantic political economy.[59]

In more recent times, a similar pattern is emerging in relations between the United States and the global South, implemented through such mechanisms as structural adjustment policies and the so-called Washington consensus, and the North American Free Trade Agreement, the model for the Free Trade Association of the Americas and the WTO. Imperialism today is synonymous with the internationalization of the state. U.S. state agencies remain central to this process, which reproduces and extends the imperialist relations between the United States and other parts of the world. To ignore this history and laud the United States as the very model of our "postimperial" world, as do Hardt and Negri, is peculiar to say the least.

In a remarkably prescient statement, James Petras and Morris Morley argued in 1981 that: "what is striking about the contemporary period is . . . the extended jurisdiction of the [U.S.] state as an imperial state far beyond its territorial borders."[60] But this U.S. state is not a unified subject. In a distant echo of Empire's "mixed constitution," Petras and Morley noted that the state must be disaggregated so as to enable us to see the various and differentiated functions carried out by its different parts. Following Poulantzas, much recent analysis focuses on the economic functions of the internationalizing state.[61] In the remainder of this chapter we briefly discuss the internationalization of the state's coercive functions and in particular policing. Even in the crudest phenomenological terms, policing is integral to the contemporary international.[62] Hardt and Negri link the importance of policing to the disappearance of an "outside" characteristic of Empire. For us, in contrast, the restructuring of policing is an indicator of the nature and increasing reach of the internationalizing state. Here too, U.S. state agencies play a central role.

In the contemporary period, policing is undergoing rapid internationalization, as institutions and practices definitive of the pacified and ordered character of domestic spaces are transformed and extended beyond sovereign borders. The policing of organized crime provides an illustration. Although organized criminal activity across state borders is not new, in the past decade transnational organized crime has been constituted as a major "national and international security issue."[63] Successive U.S. administrations have been central to this process which, predating the end of the Cold War and "globalization," has its origins in the 1960s "War on Drugs."[64]

One result is an ongoing rescaling of legal structures, both on a U.S. model and under U.S. pressure. The specifically U.S. definition of organized crime—as "mafia type structure" and "mafia type activity" threatening internal social and economic structures—has been securitized, that is, transformed from a domestic into a national security issue, with dramatic consequences for the U.S. state.[65] "'The ravages of transnational crime,'" FBI director Louis Freeh argued in 1994, are "the greatest long term threat to the security of the United States."[66] This definition has in turn been internationalized. The participants in the UN World Ministerial Conference on Organized Transnational Crime, held in Naples in 1994, for instance, adopted and deployed this U.S. construction.[67] The solution to this internationalized security threat is, of course, enhanced international coordination and increased policing at all levels. At the UN conference it was decided that the threat "can only be met if law enforcement authorities are able to display the same . . . cooperation that characterized the criminal organizations themselves."[68] Coordinated policy, in turn, requires, "international harmonization of legislation,"[69] which in practice means Americanization of legal structures. U.S.-pioneered crime-control strategies—the 1970 Racketeer Influenced and Corrupt Organizations (RICO) statute is a prime example—were the preferred methods emphasized by most speakers at the UN conference.[70]

Rescaled state apparatuses have appeared in the wake of this conceptual and legal transformation. Central has been the extraterritorialization of U.S. state apparatuses, notably the FBI, DEA, and BCIS. The FBI, like the others, now has "an active overseas presence that fosters the establishment of effective working relationships with foreign law enforcement agencies."[71] It trains foreign officers in techniques and principles of law enforcement, thus ensuring their Americanization, and builds such institutions as are "necessary to help establish and foster the rule of law in newly democratic republics."[72] At the same time, U.S.-style apparatuses are being adopted in other states. Poland is a notable example, where EU and U.S. funding have contributed to the creation of the U.S.-style policing of organized crime—to the detriment of the policing of crimes that victimize the local population.[73] Policing has been international-ized through the expansion of existing policing bodies such as Interpol and the creation of new ones such as Europol. Securitizing transnational crime has also led to significant militarization of policing at home and abroad.[74]

Existing state structures and in particular the agencies that secure domes-tic spaces are being reworked and in certain respects internationalized. As a result, we are witnessing the emergence and consolidation of a set of inter-twined and overlapping structures of governance and rule—a complex and unevenly developed internationalized state apparatus for policing organized crime, significantly modeled on and influenced by the United States and with local, national, regional, international, and transnational manifestations. As we noted above, in the process, borders too are being extraterritorialized: polic-ing of organized crime extends the U.S. state—its organizing principles and institutional-legal structures—into the territories of myriad other states. In ways strikingly similar to Poulantzas's account of U.S. economic imperialism, the state and its coercive functions are also being internationalized. This is a long way from the sovereign territoriality of the sovereignty narrative. It is also a long way from Hardt's and Negri's representation of the international as Empire, in which these practices and institutions are invisible.

Like globalization, policing too is often defined in relation to the sovereign territorial state. In a world putatively structured around a Westphalian logic of inside/outside, policing refers to those agencies—mostly public but also pri-vate—responsible for the ordering and control of domestic space. So under-stood, policing refers to the regulation and defense of a particular conception of social, cultural, economic and political order against threats arising within a sovereign territory. It is a crucial "governmental activity"[75] concerned with "law and order" and "the rule of law" that presupposes the sovereign state and its monopoly over the legitimate use of force. But the sovereignty narrative is actu-ally a poor guide to analysis of policing: even a passing acquaintance with the complex articulations between force and its constitution found in imperial relations puts such distinctions in doubt. The international coercive apparatus constructed by the United States, for instance, like that of other imperialisms before it, encompassed both military and policing practices narrowly defined. Hardt and Negri, wedded to the sovereignty narrative, misconstrue the place of force in the international. We need a different vantage point from which to make sense of the relations between coercion—in whatever form—territorial-ity, order, and the state in the context of globalization. One place to look, we would argue, is in the still largely ignored literature on the internationalization of capital and the state.

## Conclusion

Globalization, we are repeatedly told, is our present and our future. As former British prime minister Margaret Thatcher was fond of saying while in office, "there is no alternative." Such pronouncements, with their false air of certainty, overlook the contested nature of globalization: even if we are living in globalization, we cannot agree on what it is. As to the future, there too not much is certain: which imagined "international" is eventually realized "will depend upon the outcomes of current social struggles, struggles in which the meanings assigned to 'globalization' are central."[76] In this context, *Empire* makes a real contribution to contemporary political action, not least because it offers a positive and liberatory vision of globalization. Globalization is a good thing. We should aspire not to stop it but to drive it forward. The multitude is the motor of history that, through its struggles, has brought Empire into existence as the next step towards the realization of the communist dream of internationalism. All struggles are created equal under Empire: the new global logic of rule has no center and the borders that divided the multitude and privileged some struggles over others are no more. Indeed, "borders are sieves," and the new-found mobility and hybridity of the multitude, which Hardt and Negri celebrate, foreshadows a new world beyond modern sovereignty. But this heartening vision of our global future comes at a price.

At its core, Hardt's and Negri's representation of the international remains deeply indebted to the sovereignty narrative. As we have shown, the result is bad history and a poor understanding of the everyday realities of the international, not least coercive ones. It is also bad politics. It is hard to see how we can build a better future if we set out armed with a theoretical toolbox that renders invisible or marginal the very structures of power we would aspire to transform. But this is precisely what Hardt and Negri offer us. In their haste to reject modern sovereignty as a meaningful guide to our present and future, they downplay the continuing centrality of the state—and of one state in particular—to the contemporary international. And in validating modern sovereignty as history, Hardt and Negri simply miss the myriad ways in which sovereign territoriality has never been a reliable guide to the nature of power and its place in the international. As a result, for all the insight *Empire* provides into the character of the international, in a very real sense it also renders the multitude and its circumstances in a deeply misleading way. The first principle of meaningful struggle, of struggle that has some hope of success, is a realistic assessment of the situation and in particular of the nature and distribution of power. This *Empire* fails to provide.

In contrast, our alternative representation offers some hope of overcoming these difficulties. Starting with the internationalization of capital and the state, rather than the sovereignty narrative, enables us better to capture the nature of power in the world today. Restrictions on the movement of "suspect" populations and the deportation of illegal immigrants are testimony to the continuing power of the state to police its borders. In the aftermath of the attacks on the World Trade Center and the Pentagon, and the subsequent U.S. attacks on Afghanistan and Iraq, it is harder to deny the centrality of the United States to world order, at least coercively. But most of the examples of policing we pointed to above predate September 11, 2001: the growing reality of borders and the reworking of coercive structures along U.S. lines is not explicable in terms of the "War on Terrorism," however much that "war" has accelerated these changes. Elsewhere, too, the centrality of the United States to world order is apparent. In one forum after another, efforts to promote a more peaceful planet have been scuppered by the U.S. government.[77] Meanwhile, the IMF and the World Bank, dominated by the United States, continue to extract payment and policy concessions from "poorly performing" states around the world. Making sense of all this and figuring out where and how we might respond to it is not made easier by references to a "decentered and deterritorializing apparatus of rule." Beginning with capital, the state, and their internationalization offers a better understanding of the world in which we live and so a better place from which to set out as we try to change it.

## Notes

1. Slavoj Žižek, quoted in Emily Eakin, "What Is the Next Big Idea? Buzz Is Growing for *Empire*," *New York Times*, July 7, 2001, available at http://www.pastforward.org/hardt/nytimes.1.rtf; Michael Hardt and Antonio Negri, *Empire* (Cambridge, MA: Harvard University Press, 2000). Subsequent references to *Empire* are included parenthetically in the text.

2. See also Tarak Barkawi and Mark Laffey, "Retrieving the Imperial: *Empire* and International Relations," *Millennium* 31 (2002): 109–127.

3. Colin Hay and David Marsh, *Demystifying Globalization* (London: Palgrave, 2000), 1.

4. Janet Abu-Lughod, "Going beyond Global Babble," in *Culture, Globalization, and the World System*, ed. Anthony D. King (London: Macmillan, 1991), 131.

5. Quoted in Gearóid Ó Tuathail, Andrew Herod, and Susan M. Roberts, "Negotiating Unruly Problematics," in *Unruly World? Globalization, Governance, and Geography*, ed. Herod, Ó Tuathail, and Roberts (New York and London: Routledge, 1998), 9.

6. Kenichi Ohmae, *The End of the Nation State: The Rise of Regional Economies* (New York: HarperCollins Publishers, 1995), 5. Such pronouncements are not new; see Charles Kindleberger, *American Business Abroad* (New Haven, CT: Yale University Press, 1969), 207.

7. Thomas Friedman, *The Lexus and the Olive Tree* (New York: HarperCollins Publishers, 2000), xvii.

8. Ronnie D. Lipschutz, "Reconstructing Global Politics: The Emergence of Global Civil Society," *Millennium* 21 (1992): 392; cf. "Global Civil Society and Global Governmentality: or, The Search for the Missing State amidst the Capillaries of Power," presented at the Power and Global Governance conference, University of Wisconsin, Madison, April 2002.

9. Renato Ruggiero, "Managing a World of Free Trade and Deep Interdependence," Address to the Argentinian Council on Foreign Relations, Buenos Aires, September 10, 1996, p. 3, available at http://www.wto.org/wto/english/news_e/pres96_e/pr055_e.htm.

10. Linda Weiss, "Globalization and National Governance: Antinomy or Interdependence?" *Review of International Studies* 25 (1999): 61.

11. Linda Weiss, "Globalization and the Myth of the Powerless State," *New Left Review* 225 (1997): 4. The classic statement is Paul Hirst and Grahame Thompson, *Globalization in Question: The International Economy and the Possibilities of Governance*, 2nd ed. (Cambridge, UK: Polity Press, 1999).

12. Nonsovereign entities, on this view, are outside "the international pale"; Alan James, "Sovereignty: Ground Rule or Gibberish?" *Review of International Studies* 10 (1984): 4.

13. The vast state-theory literature has had little impact on the understanding of the state in the sovereignty narrative, which makes a sharp distinction between "the domestic," where state theory is understood to be relevant, and "the international," where it is not; e.g., R. B. J. Walker, *Inside/Outside: International Relations as Political Theory* (Cambridge, UK: Cambridge University Press, 1993).

14. Max Weber, "Politics as a Vocation," in *From Max Weber: Essays in Sociology*, ed. H. H. Gerth and C. Wright Mills (New York: Oxford University Press, 1946), 78.

15. Kenneth Waltz, *Theory of International Politics* (Reading, MA: Addison-Wesley, 1979), 96.

16. Robert Gilpin, *War and Change in World Politics* (Cambridge, UK: Cambridge University Press, 1981),

17. David Harvey, *The Condition of Postmodernity: An Enquiry into the Origins of Cultural Change* (Oxford: Basil Blackwell, 1989), 240ff.

18. Weiss, "Globalization and National Governance," 59.

19. See, e.g., Randall Germain, *The International Organization of Credit: States and Global Finance in the World Economy* (Cambridge: Cambridge University Press, 1997).

20. Neil Brenner, "Beyond State-Centrism? Space, Territoriality, and Geographical Scale in Globalization Studies," *Theory and Society* 28 (1999): 39–78.

21. John Agnew, "The Territorial Trap: The Geographical Assumptions of International Relations Theory," *Review of International Political Economy* 1 (1994): 53–80.

22. Martin Shaw, "The State of Globalization: Towards a Theory of State Transformation," *Review of International Political Economy* 4 (1997): 497–513.

23. See, e.g., Hedley Bull and Adam Watson, eds., *The Expansion of International Society* (Oxford: Clarendon Press, 1984).

24. Fernando Coronil, *The Magical State: Nature, Money, and Modernity in Venezuela* (Chicago: University of Chicago Press, 1997), 15.

25. See, e.g., Michael Klare, *Rogue States and Nuclear Outlaws: America's Search for a New Foreign Policy* (New York: Hill and Wang, 1995).

26. Tarak Barkawi and Mark Laffey, "The Imperial Peace: Democracy, Force and Globalization," *European Journal of International Relations* 5 (1999): 403–434.

27. See, e.g., Anthony Giddens, *A Contemporary Critique of Historical Materialism*, vol. 2, *The Nation State and Violence* (Berkeley, CA: University of California Press, 1985).

28. Robert Latham, *The Liberal Moment: Modernity, Security, and the Making of Postwar International Order* (New York: Columbia University Press, 1997), 65–70.

29. Darel Paul, "Sovereignty, Survival, and the Wesphalian Blind Alley," *Review of International Studies*, 25 (1999), 218–219.

30. Quoted in Nicholas Brown and Imre Szeman, "The Global Coliseum: On *Empire*," *Cultural Studies* 16 (2002): 180–181.

31. Hardt's and Negri's most explicit and detailed discussion of the international is found in their account of the political constitution of Empire (ibid., 304–324).

32. This paragraph draws on Barkawi and Laffey, "Retrieving the Imperial."

33. On autonomism and *Empire*, see Alex Callinicos, "Toni Negri in Perspective," *International Socialism Journal* 92 (2001).

34. The Schengen area, which came into effect in 1995, encompasses thirteen EU states. It abolished the internal borders of the signatory states and created a single external border where immigration checks are carried out in accordance with a single set of rules.

35. "Schengen," Swedish Civil Aviation Administration, March 25, 2001, available at http://www.lfv.se/site/journey/eng/schengen/index.asp

36. Thanks to Neta Crawford for this example.

37. Peter Andreas, *Border Games: Policing the U.S.-Mexico Divide* (Ithaca, NY: Cornell University Press, 2000), 6.

38. Tony Bunyan, quoted in "Secret US-EU Meeting on Asylum: The Construction of a Common EU-US Area of Migration, Asylum, and Borders?" *Statewatch News*, February 2002, available at http://www.statewatch.org/news/2002/feb/03useuim.htm; see also "Text of US Letter from Bush with Demands for EU for Cooperation," *Statewatch News*, November 2002, available at http://www.statewatch.org/news/2001/nov/06uslet.htm.

39. Quoted in Brown and Szeman, "The Global Coliseum," 180.

40. *Empire*, 347. Hardt and Negri acknowledge that global military and financial power might be plausibly represented as centralized in the United States (in Washington and New York, respectively) but insist that this is not true for their third mechanism of global power, communications. This is a contentious claim: aside from the global reach of Los Angeles (which they do recognize) and New York, national communication regimes and cultural forms are increasingly modeled on U.S. forms. See, e.g., Edward S. Herman and Robert W. McChesney, *The Global Media: The New Missionaries of Corporate Capitalism* (London: Cassell, 1997).

41. On U.S. sovereignty (imperial) versus European sovereignty (imperialist), see *Empire*, 172–182.

42. Andreas Osiander, "Before Sovereignty: Society and Politics in *Ancien Regime* Europe," *Review of International Studies* 27 (2001): 19.

43. Stephen D. Krasner, "Rethinking the Sovereign State Model," *Review of International Studies*, 27 (2001): 17.

44. "Structuralism and Post-Structuralism: An Interview with Michel Foucault," interview by Gerard Raulet, translated by Jeremy Harding, *Telos* 55 (1983): 206.

45. Leo Panitch and Sam Gindin, "Gems and Baubles in *Empire*," *Historical Materialism* 10 (2002): 12.

46. Leo Panitch, "Rethinking the Role of the State," in *Globalization: Critical Reflections*, ed. James H. Mittelman (Boulder, CO: Lynne Rienner, 1996), 85.

47. Neil Brenner, "Global, Fragmented, Hierarchical: Henri Lefebvre's Geographies of Globalization," *Public Culture*, 10 (1999): 40 and 156, emphasis added; Brenner, "Beyond State-Centrism?," 41.

48. Roger Benjamin and Raymond Duvall, "The Capitalist State in Context," in *The Democratic State*, ed. Roger Benjamin and Stephen L. Elkin (Lawrence, KS: University Press of Kansas, 1985), 23.

49. Ibid., 25, 26.

50. This allows us to recognize both the often incoherent and inconsistent policies and actions taken by diverse "agencies of government," and coherent underlying structuring principles; ibid., 24.

51. Robert Cox, *Production, Power, and World Order: Social Forces in the Making of History* (New York: Columbia University Press, 1987), 254.

52. See, e.g., Stephen Gill, "New Constitutionalism, Democratisation and Global Political Economy," *Pacifica Review* 10 (1998).

53. Barkawi and Laffey, "Retrieving the Imperial," 123–127.

54. Bruce Cumings, *Parallax Visions: Making Sense of American–East Asian Relations at the End of the Century* (Durham, N.C.: Duke University Press, 1999), 8; Karl Marx, "Bastiat and Carey," in *The Grundrisse: Foundations of the Critique of Political Economy*, trans. Martin Nicolaus (New York: Vintage Books, 1973), 885–886.

55. David Harvey, *Spaces of Hope* (Edinburgh: Edinburgh University Press, 2000), 69.

56. Leo Panitch, "The New Imperial State," *New Left Review* 2 (2000): 9.

57. Ibid, 13–14.

58. Nicos Poulantzas, *Classes in Contemporary Capitalism* (London: New Left Books, 1975), 47.

59. See Kees van der Pijl, *The Making of a North Atlantic Ruling Class* (London: New Left Books, 1984), who builds on Poulantzas's analysis.

60. James Petras and Morris Morley, "The U.S. Imperial State," in *Class, State, and Power in the Third World*, James F. Petras, et al. (London: Zed Press, 1981), 1.

61. Compare William Robinson; e.g., *Promoting Polyarchy: Globalization, U.S. Intervention, and Hegemony* (Cambridge, UK: Cambridge University Press, 1996).

62. The following draws on our "Policing and Global Governance," presented at the Power and Global Governance conference, University of Wisconsin, Madison, April 2002.

63. "Perl Warns that Globalization Facilitates Criminal Activities," Washington File, U.S. Department of State, December 13, 2000, available at http://usinfo.state.gov/topical/pol/terror/00121300.htm.

64. Christian Parenti, *Lockdown America: Police and Prisons in the Age of Crisis* (London: Verso, 1999).

65. Ole Waever, "Securitization and Desecuritization," in *On Security*, ed. Ronnie D. Lipschutz (New York: Columbia University Press, 1995), 46–86; Peter Andreas and Richard Price, "From War Fighting to Crime Fighting: Transforming the American National Security State," *International Studies Review* 3 (2001): 31–52.

66. Quoted in Michael Woodiwiss, "Organized Crime—The Dumbing of Discourse," *The British Criminology Conference: Selected Proceedings*, vol. 3, p. 10. Available at http://www.britsoccrim.org/bccsp/vol03/woodiwiss.html.

67. U.N. General Assembly, "Report of the World Ministerial Conference on Organized Transnational Crime," December 2, 1994, A/49/748, available at http://www.imolin.org/naples.htm.

68. Quoted in Woodiwiss, "Organized Crime—The Dumbing of Discourse," 10.

69. Louise Shelley, "Threat from International Organized Crime and Terrorism," Congressional Testimony before the House Committee on International Relations, October 1, 1997, Congressional Hearings, Intelligence and Security, p. 6. Available at http://www.fas.org/irp/congress/1997_hr/h971001ls.htm.

70. Woodiwiss, "Organized Crime—The Dumbing of Discourse," 10–11.

71. Louis J. Freeh, "Statement for the Record of Louis J. Freeh, Director, Federal Bureau of Investigation on International Crime before the United States Senate Committee on Appropriations, Subcommittee on Foreign Operations," Washington, D.C., April 21, 1998, available at http://www.fbi.gov/congress/congress98/intrcrime.htm.

72. Ibid., 3–4.

73. Bill Hebenton and Jon Spencer, "The Contribution and Limitations of Anglo-American Criminology to Understanding Crime in Central-Eastern Europe," *European Journal of Crime, Criminal Law and Criminal Justice*, 2 (1994): 50–61; Jon Spencer and Bill Hebenton, "Crime and Insecurity in the New Europe: Some Observations from Poland," *The British Criminology Conferences: Selected Proceedings*, vol. 2. Available at http://www.britsoccrim.org/bccsp/vol02/04spenc.htm.

74. This is apparent in the efforts to secure borders and in the so-called "War on Drugs"; see, e.g., Parenti, *Lockdown America*, chap. 7.

75. J. W. E. Sheptycki, "The 'Drug War': Learning from the Paradigm Example of Transnational Policing,' in *Issues in Transnational Policing*, ed. J. W. E. Sheptycki (London: Routledge, 2000), 201.

76. Mark Rupert, *Ideologies of Globalization: Contending Visions of a New World Order* (London: Routledge, 2000), 42.

77. See George Monbiot, "The Logic Of Empire," *The Guardian*, August 6, 2002, for a list.

# 7

Global

# Africa's Ambiguous Relation
# to Empire and *Empire*

## Kevin C. Dunn

Despite Michael Hardt's and Antonio Negri's attempt to examine the supposed changing relations of power in world politics, they surprisingly fail to provide many non-Western examples for their grand theory in *Empire*. Indeed, there seems to be a sparsity of empirical evidence in general. At the same time, Hardt's and Negri's grand narrative continues to exhibit core elements of Eurocentric thought. My goal in this chapter is to provide an examination of *Empire* through the lens of African evidence. Incorporating African experiences helps us construct a "peripheral" or subaltern perspective on international relations.[1] More specifically, incorporating African experiences provides a more nuanced vision of the current global situation than the one proffered by Hardt and Negri and helps avoid many of the presentist claims they make.

It should be stressed at the outset that I am not interested in providing *the* "African" or "Africanist" interpretation of *Empire*. Rather, I am outlining a first response to the authors' ambiguous utilization of Africa in their work. It strikes me that Africa is often treated by Hardt and Negri as a necessary but unwanted actor in their grand theater, called on to the stage when the "Dark Continent" helps illustrate their points concerning the construction of modern European sovereignty and national identity, but then sent off to wait in the wings when it becomes clear that its observable presence might disrupt the narrative they are trying to spotlight.

I see *Empire*'s ambiguous relationship with Africa prevalent in two places. First, where does Africa fit in their concept of Empire? Is the continent inside or outside this postmodern imperial project? On closer examination, it appears that Africa is, by necessity, both incorporated and excluded from Empire. Yet simultaneously, as I will show, Hardt's and Negri's attempt to construct a theory of Empire requires their marginalization of Africa. When African experiences are made explicit, Hardt's and Negri's central claims concerning sovereignty, the state, and the new spatiality of Empire are put in considerable doubt. Second, how do Africa and Africans fit into their assumptions about the "multitude"? They argue that the multitude constitutes a progressive, liberating power by which to counter Empire. Yet the arguments they make and the assumptions that they are based upon seem to be distinctly out of step with most Africans' lived experiences. I will respond to each of these general questions in the two sections that follow.

## Africa and Empire

Central to Hardt's and Negri's grand theory is the proposition that there has been a dramatic shift from the paradigm of modern sovereignty to one of imperial sovereignty and a corresponding defeat of the state by forces of global capital, which has created a smooth global space of Empire. I am unpersuaded by the claim that "a global order, a new logic and structure of rule—in short, a new form of sovereignty" (xi) has emerged. Hardt and Negri appear to take the myth of modernity—the fixity of sovereignty, the nation-state, and territoriality—at face value. But African experiences have always exposed the hollowness of the modernist myth; had Hardt and Negri incorporated this fact, they would not have assumed such a presentist conviction that we are now entering a new paradigm. Clarifying Africa's relation with Empire—that is, taking African experiences with sovereignty, the state, and territory *seriously*—disrupts Hardt's and Negri's grand narrative.

### Sovereignty

Hardt and Negri realize that modern sovereignty was "born and developed in large part through Europe's relationship with its outside" (70), thus hinting to a subaltern rereading of sovereignty. This is a point that is often lost on most international relations (IR) theorists. As Tarak Barkawi and Mark Laffey have noted: "Hardt and Negri force us to see that sovereignty, as a concept and an institution, developed in the encounter between Europe and the non-European world. The genealogy of sovereignty cannot be restricted to Europe itself but must include the imperial relations between Europe and its colonies."[2] However, Hardt and Negri do not consider the specific ways that sovereignty as a concept and institution has been produced and performed in the non-

European world. Instead, they assume that modern sovereignty functioned outside Europe in the same way as it did inside Europe. They accept the modernist myth that state borders are relatively impermeable containers of social relations. If we focus on African evidence, we expose how Hardt and Negri misunderstand the complexities in the construction and practices of "modern sovereignty." African experiences illustrate that the myth of modern sovereignty has never been an accurate description of what is actually occurring.

On the surface level, Africa only enters Hardt's and Negri's discussion of sovereignty in two major places. First, Hardt and Negri argue that the modern concepts of Western national identity and sovereignty relied on the African Other. When discussing the formation of European national identity and sovereignty, they quite correctly observe: "The dark Other of European Enlightenment stands as its very foundation just as the productive relationship with the 'dark continents' serves as the economic foundation of the European nation-states" (115). They later comment that: "Only through opposition to the colonized does the metropolitan subject really become itself" (128). This is a point that has been well established by many postcolonial theorists.

The second place in which Hardt and Negri employ African experiences vis-à-vis modern sovereignty is in their discussion of "subaltern nationalism." As Hardt and Negri point out, in the Western context: "the nation sustains the concept of sovereignty by claiming to precede it" (101). This claim always posed a problem for postcolonial African states, where the modern state was clearly a colonial creation with little or no connection to a preexisting nation. As Ernest Geller noted: "Nationalism is not the awakening of nations to self-consciousness; it invents nations where they do not exist."[3] One of the clearest African examples of the postcolonial project of "inventing" the nation is Mobutu Sese Seko's renaming of the Congo to "Zaire" and launching an *authenticité* campaign to construct an essential Zairian national identity.[4] The root of the problem was that postcolonial African societies simply could not employ the myth of modernity that posited a nation prior to national sovereignty, because often one did not exist.

Beyond these two examples, African experiences are absent from Hardt's and Negri's discussion of sovereignty, and perhaps for good reason: further incorporation of Africa into this specific discussion actually undermines one of the fundamental assumptions of their argument. At the core of *Empire* is the argument that there has been a paradigmatic shift away from modern sovereignty to postmodern or imperial sovereignty. As they argue in their Preface: "Our basic hypothesis is that sovereignty has taken a new form, composed of a series of national and supranational organisms united under a single logic of rule. This global form of sovereignty is what we call Empire" (xii). Because African experiences illustrate that modern sovereignty (as understood by Hardt and Negri) never really existed, how could such a shift have occurred?

The narratives of international relations assert that modern sovereignty was formulated in the sixteenth century and first systematically presented by Jean Bodin, as "the state's supreme authority over citizens and subjects." Hence, the state is the final arbitrator within its territory, with no higher authority or law. As Hardt and Negri correctly point out, this conception of modern sovereignty emerged to resolve the many inherent crises of modernity (83–90). Yet Hardt and Negri make the mistake that many IR theorists have also made. That is, they tend to combine the constitutive elements of sovereignty—population, territory, authority, and recognition—into a single, unproblematic actor: the sovereign state.[5] But the Westphalian sovereign-state model has never been an accurate description of the reality of international relations.[6] As Mark Laffey and Jutta Weldes also note in chapter 6, what is missing from Hardt's and Negri's analysis is the realization that sovereignty is a practice that is socially constructed within the international society. Hence, there needs to be "a consideration of the constitutive relationship between the state and sovereignty; the ways the meaning of sovereignty is negotiated out of interactions within intersubjectively identifiable communities; and the variety of ways in which practices construct, reproduce, reconstruct, and deconstruct both state and sovereignty."[7] Sovereignty is an institution or discourse that is constantly undergoing change and transformation, representing constituted and constituting power. It should never be assumed or taken as given, fixed, or immutable. While a paradigm of sovereignty has emerged in modern Western discourses, it is neither monolithic nor universally accepted and practiced.[8]

By incorporating African evidence, one finds important examples of the multiple and shifting construction of sovereignty. Siba Grovogui's work, for example, has illustrated that the production and performance of sovereignty have been highly contested affairs, particularly in Africa.[9] Grovogui highlights how global structures of economic relations and political processes and ideological contestation have led to diverse formulations of sovereignty. During colonialism, European powers delegitimated the sovereignty of non-Western polities but simultaneously inscribed their colonial holdings with a "quasi-sovereignty" that provided legal grounding for European administration and subjugation. Within colonial Africa, multiple, overlapping, and often contradictory regimes of sovereignty were produced and practiced, often through the mediation between the metropole, colonial administrators, and local elites. As Barkawi and Laffey note, in the non-Western world, modern sovereignty "was not a universal but at best only a regional practice of government and rule."[10]

After independence, African states produced new and varied discourses and institutions of sovereignty. Recent work on African state sovereignty has focused on the ways in which existing relationships of economic dependence on the Western donor agencies have led to what many consider an erosion of sovereignty. In the case of Mozambique, for instance, it has been argued that a "recolonization" process is underway due to its aid dependence on donor agencies.[11] Yet the question is not whether Mozambique's sovereignty is being eroded, for that question assumes a preexisting notion of sovereignty. Instead, the question is in what ways have Mozambique's sovereignty and autonomy been constructed and constricted within the global political economy. The answers require a historicizing of the concept of sovereignty. In cases like Mobutu's Zaire, sovereignty—rather than illustrating a "supreme authority" within a territory—primarily helped legitimize deals with foreign firms and creditors. The practice and production of sovereignty allowed nonstate actors, primarily foreign firms, to hide their partnerships behind a legal facade, simplifying questions "concerning legitimacy of contracts, insurance, and adherence to laws in the firm's home country."[12] For the international community at large, the production of many African states' sovereignty remains essential because it "leaves in place an interlocutor who acknowledges debts and provides a point of contact between foreign state officials and strongmen without raising politically disturbing questions of recognition."[13] Thus sovereignty is a resource for both African leaders and elements within the international community.

The construction and performance of state sovereignty in Africa supports Rob Walker's view that there does not exist a Western norm of sovereignty that is firmly established and historically fixed.[14] Rather, sovereignty reflects historical regimes or social compacts that give form to power and legitimacy.[15] These regimes have produced disparate constructions of sovereignty. To speak of a monolithic "modern sovereignty," as Hardt and Negri tend to do, ignores the ways in which sovereignty discourses and practices are multiple and varied. Scholars working from a non-Western perspective will doubt that a shift from modern sovereignty (as understood by Hardt and Negri) to postmodern sovereignty has occurred, because they question whether modern sovereignty ever truly existed.

## The State

Hardt's and Negri's discussion of sovereignty is intimately connected to their examination of the changing, or rather declining, power of the nation-state. Their main point regarding the state in Africa and other postcolonial societies is that colonial export of the myths and institutions of modernity has had negative implications. They argue quite clearly that "*the state is the poisoned gift of national liberation*" (134; emphasis in original). Modern notions of the nation, sovereignty, and the disciplinary models associated with them helped trap emerging postcolonial societies in subordinate positions within the international economic order. The authors argue that "national liberation and national sovereignty are not just powerless against this global capitalist hierarchy but themselves contribute to its organizing and functioning" (133). This is not a new argument and it unfortunately perpetuates the problem found in so many Marxist-oriented analyses of international relations: namely, the portrayal of Africans as helpless, agency-less victims.

But a larger problem emerges. Simply put, Hardt and Negri employ Weberian concepts of the state and power as if they were actual descriptions of reality (41). That is to say, they assume a monolithic, homogenous, and universal understanding of the state and state practices. In fact, states—like other international phenomena—are produced through relations of mutual constitution. What Hardt and Negri fail to take into account, in other words, is the *process* of state-making.[16] By paying attention to African experiences, we can see how the state, like sovereignty, has been discursively constructed and performed in new and contradictory ways (within both the colonial and the postcolonial context), thus undermining Hardt's and Negri's assumption of a universal norm of statehood.

Under the classic Weberian definition, most African states are unable to claim a monopoly on the means of violence, legitimate or otherwise. Furthermore, government claims of territorial integrity are highly dubious, as vast sections of territory remain outside the control of many African regimes. As Africans have increasingly chosen to "disengage" and distance themselves from predatory and parasitic governments, the continent is increasingly made up of "states without citizens."[17] Since citizenship, territorial integrity, and monopoly of the tools of coercion are all considered prerequisites for statehood, the disengagement of citizens raises serious doubts about whether African states are in fact "states" at all. Scholars on the African state have recently taken to producing new adjectives (such as *failed, collapsing, quasi-, soft*, and *post*-state) to describe what are distinctly non-Weberian states.[18] Yet, in one of the more insightful recent discussions of politics in Africa, Patrick Chabal and Jean-Pascal Daloz argue that the state in Africa—colonial and postcolonial—*never* met the requirements established by Weber because it failed to be institutionalized. Chabal and Daloz note that the state in Africa is not "collapsing," simply because no (Weberian) state was constructed to begin with.[19]

The concept of the state must always be historicized and contextualized. Even though African elites may have accepted the concept of the state, they have constructed and employed it according to their own needs and contexts. While international forces are constructing various discourses of the state in Africa for their own interests, Africans are often exploiting such discourses for their own enrichment. For example, the Sierra Leonean government of Valentine Strasser used the state as a legal facade by which to conduct business with the international community, specifically with the international financial institutions.[20] In the former Zaire (as well as what is left of the "new" Congo), domestic strongmen and external actors discursively produce and employ the state as a shield behind which power is generated and practiced as international affairs are conducted and legitimized. The history of the modern nation-state in Africa reveals how the very institutions and practices that constitute the "state" are produced in myriad ways. While the production and performance of the state in Africa may often seem outside the realm of Western rationality, it is important to recognize the multiplicity of the state beyond the assumed Westerncentric ideal type.[21]

Hardt and Negri thus seem to begin by privileging assumptions of the Weberian state, and when they recognize that the Weberian state does not currently exist, they mistakenly deduce that a massive shift has taken place. But this "discovery" is possible only because they ignore the way the "state" has been reconfigured and employed at the margins. Hardt and Negri correctly expose the Weberian state as a myth, but it has always been a myth in Africa. Their realization leads them to jump to a mistaken double conclusion: that the state has been defeated, and that power now operates at a universal level of Empire; that the "traditional spheres of politics" have declined, and that now "power is constitutionalized on a supranational level" (308–309). African experiences indicate a far more complicated picture of current international relations.

For example, Hardt's and Negri's discussion of the state leads them to the conclusion that it has been eclipsed in world politics by transnational corporations (TNCs) and, to a lesser extent, nongovernmental organizations (NGOs) that help advance the cause of Empire. As they succinctly assert: *"the state has been defeated and corporations now rule the earth!"* (306; emphasis in original). This is a fundamentally important element of their grand theory and one in which the incorporation of African experiences adds much texture.

Hardt and Negri assert that "large transnational corporations have effectively surpassed the jurisdiction and authority of nation-states" (306). In Africa, this is often the case. In one notable instance, a West German firm was able to gain virtual sovereignty over a 150,000 kilometer area of Zaire during Mobutu's reign.[22] Yet it is unclear to what extent this represents a fundamental change, given that European corporations were also given sovereign power over sections of territory during the colonial project. In much of contemporary Africa, one can see the increased strength of several transnational corporations, must notably Coca-Cola and the South African Brewing Corporation. But Hardt's and Negri's discussion of the increased power of TNCs tends to underemphasize the ways in which the relationships between these TNCs and the state have been reformulated. For example, the new Coke plant in Angola is co-owned by the Angolan state itself. In such instances, the privatization of African economies dictated by the International Monetary Fund (IMF) and World Bank has led to the reformulation and extension of state powers.

The literature on African international relations has also paid attention to the ways in which state power has been altered and reformulated by the increased presence of NGOs on the continent. For Hardt and Negri, many of these NGOs (and they are exclusively interested in Western NGOs) are best understood as moral instruments by which the Empire's powers of intervention are advanced by circumventing the power of the state (35–36). However, work on NGOs and Africa has focused on the highly ambiguous relations between NGOs and state. In many ways, NGOs can reinforce the power of the state, especially when NGO presence reinforces the legitimacy of state leaders. NGOs in Africa have also contributed to the discursive production of the state and sovereignty, operated as emancipatory elements within civil society, and contributed to the fostering of the neoliberal economic orthodoxy of the West. That is, African experiences with NGOs offer a more complicated and nuanced picture than the one being offered by Hardt and Negri (312–313).[23]

When Hardt and Negri observe that: "Although transnational corporations and global networks of production and circulation have undermined the powers of nation-states, state functions and constitutional elements have effectively been displaced to other levels and domains" (307), they are convincing. But scholars of African politics have long examined the fragmented, concentric nature of power, authority, and sovereignty in Africa as a *tradition*. In the postcolonial context, structures of authority and loyalty have emerged, sometimes replacing the state as the supreme territorial authority. In some African cases, these are characterized as "warlord" structures. In other cases, a resurgence of social attachments based on perceived ties of kinship, ethnicity, language, and religion have undermined and replaced territorial affiliation. Such a decentralization of politics has created a web of sociopolitical structures that integrate local, regional, and international actors, often resulting in multilayered structures of concentric circles of diminishing control, radiating from the various cores.[24] In various parts of Africa, a system of overlapping authority and multiple loyalties exists, a system in which the state must share its authority with regional, international, substate and subnational authorities to such an extent that the concept of modern sovereignty has become increasingly complicated. But this is a diffuse process, and it would be a gross overstatement to argue, as do Hardt and Negri, that power is flowing solely (or even primarily) to the supranational level. To name only one alternative view, a growing body of literature addresses the complexities of power and authority in Africa not through the globalizing generalizations found in *Empire* but through a focus on the importance of "new regionalisms."[25] Such approaches work because they are more driven by realities on the ground than by ideologies in the air.[26]

## Spatial Demarcations

*Empire*'s ambiguous treatment of Africa is perhaps most visible in the way Hardt and Negri construct Empire spatially. The authors suggest that everything is inside Empire, and there is no outside. As they state at the outset: "First and foremost . . . the concept of Empire posits a regime that effectively encompasses the spatial totality, or really that rules over the entire 'civilized' world" (xiv). For them, Empire is a universal space; a "smooth" space (190; 332–333); a "continuous, uniform space" (190) with "progressively less distinction between inside and outside" (187). Central to this thesis is the proposition that the entire world has been incorporated into Empire because, through the progressive "proletarianization" of noncapitalist environments, "*the outside is internalized*" (226; emphasis in original). Hardt and Negri argue that the modernist system created a space of "global striation, channeling, coding, and territorializing the flows of capital, blocking certain flows and facilitating others," but that it has been displaced by Empire's production of "a smooth space of uncoded and deterritorialized flows" (332–333). African evidence, however, illustrates that the globe is still made up of rough, fragmented spaces. Africa is positioned ambiguously, placed both inside and outside—incorporated but not "civilized."

For Hardt and Negri, the shift to Empire means that modernist distinctions between Worlds have been erased: "the spatial divisions of the three Worlds (First, Second, and Third) have been scrambled so that we continually find the First World in the Third, the Third in the First, and the Second almost nowhere at all" (xiii). Such a view subtly presupposes that a recognizable First/Third World dichotomy once existed. Yet a historical examination would illustrate that those spatial delineations never held. Postcolonial theorists have pointed out that the European colonial project was largely concerned with creating and reifying these imagined boundaries.[27] Well before the advent of Hardt's and Negri's Empire, the "First" world was in the "Third" world and vice versa. For example, the process of transculturation between European and African societies was occurring long before colonialism and the Atlantic slave trade. Although much of the modernist project has entailed defining, demarcating, and policing those boundaries, they were "scrambled" then and they remain "scrambled" now. What Hardt and Negri observe may be a difference in degree, but this difference does not constitute a paradigm shift.

The argument that global spatial divisions have been scrambled also does not necessarily lead to the conclusion that global space has therefore become "smoothed" over.[28] In fact, spatial demarcations of Africa and the West continue to be politically significant for international relations. The key to understanding Hardt's and Negri's ambiguous treatment of Africa is to focus on the notion of "civilization," which is fundamental to the authors' discussion of Empire. As they say, Empire "rules over the entire 'civilized' world" (xiv). Later they stress that "once a segment of the environment has been 'civilized,' once it has been organically incorporated into the newly expanded boundaries of the domain of capitalist production, it can no longer be the outside necessary to realize capital's surplus value" (227). Yet contemporary Western discourses illustrate that Africa is both partly "incorporated" and also partly outside "civilization." Defining Empire through a "universal civilization" is not only Eurocentric but deeply problematic when one recognizes that many dominant Western discourses and practices continue to exclude Africa from the "civilized" realm.

To a limited extent, Hardt and Negri recognize this tension. Not long after they argue that the globe has been "civilized" by being incorporated into the domain of capitalist production, they state that the "most subordinated regions, such as areas of sub-Saharan Africa, are effectively excluded from capital flows and new technologies, and they thus find themselves on the verge of starvation" (288). But Hardt and Negri ignore the ways in which Africa continues to be discursively constructed outside of Western "civilized" space; that is, outside Empire.

This attempt to portray parts of Africa as uncivilized is a trope known as the "New Barbarism" thesis and has been applied to numerous African contexts, including Sierra Leone, Liberia, Rwanda, Zaire/Congo, and Somalia. The basic tenet of this thesis is that Africa is an inherently wild and dangerous place, plagued by politically meaningless violence brought about by culture and the environment.[29] One of the foremost proponents of this perspective has been Robert Kaplan, particularly in his 1994 *Atlantic Monthly* article "The Coming Anarchy." Kaplan paints a picture of the world going to hell in a handbasket, often using Africa as his "evidence." The continent, he suggests, is undergoing a breakdown of its social fabric because of African cultural beliefs and practices. In the rhetoric of New Barbarism, Africa simply cannot sustain basic elements of civilization.

The predominance of the New Barbarism trope in Western discourses largely explains why Western powers have been reluctant to intervene in recent African crises. Hardt and Negri argue that the legitimacy of Empire is supported through intervention, or the right to engage in "police action" (17). Yet, with the notable exception of the Somalian failure, the "international community" has largely chosen to ignore recent African crises, including the enormously destructive war in the Congo. Western confidence in its ability to "civilize" and "develop" Africa appears to have been deeply shaken. The employment of the New Barbarism discourse allows for this "isolation" of Africa by the West. Within Western discourses, parts of Africa are characterized by references to AIDS, the Ebola virus, inherent savagery, and barbarism; an apolitical chaos beyond the rational comprehension of the "civilized" West.[30] Hence, parts of Africa are excised from the spatial domain of "civilization" which constitutes Hardt's and Negri's Empire.

The continued spatial exclusion of Africa (both discursively and economically) could possibly be addressed by two arguments found in *Empire*. First, Hardt and Negri argue that racism has undergone a shift away from biological to cultural determinism: "biological differences have been replaced by sociological and cultural signifiers as the key representations of racial hatred and fear" (191). Hence, "culture is made to fill the role that biology had played" (192). This, it would seem, means that Africans are not being excised from "civilization" because of their skin color but because of their cultural practices. This is a rather astute observation that helps illustrate the shifting discourses and dynamics of race in the current era. However, this new form of racism still produces and maintains spatial demarcations and the excising of African alterity. Because African culture is posited as existing primarily but not exclusively in Africa, Africa is again constructed as outside the spatial domain of Western "civilization."[31]

Second, Hardt and Negri assert that continuing global inequalities reflect "new segmentations" within Empire (336–339). This is an interesting conceptual balancing act, for it posits that global space has simultaneously become "smooth" and "segmented."[32] The contradictions in this image become apparent when one recognizes that the segments represent unequal, fragmented spaces. In fact, Hardt's and Negri's introduction of spatial segmentations raises important questions about boundaries and borders. For the authors, the move to Empire has meant the erasure of borders: "In the passage of sovereignty toward the plane of immanence, the collapse of boundaries has taken place both within each national context and on a global scale. . . . The establishment of a global society of control that smooths over the striae of national boundaries goes hand in hand with the realization of the world market and the real subsumption of global society under capital" (332). Yet African evidence indicates more complicated processes at work.

*Within* parts of Africa, it is clear to see that nation-state borders are often porous, with the flow of people, weapons, goods, and resources largely unrestricted.[33] The boundaries *between* Africa and the West, however, remain extremely important. In fact, one could argue that Western governments' attempts to demarcate and police those borders have actually increased in recent years, with massive efforts to stem the flow of asylum seekers, illegal economic migrants, drugs, weapons, contraband, and other undesirables. As Hardt and Negri point out: "Fear is the ultimate guarantee of the new segmentations" (339). Perhaps the best example of this is Robert Kaplan's "Coming Anarchy" thesis, which demarcates a modern West needing protection from the barbaric Third World contagion. Again, the spatial demarcations of the "new segmentations" and the fear underpinning them are founded partly upon African alterity. Spain's heightening and militarizing its southern borders to keep out African refugees is but one example of how European and American states have responded to this fear by strengthening rather than weakening the boundaries between themselves and the African Other. Not only do these actions indicate that the nation-state and the modern project of sovereignty are still extremely important for the West, but they also belie Hardt's and Negri's claim that there exists a "smooth" global space with no outside. In the end, we are left with Africa occupying an ambiguous relationship with Empire—simultaneously incorporated and excised.

## Africa and Multitude

Hardt's and Negri's work not only seeks to be descriptive but is also self-consciously prescriptive. Central to their schema is the "multitude," their term for the masses or proletariat. In the authors' grand narrative, both Empire and preimperial world orders have been created by constant struggles between the communism of the multitude and the reactionary forces of capitalism (43). Unfortunately, Hardt's and Negri's multitude is vaguely defined. As such, it is less an analytic tool than "an expression of good intentions."[34] Despite being a nonconcept, the multitude is Hardt's and Negri's theoretical agent for resisting and overcoming the repressive powers of Empire. Yet their discussion of the multitude often reveals their Eurocentrism.[35] Focusing on African evidence leads us to question the progressive assumptions Hardt and Negri make about the emancipatory power of the multitude. In this section, I focus on two of the primary elements of the multitude presented by Hardt and Negri: nomadism and the generative/constituent power of the multitude.

### Nomadism

Hardt and Negri argue that the multitude's ability to become mobile provides enormous emanicipatory and liberatory possibilities.[36] They argue that the "power to circulate is a primary determination of the virtuality of the multitude, and circulating is the first ethical act of a counterimperial ontology" (363). Hardt and Negri hold that mobility allows the multitude to resist global capital's attempts to control their labor power: "The new transversal mobility of disciplinary labor power is significant because it indicates a real and powerful search for freedom and the formation of new, nomadic desires that cannot be contained and controlled within the disciplinary regime" (253). For the authors, this mobility of the multitude is nothing less than an "ethical practice" (362) aimed at achieving "global citizenship" (361).

They are able to make this argument largely because of their earlier claim that nation-state borders have become more porous, tied to the conviction that labor has become increasingly mobile. As I discussed earlier, this view of the porousness of state borders is more complicated than they allow for. Clearly some state borders have become more fluid. Within Europe, the porousness of the borders has largely been realized through the institutional changes wrought by the European Union. In many parts of Africa, the fluidity and porousness of many state borders are grounded in colonial and precolonial practices. It is a mistake to assume that a paradigmatic shift has occurred because Hardt and Negri suddenly realize that borders are not as concrete as they have been purported to be within the modernist myths. Moreover, as the previous section illustrated, even though some boundaries are less important, there still remain other significant boundaries, such as the ones between Africa and the West. The vision of a "smooth," "flattened" global space is a myth. Hardt's and Negri's claim that "*space is always open*" (176; emphasis in original) clearly does not hold true for Africans.

Moreover, I question the validity of the second half of their proposition—that labor is now more mobile. In discussing the mobility of labor, Hardt and Negri claim: "[e]conomic geography and political geography both are destabilized in such a way that the boundaries among the various zones are themselves fluid and mobile" (254). However, the experience of the North American Free Trade Agreement (NAFTA) indicates that, while capital has become more mobile, labor has not. After September 11, immigration controls in the United States increased, leading to an even greater clampdown on the flow of labor in North America. Taking the example of southern Africa, we can see a far more complicated image than the one being offered by Hardt and Negri. Under colonialism, southern African labor was highly regulated, with men primarily from Mozambique, Malawi, Lesotho, and Swaziland shipped into South Africa to work in the mining sector.[37] But with the end of apartheid in South Africa, there have been even greater state controls placed on labor movements. With the strengthening of its northern borders and increased regulation on immigration, the South African case indicates that labor may be *less* mobile today than it was before.

Setting aside questions about porous borders and the mobility of labor, we need to examine the core assumption being put forth by Hardt and Negri, namely that nomadism is a liberating act. Discussing the multitude's choice to become mobile, Hardt and Negri argue that this movement reflects "a desire of liberation that is not satiated except by reappropriating new spaces, around which are constructed new freedoms" (397). In one of their more prophetic moments, they claim that passports will increasingly become less important (397).

From the perspective of African evidence, one cannot help but feel these arguments are disconnected from reality. I do not mean to call into question the potential liberating effect of movement. But with around 14 million refugees and displaced persons in Africa,[38] nomadism is far more about survival than liberation. Hence, it seems difficult to image that Sudanese refugees, displaced Congolese, or the many Africans engaged in smuggling goods across state borders for economic survival are part of what Hardt and Negri would consider a "counterimperial ontology" (363). Moreover, the state's regulation and documentation of this movement remain one of the ways in which state power is performed and strengthened. While Hardt and Negri are correct in recognizing that this disciplinary power is never complete, that should not lead one to assume that it is necessarily declining.

Hardt and Negri argue that *"The general right to control its own movement is the multitude's ultimate demand for global citizenship"* (400; emphasis in original). Rather than the African refugee, their idealized "global citizen" seems to be the "global soul" discussed by Pico Iyer.[39] In that work, Iyer focuses on the emergence of a global elite, whose constant world-traveling has created a new class of displaced individuals living in a globalized "transnational village" of cultural fusion. Iyer, like Hardt and Negri, discusses how these "global souls" do not belong to a specific nation-state but exist in a multicultural nonplace. However, there is a sharp contrast between Iyer's "global soul" and the image of the African refugee. The latter seems to be caught within the web of modernity's violent contradictions while the former successfully employs and manipulates the symbols and signs of the modern nation-state (passports, visas, currencies, etc.) actually to further capitalism. One is left wondering how either image fulfills Hardt's and Negri's vision of the emancipatory and counterimperial power of nomadism.

## The Creative and Generative Power of the Multitude

For Hardt and Negri, the true liberatory power of the multitude derives from its generative power. This element of their grand theory is perhaps best expressed when they focus on "the constituent power of the multitude—or really . . . the product of the creative imagination of the multitude that configures its own constitution. This constituent power makes possible the continuous opening to a process of radical and progressive transformation" (406; see also 47, 60–61; 65–6; 395–396). For Hardt and Negri, this constituent power can lead to progressive transformation of the sociopolitical order, because the multitude is driven by two internal desires. The first is the constant desire to resist domination: "The desires of the multitude and its antagonism to every form of domination drive it to divest itself once again of the processes of legitimation that support the sovereign power" (90). The second desire is more specific. The multitude, Hardt and Negri argue, is driven by a primary desire of "*getting out of modernity*" (251; emphasis in original). For Hardt and Negri, this desire is partly linked to their view that the teleology of the multitude is toward increasing their own joy and power (396); that is, the multitude as driven towards the realization of an *Earthly* City rather than a *City of God* (396).

Upon examination, Hardt's and Negri's embrace of these assumptions—and their optimism for a liberatory politics—is largely based on the view that modernity's disciplinary institutions—particularly those found in civil society—are declining and collapsing with the shift to Empire: "Today the social institutions that constitute disciplinary society (the school, the family, the hospital, the factory), which are in large part the same as or closely related to those understood as civil society, are everywhere in crisis" (329). For Hardt and Negri: "The withering away of civil society and the general crisis of the disciplinary institutions coincide with the decline of nation-states as boundaries that mark and organize the divisions in global rule" (332). This crisis of civil society opens spaces for the multitude to engage in virtual, constitutive actions for a counterimperial politics.

While it may be true that there is a withering away of civil society in Western societies, this is not the case in many African societies. In European and American societies, the institutions of civil society indeed seem to be in decline, and people may be "bowling alone"—to use Robert Putman's notorious expression.[40] However, a great deal of scholarly attention has been paid to the resurgence of an energetic—though conflictual—civil society in many parts of Africa.[41] In fact, religious institutions—arguably the most important disciplinary institutions of modernity—are increasing in their importance and vitality in many African civil societies. This significant fact challenges Hardt's and Negri's claims that the multitude desires liberation from domination, struggles to get out of modernity, and seeks the Earthly City rather than the City of God.

In Philip Jenkins's examination of the rise of conservative Christianity around the world, he notes: "Christianity as a whole is both growing and mutating in ways that observers in the West tend not to see."[42] While much media attention has been paid to the spread of Islam in the Third World, particularly to its more conservative and fundamentalist strains, it appears that the spread of conservative Christianity will have a far greater impact for the postmodern global community. The Christian population may be shrinking in the West, but it is surging in the South. For example, there are currently around 360 million Christians in Africa, compared to 480 million in Latin America, 313 million in Asia, and 260 million in North America.[43] Within the last century, the percentage of Christians in Africa has increased from 9 percent to 46 percent of the total population. Within the next twenty-five years, it is estimated that the world's Christian population will grow to 2.6 billion, making Christianity by far the world's largest faith. Hardt and Negri envision a smooth global space of Empire. In contrast, Jenkins argues that the declining autonomy of the nation-state is leading to "a new transnational order in which political, social, and personal identities are defined chiefly by religious loyalties."[44] Does this evidence not disrupt both Hardt's and Negri's vision of Empire and their view of the multitude?

While this dramatic increase in the Christian population is significant, for our discussion it is more important to recognize that Southern Christianity is far more conservative than the Northern version. The surge occurring in the South is predominantly among the Evangelical, Pentecostal, and Catholic communities, which stress supernaturalism and neo-orthodoxy. Given the increased tension between the more liberal Northern Christians and the growing Southern religious revolution, a global schism within Christianity is likely to erupt. As Jenkins specifies: "The denominations that are triumphing across the global South—radical Protestant sects, either evangelical or Pentecostal, and Roman Catholicism of an orthodox kind—are stalwartly traditional or even reactionary by the standards of the economically advanced nations."[45]

While I resist Jenkins's rather alarmist presentation of the spread of Christianity in the South, he does provide important evidence that troubles Hardt's and Negri's pronouncements about the generative power of the multitude. Rather than seeing the withering away of modernity's disciplinary institutions, we see the multitude embracing these institutions, particularly conservative ones that stress traditional authority and neo-orthodoxy. How does the enormous growth of conservative Christianity in Africa fit into Hardt's and Negri's optimistic vision of the multitude? I am not suggesting that conservative Christianity should necessarily be feared or that the multitude does not possess the potential for generative, constituent, or even emancipatory powers. But if one is to accept Hardt's and Negri's proposition that the multitude produces its own singularity (395), then the current direction of the multitude in many parts of Africa is clearly at odds with the liberatory project that Hardt and Negri envision.

## Conclusion

One of *Empire*'s most worthy contributions is its attempt to rectify IR theory's parochialism—both geographical and disciplinary. To its credit, *Empire* rejects many of the basic starting points of traditional IR theories (anarchy, human nature, interdependence, etc.) and recognizes the need to examine the relations of global power outside the narrow confines of Europe. Hardt and Negri also offer many insights into the shifting discourses of sovereignty and authority in Europe and America. Their discussion of how capital continues to reconfigure social and political space in the West charts especially useful paths for future analyses. However, Hardt and Negri make two major mistakes. First, they succumb to the presentist impulse, arguing that the world today is somehow radically different from the world of yesterday. In order to make their arguments convincing, Hardt and Negri ignore or erase the multiplicity and contestedness of the historical record to posit a uniform and monolithic "modern condition" of fixed disciplinary institutions and practices, such as sovereignty and the nation-state. Second, they assume that what is true in their Western context must be true for the world at large. These two mistakes could have been avoided by employing greater historical sensitivity and non-Western examples. Hardt's and Negri's discussions of sovereignty, the state, and the new Empire of global capitalism expose their own Westerncentric assumptions.

Despite its insights and deft syntheses, *Empire* constructs a global vision strangely disconnected from global realities. In their desire to create a grand theory of contemporary world politics, Hardt and Negri frequently overgeneralize and ignore contradictory evidence. These problems become visible when one considers Africa's ambiguous relation to Empire and to *Empire*. If Hardt and Negri had taken African historical examples seriously, for example, they would have avoided the numerous presentists and universalizing flaws that plague—and ultimately undermine—their work. Undoubtedly this would have disrupted the smooth grand theory of Empire they were trying to construct. But it would have given their readers a greater appreciation of the complicated and frequently contradictory state of today's world.

## Notes

1. Kevin C. Dunn and Timothy M. Shaw, eds., *Africa's Challenge to International Relations Theory* (Basingstoke, UK: Palgrave, 2001). References to *Empire* (Cambridge, MA: Harvard University Press, 2000) are inserted parenthetically throughout.

2. Tarak Barkawi and Mark Laffey, "Retrieving the Imperial: *Empire* and International Relations," *Millennium* 31; 1 (2002): 121.

3. Ernest Geller, *Thought and Change* (London: Weidenfeld and Nicolson, 1964): 168.

4. Kevin C. Dunn, "Imagining Mobutu's Zaire: The Production and Consumption of Identity in International Relations," *Millennium* 30; 2 (2001).

5. Thomas Biersteker and Cynthia Weber, eds., *State Sovereignty as Social Construct* (Cambridge, UK: Cambridge University Press, 1996): 5.

6. Stephen D. Krasner, "Rethinking the Sovereign State Model," *Review of International Studies* 27, special issue (2001): 17. This is a point echoed by Barkawi and Laffey in their critique of *Empire*. They point out that sovereignty, "as understood in disciplinary narratives derived from Westphalia, applies only to limited periods of history and in particular regions, principally Europe." See Barkawi and Laffey, "Retrieving the Imperial," 110.

7. Biersteker and Weber, *State Sovereignty as Social Construct*, 11.

8. Richard Ashley, "The Power of Anarchy: Theory, Sovereignty, and the Domestication of Global Life," in *International Theory: Critical Investigations*, ed. James Der Derian (New York: New York University Press, 1995), 112–113.

9. Siba Grovogui, *Sovereigns, Quasi Sovereigns, and Africans* (Minneapolis: University of Minnesota Press, 1996); and "Sovereignty in Africa: Quasi-Statehood and Other Myths in International Theory" in *Africa's Challenge to International Relations Theory*, eds. Dunn and Shaw.

10. Barkawi and Laffey, "Retrieving the Imperial," 123.

11. Merle Bowen, "Beyond Reform: Adjustment and Political Power in Contemporary Mozambique," *Journal of Modern African Studies* 30; 2 (1992); David N. Plank, "Aid, Debt, and the End of Sovereignty: Mozambique and Its Donors" *Journal of Modern African Studies* 31; 3 (1993); Joseph Hanlon, *Mozambique: Who Calls the Shots?* (London: James Currey, 1991); Joseph Hanlon, *Peace without Profit: How the IMF Blocks Rebuilding in Mozambique* (Oxford: James Currey, 1996); and Chris Alden, *Mozambique and the Construction of the New African State* (Basingstoke, UK: Palgrave, 2001).

12. William Reno, "Sovereignty and Personal Rule in Zaire," *African Studies Quarterly* 1; 3 (1997).

13. Ibid.

14. R. B. J. Walker, *Inside/Outside: International Relations as Political Theory* (Cambridge, UK: Cambridge University Press, 1993). In his critique of Hardt's and Negri's *Empire*, Walker astutely observes: "As with so many other texts, a version of history as modernisation is deployed to solve problems identified in a reading of modernity as history." See R. B. J. Walker, "On the Immanence/Imminence of Empire," *Millennium* 31; 2 (2002): 341.

15. Jens Bartelson, *A Geneology of Sovereignty* (Cambridge, UK: Cambridge University Press, 1995), 186–248.

16. Recognizing the limitations of the Weberian state model is not a particularly new insight but it is a fundamentally important one for international relations. Robert Cox, for instance, has argued that the state is not a given but emerges out of social forces, as do other social structures. Likewise, Charles Tilly, Michael Mann, and other historical sociologists have examined how specific kinds of states have been produced by multiple and competing forces at work in domestic and international societies. For them, it is important to recognize at the outset that states differ and are functionally different because of the complexities of the state as a process. See Robert Cox, *Approaches to World Order* (Cambridge, UK: Cambridge University Press, 1996); Charles Tilly, *The Formation of the Nation-State in Western Europe* (Princeton, NJ: Princeton University Press, 1975) and *Coercion, Capital, and European States, AD 900–1992* (Oxford: Basil Blackwell, 1990); and Michael Mann, *The Sources of Social Power*, vol. 1 (Cambridge, UK: Cambridge University Press, 1986) and *The Sources of Social Power*, vol. 2 (Cambridge, UK: Cambridge University Press, 1993).

17. John A. A. Ayoade, "States without Citizens: An Emerging African Phenomenon," in *Precarious Balance: State and Society in Africa*, eds. Rothchild and Chazan (Boulder, CO: Westview, 1988).

18. Jeffrey Herbst, "Responding to State Failure in Africa," *International Security* 21; 3 (1996); William Zartman, ed., *Collapsed States: The Disintegration and Restoration of Legitimate Authority* (Boulder, CO: Lynne Rienner, 1995); Robert H. Jackson, *Quasi-States: Sovereignty, International Relations and the Third World* (Cambridge, UK: Cambridge University Press, 1990); Donald Rothchild, "Hegemony and State Softness," in *The African State in Transition*, ed. Ergas (New York: St. Martin's Press, 1987); and Catherine Boone, "'Empirical Statehood' and Reconfiguration of Political Order," in *The African State at a Critical Juncture: Between Disintegration and Reconfiguration*, eds. L. Villalón and P. Huxtable (Boulder, CO: Lynne Rienner, 1998).

19. Patrick Chabal and Jean-Pascal Daloz, *Africa Works: Disorder as Political Instrument* (Oxford: James Currey, 1999).

20. William Reno, "Sierra Leone: Weak States and the New Sovereignty Game," in *The African State at a Critical Juncture*, eds. Villalón and Huxtable.

21. Kevin C. Dunn, "MadLib #32: The (blank) African State: Rethinking the Sovereign State in International Relations Theory," in *Africa's Challenge to International Relations Theory*, eds. Dunn and Shaw.

22. Crawford Young and Thomas Turner, *The Rise and Decline of the Zairian State* (Madison: University of Wisconsin Press, 1985), 387–388.

23. See Christopher Clapham, *Africa and the International System: The Politics of State Survival* (Cambridge, UK: Cambridge University Press, 1996); Anna C. Vakil, "Confronting the Classification Problem: Towards a Taxonomy of NGOs," *World Development* 25; 12 (1997); Stephen N. Ndegwa, *The Two Faces of Civil Society: NGOs and Politics in Africa* (Bloomfield, CT: Kumarian Press, 1996); Thomas G. Weiss and Leon Gordenker, eds., *NGOs, the UN and Global Governance* (Boulder, CO: Lynne Rienner, 1996); and Susan Dicklitch, *The Elusive Promise of NGOs in Africa: Lessons from Uganda* (Basingstoke, UK: Macmillan, 1998).

24. Igor Kopytoff, "The Internal African Frontier: The Making of African Political Culture," in *The African Frontier: The Reproduction of Traditional African Societies*, ed. Kopytoff (Bloomington, IN: Indiana University Press, 1987), 29.

25. J. Andrew Grant and Frederick Söderbaum, eds., *New Regionalisms in Africa* (London: Ashgate, 2003); Michael Niemann, *A Spatial Approach to Regionalisms in the Global Economy* (Basingstoke, UK: Macmillan, 2000); Morten Bøås, Marianne Marchand, and Timothy M. Shaw, eds., *Third World Quarterly* 20, special issue on "New Regionalisms in the New Millennium" (1999); and Björn Hettne, András Inotai, and Osvaldo Sunkel, eds., *Globalism and the New Regionalism* (Basingstoke: Macmillan, 1999).

26. In many ways, a more useful conceptual model of African international relations may be found in Hedley Bull's discussion of a "New Medieval" system:

> In [the Medieval] system no ruler or state was sovereign in the sense of being supreme over a given territory and a given segment of the Christian population; each had to share authority with the vassals beneath, and with the Pope and (in Germany and Italy) the Holy Roman Emperor above. . . . [I]t is not fanciful to imagine that there might develop a modern and secular counterpart of it that embodies its central characteristic: a system of overlapping authority and multiple loyalty. . . . If modern states were to come to share their authority over their citizens, and their ability to command their loyalties, on the one hand with regional and world authorities, and on the other hand with sub-state or sub-national authorities, to such an extent that the concept of sovereignty ceased to be applicable, then a neo-mediaeval form of universal political order might be said to have emerged.

(see Hedley Bull, *The Anarchic Society* (New York: Columbia University Press, 1997), 254–255. African postcolonial experiences, particularly with the contested nature of the state, sovereignty, and authority, may align more with Bull's "New Medievalism" than with the conceptual model espoused by Hardt and Negri.

27. Anne McClintock, *Imperial Leather: Race, Gender and Sexuality in the Colonial Contest* (London: Routledge, 1995); and Frederick Cooper and Ann Laura Stoler, *Tensions of Empire: Colonial Cultures in a Bourgeois World* (Berkeley, CA: University of California Press, 1997).

28. As Rob Walker has noted, Hardt's and Negri's assertion is based on a conflation of two different sorts of claims: "claims that we are seeing a shift from a specifically modern articulation of relations of identity and difference in a territorially organized political space . . . and claims that this different kind of order has now become radically immanent, having to outside, no Others." See R. B. J. Walker, "On the Immanence/Imminence of Empire," 343. The "immanent" critique of modernity that Hardt and Negri provide does not automatically translate into an account of a politics that involves bringing the outside inside. As Walker states: "One can no more move inside an inside/outside problem than move outside of it" (Ibid., 344).

29. Paul Richards, *Fighting for the Rain Forest* (Oxford: James Currey, 1996), xiii–xv.

30. Western, particularly American, responses to the events in Zaire during the 1990s, for example, were largely informed by this trope. Media coverage was steeped in the language of "New Barbarism"— employing the rhetoric of "chaos," tribalism and irrational African violence (*Time*, November 25, 1996, March 24, 1997, and May 12, 1997; *Newsweek*, December 2, 1996, March 31, 1997, April 21, 1997 and May 12, 1997; *Economist*, July 8, 1995, February 15, 1997, and May 24, 1997). Zaire was represented as wallowing in the "law of the jungle" (*New York Times*, March 17, 1997). There was a clear attempt to conjure up images of a society that had reverted to a prehistorical condition. In an extremely telling

example, *Newsweek* greeted the collapse of Mobutu's regime with a headline lifted directly from Conrad's *Heart of Darkness*: "The Horror, The Horror" (March 31, 1997).

31. Samuel Huntington, *The Clash of Civilizations and the Remaking of World Order* (New York: Simon and Schuster, 1996).

32. As an aside, this conceptual model of a segmented but universal global space, under the sway of global capital is surprisingly similar to the images that Immanuel Wallerstein and other world-system theorists have been constructing for some time. See Immanuel Wallerstein, "The Rise and Future Demise of the World Capitalist System," *Comparative Studies in Society and History* 16; 4 (1974). Hardt and Negri argue that their vision is more nuanced because they recognize that social divisions and geographical borders do not strictly correspond. But this point was well recognized by world-system theorists, who rarely if ever employed the core/semi-periphery/periphery distinctions as ham-fistedly as their critics claimed. They recognized that within regions, elements of each sphere existed. To be fair, Hardt himself has recognized *Empire*'s debt to previous theorists: "Toni and I don't think of this as a very original book. We're putting together a variety of things that others have said" (quoted in Emily Eakin, "What Is the Next Big Thing? Buzz is Growing for 'Empire,'" *New York Times*, July 7, 2001).

33. Christopher Clapham, "Boundaries and States in the New African Order" in *Regionalisation in Africa: Integration and Disintegration*, ed. D. Bach (London and Bloomington, IN: James Currey/Indiana University Press, 1999); Paul Nugent and A. I. Asiwaju, eds., *African Boundaries: Barriers, Conduits and Opportunities* (London: Pinter, 1996). Yet, moving beyond considering only state borders, these regions appear as a complicated web of socially constructed borders: linguistic, political, ethnic, cultural, economic, and so forth. At the end of the twentieth century, these boundaries were often more important than the borders of sovereign states.

34. Alex Callinicos, "The Actuality of Imperialism," *Millennium* 31; 2 (2002): 320.

35. For example, they state that one of the multitude's political demands should be "*a social wage and a guaranteed income for all*" (403; emphasis in original). While I do not question the importance of such a demand, it reflects a Westerncentric understanding of labor and the multitude and appears unconnected to the lived experiences and needs of many Africans who are not wage laborers.

36. For their distinction between emancipation and liberation, see Hardt and Negri, 362.

37. Dunbar Moodie, *Going for Gold: Men, Mines, and Migration* (Berkeley, CA: University of California Press, 1994).

38. In its *World Refugee Survey, 2000*, the U.S. Committee for Refugees estimated that there are around 3.6 million refugees in Africa and around 10.6 million displaced people.

39. Pico Iyer, *The Global Soul* (New York: Vintage, 2000).

40. Robert D. Putman, "Bowling Alone: America's Declining Social Capital," *Journal of Democracy* 6; 1 (1995).

41. Nelson Kasfir, ed., *Civil Society and Democracy in Africa* (London: Frank Cass, 1998); John Harbeson, Donald Rothchild, and Naomi Chazan, eds., *Civil Society and the State in Africa* (Boulder, CO: Lynne Rienner, 1994); and Donald Rothchild and Naomi Chazan, eds., *Precarious Balance: State and Society in Africa* (Boulder, CO: Westview Press, 1988).

42. Philip Jenkins, "The Next Christianity," *The Atlantic Monthly* 290; 3 (2002): 54.

43. Ibid.

44. Ibid., 55.

45. Ibid., 59.

# Intermezzo: The *Theory & Event* Interview

## Sovereignty, Multitudes, Absolute Democracy: A Discussion between Michael Hardt and Thomas L. Dumm about Hardt's and Negri's *Empire*

**Thomas L. Dumm**: First of all it seems important to ask; How is Professor Negri? When might he be released?

**Michael Hardt**: Negri now has a work-release arrangement whereby he is free to go where he pleases during the day but must return each night to the Rebibbia prison near Rome. After spending fourteen years in exile in France, he returned to Italy and prison in 1997 in the hope that he could both resolve his own case and work for a general amnesty for all those accused of crimes on the basis of their political activities in the 1960s and seventies. There has been no movement in the Italian Parliament toward such an amnesty, however, and Negri's own case has proceeded according to normal criminal procedures. In 1998, he reached the midpoint of his sentence (including the four and a half years he served before going to France) and he was thus eligible for work release. In 2001, when he reaches the point when three years remain on his sentence, he will be eligible for parole.[1]

**TD**: It is good to know that despite his status it is possible for him to be able to continue his work, which includes the collaborative projects he has completed with you.

One of my favorite aphorisms is the opening sentence from Deleuze's and Guatarri's *A Thousand Plateaus*: "The two of us wrote *Anti-Oedipus* together.

Since each of us was several, there was already quite a crowd." Some may already be aware that the two of you have already written *Labor of Dionysus* together and have worked on the French journal *Futur Antérieur* for some time, but could you tell us a little bit about how you and Antonio Negri came to collaborate on *Empire?*

**MH**: Negri has worked collaboratively for a long time in journal collectives and political organizations. He also wrote a book together with Félix Guattari. I imagine that I learned how to write collaboratively largely from him.

I profit enormously from collaboration and I think collaborative writing should be encouraged more in the humanities. (It is already necessary in the natural sciences and many areas of the social sciences due in part to the technologies of research.) It is obvious, I imagine, how much collaborators learn from each other. Negri and I have very different disciplinary training—he in political science and I in comparative literature—and we refer primarily to different national literatures. Our writing projects thus always begin by making reading lists for the other person of what each of us consider to be the relevant literature. The collaboration is in this way a kind of mutual education process.

What is most exhilarating and challenging about collaborative writing is the negotiation involved in the writing itself. But really negotiation is not the right concept, because that would involve some kind of dialogue between two individuals. Alchemy is a better notion for the process. In cooperation, Marx says, humans are stripped of the fetters of their individuality. And this is why so many people have difficulty embarking on collaborative writing projects—it is so hard to abandon our individuality! I have found that there is a tendency when writing collaboratively to think like the other person and construct sentences that he or she would form. I feel the resulting prose is both mine and not mine. That is why it is futile to try to divide collaborative texts into passages written by this author or the other. Each author is adopting the other's voice or, really, they are both adopting some third voice or numerous other voices. This is what I think Deleuze and Guattari mean when they refer to the crowd who wrote *Anti-Oedipus*. The alchemy of collaboration does not merge the two authors into a single voice but rather proliferates them to create the chorus of a multitude.

**TD**: The way you describe your process of collaboration sounds very much like the way you and Negri imagine labor having new opportunities to realize itself in the rhizomatic model of communication anticipated by Deleuze and Guatarri, a model that seems crucial to your vision of absolute democracy in *Empire*. Indeed, your reference above to a "multitude" gestures toward the decentered hybrid of the new revolutionary subject, one perhaps not identified with the either/or of the citizen or laboring body but with a yet-to-be-realized emergent being. The realization of this project seems to require a new vocabulary, and "the multitude" seems to be one of your most crucial conceptual interventions in that regard. One is reminded of Marx's comment in the 1844 manuscripts about how the authentic language of humanity would, in present circumstances, be heard as a scream.

**MH**: Perhaps Marx's notion of a general intellect captures best this process of collective theorizing. It is easy to see that all of us stand on the shoulders of others when we think, using concepts, logics, and knowledges that we have inherited. What Marx's notion of general intellect does for me is to pose this observation in social rather than individual terms. We are all part of a general intellect or a collective intelligence that produces concepts and knowledges. It is difficult and finally pointless to try to determine which idea was mine and which yours. We're thinking together. (And that is why private property in the realm of the intellect is such a tenuous proposition.) That doesn't mean that we all think the same or even less that we all agree, just that the process of thought is a social process.

**TD**: Perhaps it is partly a result of your collaborative process that *Empire* doesn't dwell so much in the realm of negative critique. Instead, it appears as both a critical history of the present and a vision for the future. But whereas other recent interventions in theory seem to focus on one side of the problem of politics, perhaps too reductively, we could call this the problem associated with techniques of normalization—say, Habermas's theory of communicative action, Derrida's deconstruction, Foucault's genealogy of disciplinary society and governmentality, and even Deleuze's and Guatarri's nomadology—you and Negri seem to focus your most important critical energies and constructive efforts on understanding and providing ways of resisting sovereignty as it migrates away from the nation-state and to its newest networks. In this sense, the work you have done and the work of other thinkers like Giorgio Agamben concerning an immanent rather than transcendent mode of thinking politically seem both to resurrect an idea of history as movement and to resist Hegelianism while trying to use Hegel still. Why do you think sovereignty is now appearing as such a central problem for political theory?

**MH**: I assume that the renewed interest in the concept of sovereignty in the field of political theory is related in part to the analyses of the autonomy of the political that first focused on the work of Hannah Arendt and more recently on that of Carl Schmitt. Sovereignty does identify what is distinctive about the political or at least about the nature of rule and resistance. Another reason for increased interest today in the concept of sovereignty, not only among political theorists, is the decline of the sovereignty of nation-states. It is quite clear that in the various processes of globalization, the locus of sovereignty has shifted away from the nation-state, at least in part, but it is not so easy to identity its new locus, if indeed it can be located at all. Furthermore, and this is the much more interesting question, perhaps the nature itself of sovereignty has changed in this passage. We claim that indeed there has been a shift from the modern form of sovereignty, theorized by authors from Bodin and Hobbes to Schmitt, to what we call an imperial sovereignty. The form of modern sovereignty can be characterized schematically by the dialectic of inside and outside that I mentioned earlier. (Think of Schmitt's friend/enemy distinction as its basic unit, if you like.) Imperial sovereignty, in contrast, operates on a network model and functions through hybrid identities and differences of degree.

Our perspective, of course, is against sovereignty in all its forms: imperial sovereignty, the nation-state, even the "popular" forms of sovereignty that arose in modernity. Absolute democracy is incompatible with sovereignty. But in order to challenge sovereignty and pose an alternative to it, one must understand first its contemporary form. Resistances to old, outdated forms of rule often tend not only to be ineffective against the present form but to contribute to its functioning.

**TD**: In that regard, my sense is that you both recognize the power of Giorgio Agamben's argument in *Homo Sacer* concerning the extraordinary violence of sovereignty at the end of modernity and yet you seek to overcome what may (not too unjustly) be thought of as a terrifying passivity that his position could result in.

**MH**: Our argument in *Empire* does share some central concerns with Agamben's *Homo Sacer*, particularly surrounding the notions of sovereignty and biopower. Agamben brilliantly elaborates a conception of modern sovereignty based on Carl Schmitt's notions of the decision on the exception and the state of emergency, in which the modern functioning of rule becomes a permanent state of exception. He then links this conception to the figure of the banned or excluded person back as far as ancient Roman law with his usual spectacular erudition. The pinnacle and apotheosis of modern sovereignty thus becomes the Nazi concentration camp; the zone of exclusion and exception is the heart of modern sovereignty and grounds the rule of law. My hesitation with this view is that by posing the extreme case of the concentration camp as the heart of sovereignty it tends to obscure the daily violence of modern sovereignty in all its forms. It implies, in other words, that if we could do away with the camp, then all the violence of sovereignty would also disappear.

The most significant difference between our projects, though, is that Agamben dwells on modern sovereignty, whereas we claim that modern sovereignty has now come to an end and transformed into a new kind of sovereignty, what we call imperial sovereignty. Imperial sovereignty has nothing to do with the concentration camp. It no longer takes the form of a dialectic between Self and Other and does not function through any such absolute exclusion but rules, rather, through mechanisms of differential inclusion, making hierarchies of hybrid identities. This description may not immediately give you the same sense of horror that you get from Auschwitz and the Nazi *Lager*, but imperial sovereignty is certainly just as brutal as modern sovereignty was, and it has its own subtle and not-so-subtle horrors.

But still none of that addresses the passivity you refer to. For that we have to look instead at Agamben's notions of life and biopower. Agamben uses the term "naked life" to name that limit of humanity, the bare minimum of existence that is exposed in the concentration camp. In the final analysis, he explains, modern sovereignty rules over naked life, and biopower is this power to rule over life itself. What results from this analysis is not so much passivity, I would say, but powerlessness. There is no figure that can challenge and contest sovereignty. Our critique of Agamben's (and also Foucault's) notion of biopower is that it is conceived only from above, and we attempt to formulate instead a notion of biopower from below, that is, a power by which the multitude itself rules over life. (In this sense, the notion of biopower one finds in some veins of ecofeminism such as the work of Vandana Shiva, although cast on a very different register, is closer to our notion of a biopower from below.) What we are interested in finally is a new biopolitics that reveals the struggles over forms of life.

TD: How are people to be convinced that the relevant opposition is to sovereignty, though? That is, to put it maybe too simplistically, beyond the call for the end of big government, a call which has its ironies, through what communicative means do you see the constituent power of the multitude realizing itself against the nation-state?

MH: It is not a matter of convincing anyone to oppose sovereignty. It is natural to refuse authority, and the refusal of authority is going on every day at all levels of society. And all of the various forms of modern and contemporary liberatory politics are at base a refusal of servitude, a refusal to accept as natural our subordination to rulers. I see the opposition to sovereignty as a way to name the generality of all these activities.

**TD**: Your resistance to all forms of sovereignty is certain to provoke some very strong responses, I would think especially among postcolonial thinkers who still see in the nation-state a way of advancing a progressive agenda. You and Negri are very appreciative of this position in *Empire*, yet you also urge people not to "harbor any nostalgia for the powers of the nation-state or to resurrect any politics that celebrates the nation" (336).

**MH**: Anticolonial and postcolonial thinkers have certainly not been united in their political evaluations of the nation-state. Franz Fanon's work itself demonstrates the numerous complexities that surround the question. And the Marxist tradition, too, has been divided (the conflict between Lenin and Luxemburg was one powerful instance). But these were all tactical matters. The only logical and honest argument for the nation-state in these contexts is as a defense weapon against more powerful foreign forces, such as colonialist armies or transnational capital. The state itself, however, is at its base an apparatus of domination; it establishes a ruling authority that stands separate from and above society. The question is not: Should the state be destroyed in order to establish a democratic society? but: When is the right time to do so?

**TD**: But some postcolonial theorists—here I am thinking of Homi Bhabha's essay "The Postcolonial and the Postmodern"—might argue that the question of the nation-state is not a tactical one but a cultural one in the deepest possible sense. For Bhabha, the emergence of a postcolonial episteme may offer up a hybrid subjectivity that might allow us to evade the fate of the normalized subject. How would you respond to this argument?

**MH**: First of all, nation is the wrong concept to use to name cultural heritage, identity, and community in this case. There may exist nations without states, but every nation contains within itself the dream of a state. I sometimes think that Benedict Anderson's motto should be reversed: the nation sometimes seems to be the only form in which we can imagine community. And that is only testament to our poverty of imagination. Nation, of course, is a specific form of community, one that is inevitably characterized by exclusion of others, internal hierarchy, and ultimately sovereign authority.

More important for our argument in *Empire*, however, is the question of hybridity. Homi Bhabha's work is rich and complex, but many readers come away from it with the impression that hybridity itself is liberatory because it defies the binaries through which power functions: white/black, male/female, and so forth. We claim, however, that imperial sovereignty is not threatened in the least by hybrid subjectivities. In fact, *Empire* rules precisely through a kind of politics of difference, managing hybrid identities in flexible hierarchies.

From this perspective, then, a politics of hybridity may have been effective against the now-defunct modern form of sovereignty but it is powerless against the current imperial form.

**TD**: Let's shift gears slightly to discuss some of the methodological features of your book. One way of describing *Empire* might be to say that you and Negri challenge your readers to follow you to the green pastures of a new communism, one nurtured by what might be thought of as a certain eclecticism at the level of method. You combine a rigorous resistance to modern formulas of transcendence through both a continued adherence to critique and the embrace of an immanence indebted to Spinoza (among others) while admittedly, as you say, continuing to "flirt with Hegel." Indeed, you present as your twin models Marx's *Capital* and Deleuze's and Guatarri's *A Thousand Plateaus*. This makes the book a great adventure to read, if not the least because of the surpassing juxtapositions of thinkers and categories of thought usually thought to be utterly incompatible. Are you concerned that some may find *Empire* too eclectic, that is to say, not rigorous enough? Or do you find such a concern itself to be misplaced?

**MH**: I think the greater danger, if one had to choose between the two, would be dogmatism rather than eclecticism. Dogmatism narrows our range of theoretical possibilities; the dogmatic calls eclectic any effort to read thinkers and traditions differently and arrange them in new constellations. The charge of eclecticism really assumes that the writer has no method or perspective of her or his own; moving among different traditions thus appears as an incoherent combination. When the writer does have his or her own method and perspective, however, the various traditions and thinkers enlisted in the argument are organized by its overall coherence. In this case, what is really at stake is the formation of a new canon, a new constellation of political and philosophical traditions. Our project aims at such a new constellation and, perhaps for that reason, may appear to some as eclectic.

The dogmatic division that I find most prevalent and troublesome today is the one that separates Marxism from poststructuralism. First of all, the division is simply historically inaccurate. Poststructuralism is a vague term, but the majority of the French philosophers who are generally grouped under that rubric developed their thought within one vein or another of the Marxist tradition. The fact that many of them at various points of their careers challenged established Marxist doctrines or Marx's own writings does not warrant our posing some theoretical opposition; such challenges are what commonly keep traditions alive. Poststructuralism in the United Statas is not so easily characterized, but recently someone criticized me of eclecticism when I crossed the Marxist/poststructuralist divide and discussed Donna Haraway's "Cyborg Manifesto" in the context of a communist project. There is obviously some historical amnesia involved when we cannot remember that Haraway's "Cyborg Manifesto" was explicitly a project of socialist feminism.

Second, and more important than any such historical arguments, enforcing an intellectual division between poststructuralism and Marxism distorts the content of both traditions and deprives us of many significant theoretical and practical possibilities. I must admit that I have only recently become aware of the division and the dedication many have to it. Previously I crossed the lines in blissful ignorance. The Left Conservatism debate (featured in an earlier issue of *Theory & Event*) and reactions to my own work have forced me to recognize the problem. Negri and I often prefer to conceive of our orientation as communist rather than Marxist and, for us at least, this serves to circumvent this kind of dogmatic division. Dedicating a tradition to a single thinker rather than a set of methods, principles, and ideas always runs the risk of precluding innovation and creating a new dogmatism. We certainly have as substantial criticisms of Marx as we do of Spinoza, Deleuze, Machiavelli, and others. In fact, the tradition of communist thought and practice has perhaps been too dominated by the name of Marx, eclipsing its various alternatives and possibilities. Communist thought, in other words, is much bigger than Marx. We claim, for example, that Spinoza was a communist thinker long before Marx—how else can we understand his proposal of an "absolute democracy"—and Deleuze was a communist thinker even if he did not conceive of himself as one.

**TD**: The Left Conservatism debate has seemed to hinge on claims about differences between culture and economy among some of the protagonists (such as the interesting and productive debate between Judith Butler and Nancy Fraser, which you cite in *Empire*), and arguments about the powers of identity and the claims of recognition advanced by critical race theorists and some others and a more traditional unionism and nationalism as represented these days by Richard Rorty and Adolph Reed, to name few. More than simply naming yourselves as communists, in *Empire* you and Negri seem to be suggesting that these differences are bound to dissolve in the crucible of the informatization of labor.

**MH**: You're probably right that the most substantial aspect of these debates was the question of whether culture or economy should serve as the primary field of explanation in such political discussions. It seems to me, though, that the question is poorly posed, because in separating economy from culture, we end up with false notions of both economy and culture. Moreover, if in the recent transformation, as we claim, economic production is becoming increasingly cultural and cultural production increasingly economic, then the entire problematic would be significantly displaced. We try to think this shift under the rubric of immaterial labor, which includes not only work with images and analytical-symbolic tasks but also affective labor and caring labor. In immaterial labor, the economic and the cultural are inseparable.

**TD**: In this sense you make respectable yet another term that has fallen on hard times: postmodernism. Nietzsche once claimed that the only word with a clear meaning is one without a history. What work does that term do for you, especially since you are so aware of its troubled history?

**MH**: Well, our entire project is indeed based on the recognition of an epochal break or an historical passage that brought modernity and modernization to an end. Foucault was brilliant at naming for such shifts a very specific date or event, which appeared absurd for its very specificity; we might seem equally absurd for indicating too many events as the marker of this passage. At times we locate the shift in the victorious national liberation struggles of the 1960s and the end of European colonialism, at other times we point to the explosion of workers movements, liberation struggles, and feminist movements throughout the world in 1968, at still other times we indicate Nixon's decoupling of the dollar from the gold standard in 1971, at others we conceive the 1989 fall of the Berlin Wall as the central event, and so forth. We try to demonstrate that all of these events are elements of the passage. So if the postmodern is meant to indicate the end of modernity and modernization, then yes our project is certainly postmodern. On the other hand, it bears little resemblance to the various postmodernist theories that seemed so urgent a few years ago. Perhaps in retrospect we should reread those postmodernist theories as symptoms of a passage rather than as a model or paradigm for thought.

**TD**: A compelling feature of *Empire* is the explanatory framework it provides for understanding the contemporary transformations that are taking place in the production of space and how this change is crucial to the emergence of a new imperial sovereignty. To quote:

> The striated space of modernity constructed places that were continually engaged in and founded on a dialectical play with their outsides. The space of imperial sovereignty, in contrast, is smooth. It might appear to be free of the binary divisions or striations of modern boundaries, but really it is crisscrossed by so many fault lines that it only appears as a continuous uniform space. In this sense, the clearly defined crisis of modernity gives way to an omnicrisis of the imperial

world. In this smooth space of Empire, there is no place of power—it is both everywhere and nowhere. Empire is an *ou-topia*, or really a non-place. (190; emphasis in original)

This passage, with its multiple debts both explicit and implicit—to Deleuze, to Foucault (the description is redolent with gestures to Deleuze's "diagram of Foucault" in *Foucault*), to Lefebvre, to Debord, among others—underlines the point that: "The modern dialectic of inside and outside has been replaced by a play of degrees and intensities, of hybridity and artificiality" (187–188). It seems that for this reason the postmodernist writers you are most enthusiastic about are those who have tried to apply the lessons of poststructuralism to international relations theory. Why do you think that there has been no correspondingly powerful critical insight achieved in other domains of theory?

**MH**: I do see the reconceptualization of space as a general project that is being pursued across various domains of theory. For example, the increasing importance of geography to theory more generally—the work of David Harvey, Edward Soja, and Doreen Massey come to mind—is perhaps a symptom of this renewed focus on space. But you may be right that this reconceptualization of space is often not recognized explicitly as such.

As is evident from the passage you cite, we try to capture the various ways in which space had been transformed in the transition from the modern to the postmodern, or the imperialist to the imperial, with the claim that "there is no more outside," by which we mean that the distinction between inside and outside becomes increasing less clear. (I had been intrigued by Fred Jameson's claim that in postmodernity there is no more nature, and this is one way of interpreting that.) It is perhaps most obvious, as you say, to examine our claim in the context in international relations, because one effect of the contemporary processes of globalization is to blur national boundaries, that is, to make less clear what should be situated inside and what outside the nation-state. This blurring clearly poses a challenge to the realist tradition of international relations theory because it makes reading the world scene as if state actors were the primary agents acting as individuals more and more implausible.

It is more challenging and perhaps more important to bring this observation down to the level of the subject itself. The claim that there is no more outside means here that identity and difference are no longer the adequate concepts for recognizing the constitution and interaction of subjects. But here too our claim is not particularly original. In fact, I consider this—the conception of the subject beyond the boundaries of identity and difference—one of the central propositions of queer theory in its best formulations. What is distinctive about our contribution in this regard, I think, is our proposal of a general framework that demonstrates the continuity among these different realms in which there is no more outside.

**TD**: This observation may be a key to understanding how the multitude is different from the masses. That is, it ties back to the explanation for the need for progressive forces to "get over" the nation-state.

**MH**: For us it is most important, first of all, to distinguish the concept of the multitude from that of the people. The people is a single identity, a representation or synthesis of the population, whereas the multitude is a multiplicity. The people cannot exist without the nation, and vice versa. On the other hand, the concept of the multitude is also different from that of the masses or the mob. The masses and the mob are most often used to name an irrational and passive social force, dangerous and violent because so easily manipulated. The multitude, in contrast, is an active social agent—a multiplicity that acts. It is in fact the foundation of all social creativity.

This may be relatively clear conceptually, but it is still not at all evident how to understand the multitude in social and sociological terms. This appears to us now as the most significant shortcoming of our book. After a theory of Empire, we now need to write a theory of the multitude. We have started to  work on this along two axes: first, the various recent theorizations of the body, particularly among feminist theorists, and second, the innovative forms of political organization that are emerging in the new social struggles around the world. I hope you can see how these two axes fit together. The multitude is not a body in the sense that Hobbes theorized the body politic; it is rather a corporeal assemblage that acts as a living multiplicity. But this is already a question of political organization. It may involve finding a way to set up a dialogue between these theoretical problematics on the one axis and the practical experiments on the other.

**TD**: I'm sure a lot of people will be looking forward to this next step. Thank you very much.

## Note

1. Antonio Negri was released from prison in the summer of 2003. He is now free with a passport.

## 8

Space

# The Repositioning of Citizenship: Emergent Subjects and Spaces for Politics

## Saskia Sassen

### Connections to *Empire*: Thoughts on Place, Scale, and Deterritorialization

One set of themes in *Empire*[1] concerns the formation of the multitude as a political subject. Of direct interest to the paper that follows this brief introduction are Hardt's and Negri's propositions about the new geographies constituted through the movements and mixing of the multitude and the latter's territorial reappropriations through these movements. A first step in the formation of political subjectivity is described by Hardt and Negri as the right of the multitude to govern its own movements and its appropriation of space; this is also a first step in the formation of global citizenship.

The authors insist throughout the volume that this political work, this forming of a political subject out of the multitude, needs to take place on the global scale: "Empire can be effectively contested only on its own level of generality and by pushing the processes that it offers past their present limitations . . ." (206). The multitude needs to "learn to think globally and act globally" because the Empire is a nonplace and because locality is likely to harken back to the old regressive categories of race, nation, religion. Empire is everywhere, in networks, in a space of communication that is deterritorialized. The multitude can become a political subject only if it also is global in its scale.

I want to argue that both Empire and the mobility and mixing of the multitudes can be constitutive of placeness and that the latter is one of the strategic sites for the formation of new political subjectivities. This is a type of place-ness that is partial, not totalizing, in that it is constructed as part of global networks and new geographies that cut across old divides of North and South. In my reading, there are several mentions in *Empire* that can be interpreted as accommodating at least some aspects of my argument, though I recognize immediately that the authors might disagree.

Indeed, to get from Hardt's and Negri's macro- and meta-analyses to my very particularized and microanalyses takes some conceptual acrobatics. It also means engaging some of the more lateral elements of their argument, ones that easily slip out of view in reading the volume. If I refer to my past work in this brief introduction, it is to emphasize the depth of my agreement with much of the argument and the extent to which I view the article that follows as a partial elaborating of a particular theme in *Empire*, even though at the time of writing this was not my purpose (hence this brief introduction).

A first issue concerns Hardt's and Negri's assertions about the need for the multitude to act globally because Empire is global. Let me start with a question: Can the global be conceived, constituted, and enacted only on the self-evident global scale? Or is the global actually multiscalar in that it can also be  constituted and engaged at the subnational scale—the locality, or particular national state institutions that may look national but have in fact ceased to be so? My answer to this question has long been that the global is multiscalar, and this has been one of my key foci for research. The work of capturing the multiscalar character of the global comes through in constructs such as that of the global city,[2] that of place-centered politics of the global that include noncosmopolitan forms of global,[3] and the denationalizing of particular state institutions and aspects of the work of states.[4]

The focus in the article that follows is on how the space of large cities, especially global cities, brings together two of the critical actors in today's world: on the one hand, global corporate capital and, on the other, those who are not fully at home in the modern nation-state (immigrants, internal minorities, discriminated groups, and postsocial subjects). Each of these two major, amalgamated actors finds in the space of the global city a strategic terrain for its political and economic operations. In this engagement, political subjectivities are formed. In some respects, the space of the global city illustrates one of the key dynamics identified by Hardt and Negri: the progressive lack of distinction between inside and outside which has important implications for the social production of subjectivity (195). The global city is a denationalized space where people from all over the world come together and claim-making is not confined to formal citizens.

Why the space of the global city is strategic and is so both for global corporate capital and for the multitude, in its political work of reappropriating space, engages a second set of themes in Hardt and Negri. They concern the features attributed to Empire: its diffuseness, its networked quality, its being a non-place, a deterritorialized space of communication. The multiscalar quality of the global entails two dynamics not necessarily developed or accommodated by the analysis in *Empire*; one of these is that global power, global control, global order and coordination, all need to be produced, designed, serviced, and so on, and that for various reasons I develop at length elsewhere, some of this work is place-bound and indeed reappropriates and reconstitutes urban space as strategic for Empire. Global cities are preeminent here. This is a partial condition, not an absolute or totalizing one. But it means that there is a reterritorializing of key components of the new global order—a fact evicted from mainstream accounts and also from most critical accounts about globalization today. Deterritorialization, space-time compression, and non-places are all features of the new order. But it takes a specific type of production regime (to use Hardt's and Negri's term) to produce these three features. Much mainstream and critical analysis misses this point. There are multiple references in Hardt and Negri to the importance of production. The new global order "would be merely a hollow husk if we were not to designate also a regime of production" (205). I do not think it is misplaced to include here the production of the capabilities for global control and operation, but the authors may well disagree.

Further, global cities also emerge as strategic for the multitude because they are major destinations for many of its segments, whether immigrants or internal minorities, because they become sites for the mixing of people from all over the world who are not likely to meet elsewhere, and, finally, but importantly, because they are venues for their minoritizing—one element in the shaping of political subjectivity across groups.

The joint presence of these two strategic types of actors partly shapes and is also shaped by an explosion of new types of segmentations internal to these cities. These cities are traversed and located on new geographies that cut across the old divides of North/South or center/periphery—which continue to exist as well, as part of older geographies of power and domination. These are geographies of centrality constituted through the movements of global capital and the recurrence of particular urban settings in a growing number of cities across the world—urban glamor zones and urban citadels for the new transnational global elite we find in New York and in Bombay, in Paris and in Shanghai. And they include new geographies of marginality constituted by migrations and the recurrence of certain patterns of poverty, exploitation, and segregation also in the cities of the global North—the "peripheralization at the core" as I put it in 1982 in one of my first articles.

Hardt and Negri in fact critique notions of South and North, First and Third World, core and periphery. They emphasize new global divisions and distributions of production, accumulation, and social forms; they observe that new international divisions and flows of labor and capital have fractured and multiplied, so that we can no longer demarcate these large geographical zones: "The geography of uneven development and the lines of division and hierarchy will no longer be found along stable national and international boundaries, but in fluid infra- and supranational borders" (335). And they speak of the new segmentations inside cities (336). But they do not seem to think that these are constructed geographies that are a form of placeness for the Empire and for the multitudes.

Hardt and Negri do allow for the fact that the type of place we might refer to as the local need not be regressive and that it can be a site for politics: "The concept of the local, however, need not be defined by isolation and purity. In fact, if one breaks down the walls that surround the local (and thereby separate the concept from race, religion, ethnicity, nation, and a people), one can link it directly to the universal" (262). There is also a recognition formulated rather clearly—at least once, that I could find—about something akin to what I call noncosmopolitan forms of global politics: "The concrete universal is what allows the multitude to pass from place to place and make its place its own. This is the common place of nomadism and miscegenation . . . the desire of the multitude is not the cosmo-political state but a common species . . ." (362). "An effective notion of postmodern republicanism will have to be constructed *au milieu*, on the basis of the lived experience of the global multitude" (210). But these elements are not part of the main body of the argument developed. I am thus picking up on a set of themes that are present but not elaborated.

One of my hypotheses, partly worked out in the paper that follows, is that in these types of cities we can detect emergent types of political subjects and political spaces. Their emergence is partly enabled by the destabilization of key elements in nation-based politico-legal architectures, a result of what Hardt and Negri call the "new global order."

While subjectivity is crucial in Hardt's and Negri's analysis, the concrete and particularized mediation of places such as global cities is not. They have much to say on subjectivity. "History has a logic only when subjectivity rules it, only when (as Nietzsche says) the emergence of subjectivity reconfigures efficient causes and final causes in the development of history. The power of the proletariat consists precisely in this" (235). And they also recognize the need for theorization to get at this:

> We still need to identify, however, a theoretical schema that can sustain us in this inquiry. The old analyses of imperialism will not be sufficient here because in the end they stop at the threshold of the analysis of subjectivity and concentrate rather on the contradictions of capital's own development. We need to identify a theoretical schema that puts the subjectivity of the social movements of the pro-

letariat at center stage in the processes of globalization and the constitution of global order. (235)

The way in which place is constructed in the global city—its strategic character for both the Empire and the multitude, its location on the new cross-border geographies of centrality and marginality—makes it a mediated space. That is to say, it is a space where complex national legal architectures (i.e., the formal institution of citizenship) and global dynamics (global capital, migrations, minoritization) get instantiated. But placeness does not seem to figure in Hardt's and Negri's analysis of political subjectivity: "Having achieved the global level, capitalist development is faced directly with the multitude, without mediation."

I should say that in emphasizing this particular type of mediation that is the global city, I do not mean to disagree with Hardt's and Negri's proposition about the relocation of state power to the global level. Hardt and Negri indicate how easy it is to think that we are seeing the end of nation-states and constitutional order but that actually the constitutional functions have been displaced to another level: power is constitutionalized on a supranational level (309). I have myself made this argument by saying that sovereignty, far from disappearing, has been partly denationalized, dislodged from the national state and relocated to the supranational level and to new forms of private authority.[5] But I also think that the multiscalar character of the global means that also subnational levels are instantiating the global.

Hardt and Negri do ask about the where of politics: "Our ultimate objective in this analysis of the constitutional process and figures of Empire is to recognize the terrain on which contestation and alternatives might emerge. In Empire, as indeed was also the case in modern and ancient regimes, the constitution itself is a site of struggle, but today the nature of that site and that struggle is by no means clear" (319). But this question is not at the heart of the conceptual architecture they produce. The microstructurations in the formal and lived experience of citizenship analyzed in the paper below might contribute to the specification of one partial element in its answer.

## Introduction

Most of the scholarship on citizenship has claimed a necessary connection to the national state. The transformations afoot today raise questions about this proposition, insofar as they significantly alter those conditions that in the past fed the articulation between citizenship and the national state. The context for this possible alteration is defined by two major, partly interconnected conditions. One is the change in the position and institutional features of national states since the 1980s, resulting from various forms of globalization. These

range from economic privatization and deregulation to the increased promi-
nence of the international human rights regime. The second is the emergence
of multiple actors, groups, and communities partly strengthened by these
transformations in the state and increasingly unwilling automatically to identify with a nation as represented by the state.

Addressing the question of citizenship against these transformations
entails a specific stance. It is quite possible to posit that at the most abstract or
formal level not much has changed over the last century in the essential features of citizenship. The theoretical ground from which I address the issue is
that of the historicity and the embeddedness of both categories, citizenship
and the national state, rather than their purely formal features. Each of these
has been constructed in elaborate and formal ways. And each has evolved historically as a tightly packaged bundle of what were in fact often rather diverse
elements. The dynamics at work today are destabilizing these particular
bundlings and bringing to the fore the fact itself of that bundling and its particularity. Through their destabilizing effects, these dynamics are producing
operational and rhetorical openings for the emergence of new types of political subjects and new spatialities for politics.

More broadly, the destabilizing of national state-centered hierarchies of
legitimate power and allegiance has enabled a multiplication of nonformalized
or only partly formalized political dynamics and actors. These signal a deterritorializing of citizenship practices and identities and of discourses about loyalty and allegiance. Finally, specific transformations inside the national state
have directly and indirectly altered particular features of the institution of citizenship. These transformations are not predicated necessarily on deterritorialization or locations for the institution outside the national state as is key to
conceptions of postnational citizenship and hence are usefully distinguished
from current notions of postnational citizenship. I will refer to these as denationalized forms of citizenship.

Analytically, I seek to understand how various transformations entail continuities or discontinuities in the basic institutional form. That is to say, where
do we see continuities in the formal bundle of rights at the heart of the institution and where do we see movement towards postnational and/or denationalized features of citizenship? And where might as-yet-informal citizenship
practices engender formalizations of new types of rights? Particular attention
goes to several specific issues that capture these features. One of these is the
relationship between citizenship and nationality and the evolution of the latter
towards something akin to "effective" nationality rather than as "allegiance" to
one state or exclusively formal nationality. A later section examines the mix of
distinct elements that actually make up the category of citizenship in today's
highly developed countries. Far from being a unitary category or a mere legal

status, these diverse elements can be contradictory. One of my assumptions here is that the destabilizing impact of globalization contributes to accentuate the distinctiveness of each of these elements. A case in point is the growing tension between the legal form and the normative project towards enhanced inclusion, as various minorities and disadvantaged sectors gain visibility for their claim-making. Critical here is the failure in most countries to achieve "equal" citizenship—that is, not just a formal status but an enabling condition.

The remaining sections begin to theorize these issues with a view towards specifying incipient and typically not formalized developments in the institution of citizenship. Informal practices and political subjects not quite fully recognized as such can nonetheless function as part of the political landscape. Undocumented immigrants who are long-term residents engage in practices that are the same as those of formally defined citizens in the routines of daily life; this produces an informal social contract between these undocumented immigrants and the community. Subjects who are by definition categorized as nonpolitical, such as "housewives," may actually have considerable political agency and be emergent political subjects. Insofar as citizenship is at least partly shaped by the conditions within which it is embedded, conditions that have today changed in certain very specific and also general ways, we may well be seeing a corresponding set of changes in the institution itself. These may not yet be formalized, and some may never become fully formalized. Further, social constructions that mark individuals, such as race and ethnicity, may well become destabilized by these developments in both the institution of citizenship and the nation-state. Generally, the analysis in this paper suggests that we might see an unbounding of existing types of subjects, particularly dominant ones such as the citizen-subject, the alien, and the racialized subject.

A concluding section argues that many of these transformations in the broader context and in the institution itself become legible in today's large cities. Perhaps the most evolved type of site for these transformations is the global city.[6] In this process, the global city is reconfigured as a partly denationalized space that enables a partial reinvention of citizenship. This reinvention takes the institution away from questions of nationality narrowly defined and toward the enactment of a large array of particular interests, from protests against police brutality and globalization to sexual preference politics and house-squatting by anarchists. I interpret this as a move towards citizenship practices that revolve around claiming rights to the city. These are not exclusively or necessarily urban practices. But it is especially in large cities that we see simultaneously some of the most extreme inequalities as well as conditions enabling these citizenship practices. In global cities, these practices also contain the possibility of directly engaging strategic forms of power, a fact that I interpret as significant in a context where power is increasingly privatized, globalized, and elusive.

## Citizenship and Nationality

In its narrowest definition, citizenship describes the legal relationship between the individual and the polity. This relation can in principle assume many forms, in good part depending on the definition of the polity. Hence, in Europe this definition of the polity was originally the city, both in ancient and in medieval times. But it is the evolution of polities along the lines of state formation that gave citizenship in the West its full institutionalized and formalized character and that made nationality a key component of citizenship.

Today the terms "citizenship" and "nationality" both refer to the national state. In a technical legal sense, while essentially the same concept, each term reflects a different legal framework. Both identify the legal status of an individual in terms of state membership. But citizenship is largely confined to the national dimension, while nationality refers to the international legal dimension in the context of an interstate system. The legal status entails the specifics of whom the state recognizes as a citizen and the formal basis for the rights and responsibilities of the individual in relation to the state. International law affirms that each state may determine who will be considered a citizen of that state (see the Hague Convention, 1954).[7] Domestic laws about who is a citizen vary significantly across states, and so do the definitions of what it entails to be a citizen. Even within Europe, let alone worldwide, there are marked differences in how citizenship is articulated and hence how noncitizens are defined.

The aggressive nationalism and territorial competition among European states in the eighteenth, nineteenth, and well into the twentieth centuries made the concept of dual nationality generally undesirable, incompatible with individual loyalties and destabilizing of the international order. Absolute state authority over a territory and its nationals could not easily accommodate dual nationality. Indeed, we see the development of a series of mechanisms aimed at preventing or counteracting the common causes for dual nationality.[8] This negative perception of dual nationality continued into the first half of the twentieth century and well into the 1960s. There were no international accords on dual nationality. The main effort by the international system remained rooting out the causes of dual nationality by means of multilateral codification of the law on the subject.[9] It is probably the case that this particular form of the institution of citizenship, centered on exclusive allegiance, reached its high point in the twentieth century.

The major transformations of the 1980s and 1990s have once again brought conditions for a change in the institution of citizenship and its relation to nationality, and they have brought about changes in the legal content of nationality. Mostly minor formal and nonformal changes are beginning to dilute the particular formalization coming out of European history. The long-lasting resistance to dual or multiple nationalities is shifting towards a selective acceptance. According to some legal scholars,[10] in the future dual and multiple nationalities will become the norm. Today, more people than ever before have dual nationality.[11] Insofar as the importance of nationality is a function of the central role of states in the international system, it is quite possible that a decline in the importance of this role and a proliferation of other actors will affect the value of nationality.

These transformations may give citizenship yet another set of features as it continues to respond to the conditions within which it is embedded.[12] The nationalizing of the institution, which took place over the last several centuries, may today give way to a partial denationalizing. A fundamental dynamic in this regard is the growing articulation of national economies with the global economy and the associated pressures on states to be competitive. Crucial to current notions of competitive states is withdrawal from various spheres of citizenship entitlements, with the possibility of a corresponding dilution of loyalty to the state. Citizens' loyalty may in turn be less crucial to the state today than it was at a time of people-intensive and frequent warfare, with its need for loyal citizen-soldiers.[13] Masses of troops today can be replaced by technologically intensive methods of warfare. Most importantly, in the highly developed world, warfare has become less significant partly due to economic globalization. Global firms and global markets do not want the rich countries to fight wars among themselves. The "international" project of the most powerful actors on the world stage today is radically different from what it was in the nineteenth and first half of the twentieth centuries.

Many of the dynamics that built economies, polities, and societies in the nineteenth and twentieth centuries contained an articulation between the national scale and the growth of entitlements for citizens. During industrialization, class formation, class struggles, and the advantages of both employers and workers tended to scale at the national level and became identified with state-produced legislation and regulations, entitlements, and obligations. The state came to be seen as a key to ensuring the well-being of significant portions of both the working class and the bourgeoisie. The development of welfare states in the twentieth century became a crucial institutional domain for granting entitlements to the poor and the disadvantaged. Today, the growing weight given to notions of the "competitiveness" of states puts pressure on states to cut down on these entitlements. This in turn weakens the reciprocal relationship between the poor and the state.[14] Finally, the growth of unemployment and the fact that many of the young are developing weak ties to the labor market, once thought of as a crucial mechanism for the socialization of young adults, will further weaken the loyalty and sense of reciprocity between these future adults and the state.[15]

As these trends have come together toward the end of the twentieth century, they are contributing to destabilizing the meaning of citizenship as it was forged in the nineteenth and much of the twentieth centuries. Economic policies and technical developments we associate with economic globalization have strengthened the importance of cross-border dynamics and reduced that of borders. The associated emphasis on markets has brought into question the foundations of the welfare state. T. H. Marshall[16] and many others saw and continue to see the welfare state as an important ingredient of social citizenship. Today the assumptions of the dominant model of Marshallian citizenship have been severely diluted under the impact of globalization and the ascendance of the market as the preferred mechanism for addressing these social issues. For many critics, the reliance on markets to solve political and social problems is a savage attack on the principles of citizenship. Thus Peter Saunders argues that citizenship inscribed in the institutions of the welfare state is a buffer against the vagaries of the market and the inequalities of the class system.[17]

The nature of citizenship has also been challenged by a proliferation of old issues that have gained new attention. Among the latter are the question of state membership of aboriginal communities, stateless people, and refugees.[18] All of these have important implications for human rights in relation to citizenship. These social changes in the role of the state, the impact of globalization on states, and the relationship between dominant and subordinate groups also have major implications for questions of identity. "Is citizenship a useful concept for exploring the problems of belonging, identity and personality in the modern world?"[19] Can such a radical change in the conditions for citizenship leave the institution itself unchanged?

## Deconstructing Citizenship

Though often talked about as a single concept and experienced as a unitary institution, citizenship actually describes a number of discrete but related aspects in the relation between the individual and the polity. Current developments are bringing to light and accentuating the distinctiveness of these various aspects, from formal rights to practices and psychological dimensions.[20] They make legible the tension between citizenship as a formal legal status and as a normative project or an aspiration. The formal equality granted to all citizens rarely rests on the need for substantive equality in social and even political terms. In brief, current conditions have strengthened the emphasis on rights and aspirations that go beyond the formal legal definition of rights and obligations.

This is mirrored most recently in the reinvigoration of theoretical distinctions: communitarian and deliberative, republican and liberal, feminist, postnational, and cosmopolitan notions of citizenship. Insofar as citizenship is a status that articulates legal rights and responsibilities, the mechanisms through which this articulation is shaped and implemented can be analytically distinguished from the status itself, and so can the content of the rights. In the medieval cities so admired by Max Weber,[21] it was urban residents themselves who set up the structures through which to establish and thicken their rights in the space of the city. Today it is the national state that provides these mechanisms, and it does so for national political space. But these mechanisms may well be changing once again, given globalization, the associated changes in the national state, and the ascendance of human rights. In each of these major phases, the actual content and shape of the legal rights and obligations also changed.

Some of these issues can be illustrated through the evolution of equal citizenship over the last few decades. Equal citizenship is central to the modern institution of citizenship. The expansion of equality among citizens has shaped a good part of its evolution in the twentieth century. There is debate as to what brought about the expanded inclusions over this period, most notably the granting of the vote to women. For some,[22] it is law itself—and national law—that has been crucial in promoting recognition of exclusions and measures for their elimination. For others,[23] politics and identity have been essential because they provide the sense of solidarity necessary for the further development of modern citizenship in the nation-state. Either way, insofar as equality is based on membership, citizenship status forms the basis of an exclusive politics and identity.[24]

In a country such as the United States, the principle of equal citizenship remains unfulfilled, even after the successful struggles and legal advances of the last five decades.[25] Groups defined by race, ethnicity, religion, sex, sexual orientation, and other "identities" still face various exclusions from full participation in public life, notwithstanding formal equality as citizens. Second, because full participation as a citizen rests on a material base,[26] poverty excludes large sectors of the population, and the gap is widening. Feminist and race-critical scholarship have highlighted the failure of gender- and race-neutral conceptions of citizenship such as legal status to account for the differences of individuals within communities.[27] In brief, legal citizenship does not always bring full and equal membership rights. Citizenship is affected by the position of different groups within a nation-state.

Yet it is precisely the position of these different groups that has engendered the practices and struggles that forced changes in the institution of citizenship itself. Thus Kenneth Karst observes that in the United States it was national law that "braided the strands of citizenship"—formal legal status, rights, belonging—into the principle of equal citizenship.[28] This took place through a series of Supreme Court decisions and acts of Congress, beginning with the Civil Rights Act of 1964. Karst emphasizes how important these constitutional and legislative instruments are and that we cannot take citizenship for granted or be complacent about it.

There are two aspects here that matter for my argument. This history of interactions between differential positionings and expanded inclusions signals the possibility that the new conditions of inequality and difference evident today and the new types of claim-making they produce may well bring about further transformations in the institution. Citizenship is partly produced by the practices of the excluded. Secondly, by expanding the formal inclusionary aspect of citizenship, the national state contributed to create some of the conditions that would eventually facilitate key aspects of postnational citizenship. At the same time, insofar as the state itself has undergone significant transformation, notably the changes bundled under the notion of the competitive state, it may reduce the chances that state institutions will do the type of legislative and judiciary work that has led to expanded formal inclusions.

The consequence of these two developments may well be the absence of a lineal progression in the evolution of the institution. The expanding inclusions that we have seen in the United States since the 1960s may have produced conditions that make possible forms of citizenship that follow a different trajectory. Furthermore, the pressures of globalization on national states may mean that claim-making will increasingly be directed at other institutions as well. This is already evident in a variety of instances. One example is the decision by First Nation people to go directly to the UN and claim direct representation in international fora rather than going through the national state. It is also evident in the increasingly institutionalized framework of the international human rights regime and the emergent possibilities for bypassing unilateral state sovereignty.

*[handwritten margin note: yet they also often return to the national state]*

As the importance of equality in citizenship has grown and become more visible, and as the role of national law in giving presence and voice to hitherto-silenced minorities has grown, the tension between the formal status and the normative project of citizenship has also grown. For many, citizenship is becoming a normative project whereby social membership becomes increasingly comprehensive and open-ended. Globalization and human rights are further enabling this tension and thereby furthering the elements of a new discourse on rights. These developments signal that the analytic terrain within which we need to place the question of rights, authority, and obligations is shifting.[29] Some of these issues can be illustrated by two contrasting cases described below.

## Toward Effective Nationality and Informal Citizenship

### 1. Unauthorized yet Recognized

Perhaps one of the more extreme instances of a condition akin to effective, as opposed to formal, nationality is what has been called the informal social contract that binds undocumented immigrants to their communities of residence.[30] Hence, unauthorized immigrants who demonstrate civic involvement, social deservedness, and national loyalty can argue that they merit legal residency. To make this brief examination more specific, I will focus on one case, undocumented immigrants in the United States.

Individuals, even when undocumented immigrants, can move between the multiple meanings of citizenship. The daily practices by undocumented immigrants as part of their daily life in the community where they reside—such as raising families, schooling children, holding a job—earn them citizenship claims in the United States even as the formal status and, more narrowly, legalization may continue to evade them. There are dimensions of citizenship, such as strong community ties and participation in civic activities, which are being enacted informally through these practices. These practices produce at least a partial recognition of them as full social beings. In many countries around the world, including the United States, long-term undocumented residents can often gain legal residence if they can document the fact of this long-term residence and "good conduct." U.S. immigration law recognizes such informal participation as grounds for granting legal residency. For instance, prior to the new immigration law passed in 1996, individuals who could prove seven years of continuous presence, good moral character, and that deportation would be an extreme hardship were eligible for suspension of deportation, and hence for U.S. residency. NACARA extended the eligibility of this suspension of deportation to some 300,000 Salvadorans and Guatemalans who were unauthorized residents in the United States.[31]

The case of undocumented immigrants is in many ways a very particular and special illustration of a condition akin to "effective" citizenship and nationality. One way of interpreting this dynamic in the light of the discussion in the preceding sections is to emphasize that it is the fact of the multiple dimensions of citizenship that engenders strategies for legitimizing informal or extrastatal forms of membership.[32] The practices of these undocumented immigrants are a form of citizenship practices, and their identities as members of a community of residence assume some of the features of citizenship identities. Supposedly this could hold even in the communitarian model, where the community can decide on whom to admit and whom to exclude, but once they are admitted, proper civic practices earn full membership.

Further, the practices of migrants, even if undocumented, can contribute to recognition of their rights in countries of origin. During the 1981-to-1992 civil war, Salvadoran migrants, even though citizens of El Salvador, were directly and indirectly excluded from El Salvador through political violence, enormous economic hardship, and direct persecution.[33] They could not enjoy their rights as citizens. After fleeing, many continued to provide support to their families and communities. Further, migrants' remittances became a key factor in El Salvador's economy—as they are for several countries around the world. The government of El Salvador actually began to support the emigrants fight to get residency rights in the United States, even joining U.S.-based activist organizations in this effort. The Salvadoran government was thus supporting Salvadorans who were the formerly excluded citizens—they needed those remittances to keep coming and they needed the emigrants to stay out of the Salvadoran workforce, given high unemployment. Thus the participation of these undocumented migrants in cross-border community, family, and political networks has contributed to increasing recognition of their legal and political rights as Salvadoran citizens.[34]

According to Coutin[35] and others, movements between membership and exclusion and between different dimensions of citizenship, legitimacy, and illegitimacy may be as important as redefinitions of citizenship itself. Given scarce resources, the possibility of negotiating the different dimensions of citizenship may well represent an important enabling condition. Undocumented immigrants develop informal, covert, often extrastatal strategies and networks connecting them with communities in sending countries. Hometowns rely on their remittances and their information about jobs in the United States. Sending remittances illegally by an unauthorized immigrant can be seen as an act of patriotism, and working as an undocumented immigrant can be seen as contributing to the host economy. Multiple interdependencies are thereby established, and grounds for claims on the receiving and the originating country can be established even when the immigrants are undocumented and laws are broken.[36]

## 2. Authorized yet Unrecognized

At perhaps the other extreme from the undocumented immigrant whose practices allow her to become accepted as a member of the political community is the case of those who are full citizens yet are not recognized as political subjects. In an enormously insightful study of Japanese housewives, Robin LeBlanc finds precisely this combination.[37]

Being a housewife is basically a full-time occupation in Japan and restricts Japanese women's public life in many important ways, both practical and symbolical. A "housewife" in Japan is a person whose very identity is customarily that of a particularistic, nonpolitical actor. Yet, paradoxically, it is also a condition providing these women with a unique vehicle for other forms of public participation, ones where being a housewife is an advantage, one denied to those who might have the qualifications of higher-level political life. LeBlanc documents how the housewife has an advantage in the world of local politics or the political life of a local area: she can be trusted precisely because she is a housewife, she can build networks with other housewives, hers is the image of desirable public concern and of a powerful—because believable—critic of mainstream politics.

There is something extremely important in this condition that is shared with women in other cultures and vis-à-vis different issues. For instance, and in a very different register, women emerged as a specific type of political actor during the brutal dictatorships of the 1970s and 1980s in several countries of Latin America. It was precisely their condition as mothers and wives that gave them the clarity and the courage to demand justice and to demand bread, and to do so confronting armed soldiers and policemen. Mothers in the barrios of Santiago during Pinochet's dictatorship, the mothers of the Plaza de Mayo in Buenos Aires, the mothers regularly demonstrating in front of the major prisons in El Salvador during the civil war—all were driven to political action by their despair at the loss of children and husbands and the struggle to provide food in their homes.

Further, and in a very different type of situation, there is an interesting parallel between LeBlanc's capturing of the political in the condition of the housewife and a set of findings in some of the research on immigrant women in the United States. There is growing evidence that immigrant women are more likely than immigrant men to emerge as actors in the public domain precisely because of their responsibilities in the household. Regular wagework and improved access to other public realms has an impact on their culturally specified subordinate role to men in the household. Immigrant women gain greater personal autonomy and independence while immigrant men lose ground compared to their condition in cultures of origin. Women gain more control over budgeting and other domestic decisions and greater leverage in requesting help from men in domestic chores. Their responsibility for securing public services and other public resources for their families gives them a chance to become incorporated in the mainstream society—they are often the ones in the household who mediate in this process.[38] It is likely that some women benefit more than others from these circumstances; we need more research to establish the impact of class, education, and income on these gendered outcomes.

Besides the relatively greater empowerment of immigrant women in the household associated with waged employment, what matters here is their greater participation in the public sphere and their possible emergence as public actors. There are two arenas where immigrant women are active: institutions for public and private assistance, and the immigrant or ethnic community. The incorporation of women in the migration process strengthens the settlement likelihood and contributes to greater immigrant participation in their communities and vis-à-vis the state. For instance, Pierrette Hondagneu-Sotelo found that immigrant women come to assume more active public and social roles, which further reinforces their status in the household and the settlement process.[39] These immigrant women are more active in community-building and community activism and they are positioned differently from men regarding the broader economy and the state. They are the ones who are likely to have to handle the legal vulnerability of their families in the process of seeking public and social services for their families. This greater participation by women suggests the possibility that they may emerge as more forceful and visible actors and that this may make their role in the labor market more visible as well.[40]

These are dimensions of citizenship and citizenship practices that do not fit the indicators and categories of mainstream frameworks for understanding citizenship and political life. Women in the condition of housewives and mothers do not fit the categories and indicators used to capture participation in political life. Feminist scholarship in all the social sciences has had to deal with a set of similar or equivalent difficulties and tensions in its effort to constitute its subject or to reconfigure a subject that has been flattened. The theoretical and empirical distance that has to be bridged between the recognized world of politics and the as-yet-unmapped experience of citizenship of the housewife— not of women as such, but of women as housewives—is a distance we encounter in many types of inquiry. Bridging this distance requires specific forms of empirical research and of theorization.

## Postnational or Denationalized?

From the perspective of nation-based citizenship theory, some of these transformations might be interpreted as a decline or devaluation of citizenship or, more favorably, as a displacement of citizenship in the face of other forms of collective organization and affiliation, as yet unnamed.[41] Insofar as citizenship is theorized as necessarily national,[42] by definition these new developments cannot be captured in the language of citizenship.[43] An alternative interpretation would be to suspend the national, as in postnational conceptions, and to posit that the issue of where citizenship is enacted is one to be determined in light of developing social practice.[44]

From where I look at these issues, there is a third possibility beyond these two. It is that citizenship—even if situated in institutional settings that are "national"—is a possibly changed institution if the meaning of the national itself has changed. That is to say, insofar as globalization has changed certain features of the territorial and institutional organization of the political power and authority of the state, the institution of citizenship—its formal rights, its practices, its psychological dimension—has also been transformed even when it remains centered in the national state. I have argued, for instance, that this territorial and institutional transformation of state power and authority has produced operational, conceptual, and rhetorical openings for nation-based subjects other than the national state to emerge as legitimate actors in international and global arenas that used to be exclusive to the state.[45]

I distinguish what I would narrowly define as denationalized from postnational citizenship, the latter being the term most commonly used and the only one used in the broader debate.[46] In my reading, we are dealing with two distinct dynamics rather than only the emergence of locations for citizenship outside the frame of the national state. Their difference is a question of scope and institutional embeddedness. The understanding in the scholarship is that postnational citizenship is located partly outside the confines of the national. In considering denationalization, the focus moves on to the transformation of the national, including the national in its condition as foundational for citizenship. Hence it could be argued that postnationalism and denationalization represent two different trajectories. Both are viable, and they do not exclude each other.

The national, then, remains a referent in my work.[47] But clearly, it is a referent of a specific sort; it is, after all, its change that becomes the key theoretical feature through which it enters my specification of changes in the institution of citizenship. Whether or not this devalues citizenship[48] is not immediately evident to me at this point. Citizenship has undergone many transformations in its history precisely because it is, to variable extents, embedded in the specifics of each of its eras.[49] Significant to my argument here is also the fact discussed earlier about the importance of national law in the process of expanding inclusions, inclusions that today are destabilizing older notions of citizenship. This pluralized meaning of citizenship partly produced by the formal expansions of the legal status of citizenship is today contributing to exploding the boundaries of that legal status even further.

First, and most important in my reading is the strengthening, including the constitutionalizing, of civil rights that allow citizens to make claims against their states and allow them to invoke a measure of autonomy in the formal political arena that can be read as a lengthening distance between the formal apparatus of the state and the institution of citizenship. The implications, both political and theoretical, of this dimension are complex and in the making; we cannot tell what will be the practices and rhetorics that might be invented.

Second, I add to this the granting by national states of a whole range of "rights" to foreign actors, largely and especially economic actors—foreign firms, foreign investors, international markets, foreign businesspeople.[50] Admittedly, this is not a common way of framing the issue. It comes out of my particular perspective about the impact of globalization and denationalization on the national state, including the impact on the relation between the state and its own citizens, and the state and foreign economic actors. I see this as a significant though not much recognized development in the history of claim-making. For me the question as to how citizens should handle these new concentrations of power and "legitimacy" that attach to global firms and markets is a key to the future of democracy. My efforts to detect the extent to which the global is embedded and filtered through the national[51] is one way of understanding whether therein lies a possibility for citizens, still largely confined to national institutions, to demand accountability of global economic actors through national institutional channels rather than having to wait for a "global" state.

## Citizenship in the Global City

The particular transformations in the understanding and theorization of citizenship discussed thus far bring us back to some of the earlier historical formations around questions of citizenship, most prominently the crucial role played by cities and civil society. The large city of today, most especially the global city, emerges as a strategic site for these new types of operations. It is one of the nexuses where the formation of new claims materializes and assumes concrete forms. The loss of power at the national level produces the possibility for new forms of power and politics at the subnational level. The national as container of social process and power is cracked. This cracked casing opens up possibilities for a geography of politics that links subnational spaces. Cities are foremost in this new geography. One question this engenders is how and whether we are seeing the formation of new types of politics that localize in these cities.

If we consider that large cities concentrate both the leading sectors of global capital and a growing share of disadvantaged populations—immigrants, many of the disadvantaged women, people of color generally, and, in the megacities of developing countries, masses of shanty dwellers—then we can see that cities have become a strategic terrain for a whole series of conflicts and contradictions. We can then think of cities also as one of the sites for the contradictions of the globalization of capital, even though, heeding Ira Katznelson's observation, the city cannot be reduced to this dynamic.[52] Recovering cities along these lines means recovering the multiplicity of presences in this landscape. The large city of today has emerged as a strategic site for a whole range of new types of operations—political, economic, cultural, subjective.[53]

Although citizenship originated in cities, and cities played an important role in its evolution, I do not think we can simply read some of these current developments as a return to that older historical condition. The significance of the city today as a setting for engendering new types of citizenship practices and new types of incompletely formalized political subjects does not derive from that history. Nor does current local city government have much to do with earlier notions of citizenship and democracy described for ancient and medieval cities in Europe.[54] It is, rather, more connected to what Henri Lefebvre was capturing when describing the city as oeuvre and hence the importance of agency.[55] Where Lefebvre found this agency in the working class in the Paris of the twentieth century, I find it in two strategic actors—global corporate capital and immigration—in today's global cities. Here I would like to return to the fact of the embeddedness of the institution of citizenship.

What is being engendered today in terms of citizenship practices in the global city is quite different from what it might have been in the medieval city of Weber. In the medieval city, we see a set of practices that allowed the burghers to set up systems for owning and protecting property and to implement various immunities against despots of all sorts.[56] Today's citizenship practices have to do with the production of "presence" of those without power and a politics that claims rights to the city. What the two situations share is the notion that through these practices new forms of citizenship are being constituted and that the city is a key site for this type of political work and is, indeed, partly constituted through these dynamics. After the long historical phase that saw the ascendance of the national state and the scaling of key economic dynamics at the national level, the city is once again today a scale for strategic economic and political dynamics.

In his effort to specify the ideal-typical features of what constitutes the city, Weber sought out a certain type of city—most prominently the cities of the late Middle Ages rather than the modern industrial cities of his time. Weber sought a kind of city that combined conditions and dynamics that forced its residents and leaders into creative, innovative responses and adaptations. Further, he posited that these changes produced in the context of the city signaled transformations that went beyond the city, that could have a far reach in instituting often fundamental transformations. In that regard the city offered the possibility of understanding far-reaching changes that could—under certain conditions—eventually encompass society at large.

There are two aspects of Weber's *The City* that are of particular importance here. Weber sought to understand under what conditions cities can be positive and creative influences on people's lives. For Weber, cities are a set of social structures that encourage social individuality and innovation and hence are an instrument of historical change. There is in this intellectual project a deep sense of the historicity of these conditions. For Weber, modern urban life did not correspond to this positive and creative power of cities; Weber saw modern cities as dominated by large factories and office bureaucracies. My own reading of the Fordist city corresponds in many ways to Weber's in the sense that the strategic scale under Fordism is the national scale, and cities lose significance. It is the large Fordist factory and the mines that emerge as key sites for the political work of the disadvantaged and those without power.

For Weber, it is particularly the cities of the late Middle Ages that combine the conditions that pushed urban residents, merchants, artisans, and leaders to address them and deal with them. These transformations could make for epochal change beyond the city itself; Weber shows us how, in many of these cities, these struggles led to the creation of the elements of what we could call governance systems and citizenship. In this regard, struggles around political, economic, legal, and cultural issues that are centered in the realities of cities can become the catalysts for new transurban developments in all these institutional domains: markets, participatory governance, rights for members of the urban community regardless of lineage, judicial recourse, cultures of engagement and deliberation.

The particular analytic element I want to extricate from this aspect of Weber's understanding and theorization of the city is the historicity of those conditions that make cities strategic sites for the enactment of important transformations in multiple institutional domains. Elsewhere I have developed the argument that today a certain type of city—the global city—has emerged as a strategic site precisely for such innovations and transformations in multiple institutional domains.[57] Several of the key components of economic globalization and digitization instantiate in this type of city and produce dislocations and destabilizations of existing institutional orders and legal, regulatory, and normative frames for handling urban conditions. It is the high level of concentration of these new dynamics in these cities that forces creative responses and innovations. There is most probably a threshold effect at work here.

The historicity of this process rests in the fact that under Keynesian policies, particularly the Fordist contract, and the dominance of mass manufacturing as the organizing economic dynamic, cities had lost strategic functions and were not the site for creative institutional innovations. The strategic sites were the large factory and the whole process of mass manufacturing and mass consumer markets, and, second, the national government, where regulatory frameworks were developed and the Fordist contract instituted. The factory and the government were the strategic sites where the crucial dynamics producing the major institutional innovations of the epoch were located. With globalization and digitization—and all the specific elements they entail—global cities emerge as such strategic sites. While the strategic transformations are sharply concentrated in global cities, many of the transformations are also enacted, besides being diffused, in cities at lower orders of national urban hierarchies. Furthermore, in my reading, particular institutions of the state also are such strategic sites even as there is an overall shrinking of state authority through deregulation and privatization.

A second analytic element I want to extricate from Weber's *The City* is the particular type of embeddedness of the transformations he describes and renders as ideal-typical features. This is not an embeddedness in what we might think of as deep structures, because the latter are precisely the ones that are being dislocated or changed and are creating openings for new fundamental arrangements to emerge. The embeddedness is, rather, in very specific conditions, opportunities, constraints, needs, interactions, contestations, interests. The aspect that matters here is the complexity, detail, and social thickness of the particular conditions and the dynamics he identifies as enabling change and innovation. This complexity and thickness also produce ambiguities in the meaning of the changes and innovations. It is not always clear whether they are positive—where we might interpret positive as meaning the creation or strengthening of some element, even if very partial or minor, of participatory democracy in the city—and in what time frame their positiveness would become evident. In those cities of the late Middle Ages he saw as being what the city is about, he finds contradictory and multivalent innovations. He dissects these innovations to understand what they can produce or launch.

The argument I derive from this particular type of embeddedness of change and innovation is that current conditions in global cities are creating not only new structurations of power but also operational and rhetorical openings for new types of political actors that may have been submerged, invisible, or without voice. A key element of the argument here is that the localization of strategic components of globalization in these cities means that the disadvantaged can engage the new forms of globalized corporate power, and second, that the growing numbers and diversity of the disadvantaged in these cities under these conditions assume a distinctive "presence." This entails a distinction between powerlessness and invisibility or impotence. The disadvantaged in global cities can gain "presence" in their engagement with power but also vis-à-vis each other. This is different from the 1950s-to-1970s period in the United States, for instance, when "white flight" and the significant departure of major corporate headquarters left cities hollowed out and the disadvantaged in a condition of abandonment. Today, the localization of the global creates a set of objective conditions of engagement. This can be seen, for example, in the struggles against gentrification—which encroaches on minority and disadvantaged neighborhoods and led to growing numbers of homeless beginning in the 1980s—and the struggles for the rights of the homeless, and also in demonstrations against police brutalizing minority people. These struggles are different from the ghetto uprisings of the 1960s, which were short, intense eruptions confined to the ghettos and causing most of the damage in the neighborhoods of the disadvantaged themselves. In these ghetto uprisings there was no engagement with power.

The conditions that today mark the possibility of cities as strategic sites are basically two, and both capture major transformations that are destabilizing older systems organizing territory and politics. One of these is the rescaling of what are the strategic territories that articulate the new political-economic system. The other is the partial unbundling or at least weakening of the national as container of social process due to the variety of dynamics encompassed by globalization and digitization. The consequences for cities of these two conditions are many: what matters here is that cities emerge as strategic sites for major economic processes and for new types of political actors. Insofar as citizenship is embedded and in turn marked by its embeddedness, these new conditions may well signal the possibility of new forms of citizenship practices and identities.

There is something to be captured here—a distinction between powerlessness and the condition of being an actor even though lacking power. I use the term "presence" to name this condition. In the context of a strategic space such as the global city, the types of disadvantaged people described here are not simply marginal; they acquire presence in a broader political process that escapes the boundaries of the formal polity. This presence signals the possibility of a politics. What this politics will be will depend on the specific projects and practices of various communities. Insofar as the sense of membership of these communities is not subsumed under the national, it may well signal the possibility of a politics that, while transnational, is actually centered in concrete localities.

## Acknowledgments

The article that follows this introductory note is based on my keynote lecture from the March 7, 2002, conference of the *Berkeley Journal of Sociology*, "Race and Ethnicity in a Global Context," at the University of California, Berkeley, published in the *Journal*. Thank you to the *Journal* for allowing us to reprint it here. I would like to thank Ryan Center at Berkeley and Emiko Kurotsu at the University of Chicago for their help with the production of this essay.

## Notes

1. Michael Hardt and Antonio Negri, *Empire* (Cambridge, MA: Harvard University Press, 2001). All future references to *Empire* will be made parenthetically through the text.

2. Saskia Sassen, *The Global City: New York, London, Tokyo*, 2nd ed. (Princeton, NJ: Princeton University Press, 2001).

3. Saskia Sassen, *Globalization and Its Discontents* (New York: New Press, 1998), chap. 1.

4. Saskia Sassen, *Losing Control? Sovereignty in an Age of Globalization* (New York: Columbia University Press, 1996), chap. 1.

5. Ibid., 29–30.

6. For the fullest treatment of my concept of the global city, see the updated second edition of *The Global City*.

7. Hague Convention, 1954, Available at http://exchanges.state.gov/education/culprop/hague.html.

8. Michael R. Marrus, *The Unwanted: European Refugees in the Twentieth Century* (New York: Oxford University Press, 1985).

9. Kim Rubenstein and Daniel Adler, "International Citizenship: The Future of Nationality in a Globalized World," *Indiana Journal of Global Legal Studies* 7 (2000): 519–548.

10. Peter Spiro, "Dual Nationality and the Meaning of Citizenship," *Emory Law Review*, 46 (1997): 1412–1485; Kim Rubenstein and Daniel Adler, "International Citizenship: The Future of Nationality in a Globalized World," *Indiana Journal of Global Legal Studies* 7 (2000): 519–548.

11. Peter Spiro, "Dual Nationality and the Meaning of Citizenship," *Emory Law Review* 46 (1997): 1412–1485.

12. Saskia Sassen, *Losing Control?* chap. 2.

13. Brian Turner, "Cosmopolitan Virtue: Loyalty and the City," in *Democracy, Citizenship and the Global City*, ed. Engin Isin (New York: Basic Books, 1985).

14. E.g., Frank Munger, ed. *Laboring under the Line* (New York: Russell Sage Foundation, 2002).

15. Laurence Roulleau-Berger, ed., *Youth and Work in the Postindustrial Cities of North America and Europe* (Leiden, Netherlands: Brill, 2002).

16. T. H. Marshall, "Citizenship and Social Class," in *Class, Citizenship and Social Development* (Chicago: University of Chicago Press, 1977 [1950]).

17. Peter Saunders, "Citizenship in a Liberal Society," *Citizenship and Social Theory*, ed. Bryan Turner (London: Sage, 1993).

18. Saskia Sassen, *Guests and Aliens* (New York: New Press, 1999); Karen Knop, *Diversity and Self-Determination in International Law* (Cambridge, UK: Cambridge University Press, 2002).

19. John Shotter, "Psychology and Citizenship: Identity and Belonging," in *Citizenship and Social Theory* ed. Bryan Turner (London: Sage, 1993); Aihwa Ong, "Strategic Sisterhood or Sisters in Solidarity? Questions of Communitarianism and Citizenship in Asia," *Indiana Journal of Global Legal Studies* 4 (1996): 107–135, chaps. 1 and 4.

20. See Aihwa Ong, "Strategic Sisterhood or Sisters in Solidarity? 107–135; Linda Bosniak, "Universal Citizenship and the Problem of Alienage," *Northwestern University Law Review* 94 (2000): 963–984.

21. Max Weber, *The City* (New York: Free Press, 1958).

22. E.g. Kenneth Karst, "The Coming Crisis of Work in Constitutional Perspective," *Cornell Law Review* 82 (1997): 523–571.

23. Iris Marion Young, *Justice and the Politics of Difference* (Princeton, NJ: Princeton University Press, 1990); Charles Taylor, "The Politics of Recognition," in *Multiculturalism: Examining the Politics of Recognition*, eds. Charles Taylor and Amy Gutmann (Princeton, NJ: Princeton University Press, 1992).

24. Michael Walzer, *Spheres of Justice: A Defense of Pluralism and Equity* (New York: Basic Books, 1985); Linda Bosniak, "'Nativism' The Concept: Some Reflections," in *Immigrants Out! The New Nativism and the Anti-Immigrant Impulse in the United States*, ed. Juan Perea (New York: New York University Press, 1996).

25. In Kenneth Karst's interpretation of U.S. law, aliens are "constitutionally entitled to most of the guarantees of equal citizenship, and the Supreme Court has accepted this idea to a modest degree." Kenneth Karst, "Citizenship, Law, and the American Nation," *Indiana Journal of Global Legal Studies* 7 (2000): 595–601, 599, and n.20, where he cites cases). Karst also notes that the Supreme Court has not carried this development nearly as far as he might wish. Kenneth Karst, "The Coming Crisis of Work in Constitutional Perspective," *Cornell Law Review* 82 (1997): 523–571.

26. T. H. Marshall, "Citizenship and Social Class"; Joel Handler, *The Poverty of Welfare Reform* (New Haven, CT: Yale University Press, 1995).

27. Seyla Benhabib et al., *Feminist Contentions: A Philosophical Exchange* (New York: Routledge, 1995); Kimberly Crenshaw et al., eds., *Critical Race Theory: The Key Writings that Formed the Movement* (New York: New Press, 1996); Richard Delgado and Jean Stefancic, eds., *Critical Race Theory: The Cutting Edge* (Philadelphia: Temple University Press, 2001); Seyla Benhabib, *Democratic Equality and Cultural Diversity: Political Identities in the Global Era* (Princeton, NJ: Princeton University Press, 2002).

28. Kenneth Karst, "The Coming Crisis of Work in Constitutional Perspective."

29. Saskia Sassen, *Losing Control?* chap. 2; Saskia Sassen, *Denationalization: Territory, Authority, and Rights in a Global Digital Age* (Princeton, NJ: Princeton University Press, 2003).

30. Peter Schuck and Rogers Smith, *Citizenship without Consent: Illegal Aliens in the American Polity* (New Haven, CT: Yale University Press, 1985).

31. NACARA is the 1997 Nicaraguan Adjustment and Central American Relief Act. It created an amnesty for 300,000 Salvadorans and Guatemalans to apply for suspension of deportation. This is an immigration remedy that had been eliminated by the Illegal Immigration Reform and Immigrant Responsibility Act in 1996. See Susan B. Coutin, "Denationalization, Inclusion and Exclusion: Negotiating the Boundaries of Belonging," *Indiana Journal of Global Legal Studies* 7 (2000): 585–594.

32. Yasemin Nuhoolu Soysal, *Limits of Citizenship: Migrants and Postnational Membership in Europe* (Chicago: University of Chicago Press, 1994); Susan B. Coutin, "Denationalization, Inclusion and Exclusion."

33. Sarah Mahler, *American Dreaming: Immigrant Life on the Margins* (Princeton, NJ: Princeton University Press, 1995).

34. Susan B. Coutin, "Denationalization, Inclusion and Exclusion"; Sarah Mahler, *American Dreaming.*

35. Susan B. Coutin, "Denationalization, Inclusion and Exclusion."

36. Linda Basch et al., *Nations Unbound: Transnational Projects, Postcolonial, Predicaments, and Deterritorialized Nation-States* (Langhorne, UK: Gordon and Breach, 1994); Hector R. Cordero-Guzman et al., eds., *Migration, Transnationalization, and Race in a Changing New York* (Philadelphia: Temple University Press, 2001).

37. Robin Leblanc, *Bicycle Citizens: The Political World of the Japanese Housewife* (Berkeley, CA: University of California Press, 1999).

38. E.g., Norma Chinchilla and Nora Hamilton, *Seeking Community in the Global City: Salvadorans and Guatemalans in Los Angeles* (Philadelphia: Temple University Press, 2001).

39. Pierette Hondagneu-Sotelo, *Gendered Transitions: Mexican Experiences of Immigration* (Berkeley, CA: University of California Press, 1994).

40. For the limits of this process, see, e.g., Rhacel Salazar Parreñas, *Servants of Globalization: Women, Migration and Domestic Work* (Stanford, CA: Stanford University Press, 2001).

41. Linda Bosniak, "Universal Citizenship and the Problem of Alienage," *Northwestern University Law Review* 94 (2000): 963–984.

42. E.g., Gertrude Himmelfarb, *One Nation, Two Cultures: A Searching Examination of American Society in the Aftermath of Our Cultural Revolution* (New York: Vintage Books, 2001).

43. Thus for Karst "In the United States today, citizenship is inextricable from a complex legal framework that includes a widely accepted body of substantive law, strong law-making institutions, and law-enforcing institutions capable of performing their task." Kenneth Karst, "Citizenship, Law, and the American Nation," 600. Not recognizing the centrality of the law is, for Karst, a big mistake. Postnational citizenship lacks an institutional framework that can protect the substantive values of citizenship. Karst does acknowledge the possibility of rabid nationalism and the exclusion of aliens when legal status is made central.

44. E.g., Yasemin Nuhoolu Soysal, *Limits of Citizenship*; David Jacobson, *Rights Across Borders: Immigration and the Decline of Citizenship* (Baltimore, MD: Johns Hopkins Press, 1996); Maria de los Angeles Torres, "Transnational Political and Cultural Identities: Crossing Theoretical Borders," in *Borderless Borders*, ed. Frank Bonilla, et al. (Philadelphia: Temple University Press, 1998); Rodolfo D. Torres, et al., *Race, Identity, and Citizenship* (Oxford: Blackwell, 1999).

45. See *Indiana Journal of Legal Studies*, special issue on "Feminism and Globalization: The Impact of the Global Economy on Women and Feminist Theory," 4 (1996).

46. Bosniak uses the term "denationalized" interchangeably with "postnational." I do not. Linda Bosniak, "Universal Citizenship and the Problem of Alienage," *Northwestern University Law Review* 94 (2000): 963–984.

47. E.g. Saskia Sassen, *Denationalization: Territory, Authority, and Rights in a Global Digital Age* (Princeton, NJ: Princeton University Press, 2003).

48. David Jacobson, *Rights across Borders: Immigration and the Decline of Citizenship* (Baltimore, MD: Johns Hopkins Press, 1996).

49. In this regard, I have emphasized as significant the introduction in the new constitutions of South Africa, Brazil, Argentina, and the Central European countries of a provision that qualifies what had been an unqualified right—if democratically elected—of the sovereign to be the exclusive representative of its people in international fora. Saskia Sassen, *Losing Control?* chap. 2.

50. See ibid., chap. 2.

51. E.g. the concept of the global city, Saskia Sassen, *The Global City*; Saskia Sassen, "Spatialities and Temporalities of the Global: Elements for Theorization," *Public Culture* 12 (2000): 215–232.

52. Ira Katznelson, *Marxism and the City* (Oxford: Clarendon, 1992).

53. Engin Isin, "Introduction: Democracy, Citizenship and the City," in *Democracy, Citizenship and the Global City*, ed. Engin Isin (New York: Routledge, 2000); John Allen et al., eds., *Unsettling Cities* (London: Routledge, 1999); Gary Bridge and Sophie Watson, eds., *A Companion to the City* (Oxford: Blackwell, 2000).

54. Engin Isin, "Introduction: Democracy, Citizenship and the City," 7.

55. Henri Lefebvre, *The Production of Space* (Cambridge: Blackwell, 1991); Henri Lefebvre, *Writing on Cities* (Cambridge: Blackwell, 1995).

56. Only in Russia—where the walled city did not evolve as a center of urban immunities and liberties—does the meaning of citizen diverge from concepts of civil society and cities, and belongs to the state, not the city. Max Weber, *The City*.

57. Saskia Sassen, *The Global City*.

# 9

Place

# The Irrepressible Lightness and Joy of Being Green: *Empire* and Environmentalism

## William Chaloupka

*Empire* has an odd concluding sentence. At the end of their 413 page reframing of the political, Hardt and Negri announce, "This is the irrepressible lightness and joy of being communist." Perhaps this ending plays well in Europe. In the United States, however, it falls flat, not least because of the pronounced antileft sentiment that has only increased over the past decade. But what if we read this concluding sentence for its surprising "irrepressible lightness and joy" rather than for its communism? The phrase suggests that politics be thought as it has so often been acted, with a buoyant sense of possibility, a delight in intellectual speculation over openings. Such a joyful reading would displace the odd commitment to the dismal that Marxism imposed on radicals, including greens, for a century and a half. Indeed, this displacement, this redirection of left politics, is arguably *Empire*'s most significant contribution.

Yet this very contribution suffers from Hardt's and Negri's failure to attend to environmental politics, one of the most promising avenues of anticapitalism today. In searching for international anticapitalist critique, one would have expected Hardt and Negri to consider environmentalism. But even as *Empire* has dispensed with so much vestigial left dogma and error, it has still preserved one of the left's most intriguing blind spots, the green politics likely to be at the center of any foreseeable left resistance to global capitalism.

In this chapter, I aim to open up this blind spot, extending Hardt's and Negri's challenge to left politics (postmodernism, identity politics, postcolonialism, and the vestiges of class politics) to green politics. I focus on the modernism that continues to structure green thought, specifically regarding green conceptions of agency (its model of citizenship and collective action), knowledge (its biocentrism), and place (its emphasis on locality). As I endeavor to open up green politics to its own buoyant possibility, moreover, I find that Hardt and Negri need more openness as well. Despite their embrace of multiplicity, fluidity, and hybridity, Hardt and Negri sometimes neglect their own advice, missing political opportunities that might help make their case. The question of locality is particularly intriguing in this respect.

## Modern Greens

Modernism insists on the most general explanations, thus tending to drive political talk to extremes that are then defended as normal, natural, and inevitable. Often, modernism is reduced to its favorite shorthand forms, science and technology. And it is the case that sciences and technologies are primarily modernist (although, arguably, this might be changing). But modernism is broader than that; abstractly, it refers to systems that defer to universal forms of knowledge. Previously diverse practices begin to converge in modernity, and that pattern is political and cultural as well as technological.

Environmentalists may seem, at first, very unlikely modernists. After all, greens continually criticize technology. They joke about being premodern druids or Luddites. They valorize (and sometimes implement) systems of barter and cooperation in the face of modern capitalism. But there is a sense in which greens are precisely modernist. To perceive this green modernism, one must trace the green relationship to nature. Greens privilege nature much as Marxists privileged the proletariat or liberals privileged human nature and individualism (each a relationship that encodes modernism). In this view, green aspirations to "speak for" nature reveal arrangements involving knowledge and power—in all, a far more modernist approach than all the green critiques of technology could neutralize. In short, the pursuit of an authoritative "outside" perspective from which to criticize the political world is a distinctively modernist project.

But modernism involves more than a preference for nature (or technology, or change). The complex and perhaps even confounding stability of modernism often functions by absorbing seemingly contradictory commitments. Modernism is dualist in it promotion of omniscient perspective, judgment, and logic. But the monism this implies can appeal to antidualists, too. In the present instance, environmentalists oppose (often vociferously) the idea of a nature-culture dualism. But green culture is constantly approaching nature as "other"—as inspiration, danger, resource, or opportunity. Culture is inevitably cast as nature's adversary and simultaneously as its only hope.

It is easy to find different arguments. *Empire* argues that human nature cannot be understood as separate from nature in general. This claim implicitly contests greens, who often seem comfortable with that distinction. If Marx had appropriated nature, redefining it as social, greens enlarged the left's anticapitalist naturalism, arguing that human activity endangered (nonhuman) nature itself. This mobilized activists, but (like most mobilizations) it had a serious downside. The almost automatic implication was that greens necessarily understood themselves as saviors (and were thereby invested in particular accounts of agency and knowledge). Saviors preach, denounce, and prophesize.

In similar fashion, crisis becomes linked with the form of political activity that responds to crisis. Properly speaking, the response is not a response at all; once one sees the issues at hand as ongoing crises, the crisis response is inevitable. The crisis and the response become inextricably linked, propping each other up. This leads to a proliferation of unlikely pairs. To cite just one example, utopia, paired with a bent toward monolithic ideological positions, made it inevitable that adversaries—that is, anyone who needed to justify any significant level of struggle, thus threatening to disrupt the utopian peace— had to become horrific enemies, enhancing the prospect for crisis. Utopia thus becomes the partner of enmity and the best friend of ongoing crisis.

When Hardt and Negri address one of their main foils, Francis Fukuyama, the issue is precisely this question of fundamental crisis. Fukuyama's "end of history . . . is the end of the crisis at the center of modernity, the coherent and defining conflict that was the foundation . . . for modern sovereignty" (189). For this crisis, this battle of pure peace and utter evil, to persist, there must be a convincing, external critique—a perspective from which the crisis could be narrated. As Hardt and Negri explain (citing Deleuze and Guattari), "The outside is what gave the crisis its coherence. Today it is increasingly difficult for the ideologues of the United States to name a single, unified enemy; rather there seem to be minor and elusive enemies everywhere"(189). This passage suggests that the historical, contingent struggles have now accumulated into a body of evidence that dissolves the single-crisis model.

Deploying Foucault's central insight, *Empire* explains that while the left waited for a catastrophic collapse of an utterly unified system of capital, power had actually dispersed: "imperial sovereignty . . . is organized not around one central conflict but rather through a flexible network of microconflicts"(201). Finally, with the left in utter eclipse, it is possible to understand that the monolithic, modernist analysis no longer holds; there is no single force of nature that can only be overturned by its antithesis (a similarly monolithic, but dialectically opposed force of nature). In this way, green modernism becomes problematical, and *Empire* provides a useful guide in unpacking that problem.

The role of the crisis in political strategies and understandings is particularly acute. With global circulation of technologies and power, catastrophic events have happened and will continue to happen. Hardt's and Negri's argument must not be misunderstood as suggesting that a rhetorical change (perhaps, all modernist partisans of realism continually suggest, enforced by "political correctness") alters political reality as if by magic. The goal of the present discussion is to highlight the role that investment in crisis plays in the left's political strategies. In general, modernism tends to understand any challenge to its hegemony as dangerous crisis. It is this tendency that Marx exploited so adroitly, flipping it to his advantage. Now, the problem with that approach is too visible to miss; opportunities are missed, contingencies unexamined, and openness foregone as modernist critics wager all on the efficacy of the next crisis. Ironically, as the left waited for capitalist crisis, it exacerbated its own crisis, hanging on to understandings that debilitated it.

Environmentalism remains more vital than the left in general, especially in the United States. Accordingly, it is more difficult for greens to acknowledge that their monolithic-nature argument has run its course. On the contrary, green intellectuals have bitterly complained that critics who insist on historical contingency represent "the high end of the Wise Use movement."[1] Every modernist approach spends extraordinary effort in defense; the sense of certainty and rationality cannot be allowed to slip. This helps to explain the term "postmodernism;" arrangements as durable and universal as those that emerge in the modern era are not refuted (modernist style) so much as they exhaust themselves until they can be revealed and surpassed. But this elaborate set of defenses also explains why the exhaustion of modernism is no simple matter. The defenses are powerful. As Hardt and Negri understand, the arguments that intend to reorient leftism will have to attend to many dimensions of politics. It will not do simply to point out modernism's exhaustion or absurdity; there are many other elements to consider. Subsequent sections of this chapter consider two of these elements: agency and knowledge.

## Agency

Thoroughly committed to their understanding of ecological crisis, greens make thoroughly modernist assumptions about agency—about who will be key to any political response. With remarkable solidarity, environmentalists tend to assume that the public is passive, uninformed, yet possible to mobilize, primarily through calls to action. Environmentalism has seldom ventured far from its transcendentalist principles and its love of the jeremiad as a rhetorical form. The maintenance of such a green position of authority requires that there must be an authoritative way to judge. The citizen, thus conceptualized, is thus firmly cast in the god and judge role rather than the resisting multitude role that *Empire* introduces as an alternative notion of agency.

Environmentalists sometimes seem to imagine a bourgeois horizon class, led by a transcendentalist cadre (who recycle, bike, hang inspiring Sierra Club calendars, and know the biological names for plants and animals). Rather than noticing the resistance offered everywhere to capitalist imperialism, environmentalists assume that if resistance fails to match the green cultural model, it is not actually resistance. It is not a very hopeful outcome for greens if, say, some external event forces heating oil prices up and thus fosters conservation and innovation. For greens, true change only happens by dint of stern conviction. "Happy accidents" are occasions for increased moralizing, not for strategizing the next move. Environmentalists learned from Marxists, assuming that a vanguard class with a sophisticated scientific approach to politics was the precondition of radical change. Class consciousness (along with its inevitable implication, false consciousness) leant a tight but ultimately misleading political coherence to Marxism.

This was one of the parts of Hegel that Marx kept standing on its feet, if with its head turned. Political struggle had to be resolved at the level of (some subdivision of) the people's will.[2] With "multitude," Deleuze opened political understanding to the possibility that masses are always a source of potentially resistant agency, while he also defused the utopianism that lurked in the heavy burden of scientific rationality that Marxism had imposed on the proletariat. Marx derided the (lumpen) multitude, since his politics required that its privileged subjects must have a rational, abstract knowledge of their goals and methods. Any number of bad political moves intersected at this commitment, not the least of which was a misleading and largely unfortunate discussion of leadership and elitism, cadres and vanguard. Hardt and Negri imagine a resistance less clouded by middle-class assumptions and culture.

These are matters of agency. Humanity has functioned as a transcendental category for greens. One of *Empire*'s most sweeping gestures  is to dispense with "the people." Imagine a leftism that knew enough to shut up, already, with "the people, united, will never be defeated." The people are always united in the formulation promoted by this tiresome chant, but they are continually defeated, since *the people* do not exist, in that their unification is always in process (and frequently, for various reasons, in eclipse). Greens know "the people," too—they have a very specific ideal of the citizen (a recycling, guilty, middle-class citizen-scientist). To assert this category is to assume that its touch transforms politics. But nothing calls "the people" into this single, unified presence.

"The people" is a term fraught with problems that have avoided critical examination, especially since the most vocal critics are often partisan, capitalist individualists. Hardly vulnerable to charges of collaboration, Hardt and

Negri effectively deconstruct "the people," a notion that has been naturalized and should be unlearned: "Many contemporary analyses . . . go wrong precisely because they rely unquestioningly on the naturalness of the concept and identity of the people"(102). Perhaps under the spell of class, we have failed to notice a whole set of family resemblances that cluster around "the people": "The concepts of nation, people, and race are never very far apart"(103).

Instead of a hegemonic class, *Empire* posits multitude as another key to political agency, one that leads with its hybridity, rather than its hegemony:

> Just when the proletariat seems to be disappearing from the world stage, the proletariat is becoming the universal figure of labor. This claim is not actually as paradoxical as it may seem. What has disappeared is the hegemonic position of the industrial working class. . . . We understand the concept "proletariat," however, to refer not just to the industrial working class but to all those who are subordinated to, exploited by, and produce under the rule of capital. From this perspective, . . . all forms of labor tend to be proletarianized. (256)

While this may seem minor, Hardt and Negri make the point loom large. The entire political calculation begins to shift: "Against the common wisdom that the U.S. proletariat is weak because of its low party and union representation with respect to Europe and elsewhere, perhaps we should see it as strong for precisely those reasons." Class blinds, making some forms of resistance and autonomy harder to recognize: "Working-class power resides not in the representative institutions but in the antagonism and autonomy of the workers themselves. This is what marked the real power of the U.S. industrial class"(269). Marxists identified labor with its organizations; *Empire*'s critique of that is profound.

Environmentalism has not been absorbed by any party as Marxism often has. On agency, greens resemble the left displaced by *Empire* primarily in their commitment to a vanguard mobilized by modernist conviction. That the green model more closely resembles middle-class liberalism might help explain its success, which has certainly surpassed the left's, especially in the United States. On the one hand, this serves as a reminder that it is more often a movement's success—rather than errors or weaknesses—that becomes debilitating.[3] But this observation also sends us off into other questions, specifically the form of knowledge integral to green agency.

## Knowledge

The use of biological figures exemplifies the differences between green knowledge and *Empire*'s response to modernism, while also displaying the role knowledge plays in green political agency. A specific form of knowledge has long been central to green politics, and without doubt, that arrangement has produced impressive political results. A wellspring of positive public opinion attaches to environmental positions—and has persisted, often surprising mainstream commentators, virtually since the first Earth Day. It is not that people don't agree with the environmentalists, but that the environmentalists have stumbled into some sort of pathology when it comes to mobilizing that resistance and now find it difficult to escape a trap they helped set. Greens seem hedged in, somehow stunted in their effort to mobilize public policy. Especially in the United States, greens are subjected to resentful antagonism and now seem relegated to the status of one issue among many, despite green arguments claiming much more. Reading green politics through *Empire* lets us ponder whether green frustrations might not be entirely attributable to the strength of the movement's adversaries but might have roots in core green arrangements.

When greens pursue a material basis for political organizing, they have long preferred the biological sciences to other viable alternatives such as economics. Environmentalists are persistently committed to the goal of public (mostly biological) science as a political form. In its fullest modernism, the environmental movement promotes several knowledge claims, each implying a universal, ethical basis for politics. Perhaps prime among these key claims is biocentrism.[4] American greens trace the origins of biocentrism to Thoreau and Muir, for whom the biological (and, especially for Muir, the geological) provided an occasion for transcendental enlightenment.[5] Walking in the woods provided an opportunity for reflection on the relationship of spirit and nature, informing one's return to human society and subsequent efforts to change policies and inform fellow citizens. In this way, nature was central to a political scenario, powering an ethical perspective that could generate social change.

As the spiritual came under general attack in the early twentieth century, conservationists nimbly adapted. Most dramatically, the search for a persuasive, external perspective (the transcendental, discovered amid natural landscapes) for criticizing society attached itself to scientific explanations. Eventually, biochemistry became a political force. Rachel Carson epitomized this shift, creating a bond between the ethical and the biological that would be among the most important precedents for the emergence of contemporary environmentalism. The gathering movement never abandoned the hope for an external, ethical perspective from which to criticize the existing order; instead, it absorbed the rhetorical force of science within an existing transcendental framework that was already infused with the jeremiad form of argument.

As greens increasingly accommodated their moralism to lobbying and litigating, the scientific arguments became more important, but the transcendental core was hardly ever challenged; it was absorbed. New sciences, including "conservation biology," were invented to fill the gaps in preservation arguments and to augment green advocacy. But green science comfortably retained the transcendental political scenario; enlightenment would drive change, informed by science. Contemporary environmentalism has a canniness, nowhere more visible than at this point. The nature arguments preserve God (as Nature), while they also introduce the scientific authority necessary to win those truly crucial lobbying battles and court cases.

Given *Empire*'s general silence on green politics, it is unsurprising that the form of biopolitics it addresses avoids the common green form. Rather than depending on the "biocentrism" that is so popular among greens, Hardt and Negri invoke the "biopower" arguments developed by Foucault, Deleuze, and Guattari. Despite the largely coincidental similarity of the words, biocentrism and biopower signify entirely distinct political concepts. In short, biopower deploys a more open political strategy, more attuned to the contingent ebb and flow of the political world. By contrast, biocentrism locks greens into dualistic modernism, consigning them forever to the role of the frowning god, pronouncing the dismal end attached to various everyday human practices.

As articulated by Foucault, "biopower" responds to an entirely different set of questions from those of biocentrism, which is unsurprising, since Foucault barely thought about green issues at all. He introduced biopower as a way to explain how power develops and extends its actual influence over human affairs. No longer so clearly a matter of sovereign laws and armies, power had learned to inscribe habits of behavior and understanding directly into the bodies it hopes to control, as if by capillary mechanism. Rather than exclusively a matter of sovereign laws that announce what citizens must not do, power works through micropractices and habits of speech; power moved to body scale, becoming biopower. Foucault deployed the concept of biopower as a way to explain the surprising nimbleness of power, its capacity to reroute around the prevailing forms of resistance and critique. He cut through the modernist limits Marxism had carried with it, to recognize that the agents of power had changed and that resistance to power would have to change, too. This newly agile power undermined the modernist search for an external perspective from which to issue denunciations that would mobilize resistance.

While Foucault was formulating this argument in the 1970s, greens were assembling another and, it is hoped stronger and more comprehensive external perspective summarized by biocentrism. Unwilling to accept Foucault's diagnosis, greens continued to emphasize the massive corporate and sovereign forces they perceived as their opposition. They championed biocentrism as a way to reempower anticapitalist and antitechnological critique with a yet more comprehensive external perspective. Environmentalists reacted to the changes in the functioning of power by perfecting ever stronger modernist critiques. The implied position on agency differs entirely from Foucault's more open initiatives.

Firmly established in the green pantheon by Muir, the biocentric argument lives on in distilled political form as "deep ecology," even if a number of variants have also emerged.[6] Deep ecologists insist on a universal dualism between "anthropocentrism" and "biocentrism." That dualism has been remarkably successful within environmentalism; the terms seem immune to criticism. The dualism is made more stable because it is promoted in the name of antidualism, obscuring its Enlightenment origin. But those roots still show; there must be some kind of transcendental vision required so utterly to sort the things, practices, and thoughts of humans. In short, the anthro-/biocentrism split carries with it the implication that there must be a god position, an external vantage point from which to make judgments. In promoting the division, greens must also promote their capacity to interpret a wide range of human practices.

Nervous about such metaphysical stances in general, Hardt and Negri side with the more political postmodernists, giving nary a glance at deep ecology or biocentrism. Instead, they alter the distinction carried by Foucault's use of the term biopower, thus again developing the openness their book continually advocates. In *Empire*, biopower implies the source of resistance itself. Negri has described his notion of biopower as an aspect of the "new nature of work," which "is still 'bios,' an entire life made of needs and desires, of singularities and of generations succeeding each other."[7] In short, "bios" has been moved from disciplinary biology (a category Hardt and Negri criticize repeatedly) to a transposition of "labor power." In *Empire*, "biopolitics" connotes the importance of bodies (including the politics of reproduction), but also the full, embodied involvement of political agents (including *Empire*'s "multitude") who are not limited to the rational calculators implied in Marxist labor-power arguments. As Negri explained in an interview: "This 'biopolitical' paradigm invests both work and life, along with the relationships among people. And therefore it is 'full' of cognitive facts, of organizational, social, and political facts, and emotional, affective facts."[8] This implies a cacophony that resists the monolithic perspective greens and Marxists require. It also poses biopower as a response to questions Foucault had not much considered.[9]

This biopower, as opposed to biocentrism, encloses both positive and negative moments, while also promising radical pluralism, due to its location in the many dispersed *bodies*. *Empire* credits Deleuze and Guattari for presenting an "understanding of biopower that renews materialist thought and grounds itself solidly in the question of the production of social being" (28). Further underscoring their radically pluralist sense of the bios, Hardt and

Negri explain that communication plays a crucial role: "If communication is one of the hegemonic sectors of production and acts over the entire biopolitical field, then we must consider communication and the biopolitical context coexistent" (33). In *Empire*, then, "bios" is a figure for openness in both agency and knowledge—a reminder of the biological (and communicative) multiplicity of bodies rather than the disciplinary unity of biology. In an interview, Negri explained the use of biopower as a way to conceptualize political movement:

> our present problematic has to do with biopolitics and how within the biopolitical order, we can understand the concept of organization; that is, in what way we can understand the new social struggle or revolution. The question then is a matter of recognising the emergence of powerful organisations, and really a question in our terms of how to organise an exodus. (33)

In his *Theory & Event* interview with Thomas Dumm, Hardt invokes Agamben's sense of the object of power's ambitions: "Agamben uses the term 'naked life' to name that limit of humanity, the bare minimum of existence that is exposed in the concentration camp. In the final analysis, he explains, modern sovereignty rules over naked life and biopower is this power to rule over life itself."[12] Hardt distinguishes *Empire*'s sense of biopower from Foucault's because the latter does not carry an implicit or explicit response to the power it describes: "There is no figure that can challenge and contest sovereignty. Our critique of Agamben's (and Foucault's) notion of biopower is that it is conceived only from above and we attempt to formulate instead a notion of biopower from below, that is, a power by which the multitude itself rules over life."[13] Explicitly, this biopower is "from below" in the sense that it is not solely about how power disciplines individuals. It is also "from below" in the sense that it carries no hope for a single, monolithic, and effective critique of the powers that be (although *Empire* clearly hopes it will challenge those powers).

In an aside during his interview with Dumm, Hardt connects this comment with a mainstay of green theory. This is one of very few references to a green theorist by the authors of *Empire*: "In this sense, the notion of biopower one finds in some veins of ecofeminism such as the work of Vandana Shiva, although cast on a very different register, is closer to our notion of a biopower from below. . . . What we are interested in finally is a new biopolitics that reveals the struggles over forms of life."[14] Hardt's choice of Shiva is in some ways an odd one. Politically, Shiva champions an ethical modernism that shares little but anticapitalism with *Empire*. I have yet to find any mention of the term "biopower" in Shiva's work.[15] What Hardt is calling forth, however, is something cannier than the moralistic condemnations that Shiva sometimes favors. He identifies with the sense of open, biopolitical ferment that confounds global technologies and political forms, generating resistance at all sorts of points, regardless of ideology or direction. Foucault had used biopower to show the limits of grand critique; Hardt and Negri appropriate it, through intermediaries, to show potential sources of resistance to global capitalism.

A green theory that understood this reading of Shiva would be ready to engage left politics in a remarkably new register. As it is, *Empire*'s "bios" and the green "bio-" miss each other entirely—even spectacularly. For all the success that green politics has achieved, there remains a nagging worry that the green position has been stunted, somehow prevented from accomplishing realistic (and necessary) goals. While much attention is given to the environmental movement's adversaries as a source of its frustrations, the possibility that the basic configuration of the movement should share some blame is less often considered. Where the left is concerned, the difficulties of a modernist left challenge against capitalism are well understood and, if *Empire*'s success says anything, are beginning to be taken seriously. Modernism absorbs modernist challenges, forcing them into ever more marginal and dismal stances. Successful challenges to modernism will have to be particularly adroit at finding the right opportunities for action. Open political approaches—for example, those not encased by modernism—may have the better chance. Comparing biopower to biocentrism, the openness, radical pluralism, and joyousness of the first compared to the second are hard to miss. But these are abstract judgments; it is time to move to more political grounds.

## Place

The core of what those on the left sometimes perceive as green conservatism has long been its attachment to place. *Empire* is hardly the first work to challenge this core commitment. Europeans especially have been notably nervous about the green preference for moralistic, lyrical evocations of landscape as political justification.[16] But place persists as a green commitment of the highest order. Greens identify special places, justify radicalism to defend them, and argue that these places usefully contradict the mobility of contemporary capitalism.[17] As such, greens pose a rather specific challenge to *Empire*'s delight in motion and circulation.

Building on the nomadism argument developed by Gilles Deleuze and Félix Guattari, *Empire* inverts the commitment to place, opening the possibility that mobility itself holds special political promise: "Whereas in the disciplinary era sabotage was the fundamental notion of resistance, in the era of imperial control it may be desertion. . . . Battles against the Empire might be won through subtraction and defection. This desertion does not have a place; it is the evacuation of the places of power"(212). The phrase "evacuation of the places of power" gives a clue to the stakes of this reversal. Green politics had effectively hedged its political position, maintaining not only both conservative and left positions but also a claim on the politics of sovereignty (when greens battle for reserves, parks, and wilderness designations).

While greens maintained this hedged position on sovereignty, an implicit globalism persisted within green politics. Many environmental effects are global—or at least transnational—in scope. It was environmentalists, after all, who popularized the photos of the globe taken by NASA astronauts. Large green organizations are as likely as their corporate adversaries to operate on a global scale. The phrase, "think globally, act locally" has coded green ideology from an early date, capturing the notion that one can confidently assert global principles in a local setting, knowing such an arrangement can efficiently yield positive results. Hardt and Negri understand that their mobility reversal will be troubling: "We are well aware that in affirming this thesis we are swimming against the current of our friends and comrades on the left," many of whom have "sought to recompose sites of resistance," sometimes "in terms of 'place-based' movements or politics"(44). When the left takes that path, they argue, it is "entirely reactive." While Hardt and Negri acknowledge that they "respect the spirit," they still find it "both false and damaging. . . . The problem rests on a false dichotomy between the global and the local"(44).

In this example, as elsewhere in *Empire*, the left is urged to contemplate the implications of their (often unacknowledged) success. Internationalism has long been the dream of the left. Now, *Empire* suggests, it has been accomplished, if not quite in the manner anyone had imagined or proposed. The left had long hoped for the demise of the nation-state; it is now in decline. "World government" was a cherished left goal, but nobody could have imagined or proposed the model that actually emerged. Mobility has long been the odd counterpart of all that avowed localism on the left. While Emerson, Thoreau, and Muir all wanted to keep their travels brief (how brief varied from one to the other), leftists have always wanted to hit the road. Woody Guthrie, Joe Hill, Emma Goldman, and Mother Jones offer countermodels, itinerants who spread the word, taking the epithet "outside agitator" as a calling.

At this juncture in the green/*Empire* relationship there are two possibilities. On the one hand, one could use *Empire*'s arguments to support the view that greens should reduce their often-insistent defense of localism. On the other hand, the green ability to balance localism and globalism—arguably, a balance achieved at the expense of coherence within green theory—could present a lesson to Hardt and Negri. By this logic, the truest mobility would be one that could circulate among both localism and globalism. Allowing some slippage between the local and global, mobile resistance might sometimes speak in terms of the local. By this reading, "think globally, act locally" could always have encoded theoretical mobility, despite the ethical modernism greens have long cultivated. That awkward phrase could have been signaling ambivalence or fluidity all along. Its awkwardness meant more than clunky grammar.

To be sure, once one diminishes hopes for a universal materialist and modernist argument, the local could not have the sort of unambiguous authority that greens sometimes claim for it (for example, in Transcendentalist versions). The environmental justice movement has sometimes adopted the phrase "where we work, live, and play," which is a call to a situated localism (while it also distinguishes itself from pastoral versions of environmentalism that sometimes ignore the workplace). Now, with the arguments Hardt and Negri begin to outline in *Empire*, greens could develop a stronger intellectual basis for practices that have developed in spite of green modernism, flying against its logic and under its supposedly universal radar. For their part, Hardt and Negri could have found examples of mobile politics that they missed, if they had looked at the odd green attachment to/detachment from localism.

There are good reasons for the left to be nervous about green localism. Greens mobilize a genuinely conservative claim when they pose the value of place against the mobility of capital. Hardt and Negri remind us that the left has long understood that capital was radical on precisely this point: "What Marx explained most clearly is that capital constantly operates through a reconfiguration of the boundaries of the inside and the outside. Indeed, capital does not function within the confines of a fixed territory and population, but always overflows its borders and internalizes new spaces"(221). The left has long thought that this radicalism of capital, under which "all that is solid melts into air,"[18] presented an opportunity for rallying resistance. *Empire* responds that this line of defense is no longer tenable and that overcoming this tendency toward left conservatism is crucial to future left prospects.[19]

But against this nervousness over green conservatism, there are also good reasons to consider a fluidity theme in the local/global relationship. Although *Empire* sometimes seems to argue that the left has been solidified on the question of localism, it would probably be more precise to acknowledge that the local has been a matter of ambivalence for the left, which wishes to mobilize local energies while it also proposes explicitly global explanations. The circulatory metaphors brought into the left through identity politics and postcolonialism taught the left how to negotiate the local and global.[20] Globalism presents opportunities for the left, even if those opportunities are more intangible, more nuanced than the well-touted advantages gained by capital in the era of globalism.

If this discussion seems arcane, we should remember that resistance to capitalism always arises in relationship to historical resistance. The instability foreseen in *Empire* arises in a context, and that is what makes preexisting green resistance so relevant. *Empire* opens ground for a far more mobile, diffuse and, ultimately promising space for left politics. But the book is frustrating because it seems to stall almost immediately when it has reached the point from which readers can perceive the opportunity it has opened. In this sense, *Empire* is almost the mirror image of green politics, which has ready at hand a whole (reusable) shopping bag of projects it sees as political: conserve resources, recycle, get outdoors, be nice to animals, be conscientious about the fate of the earth, and so on. Reassurance is granted to greens by their mostly unquestioned sense of what is to be done. But greens hardly ever seem to examine and debate their ideological commitments the way *Empire* engages the left.

*Empire* suggests repeatedly that resistance might be more important to political action than ideology, that mobilizing action may not privilege knowledge in the way we have assumed that it does. Even if Chinese students in Tiananmen, youthful protestors in Eastern Europe, and antiapartheid forces in South Africa did not share an ideological identity with each other (i.e., did not utter some specific "magic words"), the actions of each still influenced and motivated subsequent actions.[21] The new green talent for mobilizing resistance against globalization makes the intellectual challenge more acute. There should be a better way to relate event and multitude as successors to class, biology, and the wide array of liberal values. *Empire* takes remarkable steps toward reorienting the left, but there are more steps to be taken.

## Theory and Strategy

The actual terrain of politics may be more difficult than either the green or *Empire* position suggests. Is trade protectionism appropriate to a global green agenda? How important is it to form coalitions with old-economy agents such as labor unions? Is coalition with ideologically unsympathetic but potentially useful allies (such as supporters of the third-party candidate Ross Perot) permissible? How about partnerships with budget-cutters such as John Kasich, the Ohio Republican who tried to establish his moral credibility as a congressional budget-cutter by opposing logging roads and convinced some greens to help him? Who is right: the Makah tribe or the prowhale activists? Should we trade land for peace in the rural West?

*Empire* charts a conceptual framework the left could employ in its consideration of such questions. Of course, greens have tended toward forms of normative argument that are less political. Often, the movement has driven hard toward a scientific discourse, even creating whole new scientific disciplines to address questions that had been ignored.[22] But science in this sense is more tactical than strategic; it abets strategies but it also resolves debates over strategy too quickly, pushing environmentalists relentlessly in a utopian direction, almost always advising absolute responses. Other greens, notably those based in Washington, D.C., speak of the established institutional culture there as the appropriate arbiter of green ambition, but that position has problems that even most greens now understand.[23] Yet other greens emphasize ethics, sometimes so zealously that politics wanes in the face of calls to personal conscience and enlightened personal practice.[24] In short, greens have negotiated, often implicitly, such dichotomies as the closing impulses of modernism and the open possibilities that might result from modernism's exhaustion. This is precisely what makes environmentalism such a rich trove of examples and cases.

What we might begin to learn, reading greens and *Empire* through and against each other, is that greens have a history they barely know (or have suppressed), and that the seemingly new politics of *Empire* has precedents that its authors and many readers might not have given sufficient attention. From the green side, *Empire* prepares us to perceive a trajectory of green history that has heretofore been ignored. In this story, the crucial green moment came on Earth Day, not in Muir's fight with Pinchot to establish the Green Transcendental. Greens had thought they needed the absolute justification promised by their modernist roots, but those precedents end up being less than mandatory.

What they did need, and what Rachel Carson and Earth Day finally delivered, was a rhetorical form that promised a coherent political approach while also opening space for a mass movement closer to *Empire*'s multitude. The first Earth Day in 1970 was an almost entirely distinct phenomenon from the conservation movement that preceded it.[25] Earth Day brought the multitude to the Capitol Mall; before that, one of the central conservation organizations, the Wilderness Society, had been organized around the principle articulated by Bob Marshall (who also gave the group its financial endowment) that only those who understood the organization's issues would be allowed to join.

The shift from Marshall to Earth Day hints at a move to multitude. Some of the activities greens are criticized for (being "granolas," hugging trees) are in fact the cultural markers that mobilize a multitude. The resentful critique that has been the most successful antigreen tactic could be the sort of political response multitude inevitably evokes, given its unique form of mobilization and argument. *Empire*'s challenge to the greens, then, might be in asking how the movement could be composed to promote multitude rather than vanguard. Which ideas or practices push greens in one direction or the other? A discussion of those issues would highlight the green political options more than do the movement's current ways of posing political questions. (Conversely, the resentment that resists the green cultural multitude might well be a more general problem for a politics of the multitude.)

As I have argued here, there are serious questions about the fluidity of green politics, especially in its high-modernist mode. But greens cannot completely resist the emerging political world. To cite one example particularly important to *Empire*, instances of newfound fluidity are not hard to find, especially in areas related to the environment and globalism. The Ruckus Society, for example, is renovating the practice of civil disobedience, bringing fluidity to a core resistance practice that previously seemed above analysis or change.[26] The very slogan that summarized the Seattle antiglobalism demonstrations for many—Teamsters and turtles together—immediately announces a transgression of boundaries that have been tolerated far too long in green and labor circles. There has long been a green globalism, with American and European activists setting off for sites in Asia and Africa, surely with some projects more admirable than others. "Act locally" notwithstanding, greens have been globalists for some time and thus serve as the obvious bridge for the kind of organizing *Empire* hopes to promote.

The "irrepressible lightness and joy" of *Empire*'s last sentence should be read for its praise of a politics of openness and mobility—for its liberation from the dismal, moralistic modernism of the past. If, as I have suggested, Hardt's and Negri's last sentence may be a joke that flops for some of their readers, my title is an oxymoron, since the lightness and joy of the greens has usually been expressed either as smugness (over the rightness of their moralistic ethical code) or an unexamined and thus misunderstood sense of liberation that political action fosters. Situated amid so many dichotomies, misfires, and promises, the phrase recalls Donna Haraway's famous concluding sentence, "Though both are bound in the spiral dance, I would rather be a cyborg than a goddess."[27] A spiral dance impends for *Empire* and the greens, if the greens will have it. And if they do, the prospect for a joyous politics of mobility and multitude could be as unnerving and exciting as was Haraway's cyborg.

## Acknowledgments

A different version of this essay has previously appeared in *Strategies: Journal of Theory, Culture and Politics*. I wish to thank Jane Bennett, Jodi Dean, Thom Kuehls, and Paul Passavant for their invaluable comments about earlier versions of this essay. Parenthetical references throughout are to Michael Hardt and Antonio Negri, *Empire* (Cambridge, MA: Harvard University Press, 2000).

## Notes

1. Gary Snyder made the remark in a speech to a crowd of over a thousand in Missoula, Montana. Sherry Devlin, "Poet Disputes Contention that Wilderness is a Middle-Class Luxury," *Missoulian* (Missoula, MT) May 24, 1999, A1.

2. For another broad reading of "will" in liberalism and Marxism, see Bradley Bryan, "Reason's Homelessness: Rationalization in Bentham and Marx," *Theory and Event* 6.3 (2002).

3. See William Chaloupka, "The Tragedy of the Ethical Commons: Demoralizing

Environmentalism," in Jane Bennett and Michael J. Shapiro, eds., *The Politics of Moralizing* (New York: Routledge, 2002), 113–140.

4. Green theory often discusses the distinction between "biocentrism" and "ecocentrism," the latter implying an even broader ethical perspective. For purposes of trying to stage a clearer distinction with biopower, I will refer only to biocentrism here.

5. The move toward a biocentric ethic is one of the themes traced in Robert L. Dorman, *A Word for Nature: Four Pioneering Environmental Advocates, 1845–1913* (Chapel Hill, NC: University of North Carolina Press, 1998).

6. For a sophisticated and recent discussion of the philosophical issues around deep ecology, see Eric Katz, Andrew Light, and David Rothenburg, eds., *Beneath The Surface: Critical Essays in the Philosophy of Deep Ecology* (Cambridge, MA: MIT Press, 2000).

7. Toni Negri, "Reappropriations of Public Space," available at http://www.emery.archive.mcmail.com/public_html/toni_negri/december.html.

8. Antonio Negri, "Back to the Future (Interview)," available at http://lists.village.virginia.edu/~forks/exile.htm. ("Note: This text is a transcription of an interview video, *Retour vers le futur*, which was produced in the days leading up to Negri's return to Italy and to prison.") The interview is dated 1998, with translation by Hardt.

9. Still, *Empire* does not discard Foucault's intended point. Hardt's and Negri's biopower also refers to internalized discipline. "Biopower is a form of power that regulates social life from its interior. . . . Power can achieve an effective command over the entire life of the population only when it becomes an integral, vital function that every individual embraces and reactivates of his or her own accord" (*Empire*, 23–24).

10. In the same paragraph, Hardt and Negri draw a distinction from Deleuze and Guattari, who "seem to be able to conceive positively only the tendencies toward continuous movement and absolute flows."

11. They go on to explain that this goes "well beyond" Habermas, who "still relied on a standpoint outside these effects of globalization, a standpoint of life and truth that could oppose the informational colonization of being. The imperial machine, however, demonstrates that this external standpoint no longer exists. . . . The machine is self-validating, autopoetic—that is, systemic" (*Empire*, 34).

12. "Sovereignty, Multitudes, Absolute Democracy: A Discussion between Michael Hardt and Thomas L. Dumm," *Theory and Event* 4.3, paragraph 7, and in this volume.

13. Ibid.

14. Ibid.

15. For example, in her major political work, Vandana Shiva, *Staying Alive: Women, Ecology and Development* (London: Zed Books, 1989).

16. One particularly controversial example is Luc Ferry, *The New Ecological Order* (Chicago: University of Chicago Press, 1995). For another account of French political ecology, less inflected by side issues, see Kerry H. Whiteside, *Divided Natures: French Contributions to Political Ecology* (Cambridge, MA: MIT Press, 2002).

17. This tradition dates back to John Muir, but is visible in many contemporary authors, including Wallace Stegner, William Kittredge, and Wendell Berry, to cite just three. For another discussion of the green sense of place, see R. McGreggor Cawley and William Chaloupka, "The Great Wild Hope: Nature, Environmentalism, and the Open Secret," in Jane Bennett and William Chaloupka, eds., *In the Nature of Things: Language, Politics, and the Environment* (Minneapolis: University of Minnesota Press, 1993), 3–23.

18. The phrase, from the *Communist Manifesto*, was more recently popularized in Marshall Berman, *All That Is Solid Melts into Air: The Experience of Modernity* (New York: Simon and Schuster, 1982).

19. The phrase "left conservatism" is not Hardt's and Negri's but nonetheless seems to capture some sense of their reorientation of left politics. For a discussion of left conservatism, see the symposium in *Theory and Event* 2.2 (1998).

20. Scholars of postcolonial studies take this ambivalence more seriously. An extensive literature reconsiders localism and identity, examining the question of circulation (of unfixed identities, mobile cultures, etc.) along lines suggested by Paul Gilroy, *The Black Atlantic: Modernity and Double Consciousness* (Cambridge, MA: Harvard University Press, 1993). As Sankaran Krishna, *Postcolonial Insecurities: India, Sri Lanka, and the Question of Nationhood* (Minneapolis: University of Minnesota Press, 1999) explains, these questions of identity and political resistance have extraordinary resonance

and require close attention. *Empire*, which has as one of its major virtues its sweep and scope, does not connect with postcolonialism as intensely as one might expect.

21. William Chaloupka, "What If Kuwait's Main Export Was Broccoli?" in Frederick Dolan and Thomas Dumm, *Rhetorical Republic: Representing American Politics* (Amherst, MA: University of Massachusetts Press, 1993).

22. The classic example, of course, is conservation biology, endlessly promoted by Michael Soulé, whose ventures into political thought have been much less than satisfying. See Michael E. Soulé and Gordon H. Orians, eds., *Conservation Biology: Research Priorities for the Next Decade* (London, UK: Island Press, 2001). For a more political example, See Sylvia Noble Tesh, *Uncertain Hazards: Environmental Activists and Scientific Proof* (Ithaca, NY: Cornell University Press, 2000).

23. The fact that one of the best early lobbyists on wilderness issues, David Brower, spent his long and illustrious career telling the story of his gullibility on precisely this point ensured that this understanding would be encoded in green political consciousness. More recently, Mark Dowie's widely read *Losing Ground* (Cambridge, MA: The MIT Press, 1996) made the same point.

24. See William Chaloupka, *Knowing Nukes: The Politics and Culture of the Atom* (Minneapolis: University of Minnesota Press, 1992), 88–104.

25. This point is argued in Tesh, *Uncertain Hazards.*

26. For example, Ruckus has deliberately tried to alter the interaction with the working-class police and fire personnel who initially react to their actions. "Pigs" no more. See Dan Baum, "You Say You Want Revolution?" *Rolling Stone,* July 5, 2001.

27. Donna Haraway, "A Cyborg Manifesto: Science, Technology, and Socialist-Feminism in the Late Twentieth Century," in Haraway, *Simians, Cyborgs and Women: The Reinvention of Nature* (New York; Routledge, 1991), 149–181, 181.

## 10

Migration

# Smooth Politics

## Malcolm Bull

Migration presupposes a capacity to see yourself somewhere else, and the capacity to see yourself depends on the surface in which you are looking. According to Plotinus, it was because they saw themselves reflected in the world that immortal souls first migrated to the realm of matter. The idea had its origin in the myth of Dionysus Zagreus. To distract his attention, the Titans offered the infant Dionysus a mirror and some other childish baubles and then, while he was admiring his own reflected image, captured him and tore him to pieces. Dionysus later meted out the same treatment to his own victims, but it was not this aspect of the story that interested the Neoplatonists. For them, the mirror of Dionysus was the material world itself. Proclus suggested that when Plato stated that the surface of the world was created smooth, he meant that it had a reflective surface like a mirror, and Plotinus had something similar in mind when he claimed that it was when the souls saw their images in "the mirror of Dionysus" that they descended from unity into material multiplicity.[1]

The myth has obvious resonances with what Lacan described as the mirror stage. Lacan interprets the human infant's capacity to recognize itself in a mirror as simultaneously a revelatory moment of identification of and with the Ideal-I and a devastating moment in which the discrepancy between the unified image of the reflection and the uncoordinated body of the infant becomes apparent. Like the Neoplatonists, Lacan makes the experience of the mirrored image the precipitating event through which human subjectivities are formed and emphasizes that the mirror functions as a lure: captivation leads to capture. Just as Zagreus is torn apart, and Plotinus's souls lose their immaterial unity, so the infant experiences itself as a fragmented multiplicity, a *corps morcelé*.[2]

The mirror stage remains the best known of Lacan's ideas yet, unlike his later work, it barely features in current debates in political and cultural theory. Because it is presocial and prelinguistic, the mirror stage is sometimes assumed to be prepolitical as well. Commentators pass quickly to the end of the stage, when identification with the reflected image leads to a rivalry that Lacan took to prefigure the individual's relations in and with society, and interpreted in terms of Hegel's master-slave dialectic. But they are moving too fast. Hegelian readings often ignore other possible philosophical influences on Lacan's early work, and the assumption that the political always emerges from within the social creates a blind spot in political discourse.

The parallels between Plotinus and Lacan are probably more than fortuitous. Lacan's theory developed in the early 1930s through the synthesis of his teacher Henri Wallon's "mirror test" with some of the ideas he was picking up from his informal philosophical studies. At the time, Neoplatonism was undergoing a revival in France under the leadership of Émile Bréhier at the Sorbonne, and the belief that there were affinities between the philosophies of Plotinus and Bergson brought Neoplatonism into wider philosophical discussion. Lacan's attention would have been drawn to the myth of Dionysus Zagreus (and its Neoplatonic interpreters) by a book he later said all psychoanalysts should read at least once: Erwin Rohde's *Psyche*, translated into French in 1928.[3] The general fascination with Neoplatonism had waned by the years of Lacan's fame, but the scattering of references to Plotinus in the Seminars testifies to an enduring interest.[4]

If we pick up on the Plotinian imagery in Lacan's early texts, it alerts us not just to the possible range of Lacan's sources but to the potential value of the mirror stage as a political myth of comparable potency to that of Hegel's master and slave. In certain respects, it seems more relevant to the contemporary situation than Hegel's dialectic, for it hinges on image rather than status, on movement rather than struggle, and on the relation of the one and the many rather than a dyadic rivalry. Above all, it provides a model for the dynamics of migration: the smooth reflective surface of the host region, the lure of the image glimpsed within it, and the experience of alienation that frequently results.

Despite the fundamental role of migration in history, political theorists almost invariably work with a bounded social unit and the actors within it—in modern times, the nation-state and the citizen. But during the past decade, migrants have become a potent symbol of the social dislocation created by globalization and have been invested with some of the left's more romantic aspirations. There is probably an element of self-delusion in this. Migrants are heroes of the left only in the host country, not in the nations from which they come; and if you call them settlers instead, they immediately appear in a rather different light. Nevertheless, migration remains significant, for it is not only a striking manifestation of the human aspiration for change but a proven means of effecting it.

Because migration is hardly mentioned in canonical texts of political theory, discussion of the subject remains embedded within the framework of myth. The Judeo-Christian tradition is a rich source of migratory imagery, and as Michael Walzer noted, the Exodus long ago became a model for the myth of revolution.[5] But now, as the great revolutions of the West recede into history, revolutionary ideology is being translated back into the language of Exodus.[6] For Hardt and Negri, migration is both the means and the end of a political strategy: "global exodus" is, they argue, "a primary determination of the virtuality of the multitude . . . [and] the first ethical act of a counterimperial ontology."[7]

Outside the Old Testament, the politics of exodus is perhaps best expressed by Augustine's fusion of Neoplatonic and biblical motifs in his vision of the People of God as guest workers in Babylon and pilgrims to the New Jerusalem. Small wonder, therefore, that the City of God seems to have become the left's new paradigm of social change. In *Empire*, Augustine provides the model for a counterempire in which "the divine city is a universal city of aliens, coming together, cooperating, communicating" (207). And even Slavoj Žižek, who complains that "in today's critical and political discourse, the term 'worker' has disappeared, supplanted and/or obliterated by 'immigrants,'" ends *The Fragile Absolute* with the vision of "the community of believers *qua* 'uncoupled' outcasts from the social order" clinging to "the brief apparition of a future utopian Otherness."[8]

But there the similarities end, for Žižek's implicit espousal of the politics of exodus operates very differently. Augustine described the two cities, Babylon and Jerusalem, as being governed by *cupiditas* and *caritas* respectively. But whereas Hardt and Negri make desire the defining characteristic of the multitude who inhabit their secular "divine city," Žižek sticks with *caritas* (for which he uses the Greek *agape*) as the primary virtue of his community of revolutionary outcasts. Augustine argued that *cupiditas* should be reigned in, and *caritas* spurred on. Yet, as Žižek points out, both are counterproductive. Forbidding desire is the best way to maintain it; commanding *caritas*, like the Kantian ethical imperative, turns love into obedience.

The reinterpretation of *agape* that Žižek offers as a way of appropriating the Christian legacy takes the form of a paradox. According to Žižek, hate is the new love. Jesus said: "If anyone come to me and does not hate his father and his mother, his wife and children, his brothers and sisters—yes, even his own life—he cannot be my disciple." Here, hatred does not imply an irrational anatagonism, but a self-destructive act of renunciation. Giving up his or her stake in the world uncouples the subject from the social order; the sacrifice of what is most precious "changes the co-ordinates of the situation in which the subject finds himself; by cutting himself loose from the precious object through whose possession the enemy kept him in check, the subject gains the space of free action."[9]

When Žižek's revolutionaries are leaving society, they may pass Hardt's and

Negri's multitude going the other way, for the path of the multitude goes into and through Empire. Hardt and Negri accept that there is a place for refusal and exodus but complain that "refusal in itself (of work, authority, and voluntary servitude) leads only to a kind of social suicide." There must also be a new community, and for them, the way to create such a community is through movement. So whereas Žižek complains that the obsession with immigrants obscures the issue of class, Hardt and Negri argue that migration is "a powerful form of class struggle within and against imperial postmodernity." The inhabitants of their city are "a new nomad horde, a new race of barbarians" who will reappropriate global space and affirm the right to control their own movement (213).

Hardt and Negri share Augustine's assumption that the significance of the act of movement comes from its capacity to connect with a utopian otherness. But where Žižek's outcasts seem to tune in to the Absolute just by dropping out, Hardt's and Negri's multitude are on a pilgrimage to wherever their desire takes them. Returning to Augustine's source in Plotinus, they imagine the multitude saying: "Let us flee then to the beloved Fatherland." And where is the Fatherland? "Close the eyes and call instead upon another vision that is to be waked within you, a vision, the birth-right of all, which few turn to use."[10] The passage comes from a section of the *Enneads*, where Plotinus urges people to turn from the illusory images seen in the mirror of matter and embark upon the reascent to the intelligible world. Hardt and Negri naturally eschew Plotinus's idealism, but the reference is nevertheless revealing. Despite appearances, even the nomad horde has a utopian destination in which "cooperation and revolution remain together, in love, simplicity, and innocence" (413).

## A Smooth World

Exodus has traditionally involved three phases: the initial convulsive act of uncoupling; a period of wandering in the wilderness, and finally the long-awaited arrival in the promised land. But for its postmodern interpreters, it has become a two-place relation: Žižek makes exit into arrival, Hardt and Negri turn nomadism into the Neoplatonic ascent of the soul. When Marx likened the revolutionaries of 1848 to "the Jews whom Moses led through the wilderness," it was because he knew they had a long way to go.[11] But in *Empire*, the wandering becomes a goal in itself, for here Hardt's and Negri's Augustinian rhetoric intersects with Deleuze's and Guattari's nomadology.

Deleuze and Guattari distinguish between the migrant and the nomad in terms of the kind of space they occupy: "the migrant goes principally from one point to another," whereas for the nomad, "although the points determine paths, they are strictly subordinated to the paths they determine." So where the migrant moves along the paths formed by striated space, the nomad is "distributed by turbulence across a smooth space."[12] In *Empire*, however, the terms "migrant" and "nomad" are used to denote the same people, and "migration" is described as "nomadism" whenever Hardt and Negri want to emphasise its liberatory potential. The reason they felt able to do this is that they believe we now all live in a "smooth world."

Borrowing Deleuze's and Guattari's distinction between smooth and striated space, they argue that the withering of civil society has smoothed "the striation of modern social space," and that national boundaries have collapsed because the world market "requires a smooth space of uncoded and deterritorialized flows" (329, 332–333). The perception is not in itself unusual; Castells argues that contemporary society works through the "space of flows"; Bauman sees a "liquid modernity" freed of "fences, barriers, fortified borders and checkpoints."[13] But within the framework provided by Deleuze and Guattari, the smoothness of the world is more than a metaphor for it necessarily transforms every migrant into a nomad and the wilderness into the Fatherland.

The smoothing-out of the world also makes traditional forms of politics obsolete. In *The Labor of Dionysus*, Hardt and Negri claim that "the smooth spaces" of societies of control have erased the striations that gave socialist strategy a foothold and made "the idea of socialism possible." But just as smoothing obliterates some possibilities, it releases others, "the indomitable Dionysus of freedom and communism."[14] In *Empire*, the identity of this Dionysus is revealed. When Hardt and Negri announce that: "A specter haunts the world and it is the specter of migration" (213), the echoes of the *Communist Manifesto* are more than fortuitous. Dionysus is a nomad too.

We have come full circle, and yet the constellation of images has somehow stayed the same. The mirror of Dionysus may have been turned around, but it is smooth on both sides. Deleuze and Guattari claim that smooth space is "A Body without Organs" and that the Body without Organs is "exactly the opposite" of the Lacanian *corps morcelé*: "not at all a question of a fragmented, splintered body, of organs without the body."[15] So whereas, for the Neoplatonists, the smoothness of the world was the deceptive lure that led souls to fall into material fragmentation, for Hardt and Negri it is the condition of the multitude's utopian aggregation. In one case, the world looks so smooth that the migrant is drawn towards the image reflected on it; in the other, the world actually is so smooth that the nomad glides across its surface.

## Sociology

Whatever else it is, myth is always sociology. In Deleuze and Guattari, the Body without Organs is not just an inversion of the Lacanian *corps morcelé* but also an alternative to the Durkheimian concept of organic solidarity. The anti-

Durkheimian thrust of *A Thousand Plateaus* (often ignored in the secondary literature) emerges in the authors' championing of several concepts that Durkheim had relegated to primitive stages of social development—chief among them the Body without Organs. Like Deleuze and Guattari, Durkheim used biological models for social forms. He cited polyps as an example of mechanical solidarity, noting that:

> There exists in the animal world an individuality "which is produced outside any combination of organs." Now this is identical to that of societies that we have termed segmentary . . . since the parts that make up an animal colony are mechanically intertwined with one another, they can only act as a whole, at least so long as they remain joined together.[16]

In contrast, organic solidarity involves "a system of different organs," just as, in more complex organisms, "each part of the animal, once it has become an organ, has its own sphere of action, in which it moves independently, without impinging on the others."[17]

Deleuze's and Guattari's Body without Organs, which "is opposed not to the organs but to that organization of the organs called the organism,"[18] therefore corresponds closely to Durkheim's definition of mechanical solidarity. And so too does their use of segmentarity as a model of social distribution. When they suggest that "the opposition sociologists establish between the segmentary and the central is biological deep down: the ringed worm and the central nervous system" they are simply reproducing the terms that Durkheim uses in the *Division of Labour*.[19] As for the nomad horde, it is the social unit that Durkheim took to be the primal form of mechanical solidarity, "an absolutely homogeneous mass whose parts would not be distinguishable from one another and consequently not be arranged in any order in relation to one another."[20]

The distinction between the smooth and the striated, although without a Durkheimian provenance, reproduces many of the same features. Smooth space and striated space are, respectively, nomad space and sedentary space: the steppe, the desert, and the sea are smooth, while "the city is striated space par excellence."[21] It is this anti-Durkheimian sociology, in which postmodernity uncannily reproduces the characteristics of premodern social life, to which Hardt and Negri are the heirs. Like Deleuze and Guattari, they hope that the Durkheimian oppositions between the organic and the mechanical, the central and the segmentary are all illusory. They are correspondingly uncomfortable with any account of society that emphasizes its centralization, cohesion, or complexity. The transition from disciplinary society to the society of control is, they suggest, not the spread of organic solidarity but a new segmentarity (336). Nomad hordes roam the smooth spaces of Empire.

In *The Labor of Dionysus*, Hardt and Negri pointed to "Bodies without Organs" as one of "the subjective figures today capable of communism."[22] But if, in *Empire*, the nomad horde has replaced the Body without Organs as the vehicle of communism, it hardly represents a shift in the implied model of social aggregation. As Durkheim argued, a body without organs, such as a community of polyps in which each stomach communicates with all the others, is an example of communism in the fullest sense, and the horde represents an equivalent degree of shared equality, for "communism is the necessary product of that special social cohesion that swallows up the individual within the group."[23] Hardt and Negri may wish to distance their version of communism from the primitive forms of mechanical solidarity they take as models, but it is unclear on what basis they would do so. Their nomad horde is made up of those who have uncoupled from social roles and aggregated on the basis of the constituent principle, for which, by definition, consensus is always required.[24]

## Migration

The anti-Durkheimian sociology that Hardt and Negri inherit from Deleuze and Guattari has important consequences for their understanding of the politics of migration. Whether it is the absence of people or merely the lack of differentiation within a population, smoothness always signifies an absence of the social, for in a smooth world there are none of the striations that characterize complex societies. This creates an elective affinity between smoothness and migration. Migration is something that often seems to take place outside the social, not, of course, in the sense that it is presocial, but because movement between societies is not fully governed by the laws of either. Migrants reject the society from which they come and, if they move in sufficient numbers, need take little account of the society to which they go. The difference between migration and invasion is only one of degree; migration, like revolution, can be the making and the unmaking of the social, not something that happens within it.

Migration is therefore a natural model for a politics in which political agency is unfettered by preexisting social structures and a tempting substitute for the idea of revolution. Whereas traditional politics presupposes the social, in a smooth world you can have a politics without a sociology, a politics of unimpeded movement. Hardt and Negri see Deleuze and Guattari as having posited "a vision of democracy as in an absolutely horizontal social plane on which social bodies are set loose to destroy the strictures of predetermined social forms."[25] And in *Empire* they lyrically celebrate the potential of migration to effect this destruction: contemporary population movements "cannot be completely subjugated to the laws of capitalist accumulation—at every moment they overflow and shatter the bounds of measure," redrawing the map of the world so that: "A new geography is established by the multitude as the productive flows of bodies define new rivers and ports" (397).

But although a smooth politics may be unconstrained by preexisting social forms, it is, for that reason constrained in the social forms that it can take. Hardt and Negri think of migration in terms of "subtraction and defection," as though it were a zero-sum relation between distinct groups (212). One community's loss is another's gain, and the map of the world is redrawn accordingly. Citing the example of migration from former communist states, they ask: "What recent event could be a stronger example of the power of desertion and exodus, the power of the nomad horde, than the fall of the Berlin Wall and the collapse of the entire Soviet bloc?" They therefore conclude that "mobility and mass worker nomadism always express a refusal and a search for liberation" (212, 213, 214).

But, as Durkheim pointed out, the zero-sum conception of population movement works only in the case of mechanical solidarity, where, if someone finds a leader oppressive, he or she just goes off to join another group or else to form a new one.[26] It was only the attempt to impose a rigid, artificial conformity on the population of Eastern Europe that made crossing the Berlin Wall into an act of desertion. Within the context of the Cold War, East-West movement was a loss for one side and a gain for the other. But that exchange is hardly characteristic of population movement generally. (The relationship was not even symmetrical: moving from West to East did not signify in quite the same way.) Migration redraws the ideological map only when someone renounces one identity and takes on another that was impossible within the social group from which he or she came. Neither the great European migrations to the Americas nor the contemporary global flows from South to North conform to this model. Some of the Puritan settlers may have wanted to forge new identities in the New World, but many of the first generation of immigrants from Southern and Eastern Europe sought to transpose their community life unchanged. In contemporary Europe (and in the Gulf States), guest workers are often more like commuters without transport than nomads.

Although nomadism might effect political change in a world of totalitarian monoliths, in the complex societies of late modernity it is largely an attempt to keep up with capital flows, motivated as much by the desire for wealth as by Hardt's and Negri's "wealth of desire." This is not to say that free migration is not a fundamental human right or that greater freedom of movement would not be desirable. (For example, at a time when many of the American working class live in Asia, it is difficult to separate the capacity to move freely between countries from the ability of workers to take effective industrial action.) But migration between countries is not in itself any more revolutionary than movement within them. Hardt's and Negri's claim that:

"Throughout the history of modernity, the mobility and migration of the labour force have disrupted the disciplinary conditions to which workers are constrained" ignores the fact that migration is often linked with the most severe forms of labor discipline (212). The distinction between forced and voluntary migration is sometimes blurred: slaves, bonded laborers, and the first generation of factory workers were often migrants who had either moved under duress or else had harsh constraints placed upon them as a condition or result. Migration can lead to captivity as well as to freedom. The Exodus was necessary only because the Israelites had migrated to Egypt in the first place.

## Desire

Myths inevitably tend to work with a premodern understanding of society: salvation lies in mechanical solidarity; organic solidarity is sin. For this reason, Hardt's and Negri's sociology fits snugly into their Augustinian mythology. Migration between the Earthly and the Heavenly Cities is a zero-sum exchange in the heavenly direction. But it does not work like that the other way round. When souls fall into matter, they are not cut off from Fatherland, just alienated from it. Babylon, with its half-assimilated population of guest workers, is more like a modern city than the New Jerusalem, and the reality of migration is often closer to the fall of the soul in both its motivation and its consequences. Many migrants' picture of their destination is produced by burnishing its surface until they see themselves reflected in a it. European fantasies of the New World are one example, but the same process was at work in the migrations from the countryside to the city that characterized the nineteenth and twentieth centuries. Narcissistic illusion is the lure, the "future utopian otherness" that draws people from one place to another. As Thomas Friedman mordantly remarks in *The Lexus and the Olive Tree*: "the 'wretched of the earth' want to go to Disney World—not to the barricades."[27]

But if migrants are on their way to Disney World rather than the New Jerusalem, why should their wanderings be of any interest to political theorists of the left? Because they never get there. As Durkheim noted, one of the ironies of modernity is that although complex societies are heavily dependent upon migration, they are less able to assimilate immigrants than those characterized by mechanical solidarity. Like all narcissistic fantasies, the image of the self that inspires migration is forever elusive—even Disney World is not pure Disney— fragmentation and alienation are the almost inevitable outcome, for even if they manage to make the journey, many migrants discover that the Ideal-I has moved on, leaving them once more a fragmented body, a mere "inchoate collection of desires" (as Lacan describes it).[28] In the case of migration to more complex societies (which is the predominant form of migration in the modern world), there is a sociological explanation. Unlike the unified reflection glimpsed in the smoothed surface of their destination, most migrants find that movement inevitably involves a painful accommodation to the striations of modernity—division of labor and the separation of economic from social roles. But such fragmentation is lack rather than loss. And as both Lacan and Plotinus emphasize, fragmentation is also desire, and desires, unlike narcissistic fantasies, can easily be shared.

Lacan's famous insistence that desire is *le désir de l'Autre* is routinely traced to Kojève's claim that desire is either the desire for the desire of another person ("I want him to want me") or else the mimetic desire for something that is already desired by another. Plotinus reached the conclusion through a rather different route. Given that our bodies qua bodies have sensations but no volitions, while our natures have no sensations and so no desires, how is desire possible? Answer: through the relationship between the two; our nature picks up the unformed desire of the body and, like a mother who makes the inarticulate desires of a child her own, acts upon them. So for our nature, *"le désir vient d'un autre, et existe pour un autre"* (as Bréhier's translation has it).[29] This seems close to Lacan in the emphasis on the way in which identification with another results in desiring what the other desires not just because the other desires it but instead of or on behalf of another. For Lacan, the strange workings of this principle were exhibited in Anna O.'s phantom pregnancy around the time her analyst Brauer had a child.[30] But was Anna's desire for a child Brauer's, or Brauer's desire Anna's? It makes no difference; both desires are vicarious.

Desire is also of central importance to Hardt and Negri. For them, however, it is not migration that leads to desire, but desire that leads to migration (213). Like Deleuze and Guattari, for whom the Body without Organs is "that which one desires and by which one desires," they make desire immanent within the multitude.[31] Their version of "assembling, assembled desire" is the nomad horde—constituted "through the desires of the multitude" as counter-Empire.[32] In Lacanian theory, by contrast, desire is mediated rather than assembled. The desire of the other is often not so much desire of another as of the Other, the symbolic order. The conclusion usually drawn from this is that desire is always socially constructed, and that there can be no opposition between heteronomous desire (what the Other wants) and autonomous desire (what I really want). Unlike mimetic desire, vicarious desire is socially transmitted rather than constructed, and so insofar as Lacan's account carries with it traces of Plotinus's it is open to reinterpretation. Nevertheless, the essential point remains. Desire presupposes a system of difference, a striated space.

But what is its effect? One of the few political theorists to consider the possibility of something like vicarious desire was John C. Calhoun, the Southern apologist for slavery who features in Negri's *Insurgencies* as a theorist of constituent power.[33] Like others in the republican tradition, he took individual selfishness to be the basis of all political life and the motivating force behind the constituent principle. But he acknowledged that human beings also have "sympathetic or social feelings" and briefly allowed himself to imagine what might happen if people's "feelings and affections were stronger for others than for themselves, or even as strong." The result, he suggested, would be "that all individuality would be lost. . . . For each, at the same moment, intensely participating in all the conflicting emotions of those around him, would, of course, forget himself and all that concerned him immediately, in his officious intermeddling with the affairs of all others."[34]

Calhoun's thought experiment is interesting on several counts. It involves vicarious participation in the experiences of others (not merely sympathy for or recognition of the Other) and so envisages a situation in which individuality itself is redefined. Yet this is not (as with the communism of the nomad horde) a case in which the individual is swallowed up within the group but one that presupposes difference while allowing that individuality might be redistributed across it. It suggests that where desire is the desire of the other, it will become not just a hybrid desire, but the desire of a hybrid being. This is what Calhoun most feared. He was writing during the campaign for the abolition of slavery, and the vicarious sympathies he dismissed were those that led to emancipation—the very ones that allowed people, as W. E. B. DuBois later put it, "to descry in others that transfigured spark of divinity which we call Myself."[35]

## Politics

At one point in their argument, Hardt and Negri come close to admitting that the world may not be as smooth as it looks: "The space of imperial sovereignty . . . might appear to be free of the binary divisions or striation of modern boundaries, but really it is criss-crossed by so many fault lines that it only appears as a continuous, uniform space" (190). Yet, rather than working with the idea that the striation of society has become so fine and complex that it gives the illusion of smoothness, Hardt and Negri prefer to treat the appearance as though it were the reality. Indeed, their willingness to turn migration into nomadism and to substitute nomadism for more conventional forms of emancipatory politics presupposes that the smoothness is real: only in a smooth world is a migrant a nomad; only where there is mechanical solidarity is the nomad a revolutionary; only where the striations of modernity are erased is the Dionysus of communism freed from the complex web of social relations.

"Never believe that a smooth space will suffice to save us," cautioned Deleuze and Guattari.[36] Hardt and Negri fail to heed the warning and, by turning Deleuze's and Guattari's nomadism into an Augustinian pilgrimage, they smooth the world into a mirror in which the multitude can see the fantasy of its own unity. Using Lacan to rework the Neoplatonic myth on which

Augustinian pilgrimage is based and reasserting the Durkheimian conception of organic solidarity against Deleuze's and Guattari's Body without Organs help us to see the cracks in the mirror—the striations behind the illusion of smoothness. And from the pairing of Durkheim and Lacan something else emerges as well—the possibility that the political potential of migration lies not in transcending social striation, but in contributing to it.

Whereas Plotinus values unity over multiplicity and treats the mirror image of unity that precipitates the descent of souls as something quite different from the true unity to which they reascend, Lacan treats unity and multiplicity as complementary fantasies between which the subject oscillates and makes the mirror stage into the phase of infantile development that culminates in socialization. In so doing, he opens the way to a more nuanced understanding of migration. It may be inspired by deception and motivated by narcissistic fantasy; fragmentation, alienation, and exploitation may be the immediate result, but, in the long run, migration brings a potential benefit. Its very failure to change the world into a utopia creates the conditions for solidarity. You may move only because you can see yourself inhabiting a smooth space; but once there, you have the benefit of living in a striated one—a newly found capacity to form alliances with others different from yourself.

For example, the Industrial Workers of the World, better known as the Wobblies, were a revolutionary group who coordinated industrial protest across the United States in the early years of the twentieth century. In Hardt's and Negri's account, they feature as "the great Augustinian project of modern times" whose "perpetual movement . . . was indeed an immanent pilgrimage, creating a new society in the shell of the old" (207). But in fact the Wobblies gathered support amongst those who had already made the move to the place of their dreams: migrants who had gone out West but were struggling to survive; European immigrants whose fantasies of the New World had left them slaving in the kitchens of New York hotels; African Americans and Poles whose journey to freedom had ended on the waterfront in Philadelphia.

Hardt and Negri concede that the Wobblies had extraordinary success amongst immigrants. But of the two defining characteristics of the movement, "its organizational mobility and its ethnic-linguistic hybridity," Hardt and Negri make the former (which they treat as a type of migration) into the model for their counterimperial politics while remaining deeply sceptical about the significance of the latter (207). Because hybridity is identity distributed across striation, it has little place in Hardt's and Negri's smooth politics. For them, "hybridity itself is an empty gesture, and the mere refusal of order simply leaves us on the edge of nothingness—or worse, these gestures risk reinforcing imperial power rather than challenging it" (216, 217). Fragmentation is to be transcended through aggregation rather than hybrid desire. They miss the crucial point that, even though hybridity itself may be less than revolutionary, it may still be the precondition of political solidarity within a complex society.

The case of the Wobblies suggests that the descent of the soul—the fall into fragmentation and desire—may prove to be the more productive model for a contemporary politics of migration. And it is not just migration that can be be thought of in these terms. Almost all political theorists since Plato have supposed that the object of politics is to counter the degenerative and centrifugal tendencies of society and so reestablish unity and a sense of community. Comte, for example, maintained that the extension of society threatened to divide it into a host of disparate parts which hardly seem "to belong to the same species," and argued that the primary purpose of politics was to reverse or contain the "fatal trend to a fundamental dispersion of ideas, sentiments, and interests."[37]

Although utopian politics has moved from exodus to revolution and back, it has retained this presupposition. The goal is to break open the existing social structure and create a new order without the social divisions of the old. In *Empire*, the multitude's resistance to bondage is "the struggle against the slavery of belonging to a nation, an identity, and a people," and their desire is not "the cosmopolitical state but a common species," a secular Pentecost where the "nomads speak a common tongue" (362). But at the beginning of the twenty-first century, the belief that the object of politics is to reverse the centrifugal effects of the social is increasingly difficult to sustain. One of the central facts of twentieth-century history is the failure of utopian politics in complex societies. Durkheim's view that the ideal of universal human brotherhood entailed not the reversal of social diversification but its further continuation seems, in retrospect, to have been justified.[38]

The problem for Hardt and Negri, as for many other political theorists of the left, is that their secular utopianism retains the social dynamics of its mythological predecessors. The road to utopia always leads up rather than down, and the multitude is united "in love, simplicity, and innocence." But a utopianism that is truly secular rather than merely secularized must also be open to the possibility that justice is to be found in fragmentation, complexity, and confusion—on "the edge of nothingness," in Babylon.

## Notes

1. Plotinus, *Enneads* 4.3.12. See also Jean Pépin, "Plotin et le miroir de Dionysos," *Revue internationale de philosophie* 24 (1970): 304–20.

2. Jacques Lacan, *Écrits. A Selection* (London: Norton, 1977), 1–7.

3. Jacques Lacan, *The Seminar: Book VII: The Ethics of Psychoanalysis, 1959–60* (London: Norton, 1992) 284–285; Erwin Rohde, *Psyché* (Paris: Payot, 1928) 358–362.

4. Plotinus is referred to in the seminars of February 2, 1956, November 29, 1961, April 15, 1964, April 26, 1967, and May 7, 1969.

5. Michael Walzer, *Exodus and Revolution* (New York: Basic Books, 1985).

6. See Paolo Virno, "Virtuosity and Revolution: The Political Theory of Exodus," in Paolo Virno and

Michael Hardt, eds., *Radical Thought in Italy* (Minneapolis, MN: University of Minnesota Press, 1996) 189–210.

7. Michael Hardt and Antonio Negri, *Empire* (Cambridge, MA: Harvard University Press, 2000), 364, 363. Subsequent references to *Empire* inserted parenthetically in the text.

8. Slavoj Žižek, *The Fragile Absolute* (London: Verso 2000), 10, 160.

9. Žižek, *Fragile Absolute*, 120, 150.

10. Plotinus, *Enneads*, 1.6.8.

11. Karl Marx and Frederick Engels, *Collected Works*, vol. 10 (London: Lawrence and Wishart, 1978), 117.

12. Gilles Deleuze and Félix Guattari, *A Thousand Plateaus* trans. Brian Massumi (Minneapolis, MN: University of Minnesota Press, 1987), 380, 363.

13. Manuel Castells, *The Rise of the Network Society* (Oxford, U.K.: Blackwell, 1996) 376f; Zygmunt Bauman, *Liquid Modernity* (Cambridge, U.K.: Polity Press, 2000), 14.

14. Michael Hardt and Antonio Negri, *The Labor of Dionysus* (Minneapolis, MN: University of Minnesota Press, 1994), 261, 21.

15. Deleuze and Guattari, *Thousand Plateaus*, 479, 164.

16. Émile Durkheim, *The Division of Labour in Society*, trans. W. D. Hall (Basingstoke, UK: Macmillan, 1984) 140. The quotation is from Edmond Perrier's *Les colonies animales* (1881), a work also used by Deleuze and Guattari; see *Thousand Plateaus*, 522, n. 8.

17. Durkheim, *Division of Labour*, 132 and 140.

18. Deleuze and Guattari, *Thousand Plateaus*, 158.

19. Deleuze and Guattari, *Thousand Plateaus*, 210; cf. Durkheim, *Division of Labour*, 140 and 171.

20. Durkheim, *Division of Labour*, 126.

21. Deleuze and Guattari, *Thousand Plateaus*, 379, 489.

22. Hardt and Negri, *Labor of Dionysus*, 14.

23. Durkheim, *Division of Labour*, 140, 130.

24. Durkheim, *Division of Labour*, 150.

25. Hardt and Negri, *Labor of Dionysus*, 289.

26. Durkheim, *Division of Labour*, 102–103.

27. Thomas Friedman, *The Lexus and the Olive Tree* (New York: Farrar, Straus, and Giroux, 1999), 364.

28. Jacques Lacan, *The Seminar: Book III: The Psychoses, 1955–56* (London: Norton, 1993), 39.

29. Plotinus, *Enneads*, 4.4.20. Émile Bréhier, *Ennéades*, vol. 4 (Paris: Les Belles Lettres, 1927), 122.

30. Jacques Lacan, *The Four Fundamental Concepts of Psycho-analysis* (London, Norton: 1998), 158.

31. Deleuze and Guattari, *Thousand Plateaus*, 165; *Empire*, 66.

32. Deleuze and Guattari, *Thousand Plateaus*, 399; *Empire*, 214.

33. Antonio Negri, *Insurgencies* trans. Maurizia Boscaglia (Minneapolis, MN: University of Minnesota Press, 1999), 186–187.

34. John C. Calhoun, *A Disquisition on Government* in *Works* vol. 1 (New York: D. Appleton and Company, 1863), 6.

35. W. E. B. Du Bois, *The Souls of Black Folk* (New York: Penguin, 1989), 178.

36. Deleuze and Guattari, *Thousand Plateaus*, 500.

37. Auguste Comte, quoted in Durkheim, *Division of Labour*, 295.

38. Durkheim, *Division of Labour*, 337.

# 11

## Taking the Millennialist Pulse of *Empire*'s Multitude: A Genealogical Feminist Diagnosis

### Lee Quinby

*This demagoguery, of course, must be masked. It must hide its singular malice under the cloak of universals.*

—Michel Foucault, "Nietzsche, Genealogy, History"

From time to time, claims are made that we are living through a change so momentous that the world and human nature are never to be the same. Michael Hardt's and Antonio Negri's *Empire* is one such instance.[1] Hardt and Negri are hardly alone in the feeling that irrevocable forces of change are upon us. The year 2000 publication date of *Empire* coincided with what was commonly called "Millennium Madness" in the popular press. In the buildup to the year 2000, many people around the world and certainly throughout the United States reported great trepidation that the turn of the calendar would bring, if not the literal end of the world, at least the end of the world as we know it. For Christian fundamentalists, this fear was accompanied by an equally great hope that the end would be the result of divine power and would inaugurate the beginning of a new era, a millennium-long reign of peace and harmony for those who survived. For the more secularly inclined, fears of Y2K calamity were paramount. Hope was reduced to the ability to stow away in well-stocked shelters to weather the technological fallout. Either way—and these were not mutually exclusive by any means—there was a sense that some kind of calamity would descend full force upon us and out of that a new world order would begin.

It is useful to locate *Empire* within this context, not only because it reflects so many of the ideological coordinates of Millennial Madness, but also because one particularly worrisome effect of the September 11, 2001 assault on the World Trade Center and the Pentagon has been to rekindle intense levels of fear and hope that are endemic to apocalyptic and millennial belief. A June 2002 Time/CNN poll reports, for example, that 36 percent of Americans watch the evening news to see how it relates to the end of the world as foretold by God, and 59 percent believe that the events depicted in the Book of Revelation will come true.[2] Compounding this embrace of apocalyptic conviction is the astounding success of the *Left Behind* series of novels by Tim LaHaye and Jerry B. Jenkins.[3] Fusing together international political events with fictional accounts of the impending end of the world, these novels accentuate gore and violence in order to bring people into the fundamentalist fold. The series of twelve novels has so far sold over 32 million copies. Since only half of the readers are evangelicals, the series has apparently tapped into widespread cultural anxiety.[4]

The problem with such belief is that, over and over again historically, it has stirred people toward demonization, stereotyping, and scapegoating of perceived enemies and romanticized violence in the name of justified revenge.[5] As with any Grand Narrative, millennialism tends to homogenize diversity and totalize complexity through binary oppositions. Finally, these binary oppositions have been deeply gendered, providing explanations that reflect and perpetuate patriarchal/masculinist thought and practices, either disregarding or devaluing women's productive and reproductive activities.

In this essay, I want to show how Hardt and Negri incorporate those features of millennialism in their own Grand Narrative of Empire. What I want to establish is that Hardt's and Negri's millennialism weakens their analysis in precisely the two crucial arenas that would otherwise lend their theorizing its greatest strengths, namely, feminist allegiance and Foucauldian power analysis. Even though the state of the world calls for analysis from the left that inspires rather than demoralizes, millennial inspiration not only is burdened by the problems outlined above, its very optimism feeds a will to knowledge that activates demagoguery rather than building strategic awareness necessary for activism. In my view, the most effective antidote to millennialism is a genealogical feminist approach.[6] Genealogical feminism incorporates diverse coalitional politics to challenge racialized and heterosexist regimes of power/knowledge. Following Foucault's notion of genealogy, this approach seeks to "establish a historical knowledge of struggles and to make use of this knowledge tactically today."[7] Genealogical feminism is poised, in particular, to confront what Foucault derided as the "certainty of absolutes" that are part and parcel of millennial claims for the universality of truth and experiences.[8]

## The New World Order All Over Again

Demonstrating *Empire*'s millennial drift is a complicated undertaking, in no small part because of Hardt's and Negri's tendency to say one thing and yet do another. For example, even though they explicitly claim a nonprophetic stance by stating that they can see "only shadows of the figures that will animate our future" (205), much of what actually animates the book is its prophetic vision of the nature and role of the militant, the poor, the nomad, the new barbarian, and the multitude. In place of specific and concrete analysis—a hallmark of a genealogical approach—they stamp their theory with messianic categories that diminish rather than expand our understanding of productive and reproductive life.⁹ This contradiction is particularly noteworthy because *Empire*'s millennialism is what makes it compelling. Millennial rhetoric stirs the imagination toward exhilarating poles of fear and hope, promising a culminating and righteous telos to those who adhere to its tenets of belief. It is hard not to be drawn in.

A second interrelated contradiction arises from the fact that Hardt and Negri specifically reject transcendence, making numerous explicit claims for the immanence of their materialist approach, often drawing on Foucault to help make their case. In their opening pages, for example, they "rule out" the "idea that order is dictated by a single power and a single center of rationality *transcendent* to global forces" (3). Nevertheless, their recurrent appeals to certain categories of thought cast their theoretical framework back into transcendental molds integral to millennialism, which is both totalizing and abstractionist in its history and basic formulation.

As a result, Hardt's and Negri's theory of Empire may be best understood as a kind of secular millennialism or millennial immanence. As such, their formulation rests all too firmly on the twin pillars of millennialist thought: endism and electism. Their incorporation of these two foundational structures of millennial belief converts their secular ideas into messianic visions and pushes their claims of immanence toward transcendence.

Endism operates as the glue that holds together both apocalyptic fear and millennial hope. As Charles Strozier has shown, endism is different from reflection on the fact that we die, that we experience collective as well as individual endings. As he explains, "endism, or the location of self in some future, ultimate narrative, pushes such reflection into a profoundly different realm, wrapping the future in magical projections that isolate it from meaningful, human connection with the past."¹⁰ In apocalyptic and millennial belief, that magical projection typically claims transcendent authorization. The Greek word "apocalypse," which translates as "unveiling," suggests a revelation of some sort, in the sense of a disclosure. Primarily under the influence of

Christianity, however, it has come to mean the absolute truth about the final end of things. Similarly, the word "millennium" simply means a period of one thousand years, but over the past two millennia it has come to mean the particular thousand-year period that follows the divinely wrought End Times. These shifts are central to millennialism as a system of belief, that is, as a coherent worldview that has long predominated in the Christian West.

As the *Time* magazine polls indicate, for many who adhere to this view, this means a literal end to the world. In fundamentalist Christian belief, divine destruction of the earth is what makes possible a new heaven *on a new earth* in the form of the "New Jerusalem" (Revelation 21). In secular versions of millennial belief, large-scale natural or technological destruction replaces divine action, but a new era nonetheless follows in which those who survive create a new and deserving life on earth. While Hardt and Negri venture the possibility that an actual end to the world might come from inadvertent technological destruction, their greater concern and focus is on this secular version of endism, namely, the conviction that the *end of the world as we have known it* is upon us, or as they put it in their opening sentence: "Empire is materializing before our very eyes" (xi). Empire is, by their definition, a "new global form of sovereignty" (xii) that comprises "the new world order" (36).

Within millennial belief, the end of one order enables the beginning of another, most typically entailing an elect group that will prove victorious over forces of evil. Electism is the notion that there is a deserving group, the chosen, who defeat their foes and then reign supreme.[11] Typically, the chosen believe themselves to have absolute or at least greater truth on their side, while their opponents are deceived. This is what allows them to believe in their legitimacy as administrators of justice against their enemies. The identity of the elect leads to what Manuel Castells characterizes as "*the exclusion of the excluders by the excluded.*"[12] It is an identity formation that requires collective unity in order to function within the strict good-versus-evil binary logic of millennialism. The unity operates as an "either with us or against us" mentality. The new excluders see themselves as entirely justified in establishing the new and final order of the world in which they reign supreme.

Throughout *Empire*, this reactive identity formation is found most obviously in the series of figures of the future: the militant, the poor, the nomad, the new barbarian, and the multitude. These singular yet consistently stereotyped and collective figures function as the chosen within the binary schema of Empire versus counter-Empire. In particular, the category of the multitude, Hardt's and Negri's specific effort to provide a new name for what they see as a new material phenomena, is the general conception used to designate this collective plurality of singularities. In their own words, the "new bodies" (410) that house the "creative imagination of the multitude" (406) are the only agents capable of creating and living "the irrepressible lightness and joy of being communist" that is their telos (413). Such language may well be secular to the degree that is does not call for an end beyond time and an elect that has been divinely appointed, but it invokes those transcendent qualities nonetheless. Their defense of this seems to be in the insistence that the multitude is immanent because it possesses human agency. Yet is it difficult if not impossible to discern just how agency would work in this regard, especially since attempts to clarify it sound so, well, mystical, as with the "explanation" that the "universality of human creativity, the synthesis of freedom, desire, and living labor, is what takes place in the non-place of the postmodern relations of production" (210).

In concert with this puzzling notion of agency, Hardt and Negri define the multitude as "the universality of free and productive practices" (316). Their use of the term "practice" suggests their alignment with immanence. But rather than maintaining this stance, in keeping with the turn toward immanence to which they claim to adhere, their insertion of "universality" provides a hint of the totalizing tendencies that derail their theory by putting it in back on the track of transcendence. Even though they applaud Foucault's critique of "Man" as a transcendent category (91), their concept of the multitude as the universality of free practices runs against the grain of Foucauldian analysis. If we set out to examine free and productive practices, at least from a Foucauldian perspective, it would surely look more like Foucault's notion of genealogy, which pursues "the accidents, the minute deviations—or, conversely, the complete reversals—the errors, the false appraisals, and the faulty calculations that gave birth to those things that continue to exist and have value for us."[13] In Foucault's formulation, it would be difficult to know what universality might mean, other than a return to metaphysics, since genealogy uncovers a range of disparate practices in order to dislodge false claims of universality that actually exclude, discipline, or penalize those who do not or cannot manage normalized values. With the multitude, Hardt and Negri come closer to reinvigorating the category of Man than to advancing his death. The multitude is Man luminously draped "in love, simplicity, and also innocence" (413).

Far more than drawing on Foucault, the millennial disposition of *Empire* stems from its indebtedness to Augustine, whom Hardt and Negri credit as a vital precursor for their theorizing. As they put it, "we might take inspiration from Saint Augustine's vision to contest the decadent Roman Empire," adding the caveat that: "Our pilgrimage on earth, however, in contrast to Augustine's, has no transcendent telos beyond; it is and remains absolutely immanent" (207). This stated difference is a crucial one, but it does not entirely alleviate the millennial weight of their intellectual debt. This is the case, for example, in their adaptation of Augustine's binary opposition between the two cities that struggle for ultimate control, the evil decadent one versus the righteous "new city." Just how far afield is the New Jerusalem from what Hardt and Negri herald as their secular telos, "the earthly city of the multitude" (396)? Even though they declare their idea of a new city to be an immanent one, since it occurs on earth, this appeal to Augustine's divinely ordained city—which, after all, also occurs on earth once it has been made new—rhetorically lends theirs the transcendent attributes of unity that he espoused. Indeed, they do not settle just for Jerusalem; their city is fully globalized. Such millennial references make their ideas quite gripping, at least to readers immersed in Christianized, Western thought, but in the process, one gets gripped by the millennial tendency to reduce complexities to binary struggle and then declare one's own side triumphant.

This is also the case with their adaptation of Augustine's characterization of decadence to their category of imperial "corruption." The binary language of purity versus impurity is a cornerstone of millennial belief and edges its way into their secular vision as a binary opposition between "corruption" and "generation," the latter of which functions as the positive, productive desire of the multitude. "In Empire corruption is everywhere," they state with the reductive yet pervasive claims characteristic of apocalyptic belief. They decry corruption, most particularly because imperial power is "exercised in this *putrid* cloud, in the absence of *light* and *truth*" (389, emphasis mine). If one did not know that Hardt and Negri wrote those words, a good guess would be that Tim LaHaye and Jerry Jenkins had penned them. As is characteristic of millennial discourse and belief, the generative collectivity that Hardt and Negri envision emerges to exclude the previous excluders. In the binary mind-set of millennialism, a created Other is typically feminized, as with the Whore of Babylon in the New Testament's Book of Revelation. Claims for decadence of Empire take on these associations with Babylon, which resonates in Christian belief with the first Roman Empire. The new Empire thus takes the rhetorical place of the whorish Other, the decadent force that warrants annihilation.

## Premature Ejaculations

The long history of millennial belief has been a long history of gendered hatred, often compounded by disdain for sexuality and glorification of violence against one's enemies. For over two millennia, the most typical form of gender hostility has been intensely misogynistic, manifesting blatant enmity toward women or using feminized metaphors to justify violence against certain groups, as with the Whore of Babylon mentioned above. There are exceptions to this pattern. It is possible to be millennial and nonviolent, as with much New Age belief. And some millennial strains of feminism have reversed the gender hostility, representing men in general as the enemy. What is problematically retained, even in these instances, is the structure of binary division of Good versus Evil that tends to be expressed around gender and sexuality.

In its traditional and far more pervasive form, millennialism expresses a desire to be reborn without need of women and/or traits associated with them. The Book of Revelation provides the paradigm for millennialism in its most patriarchal, romantically violent glory. By its conclusion, women have been entirely removed from earth, but not before either demonizing them to the point of warranting their death, as with the woman called Jezebel in Revelation 2; idealizing them to the point of disappearance from the earth, as with the Woman Clothed with the Sun in Revelation 12; or justifying genocidal slaughter via debauched feminine metaphors, as with the Whore of Babylon in Revelation 17. The heroic elect—the 144,000 who "follow the Lamb" (Revelation 14)—are all virginal men who are to live free of suffering, illness, and death. But first, violence is waged full force as the only means to attain the utopian state of harmony. After a long series of horrific blood-soaked images of human misery—stemming from plagues, earthquakes, deadly waters, boils, locusts, warfare, satanic beasts, and sexual impurity—comes the riveting promise: "And God shall wipe away all tears from their eyes, and there shall be no more death, neither sorrow, nor crying, neither shall there be any more pain" (21:4). This ultimate defeat of need, suffering, and death is a second birth achieved without a female body, freed of the obligation of bodily care for others, and relieved of the profound uncertainty that is part of human knowing.

As the daily news indicates, it is not hard to find contemporary instances of such misogynistic versions of millennialism among extremists in the secular world as well as within all three of the world's leading religions: Christianity, Islam, and Judaism. Yet extremism should not make us miss the fact that much of today's millennial belief retains a masculinist bias without proclaiming such strident antiwoman sentiment. In this form, the millennial vision exhibits blatant gender-blindness by ignoring women as specific subjects and agents of history and/or subsuming them into so-called universal values that are actually associated with men. *Empire*'s millennialism is of this type. As such, it retains a romanticized form of violence that has long been endemic to millennial rhetoric. In this "kinder, gentler" form of millennialism, masculinist values, particularly what Barry McCarthy has called "warrior values," are universalized. Even in cultures with little firsthand experience of war, these traits are romantically associated with proper manhood; in contemporary society, warrior values are widely promoted in media representation, ranging from news coverage to futuristic films.[14] The effect is a buildup of universalizing pressure, often toward nationalistic, patriotic fervor that seemingly includes women even as it accents masculinist values in its constitution.

In *Empire*, despite its antinationalism, warrior values resonate in names such as "the militant" and the "new barbarian." Presumably, such terms are supposed to prompt a kind of bold, Nietzschean pride, an overturning of the racialized dichotomy between the "civilized" and "barbaric," but I wonder if Hardt and Negri considered how such terms might sound to feminist-attuned ears. From my feminist perspective, at any rate, it is premature to celebrate militancy and barbarianism. Too much blood has been shed, most often at the hands of men, to risk sounding glib about barbaric violence. As a point of contrast, it is worth returning to what Robin Morgan pointed out in her prescient book on terrorism from 1989, *The Demon Lover*. Reminding readers that evocations of romanticized violence occur at every point along the political spectrum, whether left, right, or center, she argues that such evocations are historically masculinist: "it is undeniable that history is a record of most women *acting peaceably* and of most men *acting belligerently*—to a point where the capacity for belligerence is regarded as an essential ingredient of manhood and the proclivity for conciliation is thought largely a quality of women."[15] On one crucial point I would disagree with Morgan, namely that history is a record of most men acting belligerently. I would say instead that, of those who have acted belligerently, most have been men. But the point I want to take from Morgan is this: from a genealogical feminist perspective, it is important not to lose sight of the ways that masculinist views of violence are constructed and renegotiated.

This is neither to say that violence must always be shunned nor that women are incapable of it. It is to stress that romanticized evocations of violence override context-specific perceptiveness about when it is necessary and when it might simply breed more senseless violence for its own sake. *Empire* not only espouses romanticized forms of violence, it also totalizes it, stating that: "If there is to be a solution to the problem, it cannot help being material and explosive" (368). A more context-bound perspective on violence may be seen in Leo Panitch's analysis of "Violence as a Tool of Order and Change" in regard to the antiglobalization movement, a movement that Hardt and Negri have themselves pointed to as a sign of a "*new place* within the dominant nonplace of Empire, a new organization of the multitude" (emphasis in original).[16] Refuting right-wing charges that the movement employs terrorist forms of violence—and pointing out that currently the use of violence is more often found on the extreme right—Panitch observes that: "what precisely characterizes this generation and this movement in contrast with earlier ones on the European and North American left is the explicit eschewal, even among its most militant elements, of either armed revolutionary struggle or terrorism (along the lines of the Red Brigades or Weathermen just a generation ago) as a means of effecting change in the advanced capitalist countries."[17] Arguing that the movement does need to get beyond protest, he calls for more concerted efforts of activism and negotiation geared toward "addressing, including through direct action, the immediate troubles facing people in their own societies, helping in this way the longterm process of class formation and political organization to begin anew in the countries of the North."[18]

Panitch's comments, like Morgan's, remind us that historically violence has most systematically been used as a tool of oppressive order. Hardt and Negri not only lose sight of this in their advocacy of violence in general, but they also confuse resistance and violence. Momentarily veering away from their poststructuralist critique of the "natural," they designate *"the will to be against"* as "one of the most natural and healthy acts" (210; emphasis in original), oddly appealing to a human nature model. In keeping with the propensity to romanticize, they point to several forms that resistance to authority might take in the era of imperial sovereignty. These range from the outright violent and resonantly macho, in their promise that the "new nomad horde, a new race of barbarians, will arise to invade or evacuate Empire" (213), to the commercially fashionable, in the "now common aesthetic mutations of the body, such as piercings and tattoos" (216). Conceding that the latter are insufficiently radical (not to mention absurd under the circumstances), they indicate that the "will to be against really needs a body that is incapable of adapting to family life, to factory discipline, to the regulations of a traditional sex life, and so forth" (216).

But this is to confuse radical politics with the 1960s escapist rhetoric that prompted a feminist rebuttal. If maladaptation to families is radical, then countless uncelebrated men have apparently been leading the way of revolt all along. The mere inability to adapt to rigid patriarchal family structures is insufficient as a politics since it has more often led to what Rhonda Hammer calls "family terrorism." Her work shows that the "expansion of poverty and abuse, especially in regard to women and children, has been escalating on a global scale," with families as primary sites for its expression.[19] This increase of abuse and poverty must be understood as a gendered effect of globalization.

More to point in regard to *Empire*, this is a key instance in which Hardt and Negri have missed a basic feminist premise. While feminists have led the charge against male violence and dominance within families as well as the exclusions and hypocrisies contained in the use of family as an oppressive concept, it does not necessarily follow that all forms of family are equally an obstacle to democratic freedom, as Hardt and Negri suggest here. Bolstered by its reliance on millennial endings and masculinist universals and avowing romanticized forms of violence and resistance, *Empire* actually ignores the pressing problem of male violence all over the world by employing a kind of "postdisciplinary" smugness.

Hardt's and Negri's gender-blindness renders their concept of resistance to authority rhetorically engorged yet methodologically flaccid. Although they uphold factory workers and migrant populations as instances of resistance, they provide almost no examination of how the practices of everyday life of such groups might operate in opposition to Empire. Nor does their theory provide for ways to assess whether these practices comprise resistance or perpetuate inequalities. Instead, rhetorical flourishes about romanticized resistance substitute for analysis of actual practices, as in the assertion that: "Mobility and mass worker nomadism always express a refusal and a search for liberation" (212). There is simply no "always" in analysis of immanent practices.

Far more fruitful is an analytical approach that allows us to recognize the concrete consequences of power relations, which can be and often are highly varied, ranging from capitulation and reinforcement of the status quo to challenge and overturning of prevailing forces. Manuel Castells's *The Power of Identity* provides an important resource in this regard, since he not only puts gender into the forefront of global power relations but also shows how diverse these power relations necessarily are. As he states, in the past quarter-century, we have "witnessed what amounts to a mass insurrection of women against their oppression throughout the world, albeit with different intensity depending on culture and country."[20] In contrast to *Empire*, Castells demonstrates that a grounded analysis of global capital *begins* with its gendered spaces of labor, sexuality, family, reproduction, and communication and *looks for* what variations of practice might tell us about globalization's operations.

To the further detriment of theoretical acumen, *Empire* also lacks a gender analysis that might differentiate the ways in which men and women confront authority over their lives. By contrast, when such genealogical feminist analysis is done, as, for example, in the work of Raka Ray on male and female domestic workers in Calcutta, there is a far less sanguine sense of the kind of resistance available to these workers. Ray demonstrates how gendered identities are differently constructed for the men and women she studied, concluding that: "it would be a mistake to romanticize these constructions as resistance, for they do not invent the content of these identities as they please. Their identities are constituted through their class location, the work they do, and their particular relationship to a domestic space, which is also their place of work."[21] Theorizing how power operates requires a specific and meticulous investigation that does not presuppose a universality of practices, free or constrained.

Adding injury to the insult of omission of gender analysis, the seemingly inclusive concepts of collectivity and community espoused throughout *Empire* become primary vehicles for promoting its millennial/masculinist values. Ironically, this is done by an analytical sleight of hand, evoking feminist critique but then turning it on its head. This twist is achieved through a discussion of women's productive and reproductive labor and appears in a crucial section of *Empire* on shifts that are occurring via the postmodernization of the global economy. As Hardt and Negri explain, this shift has two faces; one produces "informatization of production," while the other entails the "affective labor of human contact and interaction" (292). They state emphatically that affective labor is "better understood as beginning from what feminist analyses of 'women's work' have called 'labor in the bodily mode'" (293). Such an acknowledgment is promising from a genealogical feminist perspective.

As their line of thought continues, however, readers discover that while affective or caring labor may begin as corporeal, it is really, according to their theory of Empire, a feature of the "immaterial labor" integral to the multitude. This is supposedly a positive turn of events because it is ultimately the way in which the multitude acquires community. Yet it is precisely through this conceptual maneuver that the category of the multitude loses the bodily physicality through which—from a genealogical feminist perspective—power operates in any number of ways. In *Empire*'s theory, by contrast, the shift toward immaterial labor is valorized to a utopian promise of "spontaneous and elementary communism" (294). They claim that in this shift "*cooperation is completely immanent to the laboring activity itself*" (294; emphasis in original). But what could insure this, other than a turn toward a metaphysics of cooperation that assumes a link between women's affective labor and a cooperative spirit? One response might have to do with their use of Donna Haraway's concept of the cyborg to describe the "new determinations of the human, of living—a powerful artificiality" (217–218). But even if workers become cyborgs, in that their organic bodies are border-crossed with mechanized or digitalized forms, and even if their labor produces immaterial information, their cyborgian bodies are still subject to differing networks of power. Furthermore, their use of Donna Haraway's concept erases rather than incorporates her aspirations for global feminist politics. It is more in keeping with the "reward" granted to the Woman Clothed with the Sun in the Book of Revelation who, upon giving birth to the Messiah, is then rendered immaterial, in both senses of the word, by being raised into heaven.

In the meantime, the specificities of women's lives have been absorbed into the new barbarians, among others, creating a nominally unified collectivity that ignores pressing and quite particular needs of women—paradoxically in the name of singularities and community. For that matter, the gendered specificities of men's lives are largely ignored as well, and instead people are abstracted into "types" such as migrant or worker or, collectively, the poor. In the latter case, again, there is no mention of the feminization of poverty around the world, which, as Castells demonstrates, is part of the crisis of the patriarchal family. Lacking gender awareness, *Empire*'s theory is reduced to an evocation of poverty as a privileged status of knowledge and honor, as established by Francis of Assisi (413). Hardt's and Negri's telos, in other words, prematurely disavows gendered bodies, replacing them with a new collective social body that, from a feminist perspective, looks like a familiar masculinist form masquerading as a gender-free embodiment of universal values.

## Dueling Dualisms and Dialectical Echoes

Further pushing *Empire* toward unity and totality is a dialectical maneuver resolving the impasse of dualistic possibilities following the prophesized end of the world that we have hitherto known. This is despite the work's perceptive critique of the dialectic as a faulty form of metaphysical teleology. It is noteworthy that Hardt and Negri have conceded in an interview that: "despite our polemic, we too remain prisoners of various rhetorical strategies and linguistic formulations that echo dialectical terminology."[22] In my view, their usage goes far beyond an echo, but it is difficult to isolate in light of their claims to be countering the very form that their own telos tends to take. For example, some of the ways in which they evoke the future give an appearance of a welcome admission of ambiguity. Such is the case when they state that the "geography of these alternative powers, the new cartography, is still waiting to be written—or really, it is being written today through the resistances, struggles, and desires of the multitude" (xvi). And yet the ambiguity of the unknown future is subsequently reduced to a dualism endemic to apocalyptic and millennial belief because it is cast exclusively between poles of destruction versus salvation. By way of dialectical outcome, they then indicate that the multitude, which is being formed in opposition by and to the forces of Empire, will indeed overcome Empire.

The logic goes like this: once the old sovereignty of nation-states gives way to the new sovereignty of Empire—a process of history which is itself cast in terms of dialectical destiny because the antithetical seeds of destruction of the old sovereignty are produced and planted in the structure of Empire—the end of Empire becomes possible, for it too contains the seeds of its own destruction. If true to their rejection of the dialectic, given this internal dynamism, Empire could either prevail over or be defeated by the forces of opposition from within—or, far more likely from a genealogical perspective, many combinations thereof. But those various possibilities and ambiguities are then dispelled—not to reject a dialectical outcome but, rather, to foretell which outcome will happen, namely their millennial telos. As Hardt and Negri explain in regard to the third passage toward their totalizing telos: "Here consciousness and will, language and machine are called on to sustain the collective making of history. . . . Therefore the power of the dialectic, which imagines the collective formed through mediation rather than through constitution, has been definitively dissolved. The making of history is in this sense the construction of the life of the multitude" (405). While they assert that the multitude is or will be self-constituting, that stance is undercut throughout via conceptualizations that rely on a crude dialectical opposition that looks more like this: Empire (thesis) clashes with the counter-Empire of the multitude (antithesis) to produce a willed, creative telos (synthesis).

*Empire*'s millennial tendencies toward homogeneity and totalization are fostered through Hardt's and Negri's insistence on a "single logic of rule" (xii). Once again, they begin by explicitly stating what they later counter, admitting that: "Globalization, of course, is not one thing, and the multiple processes that we recognize as globalization are not unified or univocal" (xv). They then renege on this crucial insight throughout the rest of the book by treating both Empire and the multitude in terms of a single logic that is made to accommodate diversity and inconsistency within each formation. The rationale for this is that, with Empire: "there is no more outside" (186). Information technologies, global economic flows, and cyborgian life forms, they argue, have so transformed the new world order as to eradicate this distinction of modern thought. While it is true that former distinctions such as nature and culture and the public and private are undergoing legal and cultural redefinition and that we increasingly live amidst spectacle, their claims for total transformation are both hyperbolic and overextended.[23]

Recurrently, Hardt and Negri confuse conceptualization with proof that Empire really does or will soon exist exactly as they describe it. What this abstract, faith-based claim amounts to is conceptualizing an umbrella category so large that it covers all opposing forces—which might otherwise be seen as outside Empire's structures. In regard to the multitude, this tendency is evident when they state that the "multitude is not formed simply by throwing together and mixing nations and peoples indifferently; it is the singular power of a *new city*" (395; emphasis in original). In order to stave off millennial tendencies, it is worth asking, with genealogical skepticism, why the multitude *cannot* be a hodgepodge, why it *must* be a singular power, why struggles *cannot* come from forces outside the global flows (including such things as earthquakes, floods, and droughts as well as local groups), why there *can't* be forces of resistance other than the multitude.

Sidestepping consideration of such questions, *Empire*'s critique of the possibility of local groups providing resistance is a telling one. Stating accurately enough that local groups risk reinforcing "walls of nation, ethnicity, people, and the like" (362), they too quickly dismiss such risks as "regressive and even fascistic when they oppose circulations and mixture" (362). What they will tolerate is a local challenge that links up with the "concrete universal" of the multitude. But this is to reinstate a transcendental mode, resorting to prophetic claims to know in advance which resistances work to break down oppressive forces. In contrast to legislating resistances in this way, Foucault wrote, for example, that there are "resistances that are possible, necessary, improbable; others that are spontaneous, savage, solitary, concerted, rampant, or violent; still others that are quick to compromise, interested or sacrificial."[24] Underlying this range of resistances is the recognition that we really cannot guarantee or even know in advance if an action will prove to be a resistance. In *Empire*, in the face of an acknowledged plethora of contending forces of globalization, the impulse to make programmatic guarantees seems to lie in the collectivizing pressure of millennial rhetoric and categories of thought that can only produce The Multitude, writ large and increasingly transcendent. Resistances, plural, convert into The Revolution, singular.

As a point of contrast to *Empire*'s depiction of the new world order of imperial power, it is useful to keep in mind what Virginia Woolf observed, at least half-seriously, about the impact of Postimpressionist art on British culture: "On or about December 1910 human nature changed." As Woolf went on to explain, in terms of change more astutely modest than that of Hardt and Negri: "when human relations change there is at the same time a change in religion, conduct, politics and literature."[25] It was her view that such changes occur from time to time, and around 1910 was one of those times. I think it is fair to say that this is another such time, but that hardly means that the change is universal, univocal, or unified. Just as artistic movements help change the way we see and hence think about human relations and corresponding cultural institutions, so too current economic, political, communication, and other media forces are transforming the ways we think about God, love, morality, business, art, science, and each other. Nevertheless, it is important not to confuse such change with an apocalyptic or totalizing alteration of the world as we have known it, nor to postulate a millennial outcome. When it comes to theorizing the ways things change, perhaps Gertrude Stein said it best: "You can't change everything even if everything is changed."[26]

## Beautiful Theory

Much of *Empire*'s explanatory power is placed in the context of Foucault's notion of biopower, a concept that is then transformed by way of Deleuze. As Hardt and Negri put it, Foucault's work "has prepared the terrain for such an investigation of the material functioning of imperial rule" (22). While I agree with them that Foucault's concept of biopower is invaluable for understanding certain ways in which power relations operate these days, I think that many of his major contributions are in fact obscured by their millennial rendering of biopower into "biopolitical production." In keeping with the millennialism of their concepts of the multitude and Empire, they have cast biopower into a kind of theory that resembles the "beautiful theory" that Tony Kushner satirizes in *Perestroika* when his character "Aleksii Antediluvianovich Prelapsarianov, the World's Oldest Living Bolshevik" pronounces the following:

> The Great Question before us is: Are we doomed? The Great Question before us is: Will the Past release us? The Great Question before us is: Can we change? In Time? And we all desire that Change will come. And *Theory*? How are we to proceed without *Theory*? What system of thought have these reformers to present to this mad swirling planetary disorganization, to the Inevident welter of fact, event, phenomenon, calamity? Do they have, as we did, a beautiful Theory, as bold, as grand, as comprehensive a construct . . . ?[27]

Like Prelapsarianov, Hardt and Negri create in *Empire* a "beautiful theory," but at the cost of genealogical precision and materialist understanding.

Hardt's and Negri's push toward the grand construct occurs most specifically when they argue that globalization shifts biopower from "*disciplinary society* to the *society of control*" (22–23; emphasis in original), that is, when they shift from a Foucauldian conceptualization to a Deleuzian one. When they argue that Foucault's notion of biopower is "conceived only from above and we attempt to formulate instead a notion of biopower from below, that is, a power by which the multitude itself rules over life," they appear to be making a more democratic gesture.[28] But it should be noted that this is in contradiction to what Foucault says, since he expressly argues that: "Power comes from below; that is, there is no binary and all-encompassing opposition between rulers and ruled at the root of power relations."[29] What results, more importantly, is a conceptual loss of what enables democratic freedom to operate at all, namely, the dynamism of power relations. In the absence of the possibility for power relations to shift, multiply, and contradict one another, domination takes over. Foucault made an important distinction between these two concepts, indicating that power and domination are not synonymous and indeed that domination is antithetical to power relations.[30] His emphasis on resistances in place of the Revolution was to underscore the multiplicity of these relations that called for micropolitics rather than programmatic struggle. That is the gist of his oft-quoted view from volume I of *The History of Sexuality* that "there is no single locus of great Refusal, no soul of revolt, source of all rebellions, or pure law of the revolutionary."[31]

It is hard to tell whether Hardt and Negri have forgotten this important insight, especially since they incline toward celebrating resistances themselves, or whether they are rejecting it. Logic would suggest the latter, since they see Empire as overtaking the pluralities associated with power relations and resistance. In their formulation, Empire is a force that swallows up divergences by highlighting and encouraging rather than squelching them. This makes Empire especially insidious—and as apocalyptically clever as the Antichrist—because it conceals its domination by allowing and even encouraging local struggles and identity politics. "The People" thus think that they are free while they are actually being dominated through imperial forces.

The absoluteness of such claims comprises a key point of disagreement with Foucault. What makes that disagreement hard to follow is that they are inconsistent in whether they are disputing or drawing on his analysis. They sometimes criticize him for stopping short of gauging how control goes beyond disciplinary power, while at other times they say (à la Deleuze) that they are using his insight about control, carried to its logical conclusion. Regardless, it is a crucial departure from a Foucauldian approach and one that I believe to be symptomatic of millennial thought, which operates via absolutes and binary constructions between "rulers and ruled."

The key issue, of course, is not Foucault over Marx, or Deleuze, or, for that matter, Hardt and Negri, but whether "society of control" better describes an era heavily marked by forces of globalization and multinational capitalism. If it does, then Empire would be better understood as a force of domination rather than one of power relations that shift. But if that is the case, as their descriptions suggest, then resistances of any real substance become far less likely, their optimism becomes unwarranted, and a very different kind of theory should be called for.

There are two interrelated problems here. The first is the way that Hardt and Negri mix the apocalyptic rhetoric of domination with Foucauldian possibilities of freedom that reside in power relations. Like Prelapsarianov, Hardt and Negri press forward with absolutes that describe a system of domination and resolve them with declarations of theoretical purity that have little to do with the back-and-forth shifts of resistance and power relations. Such is the case when they state unequivocally that: "At this point, the disciplinary system has become completely obsolete and must be left behind" (276). There is simply too much evidence to the contrary in power networks involving education, therapy, population control, civic surveillance, and so on. Inconsistently, they say as much later when they state that the "passage to the society of control does not any way mean the end of discipline" (330). But according to their grand theory, which they seem to have become prisoners of, Empire must press forward toward complete control in order to suppress resistances; as it does, Empire actually creates the mirrored force of the multitude, which is the only force capable of overcoming it. It does this in part by delimiting the disciplinary mechanisms so that they "interweave in a hybrid production of subjectivity" (330–331). That subjectivity eventuates in the multitude. Domination reversed thus becomes, in theory anyway, absolute democracy.

The second problem stems from the way that resistance is here defined. Hardt and Negri argue that "resistance is actually prior to power" (360). This is based on Deleuze's statement to that effect in his book entitled *Foucault*: "The final word on power is that *resistance comes first*."[32] All three attribute this argument to Foucault but I would offer a different reading of his argument, one that emphasizes the relationality of resistances and power networks rather than a sequential form. Foucault states that: "Where there is power, there is resistance, and, yet, or rather consequently, this resistance is never in a position of exteriority in relation to power." This statement is perhaps what has led to their insistence on "no outside." But the way that Hardt and Negri construct Empire as a territorializing force of global flows differs from Foucault's point about the relationship between resistance and given power relations. In their construction, there can be no outside anywhere because they have subsumed all possible power relations into one sole globalized force called Empire. Foucault's conceptualization suggests that power relations operate more erratically than that, since resistance operating from within one power network may function from an outside position in relation to another.

This crucial point is ignored throughout *Empire*. "Should it be said," Foucault asks rhetorically, "that one is always 'inside' power, there is no 'escaping' it, there is no absolute outside where it is concerned, because one is subject to the law in any case? Or that, history being the ruse of reason, power is the ruse of history, always emerging the winner?" And then he remarks: "This would be to misunderstand the strictly relational character of power relationships." He goes on to explain that: "points of resistance are present everywhere in the power network" and that they "play the role of adversary, target, support or handle in power relations."[33] Rather than indicating that resistance comes first, what this means to me is that power relations become most visible to us when we witness the resistances that are present in a given power network. While we may thus see resistance prior to recognizing power relations, it does not follow that resistance precedes power, only that this is one way to recognize power at work. To lose this insight is no small matter—but it is the means by which Hardt and Negri roll their theory of power into a theory of control or domination that is inconsistent with their own valuation of resistance. As a consequence, they are back in the ballpark of the grand theory that begs the "Great Question."

## Life Itself

Just as Empire turns Foucault's more complex concept of power relations as nonuniform, multiple, and fluid into a theory of singular force and total domination, so too it takes to a hyperbolic level his insight that, within relations of biopower, life becomes "an object of power."[34] In Hardt's and Negri's hands, the phrase "life itself" is cast into all-inclusive either/or logic. Initially this state of affairs is apocalyptically ominous; it then turns millennially optimistic. As they explain: "Biopower thus refers to a situation in which what is directly at stake in power is the production and reproduction of life itself"(24). In their conceptualization of a society of control, what has happened is that biopower "extends throughout the depths of consciousness and bodies of the population—and at the same time across the entirety of social relations" (24). While it is true that potential for threat is everywhere, it is not necessarily true that everything in life is threatening, but their concept of imperial biopolitical production initially makes it seem so by unifying the concept of life itself. And then, with equally grand sweep, they indicate that once this all-encompassing threat dialectically converts into the multitude's production and generation, salvation will occur in a "revolution that no power will control" (413).

The millennial thrust of such statements diminishes what the Foucauldian concept of biopower has most to offer, namely, a way of grasping the generative and regulative nature of modern power relations in all their diversity and in contrast with the sovereign forms of centralized power that defeat, punish, and destroy to make themselves felt. That said, I want to acknowledge that the biopower discussion in *Empire* warrants special attention because of its focus on technological power investments that have taken place since Foucault and Deleuze and Guatarri offered their respective analyses of biopower. As Hardt and Negri indicate, over the past quarter-century, an "informatization of production," that is, the shift to an economy built on services and information, has become increasingly widespread, with effects extended around the globe. This shift integral to globalization does indeed affect certain power relations and is crucial for the viability of global citizenship, a goal I share with Hardt and Negri.

At this point, therefore, I want to shift my critical focus away from their apocalyptic and totalizing Grand Narrative and toward another contemporary analysis that incisively theorizes the variegated and conflicting forces of power at work today. Addressing such forces necessarily means that democratic political actions will also be multiple, constantly changing, often conflicting yet possibly coalitional, precisely because they would come from all over the place, rather than from the "non-place" of Empire that can find salvation only in the "immeasurable" virtual. Amartya Sen's work, *Freedom as Development*, achieves this and thus helps remedy the millennial and apocalyptic tendencies that undermine *Empire*. And crucially, like Castells, Sen places gender at the forefront of his analysis. By way of conclusion, therefore, I want to draw attention to his work as another valuable resource for genealogical feminist thought and practice in this era of globalization.[35]

Significantly, in his concern with forces of globalization that produce and regulate life itself, Sen avoids totalizing biopower (a term that he does not use, but one that I believe remains useful). Instead, he differentiates between biopower forces such as birth control, access to market, and the expansion of literacy, showing how each might variously affect economic empowerment and political participation. Moreover, he documents the continuation of sovereign relations of power that are recognizably distinct from biopower. He does this by looking seriously at the interrelated lives of women and children in particular. As he makes clear, a restriction on women's lives is *at the core* of global impoverishment because "the limited role of women's active agency seriously afflicts the lives of all people—men as well as women, children as well as adults."[36] His economic analysis shows clear correlations between raised levels of women's education and child survival and family prosperity; it demonstrates the links between health care for women and their lowered fertility as well as a lowering of women's "excess mortality."

What Sen's analysis makes eminently clear is that sovereign power, far from being replaced, continues to operate in men's control over women in all parts of the world and that it is intimately linked to forces of biopower. This occurs regardless of whether the predominant economy relies on the service and information sector, industry, or agriculture, though in developing countries male control is often legally sanctioned, as it was under the Taliban in Afghanistan and until the twentieth century in the United States. In order to move toward individual and collective agency—and toward global citizenship—it is necessary to grasp the intricate gendered relations between sovereign power and biopower. Theory that ignores the ways in which biopower subsumes long-standing masculinist formations is theory that reflects a masculinist bias.[37]

Sen's theory of development is committed to making those links clear and indicating to local and national governments as well as global organizations such as the World Trade Organization what kinds of practical actions are necessary to expand freedom and agency for people around the globe. According to Sen: "development requires the removal of major sources of unfreedom: poverty as well as tyranny, poor economic opportunities as well as systematic social deprivation, neglect of public facilities as well as intolerance or overactivity of repressive states" (Sen 3). He points to five instrumental freedoms that are pivotal in extending overall freedom, precisely because they allow people sufficient agency to bring about their own expansions and directions of freedom. These five are political freedoms, economic facilities, social opportunities, transparency guarantees, and protective security (Sen 38).

To my mind, what is most important for a genealogical feminist approach to globalization is to combine Hardt's and Negri's stress on the increasing centrality of information technology and services with Sen's rigorous, gender-astute emphasis on agency and freedom. Such an approach veers away from a call to arms of messianic figures of the future. Its materialist concerns seek specific ways to provide today's "missing women," to use Sen's poignant term for female infants deprived of life, and existing men and women and children who are systematically forced into militancy, migration, and poverty, with opportunities not only for life itself but, most crucially, for life with freedom.[38]

## Acknowledgments

I wish to extend special thanks to both Biman Basu and Malini Johar Schueller for lively intellectual engagement on these and related issues and to Craig McClain for his amazing industry in gathering research. I greatly appreciate the invaluable commentary and suggestions for improvement from Jodi Dean and Paul Passavant.

## Notes

1. Michael Hardt and Antonio Negri, *Empire* (Cambridge: Harvard University Press, 2000). Subsequent references are found parenthetically in the text.

2. Nancy Glass, "Apocalypse Now," *Time*, July 1, 2002: 42.

3. As a sobering point of contrast, it is worth noting that *Empire*, which is considered a huge success for an academic book, sold two thousand hardcover in 1999, four thousand in 2000, and two thousand in 2001. The paperback version was released in August 2001 and has sold 50,000 copies as of spring 2002, according to the Harvard University Press distributor.

4. Nancy Glass, "Apocalypse Now," 42.

5. For discussion of these reponses see, Chip Berlet, http://www.publiceye.org.

6. For an extended analysis of apocalyptic and millennialist belief from a genealogical feminist perspective, see my two books, *Anti-Apocalypse* (Minneapolis: University of Minnesota Press, 1994) and *Millennial Seduction* (Ithaca, NY: Cornell University Press, 1999).

7. Michel Foucault, "Two Lectures," in *Power/Knowledge*, ed. Colin Gordon (New York: Pantheon, 1972), 83.

8. Michel Foucault, "Nietzsche, Genealogy, History," in *Language, Counter-Memory, Practice: Selected Essays and Interviews*, ed. Donald F. Bouchard (Ithaca, NY: Cornell University Press, 1977), 153.

9. See Gopal Balakrishnan's critique of the "messianic streak" in *Empire*, which he attributes to Negri's "Italian past rather than an American present." America's past and present, however, are strongly messianic, being incorporated in the rhetoric and policies of Puritan colonization, the Revolutionary period, the Civil War, through to the Cold War and the current war on terrorism. Balakrishnan, "Virgilian Visions," *New Left Review* 5 (Sept/Oct 2000): 142–148. Thanks to Malini Johar Schueller for bringing this review essay to my attention.

10. Charles Strozier, *Apocalypse: On the Psychology of Fundamentalism in America* (Boston: Beacon Press, 1994), 1.

11. I coined the word "electism" in *Millennial Seduction*, where I provide an extended analysis of its place in the history and contemporary culture of the United States.

12. Manuel Castells, *The Power of Identity* (Oxford: Blackwell, 1998), 9.

13. Michel Foucault, "Nietzsche, Genealogy, History," 146.

14. Barry McCarthy, "Warrior Values: A Socio-Historical Survey," in *Male Violence*, ed. John Archer (London and New York: Routledge, 1994), 105–120.

15. Robin Morgan, *The Demon Lover* (New York: Norton, 1989), 27.

16. Interview by Nicholas Brown and Imre Szeman, "The Global Coliseum: On *Empire*," p. 6 of 11, available at http://www.humanities.mcmaster.ca/~szeman/hninterview.htm.

17. Leo Panitch, "Violence as a Tool of Order and Change: The War on Terrorism and the Antiglobalization Movement," *Monthly Review* (June 2002): 13.

18. Panitch, "Violence as a Tool of Order and Change, 32.

19. Rhonda Hammer, *Anti-Feminism and Family Terrorism: A Critical Feminist Perspective* (New York: Rowman & Littlefield Publishers, 2002), 1.

20. Manuel Castells, *The Power of Identity*, 135.

21. Raka Ray, "Masculinity, Femininity, and Servitude: Domestic Workers in Calcutta in the Late Twentieth Century," *Feminist Studies* (Fall 2000): 691–718.

22. Interview by Brown and Szeman, "The Global Coliseum: On *Empire*," 5.

23. In this respect, the concept of Empire seems to be as much indebted to *Star Trek*'s apocalyptic concept of the Borg as it is to analysis of contemporary economic, cultural, and political conditions. Like the Borg, Empire is an elaborate network of hybridity that incorporates organic life forms into its neural web. Their mirrored (and hence reversed) image of the multitude takes on a Benign Borg identity.

24. Foucault, *History of Sexuality, Vol. One: An Introduction*, trans. Robert Hurley (New York: Vintage Books, 1978) 96.

25. Virginia Woolf, "Mr. Bennett and Mrs. Brown," in *Collected Works*, Vol, 1. (Hogarth, 1924).

26. Gertrude Stein, *Ida* (New York: Vintage, 1941), 132.

27. Tony Kushner, *Angels in America: Part Two: Perestroika* (New York: Theatre Communications Group, 1992): 13–14.

28. Michael Hardt and Thomas Dumm, "Sovereignty, Multitudes, Absolute Democracy: A Discussion between Michael Hardt and Thomas Dumm about Hardt's and Negri's *Empire*," in this volume.

29. Foucault, *History of Sexuality*, 94.

30. Michel Foucault, "The Ethic of Care for the Self as a Practice of Freedom: An Interview," in *The Final Foucault*, Trans. J. D. Gautier, S. J. *Journal of Philosophy and Social Criticism* 12 (Summer 1987): 122–23.

31. Foucault, *History of Sexuality*, 95–96.

32. Gilles Deleuze, *Foucault* (Minneapolis: University of Minnesota Press, 1986), 89.

33. Foucault, *History of Sexuality*, 95–96.

34. Quoted in *Empire* (24) from Foucault, "Les mailles du pouvoir," in *Dits et Ecrits* (Paris: Gallimard, 1994), 194.

35. Amartya Sen, *Development as Freedom* (Knopf: New York, 1999).

36. Sen, "Women's Agency and Social Change," in *Development as Freedom*, 191.

37. For a range of examples of feminist analysis of the new information and biological technologies, see the special issue on "Women Confronting the New Technologies," *Women's Studies Quarterly* (Fall/Winter 2001); also see the symposium organized by Jodi Dean, "Virtually Regulated: New Technologies and Social Control," SIGNS 24 (Summer 1999): 1067–1096.

38. In his important 1992 article entitled "Missing Women," Sen provided empirical evidence that women in Asia and North Africa were "missing," that is dead, "as a result of gender bias in the distribution of health care and other necessities"; see the chapter, "Women's Agency and Social Change," in his *Development as Freedom*, 191.

# 12

Capitalism

# The Ideology of the Empire and Its Traps

## Slavoj Žižek

One of the favored intellectuals' exercises throughout the twentieth century was the urge to "catastrophize" the situation: whatever the actual situation, it *had* to be denounced as "catastrophic," and the better it appeared, the more it solicited this exercise. Heidegger denounced the present age as that of the highest "danger," the epoch of accomplished nihilism; Adorno and Horkheimer saw in it the culmination of the "dialectic of enlightenment" in the "administered world"; up to Giorgio Agamben, who defines the twentieth-century concentration camps as the "truth" of the entire Western political project. Recall the figure of Horkheimer in the West Germany of the fifties: while denouncing the "eclipse of reason" in the modern Western society of consumption, he *at the same time* defended this same society as the lone island of freedom in the sea of totalitarianisms and corrupted dictatorships all around the globe. It was as if Winston Churchill's old ironic quip about democracy as the worst possible political regime, and all other regimes worse than it, were here repeated in a serious form: Western "administered society" is barbarism in the guise of civilization, the highest point of alienation, the disintegration of the autonomous individual, et cetera, et cetera,—however, all other sociopolitical regimes are worse, so that, comparatively, one nonetheless has to support it. . . . One is thus tempted to propose a radical reading of this syndrome: what if what the unfortunate intellectuals cannot bear is the fact that they lead a life which is basically happy, safe, and comfortable, so that in order to justify their higher calling, they *have* to construct a scenario of radical catastrophe?

This catastrophism nonetheless refers to an undeniable fact: is it not that, in the last decades, the political left was ruthlessly pursuing the path of *giving way*? Of accommodating itself, of making the "necessary compromises" with the declared enemy (in the same way the Church had to compromise on the essentials in order to redefine its role in modern secular society) by way of reconciling the opposites, that is, its own position with that of the declared opponent: it stands for socialism, but can fully endorse economic Thatcherism; it stands for science, but can fully endorse the rule of the multitude of opinions; it stands for true popular democracy, but can also play the game of politics as spectacle and electoral spins; it stands for principled fidelity, but can be totally pragmatic; it stands for the freedom of the press, but can flatter and get the support of Murdoch.¹ In the early days of his rule, Tony Blair liked to paraphrase the famous joke from Monty Python's *The Life of Brian* ("All right, but apart from the sanitation, the medicine, education, wine, public order, irrigation, roads, the freshwater system and public health, what have the Romans ever done for us?") in order ironically to disarm his critics: "They betrayed socialism. True, they brought more social security, they did a lot for health care and education, etc., etc., but, in spite of all that, they betrayed socialism." As it is clear today, it is rather the obverse which applies: "We remain socialists. True, we practice Thatcherism in the economy, we made a deal with Murdoch, etc., etc., but, nonetheless, we remain socialists."

In the old days of the twentieth century, great conservatives often did the tough jobs for the liberals; after the indecisive attitude of the Socialist government which ended up in the global crisis of the French Republic itself, it was de Gaulle who cut the Gordian knot by giving Algeria independence—up to Nixon, who established diplomatic relations with China. Today, the opposite scenario is more of a rule: the new Third Way left does the job for economic liberal conservatives, dismantling the welfare state, bringing privatization to the end, and so forth. However, the stance of condemning the postmodern left for its accommodation is also false, since one should also ask the obvious hard question: *what was effectively the alternative?* If the left were to choose the "principled" attitude of fidelity to its old program, it would simply marginalize itself. The task is a much harder one: to rethink thoroughly the leftist project beyond the alternative of "accommodation" to new circumstances and sticking to the old attitude. One of the great achievements of Hardt's and Negri's *Empire* is that they accepted the challenge to break out of this debilitating deadlock.

Perhaps we should begin our critical remarks by asking a simple question: what is the spontaneous ideology of the Empire? One of the popular chocolate products on sale all around Central Europe is the so-called *Kinder*, an empty eggshell made of chocolate and wrapped up in lively colored paper; after one unwraps the egg and cracks the chocolate shell open, one finds in it a small plastic toy (or small parts from which a toy is to be put together). Is this toy not *l'objet petit a* at its purest—the small object filling in the central gap, the hidden treasure, *agalma*, in the center? A child who buys this chocolate egg often nervously unwraps it and just breaks the chocolate, not bothering to eat it, worrying only about the toy in the center. Is such a chocolate-lover not a perfect case of Lacan's motto "I love you, but, inexplicably, I love something in you more than yourself, and, therefore, I destroy you"? This material ("real") void in the center, of course, stands for the structural ("formal") gap on account of which no product is "really *that*," no product lives up to the expectations it arouses. In other words, the small plastic toy is not simply different from chocolate (the product we bought); while materially different, it fills in the gap in chocolate itself, that is, it is on the same surface as the chocolate. (In France, it is still possible to buy a desert with the racist name "*la tête de nègre*" [the nigger's head], a ball-like chocolate cake empty in its interior ["like the stupid nigger's head"]—the *Kinder* egg fills in this void. The lesson of it is that we *all* have "nigger's heads," with holes in the centers.) And this egg provides the formula for all the products which promise "more" ("buy a DVD player and get five DVDs for free," or, in an even more direct form, more of the same—"buy this toothpaste and get one third more for free"), not to mention the standard trick with the Coke bottle ("look on the inside of the metal cover and you may find that you are the winner of one of the prizes, from another free Coke to a brand new car"); the function of this "more" is to fill in the lack of a "less," to compensate for the fact that, by definition, a merchandise never delivers on its (phantasmatic) promise. In other words, the ultimate "true" merchandise would be the one that would not need any supplement, the one that would simply fully deliver what it promises—"you get what you paid for, neither less nor more."

And is not there a clear structural homology between this structure of the commodity and the structure of the bourgeois subject? Do subjects—precisely insofar as they are the subjects of universal human rights—also not function as these *Kinder* chocolate eggs? Would the humanist-universalist reply to the *tête de nègre* not be precisely something like a *Kinder* egg? As humanist ideologists would have put it: we may be indefinitely different, some of us are black, others white, some tall, others small, some women, others men, some rich, others poor, and so on—yet deep inside us there is the same moral equivalent of the plastic toy, the same *je ne sais quoi*, an elusive X that somehow accounts for the dignity shared by all humans. To quote Francis Fukuyama:

> What the demand for equality of recognition implies is that when we strip all of a
> person's contingent and accidental characteristics away, there remains some
> essential human quality underneath that is worthy of a certain minimal level of
> respect—call it Factor X. Skin, color, looks, social class and wealth, gender, cultural

background, and even one's natural talents are all accidents of birth relegated to the class of nonessential characteristics. . . . But in the political realm we are required to respect people equally on the basis of their possession of Factor X.[2]

(In contrast to transcendental philosophers, who emphasize that this Factor X is a sort of "symbolic fiction" with no counterpart in the reality of an individual, Fukuyama heroically locates it in our "human nature," in our unique genetic inheritance.) So it can be a white chocolate, a standard milk chocolate, a dark one, with or without nuts or raisins—inside it, there is always the same plastic toy (in contrast to the *Kinder* eggs, which are the same on the outside, while each has a different toy hidden inside).

To cut a long story short, what Fukuyama is afraid of is that, if we mess too much with the production of the chocolate egg, we might generate an egg without the plastic toy inside. How? Fukuyama is quite right to emphasize that it is crucial that we experience our "natural" properties as a matter of contingency and luck: if my neighbor is more beautiful or intelligent than me, it is because he was lucky to be born like that, and even his parents could not have planned it that way. The philosophical paradox is that if we take away this element of lucky chance, if our "natural" properties become controlled and regulated by biogenetic and other scientific manipulations, we lose the Factor X. This Factor X guarantees not only the underlying identity of different subjects but also the continuing identity of the same subject.

Twenty years ago, *National Geographic* published the famous photo of a young Afghani woman with fierce bright green eyes. In 2001, the same woman was identified in Afghanistan—although her face was changed, worn out from a difficult life and heavy work, her intense eyes were instantly recognizable as the factor of continuity.

Of course, the hidden plastic toy can also be given a specific ideological twist, like the idea that, after one gets rid of the chocolate in all its ethnic variations, one always encounters an American (even if the toy is in all probability made in China). This mysterious X, the inner treasure of our being, can also reveal itself as an alien intruder, an excremental monstrosity even. The anal association is here fully justified: the *immediate* appearance of the Inner is formless shit.[3] The small child who gives his shit as a present is in a way giving the immediate equivalent of his Factor X. Freud's well-known identification of excrement as the primordial form of gift, of an innermost object that the small child gives to his/her parents, is thus not as naive as it may appear: the often overlooked point is that this piece of myself offered to the Other radically oscillates between the sublime and—not the ridiculous but precisely—the excremental. This is the reason why, for Lacan, one of the features that distinguishes man from animals is that, with humans, the disposal of shit becomes a problem—not because it has a bad smell but because it came out from our innermost. We are ashamed of shit because in it we expose/externalize our innermost intimacy. Animals do not have a problem with it because they do not have an "interior" like humans. One should refer here to Otto Weininger, who designated volcanic lava as "the shit of the earth."[4] It comes from *inside* the body, and this inside is evil, criminal: "The Inner of the body is very criminal."[5] Here we encounter the same speculative ambiguity as with the penis, organ of urination *and* procreativity; when our innermost is directly externalized, the result is disgusting. This externalized shit is precisely the equivalent of the alien monster that colonizes the human body, penetrating it and dominating it from within, and which, at the climactic moment of a science-fiction horror movie, breaks out of the body through the mouth or directly through the chest. Perhaps even more exemplary than Ridley Scott's *Alien* is Jack Sholder's *The Hidden*, in which the wormlike alien creature forced out of the body at the film's end directly evokes anal associations (a gigantic piece of shit, since the alien compels humans penetrated by it to eat voraciously and belch in an embarrassingly disgusting way.)

The problematic point of this Factor X which makes us equal in spite of our differences is clear: beneath the deep humanist insight that, "deep within ourselves, we are all equal, the same vulnerable humans," is the cynical statement: "Why bother to fight against surface differences when, deeply, we already *are* equal?"—like the proverbial millionaire who pathetically discovers that he shares the same passions, fears, and loves with a destitute beggar. The well-known and highly successful animated series *The Land before Time*, produced by Steven Spielberg, provides what is arguably the clearest articulation of this Factor X ideology. The same message is repeated again and again: we are all different—some are big, some are small, some know how to fight, others know how to flee—but we should learn to live with these differences, to perceive them as something that makes our lives richer (recall the echo of this attitude in the recent reports on how the al-Qaeda prisoners are treated at Guantanamo: they are given food appropriate to their specific cultural and religious needs, allowed to pray, etc.). From and on the outside, we appear different, but inside, we are all the same—frightened individuals at a loss in the world, needing the help of others.

In one of the songs, the big bad dinosaurs sing about how those who are big can break all the rules, behave badly, squash the helpless and small:

When you're big / You can push all / The little ones around / They're looking up / While you are looking down. / . . . / Things are better when you're big. / . . . / All the rules that grown-ups made / They don't apply to you.

The answer of the oppressed small ones in the following song is not to fight the big ones but to understand that beneath their bullying appearance, they are no different from us, secretly afraid and with their share of problems:

> They have feelings just like we do / They have problems too. / We think because they're big / they don't, but they do. They're louder and they're stronger, / and they make a bigger fuss, / but way down deep inside / I think they're kids like us.

The obvious conclusion is therefore the praise of differences:

> It takes all sorts / To make a world / Short and tall sorts / Large and small sorts / To fill this pretty planet / with love and laughter. / To make it great to live in / Tomorrow and the day after. / It takes all types / without a doubt / dumb and wise types / every size types / To do all the things / That need to be done / To make our life fun.

The problem, of course, is: How far do we go here? It takes all sorts—also nice and brutal, poor and rich, victims and torturers? The reference to the dinosaur kingdom is especially ambiguous here, with its brutal character of animal species devouring each other—is this also one of the things that "need to be done to make our life fun?" The very inner inconsistency of this vision of the prelapsarian "land before time" thus bears witness to how the message of collaboration-in-differences is ideology at its purest—Why? Because any notion of a "vertical" *antagonism* that cuts through the social body is strictly censored, substituted by and/or translated into the wholly different notion of "horizontal" differences with which we have to learn to live, because they complement each other.

And the key question is: Does the Deleuzian theory that forms the philosophical background of *Empire* provide the conceptual apparatus properly to conceive this antagonism? Let us approach this question via a detour, an attempt to provide a Deleuzian theory of the social consequences of the digital revolution, Alexander Bard's and Jan Soderqvist's *Netocracy.*[6] This book is a supreme example of what one is tempted to call the new *cyber-Stalinism*: while cruelly dismissing Marxism as outdated, as part of the old industrial society, it takes from Stalinist Marxism a whole series of key features, from primitive economic determinism and linear historical evolutionism (the development of the forces of production—the shift of accent from industry to management of information—necessitates new social relations, the replacement of the class antagonism of capitalists and proletariat with the new class antagonism of "netocrats" and "consumtariat") to the extremely rude notion of ideology (in the best naive Enlightened way, ideology—from traditional religion to the bourgeois humanism—is repeatedly dismissed as the instrument of the ruling classes and their paid intellectuals destined to keep in check the lower classes).

Here, then, is the basic vision of "netocracy" as a new mode of production (the term is inadequate, because in it, production loses its key role): whereas feudalism, the key to social power was the ownership of land, legitimized by religious ideology, and in capitalism, the key to power is the ownership of capital, with money as the measure of social status, private property as the fundamental legal category, and market as the dominant field of social exchange, all this legitimized by the humanist ideology of Man as autonomous free agent, in the newly emerging "netocracy," the measure of power and social status is the access to key information; money and material possessions are relegated to a secondary role. The dominated class is no longer the working class but the class of consumerists, "consumtariat," those condemned to consume the information prepared and manipulated by the netocratic elite. This shift in power generates an entirely new social logic and ideology: since information circulates and changes all the time, there is no longer a stable long-term hierarchy, but a permanently changing network of power relations; individuals are "nomadic," "dividuals," constantly reinventing themselves, adopting different roles; society itself is no longer a hierarchic Whole but a complex open network of networks.

*Netocracy* moves here simultaneously too fast and not fast enough—as such, it shares the mistake of all those other attempts that all too fast elevated a new entity into the successor of capitalism at the same level as capitalism: postindustrial society, informational society, and so on. Against such temptations, one should insist that "informational society" is simply *not* a concept at the same level as "feudalism" or "capitalism." The picture of the accomplished rule of the netocracy is therefore, in spite of the authors' stress on the new class antagonisms, a utopia: an inconsistent composite that cannot survive and reproduce itself on its own terms. All too many of the features of the new netocratic class are sustainable only within a capitalist regime. Therein resides the weakness of *Netocracy*: following the elementary logic of ideological mystification, it dismisses as "remainders of the (capitalist and statist) past" what are effectively positive conditions of the functioning of informational society.

The key problem is that of capitalism, the way "netocracy" relates to capitalism. On the one side, we have patents, copyright, and so on—all the different modalities in which information itself is offered and sold on the market as "intellectual property," as another commodity. (And when the authors claim that the true elite of netocracy is beyond patents and so on, because its privilege is no longer based on possessing information but on being able to discern, in the confusing quantity of information, what information is relevant, they strangely miss the point: Why should this ability to discern what really matters,

the ability to discard the irrelevant balast, not be another—perhaps crucial—
sort of information to be sold? In other words, they seem to forget here the
basic lesson of today's cognitive sciences: already at the most elementary level
of consciousness, information *is* the ability to "abstract," to discern the relevant
aspects in the confusing multitude with which we are constantly bombarded.)

On the other side, there is the prospect of the exchange of information
*beyond* the property relations that characterize capitalism. This inner antagonism is realized in the basic tension within the new netocratic class between
procapitalists (Bill Gates types) and those advocating a postcapitalist utopia. The
authors are right in emphasizing that the future "class struggle" will be decided
with regard to the possible coalition between the postcapitalist netocrats and the
underprivileged consumtariat, without this coalition and support from within
netocracy, the consumtariat alone can only articulate its protest in violent negative actions lacking any positive future-oriented program. The key point is thus
that there is no "neutral" netocracy: there is either a procapitalist netocracy, part
of late capitalism, or the postcapitalist netocracy, part of a different mode of production. To complicate things further, this postcapitalist perspective is in itself
ambiguous; it can mean a more open "democratic" system or the emergence of
a new hierarchy, a kind of informational/biogenetic neofeudalism.

This struggle is already taking place. In 2001, the Microsoft Corporation
anounced that it is working on Palladium, a radically new version of Windows
with a separate security chip that would give users protection and control of
their information: "Nothing leaves your PC without your permission."
Palladium ensures through encryption that no one eavesdrops on you, all ingo-
ing mail is filtered, your outgoing messages can be opened only by those you
authorize, you can track who opened them, and so on. It is a "plan to remake
the personal computer to ensure security, privacy and intellectual property."[7] Is
this not *the* big attempt to inscribe the informational universe into the capitalist logic of private property? Opposite to this tendency are attempts to develop
a new cyberspace language, an alternative to Microsoft Windows, which would
be not only freely accessible to all but also developed through free social interaction (preliminary versions are not kept hidden, awaiting the magic moment
when the new product is revealed to the market; on the contrary, these versions
already freely circulate in order to provoke feedback from the users). The fact
that AOL supports such an alternative in order to strike at its competitor is
telling. Why should progressive forces not strategically use this support?

*Netocracy* presents the local groups of the new informational elite almost
as islands of nonalienated utopian communities, a description of the life of the
new "symbolic class" for which lifestyle, access to exclusive information, and
social circles matter more than money—top academics, journalists, designers,
programmers, and so on effectively live that way. However, are the authors of

*Netocracy* fully aware of the ultimate irony of their notion of "nomadic" subjects and thought as opposed to traditional hierarchic thought? What they are effectively claiming is that the netocrats, today's elite, realize the dream of yesterday's marginal philosophers and outcast artists (from Spinoza to Nietzsche and Deleuze)—in short and even more pointedly, that the thought of Foucault, Deleuze, and Guattari, the ultimate philosophers of resistance, of the marginal positions crushed by the hegemonic power network, is effectively the ideology of the newly emerging ruling class. In 1996, in his admirable "The Pedagogy of Philosophy," Jean-Jacques Lecercle portrayed the scene of a yuppie in the Paris Metro reading Deleuze's and Guattari's *What Is Philosophy?*:

> The incongruity of the scene induces a smile—after all, this is a book explicitly written against yuppies. . . . Your smile turns into a grin as you imagine that this enlightenment-seeking yuppie bought the book because of its title. . . . Already you see the puzzled look on the yuppie's face, as he reads page after page of vintage Deleuze. . . .[8]

What if, however, there is no puzzled look, but enthusiasm, when the yuppie reads about impersonal imitation of affects, about the communication of affective intensities beneath the level of meaning ("Yes, this is how I design my *publicities!*"), or when he reads about exploding the limits of self-contained subjectivity and directly coupling man to a machine ("This reminds me of my son's favorite toy, the Action Man who can turn into a car!"), or about the need to reinvent oneself permanently, opening oneself up to a multitude of desires that push us to the limit ("Is this not the aim of the virtual-sex video game I am working on now? It is no longer a question of reproducing sexual bodily contact but of exploding the confines of established reality and imagining new, unheard-of, intensive modes of sexual pleasure!").

Is today's popular culture not effectively permeated by Deleuzian motifs, from the Spinozean logic of *imitatio affecti* (is this impersonal circulation of affects, bypassing persons, not the very logic of publicity, of video clips, and so on where what matters is not the message about the product but the intensity of the transmitted affects and perceptions?) to new trends in children's toys (the so-called "Transformer" or "Animorph" toys, a car or a plane which can be transformed into a humanoid robot, an animal which can be morphed into a human or robot . . . is this not Deleuzian? There is no "metaphorics" here, the point is not that the machinic or animal form is revealed as a mask containing a human shape but rather the "becoming-machine" or "becoming-animal" of the human, the flow of continuous morphing. What is blurred is also the divide machine/living organism: a car transmutes into a humanoid/cyborg organism—therein resides the horror.)?

Deleuze's answer would be here the same as in the case of fascism: although, rationally, individuals can perceive that it is against their interests to follow fascism, it seizes them at the impersonal level of pure intensities; "abstract" bodily motions, libidinally invested collective rhythmic movements, affects of hatred and passion that cannot be attributed to any determinate individual . . . it is thus the impersonal level of pure affects that sustains fascism, not the level of represented and constituted reality. So the struggle against fascism should be fought at this impersonal level of intensities, undermining the fascist libidinal economy with a more radical one, not (only) at the level of rational critique. And, *mutatis mutandis*, the same goes for late capitalism: it should also be attacked at the level of micropolitics of affects. However, is this approach not all too abstract? All "bad" politics is declared "fascist," so that "fascism" is elevated into a global container, a catchall, an all-encompassing term for everything that opposes the free flow of Becoming—it is "inseparable from a proliferation of molecular focuses in interaction, which skip from point to point, *before* beginning to resonate together in the National Socialist State. Rural fascism and city or neighborhood fascism, youth fascism and war veteran's fascism, fascism of the Left and fascism of the Right, fascism of the couple, family, school, and office"[9]—one is almost tempted to add: and fascism of the irrationalist vitalism of Deleuze himself (in an early polemics, Badiou effectively accused Deleuze of harboring fascist tendencies!).

Deleuze and Guattari (especially Guattari) often indulge here in a true interpretive delirium of hasty generalizations; in one great arch, they drew the line of continuity from the early Christian procedure of confessions, through the self-probing of the Romantic subjectivity and psychoanalytic treatment (confessing one's secret perverse desires), up to the forced confessions, in the Stalinist show trials—Guattari once directly characterized these trials as an exercise in collective psychoanalysis! To such analyses one is tempted to respond by pointing out how the Stalinist trials were evidently "productive"; their actual goal was not to discover the truth but to create new truth, to construct-generate it. It is here, against such generalizations, that one should evoke the lesson of Ernesto Laclau's notion of hegemonic articulation: fascism emerges *only* when the disperse elements start to "resonate together," it *is* only a specific mode of this resonance of elements which can be inserted also in totally different hegemonic chains of articulation.

In the second part of *Harmonienlehre*, his major theoretical manifesto from 1911, Arnold Schoenberg develops his opposition to tonal music in terms that, superficially almost recall later Nazi anti-Semitic tracts: the tonal music has become a "diseased," "degenerated" world in need of a cleansing solution; the tonal system has given in to "inbreeding and incest"; romantic chords such as the diminished seventh are "hermaphroditic," "vagrant," and "cosmopolitan." Nothing is easier than to claim that such a messianic-apocalyptic attitude is part of the same "deeper spiritual situation" that gave birth to the Nazi "Final Solution." This, however, is precisely the conclusion one should *avoid*: what makes Nazism repulsive is not the rhetoric of Final Solution *as such*, but the concrete twist it gives to it.

Another popular topic of this kind of analysis is the allegedly "protofascist" character of mass choreography displaying disciplined movements of thousands of bodies (parades, mass performances in stadiums, etc.): If one finds such displays also in socialism, one immediately draws the conclusion about a "deeper solidarity" between the two "totalitarianisms." Such a procedure, the very prototype of ideological liberalism, misses the point: not only are such mass performances not inherently fascist, they are not even "neutral," waiting to be appropriated by the left or the right—it was Nazism that stole and appropriated them from the workers' movement, their original site of birth. It is here that one should oppose the standard historicist genealogy (the search for origins, influences, etc.) to the strict Nietzschean genealogy. Apropos Nazism, the standard genealogy is exemplified by the search for the "protofascist" elements or kernel out of which Nazism grew, while the Nietzschean genealogy takes fully into account the *rupture* constitutive of a new historical event. None of the "protofascist" elements is per se fascist; what makes them "fascist" is only their specific articulation—or, to put it in Stephen Jay Gould's terms, all these elements are "ex-apted" by fascism. In other words, there is no "fascism *avant la lettre*," because *it is the letter itself (the nomination) which makes out of the bundle of elements fascism proper.* The very predicate "protofascist" should be abandoned; it is the exemplary case of a pseudoconcept whose function is to block conceptual analysis. When we say that the organized spectacle of thousands of bodies (or, say, the admiration of sports that demand high effort and self-control, such as mountain climbing) is "protofascist," we say strictly nothing, we just express a vague association that masks our ignorance.

And are Hardt and Negri not caught in a similar ambiguous attitude towards the Americanized global capitalism when they celebrate its "deterritorializing" multitude? They distinguish two ways to oppose the global capitalist Empire: either the "protectionist" advocacy of a return to the strong nation-state, or the deployment of even more flexible forms of multitude. Along these lines, in his analysis of the Porto Allegre antiglobalist meeting, Hardt emphasizes the new logic of the political space there; it was no longer the old "us versus them" binary logic with the Leninist call for a firm singular party line, but the coexistence of the multitude of political agencies and positions which remained nevertheless incompatible as to their ideological and programmatic accents (from "conservative" farmers and ecologists worried about the fate of their local tradition and patrimony, to human rights groups and agents standing for the interests of immigrants and advocating global mobility). It is effectively today's opposition to global capital that seems to provide a kind of negative mirror image to Deleuze's claim about the inherent antagonism of capitalist dynamics (a strong machine of deterritorialization that generates new modes of reterritorialization). Today's resistance to capitalism reproduces the same antagonism: calls for the defense of particular (cultural, ethnic) identities being threatened by the global dynamics coexist with demands for more global mobility (against the new barriers imposed by capitalism which concern above all the free movement of individuals).

Is it then true that these tendencies (these *lignes de fuite*, as Deleuze would have put it) can coexist in a nonantagonistic way, as parts of the same global network of resistance? One is tempted to answer by applying Laclau's notion of the chain of equivalences: of course this logic of multitude functions—because we are still dealing with *resistance*. However, what about when—if this really is the desire and will of these movements—"we take it over"? What would the "multitude in power" look like? There was the same constellation in the last years of the decaying Really Existing Socialism: the nonantagonistic coexistence within the oppositional field of a multitude of ideologico-political tendencies, from liberal human-rights groups to "liberal" business-oriented groups, conservative religious groups, and leftist workers' demands. This multitude functioned well as long as it was united in the opposition to "them," the Party hegemony; once they found *themselves* in power, the game was over. Furthermore, is today the state really withering away (with the advent of the much-praised liberal "deregulation")? Is, on the contrary, the "War on Terror" not the strongest-yet assertion of state authority? Are we not witnessing now the unheard-of mobilization of all (repressive and ideological) state apparatuses?

## Notes

1. See Giorgio Agamben, *Moyens sans fins* (Paris: Payot & Rivages, 2002), 147–148.
2. Francis Fukuyama, *Our Posthuman Future* (London: Profile Books, 2002), 149–150.
3. See Dominique Laporte, *History of Shit* (Cambridge, MA: MIT Press, 2000).
4. Otto Weininger, *Über die letzten Dinge* (Munich: Matthes und Seitz Verlag, 1997), 187.
5. Weininger, 188.
6. Alexander Bard and Jan Soderqvist, *Netocracy: The New Power Elite and Life after Capitalism* (London: Reuters), 2002.
7. See the report "The Big Secret" in *Newsweek*, July 8, 2002, 50–52.
8. Jean-Jacques Lecercle, "The Pedagogy of Philosophy," *Radical Philosophy* 75 (January-February 1996): 44.
9. Gilles Deleuze and Felix Guattari, *A Thousand Plateaus* (Minneapolis: University of Minnesota Press, 1987), 214.

# 13

**The Networked Empire:
Communicative Capitalism
and the Hope for Politics**

## Jodi Dean

Global telecommunications networks are crucial to Michael Hardt's and Antonio Negri's theory of Empire. "Empire takes form," they write, "when language and communication, or really when immaterial labor and cooperation, become the dominant force" (385). Indeed, "communicative production and the construction of imperial legitimation march hand in hand and can no longer be separated" (34). How should we understand this merging of communication with domination and the seemingly inescapable autopoietic self-justification of imperial control? For clearly, Hardt and Negri are offering more than a theory of ideology and more than a description of a discursive formation of power/knowledge called Empire. Rather, their account is a political ontology, and communications networks are global technoculture's rhizomatically inter-linked fibers of being.

To sort through these claims, I examine Hardt's and Negri's account of contemporary communications networks. My examination is guided by two questions. First, what role do global communications networks play in producing and reinforcing imperial rule? Second, how might these same networks become vehicles for resistance or for the constituent power of the multitude? I find that the strength of Hardt's and Negri's answer to the first question leads to the weakness of their answer to the second.

More specifically, Hardt's and Negri's compelling description of the merging of capitalism and contemporary communications puts in stark relief the contemporary foreclosure of politics. I refer to this merging that threatens democratic politics as communicative capitalism.[1] And I agree with much of Hardt's and Negri's account of the imperial effects of communicative capitalism. At the same time, however, I find their discussion of these effects so convincing that the redeployment of networked communications by and for the multitude seems unlikely. Hardt and Negri might know this. They might even agree. I conclude with this suggestion insofar as it hints at why Hardt and Negri substitute hope for politics.

## A Virtual Empire

Like many theorists of postmodernity, late capitalism, and technoculture, Hardt and Negri emphasize the imbrications of space, capital, and networked computers. "Communication," they write, "not only expresses but also organizes the movement of globalization" (32). Hardt's and Negri's discussion of new communications technologies synthesizes a number of ideas that have gained currency in recent years (ideas that Negri in the 1980s was already working on with Félix Guattari and with the Italian theorists of autonomist Marxism).[2] In this section, I set out three key components of *Empire*'s account of globally networked communications and how each of these components impacts economics, politics, and subjectivity. Accordingly, once I have looked at information, networks, and spectacle, I turn in the following section to their effect on communication and communicability more generally.

### Information

Hardt and Negri emphasize that if industrialization was the economic paradigm of modernity, then informatization is the economic paradigm of postmodernity. They are not claiming that agriculture and manufacture are no longer economically important. Nor are they suggesting that learning, research, and the application of knowledge played no role in the Industrial Revolution. Rather, their point is that the global system has transformed in such a way that now "providing services and manipulating information are at the heart of economic production" (280). Information—its accumulation, extension, and circulation—produces and dominates economic and social relations.[3] Informatization thus changes the conditions and products of labor and exchange.

Before taking up the far-reaching economic repercussions of informatization, I want to consider informatization itself in a bit more detail. Manuel Castells is helpful in this regard, as he identifies reflexivity as the key innovation of informatization. Castells writes: "What characterizes the current technological revolution is not the centrality of knowledge and information, but the application of such knowledge and information to knowledge generation and information processing/communication devices, in a cumulative feedback loop between innovation and the uses of innovation."[4] This feedback or reflexivity differentiates information technology from other technologies. We might think here of the computer as a machine. Unlike previous technologies that were designed for specific uses, the computer was conceived as a universal machine, one that treats its own instructions as data and thus can be programmed for multiple tasks.[5] Or we might think of the combinations of work and play driving the popularization of personal and networked computing. Advances in programming were deeply interlinked with gaming, hacking, and messing around with computers just for the fun of seeing what they could do. The experiments of hobbiests and amateurs, in other words, experiments that set the stage and created the persona for the garage-based millionaire dot-com start-ups, did not simply apply existing technology, they transformed and reconfigured it into new technologies.[6] Using computers came to mean linking them, extending their capacities, and adapting them to new sorts of problems and projects, in effect reformatting the context and conditions of computer-mediated communication.

Like the computer, information technology is reflexive. And such reflexivity, Castells explains, intertwines to an unprecedented degree "the social processes of creating and manipulating symbols (the culture of society) and the capacity to produce and distribute goods and services (the productive forces)." He concludes: "For the first time in history the human mind is a direct productive force, not just a decisive element of the productive system."[7]

With the information revolution, then, technological use comes to impact further technological development in unprecedented ways. Extended practical use of information technologies involves more than the automation of a previous task and more than the application of technological know-how to a new domain. Instead, users using technologies reconfigure the tasks, the know-how, the users, and the technologies themselves.

Hardt and Negri are thus right to emphasize the way that "the increasingly extensive use of computers has tended progressively to redefine laboring practices and relations, along with, indeed, all social practices and relations" (291). They illustrate this redefining in three types of labor. The first type of labor might be understood as a sort of hybrid of service and production (293). It results from the impact of informatization on manufacturing plants. As Hardt and Negri explain, advances in networked communications have made it possible to reduce inventories and produce commodities "just in time, according to the present demand of the existing markets . . . at least in theory, the production decision actually comes after and in reaction to the market decision" (290). With respect to commodity production, then, informatization means an increase in the importance of communication for production. Production occurs in response to information about what consumers want and where and when they want it.[8]

The second type of labor Hardt and Negri consider produces immaterial goods such as services, symbols, cultural products, and communication itself. This labor includes low-level positions in data entry, word processing, and telemarketing as well as more highly paid positions in programming, research, and brokering. On the one hand, immaterial service-sector labor increases the abstraction and homogenization of work. Workers are more distanced from the specific tasks, tools, and products of their labor. And their labor tends to be the same insofar as all are required to have basic computer skills. On the other hand, the move toward service industries characteristic of informatization entails a profound polarization. Saskia Sassen details the sharp growth at opposing ends of the service sector during the 1990s.[9] Knowledge and information-intensive services generated disproportionate numbers of new jobs for college graduates as well as massive numbers of low-wage jobs not requiring a high school education. So more well-paid college graduates work in information services than in other sectors. At the same time, the lowest-paid workers labor part-time in labor-intensive service industries or hourly in the knowledge and information-intensive services.

The third type of labor associated with informatization that Hardt and Negri emphasize is "the production and manipulation of affect" (293). Here they are concerned with feelings—of, attachment, affection, excitement, fear, ease, or well-being—as products. This third type includes such seemingly diverse sectors as entertainment, health care, and women's unpaid labor. Indeed, women's affective labor is particularly important to Hardt's and Negri's account because it produces social networks, "forms of community biopower" (293). Whereas the economic instrumentalization of communication tends to reduce communication to mere data transmission, in the case of affective labor, "communication has not been impoverished, but production has been enriched to the level of complexity of human interaction" (293). Affective labor, then, suggests that informatization may well expand the very notion of production so as to value the creation of feelings and the cultivation of sociality. (To be sure, there is a certain oddness in Hardt's and Negri's articulation of women's affective labor to informatization, an oddness that springs from linking some of the oldest with some of the newest modes of work. How is women's domestic and caring work implicated in informatization to a degree that differs from its role in agriculture- or manufacturing-based economies?)

## Networks

Hardt and Negri note that informatization has had significant geopolitical consequences. In a nutshell, states and territorially based polities are not as important as they used to be. Informatized production does not require the concentration of workers and capital in central locations. Consumers and producers, workers and capital, are not constrained by territory or, more specifically, by the political boundaries given by states. Like global capital, workers too are now more mobile. (One would think that the production of community biopower through domestic and caring work would be an exception here. One could posit, in other words, a difference in the richness and power of social relationships in terms of their forms of mediation rather than collapsing all relationships into a kind of immediacy of communication. But, as we shall see below, this would take the argument in directions counter to those of Hardt and Negri.) Accordingly, Hardt and Negri read the consequences of informatization in terms of decentralization and deterritorialization. And they think both together with the notion of networks. They write: "Information technologies tend to make distances less relevant. Workers involved in a single process can effectively communicate and cooperate from remote locations without consideration to proximity. In effect, the network of laboring cooperation requires no territorial or physical center" (295). Networks of labor, then, are also networks of communication. And these networks produce more than commodities; they produce "rich and powerful social relationships" as well (210).

Hardt and Negri emphasize the function of communications networks for production in the information economy (297). Although this is not their term, central to their analysis is the way that communication has become reflexive. They write: "*The novelty of the new information infrastructure is the fact that it is embedded within and completely immanent to the new productive processes.* At the pinnacle of contemporary production, information and communication are the very commodities produced; the network itself is the site of both production and circulation" (298; emphasis in the original). As an example, one might consider how, during the dot.com boom years, buzzwords kept appearing that would announce what the Internet was for, how it would make investors rich and make life (for the wired) really great. There were multiuser dungeons, chat rooms, auctions, virtual destination sites, webcams, and business-to-business applications. It seemed like an elaborate self-reflexive web of self-marketing. Communication was—and in the information economy is—the means for achieving communication as the end.[10]

Hardt and Negri tend to refer to networked communications in the information economy in terms of one global information infrastructure. Unlike Castells, say, who emphasizes various concrete networks, the architecture of relations between networks, and the power and privilege invested in those determining the terms and conditions for switching between networks, Hardt and Negri seem to have in mind one global network or information infrastructure.[11] (Hardt's and Negri's position here is not unique. One network was the goal of the 1992 National Information Infrastructure plan pushed so enthusiastically by then–Vice President Al Gore.) This unitary model enables them to suggest that there is currently a battle for the constitution or control of *the* communications infrastructure. On one side is the rhizomatic or democratic image of the network, idealized in the history of the Internet. This network is horizontal and deterritorialized: "An indeterminate and potentially unlimited number of interconnected nodes communicate with no central point of control; all nodes regardless of territorial location connect to all others through a myriad of potential paths and relays" (299). On the other side is the treelike oligopolistic model of the network. This is the giant corporate broadcast model—and the one arguably envisioned by the 1996 Telecommunications Act and its emphasis on a market-driven Internet. Here, large corporations combine and consolidate in a scramble for control over communication and production.[12]

Together with informatization, Hardt and Negri use the idea of networks not simply to specify postmodern capitalist production but also to establish the fact of imperial political conditions. Hence they argue that globally networked computers enable the emergence of Empire as itself a "*decentered* and *deterritorializing* apparatus of rule that progressively incorporates the entire global realm within its open, expanding, frontiers*" (xii; emphasis in original). Stated perhaps too crudely, Empire arises out of capital in the informational or communicative mode of development. Or as Hardt and Negri put it: "The development of communications networks has an organic relationship to the emergence of the new world order—it is, in other words, effect and cause, product and producer" (32).

## Spectacle

The third key component of Hardt's and Negri's account of contemporary global communications is spectacle. Inspired by Guy Debord, they present the spectacle as the glue holding together the disparate screens of Empire. Spectacle is a form of social integration presupposing audiences rather than participants. In other words, social solidarity is imposed via media networks rather than secured through traditions, norms, or a discursively achieved consensus on validity claims, to invoke the terms of Jürgen Habermas. One might think here of advertising, "spin," and the cult of celebrity so pervasive in American culture. Such a form of collectivity or massness makes political action difficult—communications networks turn individuals into audiences, bypassing what we might think of as intersubjective relations or group identifications. Instead of individuals linked to one another, each is linked to the spectacle via the screen. Mass observation or, better, the broadcasting and announcement of an event as an event to masses of people, produces and determines what is common, what is to be significant to the collective (and in so doing, produces what is to be the collective).

Echoing Habermas's account of the structural transformation of the public sphere, Hardt and Negri find that "political discourse is an articulated sales pitch, and political participation is reduced to selecting among consumable images" (322). Indeed, what is so striking in the politics of the spectacle is the way that differentiated media networks, corporations, and political bodies seem to blend and unite together as if there were one hand or power guiding participation and consumption. How is it, really, that all the news shows in a seven-hundred-channel universe feature *the same things*? It seems *"as if"* all these screens and images were "consciously and explicitly directed by a single power" (323). Spectacle, we might say, makes it seem as if there were an Empire pulling everything together and turning even our efforts to resist into things that ensnare us ever more tightly in imperial networks.

Finally, although the idea of the society of the spectacle may seem rather new, a product of broadcast media and mass communications, the way it functions is, theoretically at least, as old as the liberal state. Spectacle relies on fear, and on this point Hardt and Negri rely, not surprisingly, on Hobbes. Just as fear secured the Leviathan, so is fear a fundamental guarantor of the divisions or segmentations among poor and working people through which imperial power exerts control. Hardt and Negri thus limit the content of spectacle in two moves: spectacle communicates fear, and fear is fear of violence, poverty, and unemployment (339).[13]

At first glance, informatization could seem a term primarily for the postmodern economy. Networks might seem to designate this economy but to apply more directly to the decentralization and deterritorialization of the political occasioned by the globalized economy. Spectacle would suggest the subjectivities of this new global order, dispersed and differentiated subjectivities integrated through communicative networks telling them what to fear. This order is a bit too neat, however. Each term—informatization, networks, and spectacle—actually stretches across to impact each domain of economics, politics, and subjectivity. Communication, as a hegemonic sector of production that acts across the entire biopolitical field, is, for Hardt and Negri, coexistent with the broadest biopolitical context (33).

The affective work of the entertainment industry, for example, produces fear. Deterritorialization, moreover, impacts group identities, not only bringing previously distant groups into proximity but also lessening the hold of territorially based identities. Indeed, to the extent that Empire relies on porous boundaries and migrating people, fear seems to play an integrative role more important than in the Leviathan. As Thomas Dumm writes: "*Fear* is a word rooted in the experience of being in transit. . . . The word *far*, distant, is also associated with these words. . . . The experience of fear is that of moving from protection to exposure, experiencing the vertigo of uncertainty, not knowing what threat to well-being might lay in wait. The farther one travels, the greater the fear."[14] The nomadic movements of the present, the fluidity, speed, and transitoriness of contemporary practices, seem almost preprogrammed for inscription by and through fear. My point, then, is that for Hardt and Negri, informatization, networks, and spectacle work together on behalf of a new, imperial form of domination, a form that involves the global economy, globalized sovereignty, and fluid, hybrid subjectivities that can no longer be understood in old nation-state terms of identity and belonging.

## Communication without Communicability

Hardt and Negri claim that "communication is the form of capitalist production in which capital has succeeded in submitting society entirely and globally to its regime, suppressing all alternative paths" (347). The preceding section set out the key components of this postmodern mode of production, highlighting the ways contemporary global communications structure Hardt's and Negri's analysis of Empire. In this section, I consider how these components function together. Drawing on my work on communicative capitalism, I argue that, for Hardt and Negri, Empire entails communication without communicability. Imperial communications work instrumentally to secure control and further capitalism. Communication, then, refers not to something like dialogue or an exchange of reasons; instead, it involves the global circulation of information and production of affect.

Georgio Agamben's discussion of the society of the spectacle and the "alienation of language" helps me explain the incommunicability of communication. Agamben notes that "in the old regime . . . the estrangement of the communicative essence of human beings was substantiated as a presupposition that had the function of a common ground (nation, language, religion, etc.)." Under current conditions, however, "it is precisely this same communicativity, this same generic essence (language), that is constituted as an autonomous sphere to the extent to which it becomes the essential factor of the production cycle. What hinders communication, therefore, is communicability itself: human beings are being separated by what unites them."[15] The commonality of the nation-state was thought of in terms of linguistic and religious groups. The ideal of constitutional states, moreover, in theories such as Habermas's, has been conceptualized in terms of the essential communicativity of human beings: those who can discuss, who can come to an agreement with one another at least in principle, can be in political relation to one another. Today, however, communication has detached itself from political ideals of belonging and connection to function as itself an economic form. In this precise sense, communication is a divisive force, a force of production.

As I argue elsewhere, the concept of communicative capitalism highlights the economic reconfiguration of communication in mediated technocultures.[16] In this late-capitalist mode of production, values heralded as central to democracy take material form in networked communications. Ideals of access, inclusion, discussion, and participation come to be realized in and through expansions, intensifications, and interconnections of media. For Hardt and Negri, the extensions in opportunities for communication that carry the postmodern economy and that restructure global relations into decentered and deterritorialized networks themselves justify the imperial order. In their words, "mediation is absorbed within the productive machine" as communication industries provide an "immanent" justification of the global political structure of Empire (33). Empire, perhaps paradoxically, is an immanent form of rule that relies on what modern political theories understood in terms of democratization: communicative integration enables a sort of democratization, as the mechanisms of command are distributed in productive and affective networks throughout the social field.

The idea of communicative capitalism helps explain how this democratization in fact undermines democracy by transforming communication into its opposite. Because of expanded communications networks, more people than ever before can make their opinions known. The convenience of the World Wide Web, for example, enables millions not simply to access information but to register their points of view, to agree or disagree, to vote, and to send messages. Facts and opinions, images and reactions circulate in a massive stream of content. Any given message can thus be understood as a contribution to this ever-circulating content.

One of the most basic formulations of the idea of communication is in terms of a message and the response to the message. Under communicative capitalism, this changes. Messages are contributions to circulating content—not actions to elicit responses. Differently put, the exchange value of messages overtakes their use value. So a message is no longer primarily a message from a sender to a receiver. Uncoupled from contexts of action and application—as on the Web or in print and broadcast media—the message is simply part of a circulating data stream. Its particular content is irrelevant. Who sent it is irrelevant. Who receives it is irrelevant. That it need be responded to is irrelevant. The only thing that is relevant is circulation, the addition to the pool. Any particular contribution remains secondary to the fact of circulation. The value of any particular contribution is likewise inversely proportionate to the openness, inclusivity, or extent of a circulating data stream—the more opinions or comments that are out there, the less of an impact any given one might make (and the more shock, spectacle, or newness that is necessary for a contribution to register or have an impact). In sum, communication functions symptomatically to produce its own negation. Or, to return to Agamben's terms, communication hinders communicativity.

Communication in communicative capitalism, then, is not, as Habermas would suggest, action oriented toward reaching understanding.[17] In Habermas's model of communicative action, the use value of a message depends on its orientation. In sending a message, a sender intends for it to be received and understood. Any acceptance or rejection of the message depends on this understanding. Understanding is a necessary part of the communicative exchange. In communicative capitalism, however, the use value of a message is less important than its exchange value, its contribution to a larger pool, flow, or circulation of content. A contribution need not be understood; it need only be repeated, reproduced, forwarded. Circulation is the context, the condition for the acceptance or rejection of a contribution. Put somewhat differently, how a contribution circulates determines whether it has been accepted or rejected. And just as the producer, labor, drops out of the picture in commodity exchange, so does the sender (or author) become immaterial to the contribution. The circulation of logos, branded media identities, rumors, catchphrases, even positions and arguments exemplifies this point. The popularity, penetration, and duration of a contribution mark its acceptance or success.

Thinking about messages in terms of use value and contributions in terms of exchange value sheds light on what would otherwise appear to be an asymmetry in communicative capitalism: the fact that some messages are received, that some discussions extend beyond the context of their circulation. Of course, it is also the case that many commodities are not useless, that people need them. But what makes them commodities is not the need people have for them or, obviously, their use. Rather, it is their economic function, their role in capitalist exchange. Similarly, the fact that messages can retain a relation to understanding in no way negates the centrality of their circulation. Indeed, this link is crucial to the ideological reproduction of communicative capitalism. Some messages, issues, and debates are effective. Some contributions make a difference. But more significant is the system, the communicative network. Even when people know that their specific contributions (their messages, postings, books, articles, films, letters to the editor) simply circulate in a rapidly moving and changing flow of content, in contributing, in participating, they act as if they do not know this. This action manifests ideology as the belief underlying action, the belief that reproduces communicative capitalism.[18]

Hardt and Negri understand the absorption of media and mediation in the productive machine brought about by communicative capitalism as a merging of the communicative and the biopolitical. And they agree that it comes at the cost of the use value of communicative utterances. In what they see as an imperial totality, "exploitation is the expropriation of cooperation and the nullification of the meanings of linguistic production" (385). The whole system, the machine, functions directly through circulation rather than indirectly through responses to messages. We might say that for them the idea that "we're all connected" means that connections are given rather than produced. Connections no longer need be established or interrogated, they simply *are*, part of the biopolitical fabric of our lives. At the same time, the very linguistic performances that produce the social world reinforce imperial power, a power that operates through communicative practices.

Because communicative capitalism relies on the alienation of language, it seems to foreclose the possibility of politics. Similarly, since imperial control works through communication networks gone biopolitical, it likewise suggests a fundamental crisis for aspirations to democracy. The question thus arises: If imperial control extends throughout the "entirety of social relations" as it "reaches down to the ganglia of the social structure and its processes of development" (24), can it be resisted at all? Is there an alternative to Empire?

## Flipping the Script

The multitude is Hardt's and Negri's alternative to Empire. A "new figure of collective biopolitical production," the multitude is a force that both calls Empire into being and opens up the possibility of political change, of an alternative to imperial rule (30). But how is this change supposed to come about?— especially since it hasn't. How is the flip from Empire to multitude possible?

An obvious response is that this is the wrong question; Hardt and Negri emphasize that Empire is defined by crisis. Crisis is "proper to imperial control. . . . Crisis runs through every moment of the development and recomposition of the totality" (385). Crises arising from the productive resistance and struggle of the multitude and imperial efforts to contain them erupt throughout Empire. Central to these crises—for both Empire and multitude—are networked communications. Hardt and Negri write: "Technological development based on the generalization of the communicative relationships of production is a motor of crisis, and productive general intellect is a nest of antagonisms" (386). The struggle over the shape of the network, whether it will be democratically rhizomatic or oligopolistically treelike, exemplifies this presence of conflict, this coexisting of Empire and multitude. Almost like Wittgenstein's duck-rabbit, Empire and multitude suggest two aspects of the same phenomenon, two ways of seeing the informatization of everyday life and the reconfiguring of communication through capitalism.[19] The same conditions that reinforce imperial power, informatization, decentralization, deterritorialization, and spectacle also empower the multitude.

Hardt and Negri explain how this works when they describe the loss of the autonomy of the political. As will become clear, this description serves as well as an ontologization of the political. We see the loss of the autonomy of the political in the changed relation between the state and capital brought about through communicative capitalism (307).[20] For example, just as global financial markets impact domestic currencies and policies in ways independent of national governments and citizenries, so do networked technologies challenge the abilities of states to regulate information flow. Similarly, the very media thriving off and through spectacle reconstitute politics in terms of spectacle. Political successes depend on capacities to get messages across, to make an impact; accordingly, they often rely on raising money, instilling fear, and producing the fleeting spectacular events that seem to call publics into being. Hardt and Negri argue that these changes in the conditions of political mediation mean the loss of a separate sphere of the political.[21]

But politics is not lost. In fact, Hardt and Negri imply that now it is everywhere. Faced with the foreclosure of politics, they transform it into its opposite—the inevitable, unavoidable givenness of its presence. They arrive at this ontological point via networked communications, or via the community constituted through immaterial and affective labor in the postmodern information economy. Introducing the imperial constitution as a site of contestation, they write:

> The general outlines of today's imperial constitution can be conceived in the form of a rhizomatic and universal communication network in which relations are established to and from all its points or nodes. Such a network seems paradoxically to be at once completely open and completely closed to struggle and intervention. On the one hand, the network formally allows all possible subjects in the web of relations to be present simultaneously, but on the other hand, the network itself is a real and proper non-place. (320)

Breaking this down, we find a variation on their claim regarding the struggle over the shape of the global information infrastructure. Rather than posing an alternative between "rhizome" and "tree," here they treat the rhizomatic structure of contemporary communications as a given. They thereby suggest that the problem of imperial power is more than a problem of corporations; corporate oligopolies present one specific set of controls in a larger, shifting, and complex terrain. And in this terrain, the same attributes are benefits *and* burdens, assets *and* hindrances to resistance. What opens the network to resistance and opportunities to communicate closes the network to struggle and intervention. How can one intervene when one—and everyone—is already included? How does one struggle *against* already present communicative opportunities? And what does struggle even mean in a virtual space? As Noortje Marres observes, "when it comes to the manifestation of social movements, it all depends on the presence of irreducible social actors in the streets."[22] Alternatively, Hardt and Negri suggest that constructing something ontologically new, new modes of human being, a new place in the non-place, is one of the tasks of struggle (217). Perhaps. But making the virtual world a key location of struggle risks conceding the more mundane terrains, practices, and institutions of power to those forces of conservatism and capitalism old-fashioned enough to continue their occupation. It also seems to rely a lot more on the symbolic and immaterial labor of the technologically adept than it does on the affective, caring, and domestic labor of community-building.

Be that as it may, for Hardt and Negri, the totality of communication, production, and life renders all of Empire into an "open site of conflict" (404). Resistance and struggle, they urge, are already present. In a way, politics is everywhere, and everything is political.[23] Accordingly, language is a fundamental site of struggle. The merger of the communicative and the biopolitical means that destroying "linguistic and communicative regimes of production . . . in words is as urgent as doing so in deeds" (404). A war of words, over words, is a real war, a real struggle over the means of communication. Hardt and Negri write: "If communication has increasingly become the fabric of production, and if linguistic cooperation has increasingly become the structure of productive corporeality, then the control over linguistic sense and meaning and the networks of communication becomes an ever more central issue for political struggle" (404). All of labor is already involved in this struggle over sense, meaning, knowledge, language, and the networks of communicative production. Presumably, victories in the struggle over language will be retroactively constructed in and through the victorious concepts.

Like language, subjectivity is also a site of struggle. As with the communicative networks more broadly, here again the processes of subjectivization characteristic of imperial rule are also those enabling the multitude. And here again Hardt and Negri transform failures of mediation into the immediacy of the political. Their argument draws from what they understand as the passage from disciplinary society to the society of control (329). Disciplinary logics worked primarily within the institutions of civil society to produce subjects. These mediating institutions, for example, the nuclear family, the prison, the school, the union, the local church, and the bowling league, are in crisis (197). The spaces, logics, practices, and norms previously coalescing into these institutions have broken down and apart. Hence, their efficacy is now indeterminate. (In other words, in some instances, the release of an institutional logic from its spatial constraints has given it all the more force; in other instances, the opposite has occurred.) In Hardt's and Negri's words, "The indefiniteness of the *place* of production corresponds to the indeterminancy of the *form* of the subjectivities produced" (197; emphasis in original). So today, rather than discernible identities rooted in sex or ethnicity, say, and rather than specific social roles such as housewife, worker, prisoner, or company man, there are "hybrid and modulating subjectivities" (331).

The fluidity of these subjects supports, on the one hand, the mobility of global capital and imperial control. On the other hand, insofar as these new subjectivities exceed the forms of imperial control, they present alternatives to Empire. The alternatives seem to emerge in three key sites—the gaps and crises spread throughout the society of control, the tension between the economic and the political subject, and the change in what it means to be human that Hardt and Negri designate as an "anthropological exodus."

The first location of alternatives to Empire appears in the crises and failures multiplying throughout the society of control. Biopower in the society of control extends throughout every element of social life. For Hardt and Negri this very extension means that biopower loses "its capacity effectively to mediate different social forces" (25). Instead of disciplining subjects or relying on mediating institutions to channel and manage conflict, order in the society of control is a result of direct interventions (35). Direct interventions are singular and flexible—what we might think of as a political version of just-in-time production. Similarly, whether it is juridical or moral, an aspect of media or military surveillance, such intervention is also unbounded. It can hit anything, any time, any place. But it can not hit everything, all the time, every place. There is "always a surplus" (60). Events necessarily—as events—erupt. (I think of these as being like so many leaks rupturing a giant dam. As soon as one is fixed, another springs forth.) So, Hardt and Negri argue that imperial control intervenes but does not mediate. Empire reacts to crises not only that its very mode of control cannot prevent but that it actually relies on to call it into being. Biopower "unifies and envelops within itself every element of social life," but in so doing, "at that very moment reveals a new context, a new milieu of maximum plurality and uncontainable singularization—a milieu of the event" (25). Hardt and Negri thus conclude that unification entails pluralization. Precisely because Empire encompasses everything, resistance can appear anywhere. There are more possibilities for resistance than ever before.[24]

Hardt and Negri identify a second location of alternatives to Empire in the tension that emerges between the economic and the political subject. As I mentioned, communicative capitalism necessarily affects subject formation, effects Hardt and Negri explain through the concept of the society of control. The old political subject—the citizen-subject of an autonomous political sphere, the disciplined subject of civil society, the liberal subject willing to vote in public and then return home to his private sphere—can no longer be said to exist (if he ever did). According to the standard based on the old political subject, the new fluid, mobile, hybrid subjectivites of Empire's rhizomatic information networks are ungovernable. These subjectivities, or singularities, can only be controlled. But they cannot be under too much control since they are the source of communicative production and consumption. Hardt and Negri argue that this problem of control confronts Empire with a particular dilemma: How can the economic activity of contemporary subjectivities be channeled into some kind of political subjection?[25]

Hardt and Negri think such a channeling is not possible. Precisely because communication is production, because affect and desire are production, producing and consuming subjects, they argue, are liberated from the mechanisms of political rule. Hardt and Negri write: "On the terrain of the production and regulation of subjectivity, and in the disjunction between the political subject and the economic subject, it seems that we can identify a real field of struggle . . . a true and proper situation of crisis and maybe even of revolution" (321). As an example, we might think again of battles around the Internet. The economic ideal of an information superhighway invoked the ideological fiction of citizen-subjects interested in town meetings for millions. It should surprise no one that what we got instead was cyberporn, gambling, and Web sites debating the sexualities of puppets on Sesame Street. We got, in other words, a dispersion of "linked" resistances to established political norms.

The ungovernability of imperial subjects leads to the third place where Hardt and Negri identify changes in subjectivity that present alternatives to Empire. Hardt and Negri read challenges to conventional sexualities, experiments in body modification, and cyborgian mixings of human and machine as an "anthropological exodus." "This anthropological exodus is important primarily," they write, "because here is where the positive constructive face of the mutation begins to appear: an ontological mutation in action, the concrete invention of a first *new place in the non-place*" (215–216; emphasis in original). We find hints of or early steps in this exodus in punk fashion, piercings, and tattoos. For Hardt and Negri, these are more than fads (which have been co-opted into commodity-driven teen culture). They are indications of a "will to be against" and the emergence of a body "that is completely incapable of submitting to command" (216). Transformed posthuman bodies, Hardt and Negri prophesy, will be technologically integrated and creative as well as "radically unprepared for normalization" (216). So again, we find that contemporary changes in subjectivity constitute in and of themselves a political challenge to Empire. An alternative is already in the process of emerging. The multitude is becoming.

Perhaps. But Hardt's and Negri's descriptions of already existing struggles in and around language and subjectivity seem simply that, descriptions. Why would we accept the hopeful multitude description over the gloomy Empire description? Why, other than that we are looking for hope? There is something deeply unsatisfying about Empire-multitude as duck-rabbit. It is like a weird combination of the same technophobia and techno-utopianism that always accompany the introduction of new technologies: the results, consequences, and side effects of the adoption, dispersion, and proliferation of communication technologies might be good or they might be bad. Looking at the Net, technophobes emphasize loss of intimacy, invasions of privacy, increases in surveillance, the immiseration of the workforce, and consolidations of wealth. Techno-utopians emphasize possibilities for democratic communication, expanded and immediate access, new forms of connectivity, and new opportunities for creativity. Hardt and Negri merge the two positions, recognizing that the politics of technologies are never simply given; they are never just one thing. But nor are they necessarily two. Hardt and Negri channel all too quickly the potential stemming from the insight that technologies materialize antagonism, that networks are rapidly shifting sites and lines of conflict and struggle, into the Empire-multitude binary. And with these as our choices, what other than hope would lead us to emphasize the multitude description over the Empire description? It would be like reading the increased polarization of wealth in the United States, say, cheerfully, as a sign of the renewed strength of the poor since their numbers are growing.[26] We thus seem back to my initial question as to how the flip from Empire to multitude is possible. Is it more than a matter of hope?

## Constituent Hope

Arguing that the revolutionary potential of the multitude is immanent to global technoculture, Hardt and Negri introduce two additional ideas on behalf of their political ontology. The first involves the "paradox of incommunicability" (54). The second emphasizes the constituent power of the multitude.

Recall that communicative capitalism is rooted in communication without communicability. Under these conditions, changing the meanings of words and "inventing a common language of struggle" will go only so far (55). They are unlikely to usher in radical change. Accordingly, Hardt and Negri emphasize the political force of incommunicability. We could say that they turn conditions of impossibility into conditions of possibility. Or that they take the failure of a politics rooted in communication—in rhetoric, organizing, articulating, and representing as well as in discussing and persuading—to designate the immediacy of the political. Or that they evince a great deal of hope. At any rate, changes in the conditions of communications have made it exceedingly difficult for specific instances of resistance to link together, acquire momentum, and inspire a sense of common struggle. Hardt and Negri view this failure to communicate as a political opportunity. They argue that: "We ought to be able to recognize that what the struggles have lost in extension, duration, and communicability they have gained in intensity" (54).

Hardt and Negri do not explain what they mean by intensity and what sort of actions and events are evidence of intensity. Nevertheless, it makes sense to read "intensity" as an aspect of "immediacy." So, for Hardt and Negri, local struggles do not remain local; they strike at the heart of Empire. Because Empire spreads across a global surface, any one point is as crucial as any other. Incommunicability, they write, "is in fact a strength rather than a weakness— a strength because all of the movements are immediately subversive in themselves" (58). (Although it is a necessary component of their account of the immediacy of the political, this "all" strikes me as too inclusive to be politically useful. What sort of politics fails to distinguish between, say, Zapatistas, antiabortion activists, and Mothers Against Drunk Driving?) For Hardt and Negri, struggles do not need to connect with each other, because each can impact Empire directly. And this immediacy gives struggles an intensity previously secured only through their horizontal articulation (57). What remains unclear is what sort of lasting effects are associated with intensity. Does it merely reiterate, albeit to different ends, the affective force of spectacle? In the absence of duration, extension, or articulation with other movements, how can intensity radically impact and change imperial power? What would intense politics look like?

The second idea Hardt and Negri invoke on behalf of the political potential of the multitude is constituent struggle. Strikes in France, riots in Los Angeles, the Intifada against Israel, and the uprising in Chiapas (to mention but a few) all merge political, economic, and cultural concerns. They are biopolitical—struggles over the form of life. For Hardt and Negri this means that "they are constituent struggles, creating new public spaces and new forms of community" (56). (Presumably these new forms of community lack duration and extension, although it is difficult to understand what sort of community this might be. What occurs to me is the faux community of fans called into being by branded media products—like the Pepsi Generation—or again, the community as audience interpellated through spectacle.) Understood most simply, constituent power involves the creative, productive power of the multitude to bring something new into being. Perhaps this "new" will last only a moment. Perhaps it will be manifest only in a glimpse, only as a possibility, before it is either squashed by an imperial intervention or its own instantiation confronts it as its opposite, as sterile, lifeless, constituted power—which is actually the very same thing as imperial power given that the multitude calls Empire into being.

Since the constituent power of the multitude is at the heart of Hardt's and Negri's hope for politics, it makes sense to look at the concept in greater depth. To do so, I turn to Negri's discussion in *Insurgencies.*[27] There he asserts that "the concept of constituent power is the core of political ontology."[28] Negri considers how the concept appears in juridical theory, namely, as a power that arises from nowhere to establish a new arrangement. For him, this arising from nowhere is the ideal moment of absolute democracy: the appearance of the new out of nothing and without determination in a fundamental act of innovation. Insofar as it is necessarily outside and prior to what it constitutes, constituent power is "alien to the law." Constituent power, then, can be thought of as a sort of crisis and a sort of passion. It is a sort of crisis because of its radical rupture with what came before it; indeed, insofar as it installs new principles and arrangements, it cannot be judged by what came before it. (To this extent, constituent power seems to refer to the paradox of constitution that has long plagued democratic theory and to treat that paradox as a strength and potentiality to be celebrated.) It is a sort of passion in that it is a moment of subjective action that exceeds the rational; it is a desire to open things up to the future, to possibility.

The problem for Negri in *Insurgencies* is that what is constituted ends up desiccating and perverting the passion constituting it: sovereignty and the state dilute constituent power through representation, neutralize it through the political system, and rationalize it through the organization of time.[29] Constituent power, then, loses its strength, its effects, once it is actualized, once the constituting moment has passed. For Negri, then, the fundamental political task is to find a way to retain constituent power. "The problem of constituent power," Negri writes, "is a question about the construction of a constitutional model capable of keeping the formative capacity of constituent power itself in motion: it is a question of identifying a subjective strength adequate to this task."[30]

He identifies this subjective strength in the Other of global capitalist reformations of democracy, that is, the alien, the foreigner, the outsider, the rabble, or the multitude.[31] This move, the one celebrated in *Empire*, is in keeping with a tradition in Hegelian thought, a tradition that has emphasized the force of the mob and has identified the foreclosed excess as that point at which a system can be disrupted. Slavoj Žižek notes that Hegel posited the *Poebel* as that "necessary surplus excluded from the closed circuit of a social edifice." The *Poebel*, Žižek continues, is a "nonintegrated segment in the legal order, prevented from partaking of its benefits, and for this very reason delivered from any responsibilities toward it."[32]

Negri's argument differs from the typical Hegelian line, first, in that he does not understand the multitude as an excluded element. As he and Hardt emphasize in *Empire*, under imperial conditions, there is no outside. Negri's argument differs, second, in that what makes the multitude inside is its biopolitical productivity, rendered in *Insurgencies*, as in *Empire*, as a Foucauldian version of Marx's living labor. Hence, Negri interprets biopolitics as that which enhances strength and releases productivity, creating subjects in the process. The forces or arrangements through which subjects are created, in other words, make them strong and, in effect, install in them the potential for liberation. So politics in its constituted form governs or administers productive strength like so much dead labor controlling living labor. What is *really* political thus becomes "the ontological strength of a multitude of cooperating singularities."[33]

I see three primary problems in Negri's account of constituent power, problems that call into question the political potential of the multitude as ontologically given, or, more precisely, Hardt's and Negri's hope that communicative capitalism is becoming radically transformed toward a revolutionary absolute democracy. First, the multitude is radically alienated from what it creates; constituted power, in other words, always encounters constituent power as something radically other. The result is a turn away from state and constitutional politics as not sufficiently, not immanently, political. The state—with its police, military, legislative, judicial, and surveillance powers—is left to those who still find it useful to their interests, interests that these days seem inextricable from global capital.

We might also think here of Net politics, of discussions, debates, opinions, clicks, surveys, and ever-circulating petitions. As I mentioned, a political focus on the Net that abandons representative politics altogether is a terrible strategy, insofar as it leaves the state—its courts, laws, and declarations of war—open to control by one's opponents. A primary focus on the Net presumes that what happens on the Net matters in and of itself. A proper Net politics, however, realizes that what happens on the Net has to be made to matter. One has to link the Net to state- and interstate-level actors and actions. Ignoring the state, we might say, is precisely what "they," *the powers that be,* want us to do. Investing all energy in the non-place of the Net reinforces imperial control, repeating communicative capitalism's foreclosure of the political, insofar as each click, each contribution, adds to the exchange value circulating in communicative capitalism. Net-centered activity, in other words, does not decrease the hold of communicative capitalism. It increases it. To reduce the political to a constitutive moment enacts this same foreclosure.

A second problem appears in the impossibly clean division between constituent and constituted power reappearing throughout *Empire* as well as *Insurgencies*. Indeed, in the very absence of relation between the two, we find a relation of absence in such a way that each exists only in relation to the other. There is no constituent power without that which is constituted, and clearly there can be no constituted power absent that which constitutes it. Both are hence incomplete and in need of the other. But there is an even more concrete relation between the two: the multitude itself is always constituted by that which it has constituted; its character as biopolitical reminds us of the disciplinary and controlling arrangements that govern its productivity (I use "govern" here to invoke its old technological sense of "steering" and "driving"). Likewise, contemporary communications networks—linked computers and informatization—are characterized by precisely that reflexivity that presumes systems constituting themselves—a notion Hardt and Negri embrace. Given this reflexivity, a division between constituent and constituted power makes no sense. Constituted power is of course constituent, productive, performative, generating new arrangements of bodies. To this extent, engaging within the terms of constituted power is politically imperative.

The third problem takes me, again, to the ontological claims for the constituent power of the multitude. The multitude is a multitude of "cooperating singularities." But what does it mean to say that these singularities cooperate? What sort of relation within or among the singularities is this supposed to designate? When I think of the singularities communicating on the Net, cooperation—like communication—is the last thing that occurs to me. Or, better put, I recognize that just as messages have lost their use value to become contributions, so does cooperation function as a kind of system imperative—keep it running. Although they recognize that guaranteeing the network is crucial to imperial power, Hardt and Negri argue that the cooperative relation between singularities in the multitude is generative and affective (320). The political is, they write, "the power of generation, desire, and love" (388). It involves not antagonism, decision or division but a kind of organic growth, on the one hand, and intensifying affective identifications, on the other (a result of the dissolution of the institutions of civil society in the society of control). Passions echo and reinforce each other. Feeling something intensely is political. Hope itself is political.

## Conclusion

Hardt's and Negri's *Empire* powerfully describes the absorption of mediation in the communicative spaces of global capitalist technoculture. The imperial constitution works like and through rhizomatic communications networks that are themselves biopolitical, generative, productive, of capital, of subjectivities, of life itself. And at stake in this synthesis of communication and production, of capitalist and imperial control, is politics itself. I have argued that Hardt's and Negri's political ontology is based on a transformation of the loss of political mediations into the immediacy of the political. For them, this is a hopeful move. And within the terms of their ontology, hope is itself political. I agree that hope can be a powerful political force. But I hope for more.

Although I am not sure where to look for more hope or how, in the hope of something better, to politicize existing arrangements, I find something promising in the effort to turn conditions of impossibility into conditions of possibility. To end, then, on a hopeful note, I return to the society of the spectacle, that is, to the hope Agamben finds there, albeit in a still negative and limited form. He writes:

> The extreme form of the expropriation of the Common is the spectacle, that is, the politics we live in. But this also means that in the spectacle our own linguistic nature comes back to us inverted. This is why (precisely because what is being expropriated is the very possibility of a common good), the violence of the spectacle is so destructive; but for the same reason the spectacle retains something like a positive possibility that can be used against it.[34]

In the real and proper non-place of spectacle, there is still the possibility, the hope, of a common good. To channel this positive possibility against it, against the communicative capitalism that produces, reinforces, and relies on it, is the task for politics. And this politics will not be given; rather, it will have to be constructed through a complex and multileveled politics of articulation, struggle, and representation.

## Acknowledgments

I'm grateful to Kevin Dunn, Paul Passavant, and Lee Quinby for comments on a previous draft of this paper.

## Notes

1. I take the term "communicative capitalism" from Paul Passavant, who used it during our discussion on a panel on *Empire* (Cambridge, MA: Harvard University Press, 2000) at the 2001 meeting of the Law and Society Association in Budapest. I owe many of the points raised in this paper to our three years of discussing, teaching, and writing about *Empire*. Any mistakes are thus his. References to *Empire* are given parenthetically throughout the text.

2. See Antonio Negri, *The Politics of Subversion: A Manifesto for the Twenty-First Century*, trans. James Newell (Cambridge, UK: Polity Press, 1989). For an excellent account of autonomist Marxism and information technologies, see Nick Dyer-Witheford, *Cyber-Marx: Cycles and Circuits of Struggle in High-Technology Capitalism* (Urbana, IL: University of Illinois Press, 1999).

3. For a critical examination of various notions of what an information society might be, see Frank Webster, *Theories of the Information Society* (London: Routledge, 1995).

4. Manuel Castells, *The Rise of the Network Society* (Oxford: Blackwell Publishers, 1996), 32.

5. See Martin Campbell-Kelly and William Aspray, *Computer: A History of the Information Machine* (New York: Basic Books, 1996), esp. 54–57, 90–93.

6. See Jodi Dean, *Publicity's Secret: How Technoculture Capitalizes on Democracy* (Ithaca: Cornell University Press, 2002), chap. 3.

7. Castells, *Network Society*, 32.

8. As Dyer-Witheford makes clear, the restructuring of work brought about by informatization is part of a devastating attack on the worker. Systems of computerized flow control, he explains:

> permit management to sever the solidarity of the assembly line by cutting it into competing "work teams" supplied by robot servers, shrinking the labor force, and in some cases approaches the "lights out" scenario of fully automated factory production. The strategic advantage afforded capital by this disaggregation and downsizing is then reinforced by telecommunications systems that permit the centralized coordination of dispersed operations, making feasible the transfer of work from hot-spots of instability either to domestic "greenfield" sites uncontaminated by militancy or to offshore locations. (78)

9. Saskia Sassen, *Globalization and Its Discontents* (New York: The New Press, 1998), 143–145.

10. For more elaboration, see my argument in *Publicity's Secret*.

11. Castells, *Network Society*, 469–478. Castells writes: "Networks are open structures, able to expand without limits, integrating new nodes as long as they are able to communicate within the network, namely as long as they share the same communication codes (for example, values or performance goals). . . . Since networks are multiple, the interoperating codes and switches between networks become the fundamental sources in shaping, guiding, and misguiding societies" (470–471).

12. See Nick Dyer-Witheford, "E-Capital and the Many-Headed Hydra," 129–163, and Brian Martin Murphy, "A Critical History of the Internet," 27–45, both in *Critical Perspectives on the Internet*, ed. Greg Elmer (Lanham, MD: Rowan and Littlefield, 2002).

13. This double determination of the content of spectacle is itself spectacularly under-determined. What, we might ask, is the link between contemporary communications media and spectacle? Is the argument a claim for technological determinism? Is spectacle the inevitable result of broadcast media? Why? And what is the link between fear and spectacle? Finally, why specific fears of violence, poverty, and unemployment rather than illness and loss, say? In raising these questions, I am not saying that these links are not there—clearly, as the Bush administration and the cooperating mass media urge fears of terrorism and try to push the United States into permanent war, the links seem stronger than ever. However, I am suggesting that an analysis that problematized, specified, pluralized, and contextualized these links would be much more useful. For a general discussion of fear in the society of the spectacle, see Barry Glassner, *The Culture of Fear: Why Americans Are Afraid of the Wrong Things* (New York: Basic Books, 1999). For a collection of more specific and detailed essays on fear, see Brian Massumi, ed., *The Politics of Everyday Fear* (Minneapolis: University of Minnesota Press, 1993).

14. Thomas L. Dumm, *Democracy and Punishment: The Disciplinary Origins of the United States* (Madison, WI: University of Wisconsin Press, 1987), 148. Dumm, however, associates fear more with the possibility of freedom than with a new form of control.

15. Georgio Agamben, *Means without End: Notes on Politics*, trans. by Vincenzo Binetti and Cesare Casarino (Minneapolis, MN: University of Minnesota Press, 2000), 115.

16. This is my argument in *Publicity's Secret*.

17. Hardt and Negri explicitly contrast their position with Habermas's, insofar as Habermas positions communication outside the "effects of globalization" in a "standpoint of life and truth that could oppose the informational colonization of being" (34). For them, of course, such a standpoint no longer exists—if it ever did, we might add.

18. I am relying here on the theory of ideology developed by Slavoj Žižek in *The Sublime Object of Ideology* (London: Verso, 1989).

19. See Ludwig Wittgenstein, *Philosophical Investigations*, trans. G. E. M. Anscombe (Oxford: Basil Blackwell, 1958), 194. Wittgenstein draws upon this simple figure in the course of his consideration of two uses of the word "see." Depending on the angle of the figure, it appears as either the head of a duck or the head of a rabbit. Without being shown the second aspect of the drawing, one might never see anything but the first.

20. See also Saskia Sassen's discussion of economic citizenship in *Losing Control: Sovereignty in an Age of Globalization* (New York: Columbia University Press, 1996).

21. They write: "The place of modern liberal politics has disappeared and thus from this perspective our postmodern and imperial society is characterized by a deficit of the political. In effect, the place of politics has been deactualized" (188).

22. Noortje Marres, "Why Take the Detour? A Small Exercise in Tracing Displacements of Protests, and Issues, across the Web," published as "Pourquoi prendre des chemins de traverse? De quelques déplacements politiques sur le Web," French trans. by Anne Querrien, *Multitudes* 9, "Philosophie Politique des Multitudes" (May/June 2002), available at http://multitudes.samizdat.net/.

23. For a critique of the idea that everything is political, see "The Interface of Political Theory and Cultural Studies," my introduction to my edited volume, *Cultural Studies and Political Theory* (Ithaca, NY: Cornell University Press, 2000), 1–19.

24. *Empire's* account of an explosion in sites of struggle reiterates points Negri emphasized already in *The Politics of Subversion*. Dyer-Witheford provides an excellent summary of the argument. He writes:

> In a world where capital has insinuated itself everywhere, there is now no central front of struggle. Instead, contestation snakes through homes, schools, universities, hospitals, and media; it takes the form not only of workplace strikes and confrontations but also of resistance to the dismantling of the welfare state, demands over pay equity, child care, parenting, and health care benefits, and opposition to ecological despoilation. In the newly socialized sphere of capital, a fractal logic obtains, such that each apparently independent location replicates the fundamental antagonism that informs the entire structure—capital's insistence that life-time be subordinated to profit. (82)

25. Dyer-Witheford's analysis of Negri's earlier discussion of the challenge facing capital as it attempts to appropriate the communicative capacity of the labor force can add some clarity here. In the information age, capital has insinuated itself everywhere, throughout the life span. In order to extract value, then, it has to surround the worker (the socialized worker of the social factory) with a dense web of communication technologies and media. Capital has to deliver all this media and technology to workers if it is to continue to develop. And herein lies the problem: "By informating production, capital seems to augment its powers of control. But it simultaneously stimulates capacities that threaten to escape its command and overspill into rivulets irrelevant to, or even subversive of profit" (85).

26. Paul Krugman refers to the change in real annual compensation of CEOs compared to average workers from 1970 to 1999. In 1970, the average CEO salary was 39 times the pay of the average worker. In 1999 it was more than 1000 times the pay of average workers. Likewise, from 1979 to 1997 the after-tax income of middle-income families increased 10 percent while the after-tax income for the top 1 percent of families rose 157 percent. See his account of the new guilded age, "For Richer," *New York Times Magazine*, October 20, 2002.

27. Antonio Negri, *Insurgencies: Constituent Power and the Modern State*, trans. Maurizia Boscagli (Minneapolis: University of Minnesota Press, 1999).

28. Negri, 35.

29. Negri, 313.

30. Negri, 25.

31. Negri writes:

> From the standpoint of the political, the multitude is always objectified. Its name is reduced to a curse: *vulgus*, or worse, *Poebel*. Its strength is expropriated. Nonetheless, we cannot do without the *multitudo* in social and political life—this is evident. But how can it be dominated? This is the only question that theoretical philosophy, moral philosophy, and above all political philosophy, pose to themselves. The *multitudo* has to become each time either a nature that is mechanical and deprived of spirit, a nature closer to that of brutes than men, or a thing in itself, unachievable and therefore mystifiable, or a savage world of irrational passions that only the *Vernunft* will be able to unravel and control. (325)

32. Slavoj Žižek, *Tarrying with the Negative* (Durham: Duke University Press, 1993).

33. Negri, 333.

34. Georgio Agamben, *The Coming Community*, trans. Michael Hardt (Minneapolis: Minnesota University Press, 1993), 80.

# 14

Revolution

# The Myth of the Multitude

## Kam Shapiro

In a work that mirrors the complexity and confusion of global life in (not entirely) condensed form, Michael Hardt and Antonio Negri describe a world without borders; then they take sides. As they explain, their approach has two, distinct methodological strains: "The first is critical and deconstructive, . . . the second is . . . ethico-political."[1] In the critical mode, they map the rise of Empire, a global form of sovereignty that subsumes all categories and distinctions in an encompassing relational network. In their "ethico-political" mode, they discern in this morass a struggle for liberation on the part of the "multitude," a global revolutionary subject on the verge of radical self-authorization. This essay explores tensions in play between critical, polemical, and messianic strains of Hardt's and Negri's text, tracing similar arguments in earlier departures from orthodox historical materialism. Hardt's and Negri's departure from a critical or "deconstructive" politics is highlighted in their critique of what they describe as a "postmodern" politics of difference. Instead of a plurality of local struggles over flexible discourses and technologies—too easily co-opted by equally efficient strategies of rule—they advocate a new universalism grounded in not discrete demands but the creative power of human desire and activity. Moreover, they suggest that the multitude, so understood, is on the verge of a properly global manifestation. Hardt's and Negri's analysis of the collapse of economic and discursive categories as well as their commitment to spontaneous collective action recall George Sorel's earlier anarchist departure from orthodox Leninism. In particular, their depiction of the multitude bears a strong resemblance to that of his

"General Strike." Rather than a new utopia, the multitude comprises what Sorel described as a political "myth." In light of this comparison, I question the value of such a myth for social movements implicated in the tangle of discursive, technological, and economic forces proper to Empire.

## The Deconstruction of Sovereignty and the Politics of the Multitude

Hardt's and Negri's "deconstructive" critique of contemporary sovereignty rests on a materialist ontology that dispenses with the economic determinism formerly central to Marxist dialectics. In the place of a struggle between discrete economic classes, they describe a contest between the constitutive powers of the multitude and the constituted mediations of sovereignty (*potentia* and *potestas*, in the terms Negri adopts from Spinoza) that traverses all levels of social and individual life. The notion of the multitude, developed in Negri's prison writings on Spinoza, is not easy to pin down, which is very much to the point.[2] It denotes the "immanent" power of a material multiplicity that is not reducible to a given class or subject position in the traditional (Marxist) sense. Rather, the multitude is a generative locus of production, cooperation and "desire" that generates new subjectivities. Instead of a given organization or set of demands, the multitude is identified with creative action and transformation. Indeed, as soon as it finds  itself "mediated" as a subject or people and articulated through formal procedures and apparatuses, the multitude has effectively been captured by sovereignty. The multitude thus appears in their narrative as the engine of historical change, a dynamic force of "liberation" around which the powers of sovereignty reactively coalesce but which they never manage to arrest. In fact, they argue that sovereignty itself provokes new crises even as it works to resolve others (60).

Hardt's and Negri's critical ontology serves as a lens through which they reread a broad range of historical struggles, describing a series of escapes by the multitude that provoke ever more expansive and nuanced mediations by sovereignty. "Empire" denotes the culmination of these dynamics in a "de facto" global sovereignty, a tight web of market and governmental power that leaves no genre of human activity outside its purview. Empire is comprised of both constitutional forms and the "biopolitical" technologies of order that secure and condition them, taking the form of a decentered network of juridical, governmental, and military organs that respond to local crises in a rapid and continuous fashion. Along with the collapse of spatial boundaries, Empire is characterized by the interpenetration of different realms of human activity proper to postindustrial society, where new modes of affective and communicative production result in an unprecedented "convergence of base and superstructure" (385). Hence all conflicts are effectively internalized; economic, political, and cultural authorities are consolidated in the form of a global "police power" that arises to manage the tangle of market, labor, and cultural forces proper to contemporary life. In the diffuse and encompassing networks Hardt and Negri describe, economic, technological, and cultural processes are mutually implicated, leaving no "outside" to the global system, whether geographically or discursively.[3] Driven by the failure of modern welfare states to regulate global flows of capital and culture, sovereignty has extended and intensified both its juridical and biopolitical powers, grafting itself to global flows and permeating all levels of social life. However, these institutions and technologies are essentially opportunistic and reactive. Moreover, they are invested in a bios that is fundamentally dynamic. "Desire," Hardt and Negri assure us, "has no limit" (349). In seeking to invest itself in the biopower of the multitude, therefore, sovereignty is always tending toward its limit at deeper thresholds of difference and instability.

As this last formulation indicates, a certain progressive logic is implied by Hardt's and Negri's historical narrative. As sovereignty extends ever deeper into the micro- or biopolitical forces of the multitude, the question arises whether there might be a point at which it reaches, in some sense, to the essence of production and desire. At times, their formulations recall classical Marxist narratives that subsumed various historical struggles in a series of developmental "stages," culminating in a decisive battle for self-authorization on the part of a global collective identified with the "base" level of forces of production. Hardt and Negri are sensitive to this comparison and careful to insist on the unique conditions of different struggles. Rather than a linear model of historical development, they claim their study describes a "materialist teleology" (66).

The peculiarity of this last conjunction of terms indicates Hardt's and Negri's ambiguous relation to Hegelian Marxism, an ambiguity at the center of their distinction between critical and "ethico-political" approaches. In their "critical" mode, as noted, they trace the history of the multitude and sovereignty in a series of contingent, material struggles. Here the point is precisely to break with teleological models of development. They write: "The critical approach is thus intended to bring to light the contradictions, cycles, and crises of the process because in each of these moments the imagined necessity of the historical development can open toward alternative possibilities. In other words, the deconstruction of the *historia rerum gestarum*, of the spectral reign of globalized capitalism, reveals the possibility of alternative social organizations" (48). By attending to the complex links in these struggles between diverse material processes, Hardt and Negri effectively "deconstruct" both Marxist and neoliberal teleologies, refusing the language of historical stages and unraveling the triumphal narrative of free markets and liberal values. In their place, they reveal contingent, reciprocal interactions of biology, technology, culture, language and violence. In turn, they document a host of social struggles that—despite being later subsumed by new mediations—are not presented as having foregone conclusions.[4] On the contrary, they emphasize the different potentials and surprising innovations in each crisis. In the critical approach, the multitude serves as a common name for these potentials and struggles that give rise to but also exceed every particular sovereign mediation: "The first [approach] is critical and deconstructive, aiming to subvert the hegemonic languages and social structures and thereby reveal an alternative ontological basis that resides in the creative and productive practices of the multitude" (47).

Hardt's and Negri's shift from the critical to the "ethico-political" is less easy to characterize, not least because of a slippage in its initial formulation. On the one hand, they claim to be "seeking to lead the processes of the production of subjectivity toward the constitution of an effective social, political alternative, a new constituent power"(47). On the next page, however, they appear to reverse course: "Here we must delve into the ontological substrate of the concrete alternatives continually pushed forward by the *res gestae*, the subjective forces acting in the historical context"(48). Two rather different operations are thus described. In the first, the multitude is first revealed as a substrate of potentiality beneath hegemonic languages and structures and then directed toward an actual ("social and political") alternative; in the second, we move in the other direction, from the dispersion of concrete alternatives to their basis in a common ontological substrate. In turn, the ethico-political approach itself appears torn between leading and revealing, or programmatic speculation and metaphysical exegesis.

Clearly, Hardt and Negri would refuse this dichotomy. It is precisely the unification of potential and actual that characterizes the multitude proper, as Negri argues extensively in his reading of Spinoza.[5] In turn, they reject the distinction between theory and practice, subsuming their metaphysics in the "general intellect" of the multitude itself. However, from this perspective, the two approaches outlined above should also collapse, and the deconstructive approach should itself serve the "ethico-political" function they describe. The "ontological substrate" would itself be comprised of nothing more (nor less) than a dispersion of innovations both revealed and practiced by their critical genealogy. It is here, in the space between the potential and the actual, or rather between instances of actuated potentials, that Hardt and Negri interject the teleological strain of their materialism. We have already glimpsed this operation in the historical narrative outlined above, in which a shift from critical to ethico-political formulations is identified with the historical emergence of the multitude itself as a self-constituting ethico-political subject. We are on the cusp of such an emergence, Hardt and Negri suggest, heralded by the global linkages among bodies, affects, and ideas.[6] Hence, despite its apparently total-izing and invasive character, we should welcome the intensification and expan-sion of sovereignty as the spur to this immanent and imminent realization.

Like all messianic formulations, this raises the question of the interim, that transitory state between fall and redemption in which we remain indefinitely suspended. What are we to do, what "ethico-political" program can hasten the next, or final revolution? Hardt's and Negri's answer conforms to their histori-cal logic: we can, and therefore must, only move forward. They write: "Empire can be effectively contested only on its own level of generality and by pushing the processes that it offers past their present limitations. We have to accept that challenge and learn to think globally and act globally."[7] But what kind of think-ing or action is properly "general" or "global"? According to their critical reading of Empire, after all, thinking and action is always-already global, there being no "outside" proper to the existing network. Furthermore, what are the "present limitations" of Empire, and what will result if they are tested or broken? In their deconstructive account of sovereignty, the multitude appears as a force at work within Empire, at once constitutive and destabilizing. The ruptures of limits and boundaries are moments in an ongoing process of escape and capture. It is by pushing processes "past their present limitations," after all, that the multi-tude not only attacks but also sustains sovereignty.[8] Indeed, the emergence of the present Empire was itself a response to earlier forms of proletarian interna-tionalism (51). What could it mean, then, for the multitude to, as they put it, "push through Empire and come out the other side" (218)?

## Siding against Difference

Hardt and Negri are quick to assure us that they cannot be precise regarding the nature and timing of the coming revolution. Nor can they offer a clear set of instructions for dismantling Empire. They are quite confident, however, in their rejection of obsolete approaches. In particular, they claim that the discur-sive and cultural hybridity described by postmodern or postcolonial theory no longer poses any threat to the current order: "When they present their theories as part of a project of political liberation . . . postmodernists are still waging battle against the shadows of old enemies."[9] Along these lines, Hardt and Negri endorse Frederic Jameson's and David Harvey's claims that "postmod-ernism" (understood here as a set of practices characterized by differentiated and flexible strategies rather than hierarchical and centralized modes of com-mand) is the logic of late capitalism (154). It is not immediately clear, however, which postmodernists present their theories as "part of a project of political lib-eration" or just what the latter was supposed to have looked like.

Foucault, often a central figure in attacks on postmodern theory, has been taken to task precisely for *failing* to present a set of instruction for "liberation," being content for the most part to describe changing forms and technologies of power. Lyotard, whom Hardt and Negri cite in this regard, describes post-modernity as a *condition* rather than some liberating project.[10] If anyone speaks of postmodern "liberation," it would seem to be Hardt and Negri themselves.[11] Indeed, this is the basis of Jameson's endorsement of their work—not its acute analysis of contemporary forms of power but the "ethico-political" narrative that frames it. But in what sense is this narrative part of a project of liberation? Where in Hardt's and Negri's text do we see such a project outlined, and how does it differ from what they take to be the "project" of postmodernism?

Hardt and Negri describe the aim of postmodernism as "a global politics of difference, a politics of deterritorialized flows across a smooth world, free of the rigid striation of state boundaries" (142). Hardt and Negri borrow the term "deter-ritorialization" from Gilles Deleuze and Félix Guattari, whose work, along with that of Michel Foucault and Judith Butler, is a popular target for critics of "post-modern" politics. Yet, like other so-called postmodernists—including Foucault, Butler, and Derrida—Deleuze and Guattari neither advocate nor ascribe to con-temporary political forms the dissolution of all boundaries and distinctions. Impressions to the contrary often stem from selective and tendentious readings of key terms, such as Derrida's *différance* or Deleuze's and Guattari's admittedly dif-ficult notion of deterritorialization, a term they use in reference to a wide range of biological, social, and material processes. As in the passage above, the term invites the obvious associations of "territory" with land, nation, and so on, all of which seem to be dissolving. "Deterritorialization" would thus seem an apt description of processes of globalization and the erosion of national borders. The important point to grasp, however, is that, for Deleuze, every deterritorialization is accompa-nied by new forms of *reterritorialization*. He uses territory in the verbal rather than nominative form; there is neither solid ground, so to speak, nor groundless creativity, but only dynamic compositions (assemblages, in his terms) and dislo-cations. Chastening promises of "unlimited" desire, Deleuze and Guattari remind us:

> Desire is never separable from complex assemblages that necessarily tie into molecular levels, from microformations already shaping postures, attitudes, per-ceptions, expectations, semiotic systems, etc. Desire is never an undifferentiated instinctual energy, but itself results from a highly developed, engineered setup rich in interactions: a whole supple segmentarity that processes molecular ener-gies and potentially gives desire a fascist determination.[12]

Hardt and Negri are themselves well aware of these nuances. Deleuze's work is a primary source for their depiction of the transformations at work in

Empire. In particular, their account of contemporary sovereign power closely follows a set of terms sketched in his short essay, "Postscript on the Societies ✳— of Control."[13] There, Deleuze argues that the disciplinary enclosures described by Foucault are giving way to flexible and continuous mechanisms of control that collapse any clear distinction between public and private, inside and out-side. Put in other Deleuzian terms, the "striated" spaces of normalization and exclusion have given way to a "smooth" space of perpetually modulated differ-ence, from a rigid mold to a flexible cast.

In *Empire*, Hardt and Negri flesh out these suggestive metaphors with empirical detail. They identify the basis of "postmodern" sovereignty in a "hybrid constitution" characterized by the increasing interpenetration of local and transnational governmental agencies, on the one hand, and the increas-ingly hybrid *spaces* of global cities, on the other, where Third and First World populations converge and public/private divisions collapse in enclosed walking malls and gated communities. As these examples indicate, the "rigid" territo-rial exclusions of national sovereignty have been replace by a global network of flexible controls based on modulated categories of membership and access. What results is not a "free" movement of images, bodies, or technology across space, but changing modes of regulation and restriction at key points of exchange. Anyone who thinks contemporary sovereignty no longer operates through spatial restrictions should try to find a public toilet in Manhattan.[14]

Deleuze's and Guattari's notion of reterritorialization, it should be added, while aptly applied to these cases, is not restricted to questions of physical geography. Indeed, as Benedict Anderson has argued, geography is itself "imagined" by way of diverse technologies, languages, and migrations. De- and reterritorialization can take a variety of forms and typically operate on multiple registers simultaneously. Electronic media, for example, are radically deterri-torializing at one level, allowing for the movement of images across the globe with little regard for national borders. But the geographical dislocation facili-tated by digital reproduction and high-speed transmission is met by a corre-sponding mediation and distribution of gender, sexual, ethnic, and racial types in the form of sitcom characters, film genres, and media enclaves. In the latter case, geographical deterritorialization is met with demographic reterritorial-ization: where it once contributed to shaping a national audience, television and radio programming is now often segregated according to "community standards" into "virtual enclaves" and niche markets that distinguish, among other things, "black entertainment."[15] At the same time, both content and tech-nology are increasingly consolidated and managed by multinational media conglomerates. As a component of domestic architecture, furthermore, com-mercial television is a medium of capture par excellence, generating and sus-taining a condition of bodily stasis and scripted distraction, individuating viewers and colonizing both physical and mental spaces of free association, or, if you will, turning rhizomes into couch potatoes.[16]

In response to these reterritorializations, one finds a variety of resistances and deterritorializing innovations. Multiple struggles are under way on the part of consumers, artists, pirate broadcasters, religious groups, and computer hackers. In their attempts to create avenues of popular access and/or control, these groups may have occasion not only to resist but also to use the resources of Empire, including the courts and commercially developed technologies. The Internet is clearly a medium of de- and reterritorializing struggles over access and control and itself is an example of the dissemination of military technology for commercial and public use. Consider, for example, the dissemination of no-cost "Wi-Fi" Internet access (low-output radio signal devices that are plugged into a wired network and allow computer users in a small radius with the right antenna to link to the Internet). This technology has been made available to the public by individuals and groups who share bandwidth with anyone in range of their broadcast signal. In turn, corporate ownership and control of these transmissions is being organized. Starbucks currently offers the service for a significant (20 cents per minute) fee in some stores.

At times, then, Hardt and Negri conflate the language of de- and reterritorialization with that of the multitude and sovereignty.[17] Yet it would seem that these terms, in their Deleuzian usage, describe just the sort of politics they elsewhere insist we have to supersede. A politics of "deterritorialized flows," so understood, would be an ongoing series of flights and captures, a shifting plurality of local struggles at once empowered and menaced by the weapons they share with sovereignty. On this point, to their credit, Hardt and Negri are ambivalent, shifting between an appreciation for the achievements and risks of various struggles and their promise of a pure or "universal" democratic liberation. Throughout the book, they champion many problematic struggles, including urban riots and postcolonial nationalisms. However, noting the hazards and failures of such struggles, they repeatedly circle back to a kind of "last instance," where finite and compromised struggles give way to an unmediated confrontation between the liberating power of the multitude and the domination of sovereignty. In their description of this cataclysm, all doubts fall away, and we are promised a revolution characterized only by cooperation, love, and joy.

It is in the latter mode that Hardt and Negri part ways with Deleuze and most other so-called postmodern thinkers. For Deleuze, deterritorialization is never opposed to reterritorialization; nor is it identified with liberation per se (as indicated by his reference to fascist "lines of flight"). One finds many cautions in his work against the polemical oppositions that run throughout Hardt's and Negri's text. He and Guattari write:

One can never posit a dualism or a dichotomy, even in the rudimentary form of the good and the bad. You may make a rupture, draw a line of flight, yet there is still a danger that you will reencounter organizations that restratify everything, formations that restore power to a signifier, attributions that reconstitute a subject—anything you like, from Oedipal resurgences to fascist concretions. Groups and individuals contain microfascisms just waiting to crystalize. . . . How could movements of deterritorialization and processes of reterritorialization not be relative, always connected, caught up in one another?[18]

More in keeping with Deleuzian terms, Hardt and Negri could have described the innovations of desire or the multitude in terms of dynamic stabilities and resonant potentials in play between molar and molecular levels of order. On this reading, Empire contains within itself multiple sites of instability and potential points of emergence for new political forms. At the same time, every molar opposition is traversed by strains of numerous "micropolitical" struggles, complicating all attempts to specify the terms of liberation. Indeed, this is precisely the implication, Hardt and Negri claim, of their "deconstructive" analysis. As they show, for example, the apparent oppositions of the Cold War obscured common forms of oppression (such as the Taylorist organization of industrial labor). Properly deconstructed, the multitude appears in a dispersion of singular events. The deconstructive approach, however, does not yield a political subject and a corresponding "enemy" in the way Hardt and Negri wish to. In accord with Marxist injunctions, they take it as their task to identify a central antagonism.[19] Yet the antagonism in question and the "enemy" supposedly identified have been rendered ethereal by their "deconstructive" analysis of sovereignty: "The identification of the enemy is no small task given that exploitation tends no longer to have a specific place and that we are immersed in a system of power so deep and complex that we can no longer determine specific difference or measure." And yet, they insist: "One should not exaggerate these logical paradoxes. Even though on the new terrain of Empire exploitation and domination often cannot be defined in specific places, they nonetheless exist" (211).

In a curious way, this last quote sounds a lot like something we might hear from Secretary of Defense Donald Rumsfeld in one of his jovial military press conferences, speaking not of exploitation, of course, but "terror" (though he is perfectly willing to conflate the two—citing the exploitation of women under Islamic law—in some of his more improbable attempts to rally support for bombings and extrajudicial incarcerations). Rumsfeld draws the following analogy between the current need to mobilize popular support for military vigilance and the successful mobilizations of the Cold War:

In country after country, leaders kind of rose to the top and persuaded and informed the American people so that they gained the support necessary to make investments, in a time of peace, to make investments that would enable us to defend, if necessary—but preferably deter—against a very serious, persistent, expansionist, powerful threat that was not visible, that wasn't there every minute, that people wanted to debate against as to whether it even existed, and the American people had the staying power. And they will this time. My hope is that they'll have it because of the fact that the need is there and that democratic people, free people, have a pretty good center of gravity. The other way they'll have it is if we're punctuated periodically with additional terrorist attacks that remind us that we do have an obligation to ourselves and our system and our friends and allies around the world to behave responsibly.[20]

As Rumsfeld reminds us, the legitimation of sovereign power relies as much on rupture as it does on containment. Terrorist attacks add weight to the democratic center of gravity, keeping us "responsible" by reminding us we are never truly at peace. However, he is not content to wait for new strikes. Leaders must also inform and persuade. As he says: "Sometimes I like to stick a hole in a balloon. Twice."[21] Terrorist attacks, likewise, may puncture, but they do not necessarily deflate. Rather, they serve, in Rumsfeld's words, as "punctuations," the breaks that facilitate narrative tempo, creating avenues for fear and desire.[22]

The language of the "invisible" enemy, Hardt and Negri argue, is the hallmark of Empire and the ideal object of sovereignty operating in a permanent "state of exception." A vague notion of ubiquitous danger allows for Empire's high degree of flexibility in identifying and responding to diverse crises. In the aftermath of the attacks on the World Trade Center, Hardt's and Negri's seemingly dystopian account of Empire has become increasingly realistic. The subsequent war on terror has precipitated a rapid elimination of vestigial barriers to transnational juridical authority and a remarkable intensification of "exceptional" police powers in the name of that "center of gravity" which keeps free people responsible. The United States and its former Cold War enemies are suddenly full partners, cooperating on "terrorism, arms control and international crisis management in a post–Sept. 11 world."[23] One might thus recommend Hardt's and Negri's text to Secretary of State Colin Powell, who recently remarked (regarding the entry of Russia into NATO): "We don't yet quite have a cliché to capture this all."[24]

(Of course, Rumsfeld had devoted himself to creating a more flexible, deterritorialized fighting force and decentralizing command structures well before September 11. Moreover, as he suggests, the justification of "peacetime" mobilization against a vaguely defined enemy is nothing new. In the Cold War, as in the current "War on Terror," one finds a conflation of multiple abstractions; the new conflict is alternately framed as a defense of "democracy" against "fundamentalism," a "crusade" against "evil," a fight against a "new totalitarianism," and so forth. However, the rhetorical shift from war to "polic-ing," exemplified in references to "criminal terrorists" and even "criminal states" bears out Hardt's and Negri's descriptions, situating the enemy within an encompassing global order.[25] Under the guise of this deterritorialized strug-gle, a variety of institutional, juridical, and strategic reforms have enabled the Bush administration to designate an evolving set of friends and enemies in the fight against "terror," regardless of the apparent resemblance of the two, as in the use of torture and the deliberate or careless targeting of civilians by Russian troops in Chechnya, the Chinese campaigns against Uighur auton-omy, or the Israeli army in the Palestinian territories.)

Perhaps this is what it means to confront Empire "on its own level of gener-ality?" Might Hardt's and Negri's text provide a correspondingly deterritorialized language of struggle, allowing for the flexible authorization of a plurality of eco-nomic, racial, sexual, and other struggles, no longer subjecting them to a classical Marxist hierarchy?[26] In Hardt's and Negri's historical interludes, they manage to link a vast array of struggles—from African postcolonies to Berkeley—under the sign of the multitude. Yet when it comes to the present, they hesitate, vacillating between support for various finite, particular struggles and gestures toward highly abstract subject-forms, such as the "barbarian" and the "poor."[27] Advocates of becoming, Hardt and Negri paradoxically discredit movements currently under way in favor of the genuine Revolution that is yet to be. In a casual gesture that has since become notorious, they dismiss various global nongovernmental organiza-tions (NGOs) currently working for practical humanitarian concessions as so many attempts to manage crisis rather than disrupt the system as a whole.[28]

Hardt has since identified the failure to find a plausible contemporary embodiment of the multitude as the "most significant shortcoming" of their book.[29] Yet, when pressed on this point, he has been reluctant to identify a given instance of the multitude, instead describing their work as an *anticipa-tion* of its emergence in new configurations of technology and practice.[30] In deferring to the creative power of multitude, Hardt and Negri follow Rosa Luxembourg's model of revolutionary subjectivity, in which spontaneous col-lective praxis precedes and marks the way for theoretical supports. Hardt's and Negri's deference to collective praxis admittedly does not prevent them from making a couple of concrete proposals towards the end of *Empire*; first, for global citizenship with open borders (and we were told the deterritorializing vision of postmodernism was a lost cause!), and second for a universal "social wage." Rather than follow the lead of theorists and activists working toward similar if not identical ends, however, they leave it to the immanent coopera-tion of the multitude to find the way.

Hardt's and Negri's disengagement from current movements seems at odds with both their theoretical premises and their political aspirations; it closes off potential avenues of innovation currently under way and implicates them in a distinction between theory and practice precluded by their account of the collapse of base and superstructure and their subsumption of conceptual labor in the "general intellect" of the multitude. It would seem to exacerbate rather than resolve the tension between their critical and polemical tendencies. Rather than seek out and support new subjectivities at the volatile intersection of desire and mediation, they shift from a fatalistic reading of contemporary struggles to messianic gestures toward total revolution, where the mediations of sovereignty will be transcended altogether. The multitude will appear, they promise, once "virtualities accumulate and reach a threshold of realization adequate to their power" (368). Yet it is not clear, on their own terms, that any such "realization" would not amount to a paradox, since the power of the multitude is not that of being but that of becoming. What would it mean for virtualities to be "realized" without mediation? A figure with such aspirations can only be mortified by finite, provisional appearances. This problem may explain Hardt's and Negri's curious disavowal of their own attempts to theorize the multitude. At one point, they go so far as to proclaim the demise of *all* attempts to describe an "ontology of the possible." Their predecessors' attempts at such an ontology—including Benjamin, Adorno, Wittgenstein, Foucault, and Deleuze—they roundly declare, were all "pallid." "In fact, every metaphysical tradition is now completely worn out. If there is to be a solution to the problem, it cannot help being material and explosive" (368).

What then has become of the "ontological substrate" and the purportedly ethico-political aspirations of Hardt's and Negri's text? How are we to understand their polemical departure from critical or deconstructive approaches, if that polemic works neither to direct nor even to describe the shape of leftist struggle? Here and there, they hint at a political role for their textual practice. "Today a manifesto, a political discourse, should aspire to fulfill a Spinozist prophetic function, the function of an immanent desire that organizes the multitude. There is not finally here any determinism or any utopia" (65–66). Granted, if their metaphysics proposes no particular empirical course or conclusion, but how are we to understand a prophecy that neither predicts nor even describes a future? In what sense do such vague desires "organize" the multitude?

## Vague Language and Strong Desires: George Sorel on Myth and Utopia

In this vein, a more proper predecessor to Hardt and Negri than Deleuze or Foucault would be Georges Sorel, a writer whose ontology of the possible—the General Strike—can hardly be accused of being "pallid." In his very influential yet little-read text, *Reflections on Violence*, Sorel outlines a theory of revolution that rejects both determinism and utopian programs in favor of spontaneous, instinctual, and affective forms of collective action. Sorel's departure from mechanistic versions of historical materialism derives from a reading of Henri Bergson, who embeds human agency and experience in dynamic biological and material forces:

> We must abandon the idea that the soul can be compared to something moving, which, obeying a more or less mechanical law, is impelled in the direction of certain given motive forces. To say that we are acting, implies the we are creating an imaginary world placed ahead of the present world and composed of movements which depend entirely on us. In this way our freedom becomes perfectly intelligible. . . . Edouard Le Roy, for example, says: "Our real body is the entire universe in as far as it is experienced by us. And what common sense strictly calls our body is only the region of least unconsciousness and greatest liberty in this greater body, the part which we most directly control and by means of which we are able to act on the rest." But we must not, as this subtle philosopher constantly does, confuse a passing state of our willing activity with the stable affirmations of science. These artificial worlds generally disappear from our minds without leaving any trace in our memory; but when the masses are deeply moved it then becomes possible to trace the outlines of the kind of representation which constitutes a social myth.[31]

On this account, human imagination and action inhabit a larger totality of forces in a relation of mutual determination. Understanding and bodily practice carve out an imaginary space of agency from within the larger totality that is partial and conditioned but also effective on the rest. This conception of subjectivity precludes, we can see, the two sides of Marxism that had always lived in an uneasy relation: both the economic determinism that rendered consciousness an epiphenomenal manifestation of "forces and relations of production," and the Enlightenment-inspired promise of rational self-determination. Our motor-imaginary (or what Althusser called our "lived") relation to the world, on this account, while it cannot apprehend the totality within which it operates from an Archimedian point, works on that totality and can at times be a locus of significant transformation. In the terms of Bergson that Hardt and Negri (following Deleuze, among others) also adopt, we could call this a theory of "virtual" freedom. It is also a theory of actual freedom, as for Bergson the two are not opposed. The virtual is not potential, in the sense of a force yet to be released, but *entelechial*, manifest in a dispersion of effects that indicates but does not express underlying forces (in the sense that the former cannot be traced to the latter in a mechanical fashion). The virtual is always at play in more or less stable patterns of determination—just as thought and action participate in a larger set of causes and effects—but occasionally it "flashes up" in extraordinary experiences of liberation and disruption, reshaping the larger environment in which it takes part.[32]

The paradigm for such a rupture at the level of politics, or what Sorel calls a "social myth," is the General Strike. Throughout *Reflections on Violence*, Sorel distinguishes the "myth" of the General Strike from "utopian" political programs. A myth, he explains, is "not a description of things, but expressions of a determination to act." It is "unanalysable." "A Utopia is, on the contrary, an intellectual product. . . . It is a combination of imaginary institutions having sufficient analogies to real institutions for the jurist to be able to reason about them; it is a construction which can be taken to pieces."[33] Utopias, for Sorel, are inherently reactionary, insofar as they offer a guide to the perfect society in the name of which popular forces can be subject to technocratic and authoritarian designs. The General Strike, on the other hand, manifests an affective and motor intensity purified of symbolic or institutional authority. The sole aim of the General Strike is to free the masses from the tutelage of all given institutions and authorities; it refuses all mediation, suspending instrumental calculations in the course of immediate action.

So understood, of course, the General Strike can be only a passing moment. Just as the virtual is always at work in the actual and only occasionally ruptures the surface of their continuous exchange, the distinction between utopia and myth, or reform and revolution, breaks down in political practice. In the French Revolution, Sorel notes, myths of a radical break from authority and the installation of popular sovereignty gave way to institutions and legal experts that closely resembled those they replaced following the violent revolts. Moreover, Sorel argues that utopian designs and institutional reforms are themselves sustained by mythological abstractions.[34] He identifies a blending of myth and utopia in the parliamentary socialism for which he reserves much of his eloquent contempt. The demagoguery of socialist politicians, he writes, is "stopped by no contradiction, experience having shown that it is possible in the course of an electoral campaign, to group together forces which, according to Marxian conceptions, should normally be antagonistic."[35] This rhetorical confusion of groupings is no trivial matter. The failure of Marxism as a predictive device, Sorel suggests, can be attributed to this corruption of class affiliations. The development of class antagonism crucial to revolutionary crisis, he suggests, may be derailed by the emergence of an "enlightened" middle class willing to adjust its interests to accommodate workers' unrest, a regrettable development he traces in part to the "chatter of the preachers of ethics and sociology" (or what he calls the "*little sciences*"). Under such conditions: "An arbitrary and irrational element is introduced, and the future of the world becomes completely indeterminate."[36]

Rather than reconcile himself to the indeterminacy of parliamentary politics (or—as Habermas would later do—seek a form of compromise immanent in discursive forms), Sorel undertakes what he describes as an "empirical" search for a material solution that might set history back on its proper antagonistic track. The danger of indeterminacy and class compromise can be averted most effectively, he finds, when proletarian strikes take a violent form. Proletarian violence derails the class compromise that otherwise wards off capitalist crisis. Violence provokes the baser instincts of the middle class, undermining their philanthropic sentiments and creating the reactionary orientation that in turn spurs further unrest on the part of the exploited: "Proletarian violence confines employers to their role as producers, and tends to restore the separation of the classes, just when they seemed on the point of intermingling in the democratic marsh. Proletarian violence not only makes the future revolution certain, but it seems also to be the only means by which the European nations—at present stupefied by humanitarianism—can recover their former energy."[37]

By blows, the future once again becomes "certain." But as Sorel understands, the proletariat can all too easily be pacified and co-opted by their political representatives. Violence may guarantee class struggle, but what guarantees violence? Indeed, what will prevent the violent energies of class struggle from being channeled for other means, namely patriotism, by the parliamentarians? The short answer would seem to be, nothing, since the "objective" economic basis of crisis is dissolved by rhetorical confusions. Yet, despite his account of the collapse of economic and discursive determination, Sorel retains the Marxist premise of a cataclysmic transformation leading to new social forms. While it may not proceed mechanically from economic processes, proletarian violence, and all that follows from it, is rescued from parliamentary mediations by the myth of the General Strike. Of the syndicalists, he writes:

> They have been led to deny the idea of patriotism by one of those necessities which are met with at all times in the course of history, and which philosophers have sometimes great difficulty in explaining—because the choice is imposed by external conditions, and not freely made for reasons drawn from the nature of things. This character of historical necessity gives to the existing antipatriotic movement a strength with it would be useless to attempt to dissimulate by means of sophistries.[38]

As he explains:

> [The strikers] may be deceived about an infinite number of political, economical, or moral questions; but their testimony is decisive, sovereign, and irrefutable when it is a question of knowing what are the ideas which most powerfully move

them and their comrades, which most appeal to them as being identical with their socialistic conceptions, and thanks to which their reason, their hopes, and their way of looking at particular facts seem to make but one indivisible unity.[39]

At one level, Sorel appears caught in the same paradoxes as Hardt and Negri, combining an ontological critique that qualifies both historical determination and human agency with a messianic promise of radical self-authorization. Historical necessity, it would seem, is here not so much expelled as displaced, shifted from objective antagonism to irrefutable myths. Furthermore, Sorel's conception of the General Strike as a radical rupture from all institutions and authorities, like the notion of an "adequate expression" of virtual energies, seems compromised by his account of the comingling of utopia and myth in political practice. Our perspective changes, however, if we treat Sorel's depiction of the General Strike as *itself* a form of imagination internal to a larger set of forces, in accord with the conception of myth outlined above. As Sorel explains in his letter to Daniel Halvey:

> In the course of this study one thing has always been present in my mind, which seemed to me so evident that I did not think it worth while to lay much stress on it—that men who are participating in a great social movement always picture their coming action as a battle in which their cause is certain to triumph. These constructions, knowledge of which is so important for historians, I propose to call myths; the syndicalist "general strike" and Marx's catastrophic revolution are such myths.[40]

On the latter reading, the function of Sorel's account of the General Strike is not so much to comprehend or predict as to act on those forces. Indeed, Sorel treats Marx's theory of capitalist crisis as itself such a myth:

> The accuracy [of Marx's account of the development of capitalist crises] has been many times disputed . . . but this objection must not stop us, and it may be thrust on one side by means of the theory of myths. The different terms which Marx uses to describe the preparation for the decisive combat are not to be taken literally as statements of fact about a determined future; it is the description in its entirety which should engage our attention, and taken in this way it is perfectly clear: Marx wishes us to understand that the whole preparation of the proletariat depends solely on the organisation of a stubborn, increasing, and passionate resistance to the present order of things.[41]

The prophecy of capitalist crisis, in other words, becomes an instrument in its own realization. While the deconstructive and messianic strains in his argument are logically at odds, they might be said to achieve—adapting

Habermas's popular locution—a performative consistency.[42]

It would appear that a programmatic or descriptive narrative can itself serve as a social myth, as long as it is not taken "literally." But how can we know when that will be the case? How, practically speaking, can we distinguish between a myth and a utopia? How can we know which rhetoric will serve authority and which anarchy?

> The attempt to construct hypotheses about the nature of the struggles of the future and the means of suppressing capitalism, on the model furnished by history, is a return to the old methods of the Utopists. . . . And yet without leaving the present, without reasoning about this future, which seems for ever condemned to escape our reason, we should be unable to act at all. Experience shows that the framing of a future, in some indeterminate time, may, *when it is done in a certain way*, be very effective, and have very few inconveniences; this happens when the anticipations of the future take the form of those myths, which enclose with them all the strongest inclinations of a people, of a party or of a class.[43]

We cannot help imagining a future on the basis of past experience. But our projections can take different forms, some more suited than others to creative action. When framed "in a certain way," the imagined future can have radical effects on the present. A myth, it would seem, differs from a utopia not so much in nature as in kind. The crucial difference for Sorel concerns the degree of specificity with which the future is imagined: "It must never be forgotten that the perfection of this method of representation would vanish in a moment if any attempt were made to resolve the general strike into a sum of historical details; the general strike must be taken as a whole and undivided, and the passage from capitalism to Socialism conceived as a catastrophe, the development of which baffles description."[44]

Sorel attributes the usefulness of Marx's account of capitalist crisis for the struggles of the syndicates to a similar absence of explicit utopian projections.[45] For Sorel, Marxist claims regarding the inevitability of crisis serve the "prophetic" role that Hardt and Negri recommend for political manifestos, organizing passionate resistance to the existing order.[46] Prophecy here is not to be confused with prediction; it is to be judged not by the accuracy of its vision but by the intensity of its effect. Likewise, the myth of the General Strike does not instruct; it inspires.[47] It helps to instill the heroic, sacrificial orientation without which, Sorel presumes, the strikes themselves—given the hardships they involve and their uncertain results—cannot proceed.[48] Sorel finds an exemplary precursor in messianic Protestantism, a movement characterized by a "will to deliverance" not prevented from exerting tremendous power by its failure to predict Christ's return.[49] Indeed, would Christianity have survived so long had a date of arrival been fixed? For centuries, its messianic vision has thrived on a savior who is always "coming soon."

Despite his claims regarding the collapse of description and inspiration, Sorel hesitated to grant his work any significant place in the larger struggles he described. Rather than champion the work of intellectuals, he generally defers to the syndicates who work out their strategy in the street. Yet on this point, as well, he is hardly consistent. In his preface, he restricts the role of the Marxist intellectual to a critique of bourgeois rhetoric and a defense of the spontaneous ideology of the proletariat class.[50] However, he later allows that the proper role of socialists may be to "explain to the proletariat the greatness of the revolutionary part they are called upon to play."[51] Of course, in accord with his rejection of utopian schemes, this will not be an "explanation" per se: "Use must be made of a body of images which, by intuition alone, and before any considered analyses are made, is capable of evoking as an undivided whole the mass of sentiments which corresponds to the different manifestations of the war undertaken by Socialism against modern society."[52]

Given the contingent material conditions on which the power of myth depends, as we have seen, it cannot be certain which images will have the power to move the masses. However, Sorel argues that the force of myth can still be an object of reasoning and calculation. His commitment to the General Strike, after all, is based on an empirical observation of its function in syndicalist politics. As such, he argues it is just as "scientific" and just as provisional as any generalization from particulars destined to be rendered antiquated by further discoveries:

> Our situation resembles somewhat that of the physicists who work at huge calculations based on theories which are not destined to endure forever. . . . To proceed scientifically means, first of all, to know what forces exist in the world, and then to take measures whereby we may utilise them, by reasoning from experience. That is why I say that, by accepting the idea of the general strike, although we know that it is a myth, we are proceeding exactly as a modern physicist does who has complete confidence in his science, although he knows that the future will look upon it as antiquated.[53]

Myth and violence, for Sorel, are not part of a final solution but provisional tactics aimed to release destructive (and thus creative) potentials with uncertain results. His messianic rhetoric, in turn, is itself experimental, calculated, and thus "scientific."

For contemporary readers, of course, Sorel's text cannot help but raise the specter of the fascist and totalitarian movements that followed shortly on the heels of his pronouncements. His remarks concerning the recovery of

European *nations* are particularly foreboding in this regard, as they point in the direction toward which antiparliamentarianism was shortly to turn in Germany. As Carl Schmitt would later argue: "Sorel's . . . examples of myth also prove that *when they occur in the modern period*, the stronger myth is national."[54] Sorel was cognizant of these dangers, having witnessed the exploitation of the syndicates by would-be dictators of the left. Vague slogans and popular enthusiasm, he understood, can also serve authority. He hated the attempts by his contemporaries to harness the power of workers' struggles to political authorities, and wrote caustically of the "patriotic" movements of his day. True to his understanding of the contingent powers of imagination, however, he was reconciled to the indeterminate effects of the General Strike. It is quite possible, he acknowledges, that "we should see the social revolution culminate in a wonderful system of slavery."[55]

Hardt and Negri bear a complex relation to these traditions and diverge from Sorel in a number of important respects, including their global emphasis and their more radical departure from Marx's class categories. However, they share a dynamic materialist ontology that presumes the reciprocal determination of economic and discursive registers. Additionally, a variety of parallels support a reading of the multitude as a myth akin to that of the General Strike. Hardt and Negri share Sorel's rejection of programmatic utopias and his preference for spontaneous collective action and loose coalitions over disciplined party structures. Furthermore, they also share an affinity for chiliastic Christianity, a movement that, Hardt and Negri claim, "offered an absolute alternative to the spirit of imperial right—a new ontological basis" (21). In accord with this model, they figure the coming emergence of the multitude as a catastrophic or "explosive" development that exceeds all contemporary understanding. Along these lines, Hardt and Negri have since described the absence of programmatic specificity as a virtue of their own text:

> Some lament in a more general way that Empire provides no clear program or guide for political action, but in our view this is not a shortcoming of the book but rather an indication of its prudence. Political practice is better suited than theory to answer certain questions. New forms of political organization are being developed today and theoretical projects should be sensitive to their powers of invention.[56]

In light of a comparison with Sorel, Hardt's and Negri's shift from critical analysis to polemical, vague hortatory might appear to exhibit a peculiar kind of sensitivity and a questionable brand of prudence. At the same time, a reading of Sorel may clarify the reasoning behind such an approach. The deconstructive analysis of Empire that subsumes language, affect, will, and imagination in a larger totality, while it allows for the creative power of desire, may not be enough on its own to stimulate the enthusiasm Hardt and Negri require of the multitude. How can militant action be undertaken in the name of ideals with avowedly contingent, uncertain consequences? By positing an imminent future in which the virtual freedom of human imagination can be realized without constraint, Hardt and Negri hope to inspire the faith and resolve required for a struggle against the overwhelming forces of capitalist sovereignty. The uncertain future of any such struggle, it might be argued, is precisely what demands a militancy capable of suspending critical analysis in favor of creative action.

As we have seen, Hardt and Negri stop short of describing the multitude as a constitutive myth. Like Sorel, they are conflicted in their role as prophets, deferring to "political practice" when it comes to practical aims and tactics. Whereas Sorel's embrace of the General Strike as the social myth of his day was based on his familiarity with syndicalist strategies being tested in the streets, of course, Hardt's and Negri's multitude has no direct empirical source or referent. However, they have since aligned themselves with the "antiglobalization" protesters, a loose coalition of groups who have been taken to task precisely for failing to congeal into a discrete (utopian) program and set of demands.[57] In an editorial, Hardt and Negri have described the role of the protests at the 2001 G-8 meetings in Genoa in precisely the terms they apply to their own manifestos: "Protest movements do not provide a practical blueprint for how to solve problems, and we should not expect that of them. They seek rather to transform the public agenda by creating political desires for a better future."[58]

It would seem we have come full circle, resolving the distinction between critical ontology and ethico-political action, or theory and practice, in practical (performative) as well as theoretical terms. But where does that leave us? What will come of these protests and polemical manifestos? No doubt they can have important effects on reformist agendas, even if their more vague demands cannot be realized as such.[59] But what prevents us from specifying a set of demands, even if the results will (also) be unpredictable? Hardt and Negri describe the protesters' aims not as "antiglobalization," but for alternative, more democratically accountable forms. This crucial distinction—though surprisingly ignored by some critics[60]—is hardly original. And what political agendas are not driven by vague desires for a better future? How are we to link these desires to popular criticism of legal, economic, and military systems or to prevent the rhetoric of democracy from becoming a "center of gravity" for reactionary territorial alternatives to global liberation?

Unlike Sorel and Deleuze, Hardt and Negri never allow that the liberating flights of the multitude could give way to reactionary capture, much less harbor fascist tendencies. One might say Sorel is at once more daring and more pessimistic than they are. To call Sorel a pessimist, however, requires some clarification:

> Pessimism is quite a different thing from the caricatures of it which are usually
> presented to us; it is a philosophy of conduct rather than a theory of the world; it
> considers the *march towards deliverance* as narrowly conditioned, on the one hand,
> by the experimental knowledge that we have acquired from the obstacles which
> oppose themselves to the satisfaction of our imaginations (or, if we like, by the feel-
> ing of social determinism), and, on the other hand, by a profound conviction of our
> natural weakness. These two aspects of pessimism should never be separated,
> although, as a rule, scarcely any attention is paid to their close connection.[61]

If anything, it is this experimental, scientific, active pessimism that is lacking
in Hardt's and Negri's "ethico-political" approach to the multitude. It is similarly lacking, of course, in the ideology Sorel recommends for the syndicalist
strikers. In both cases, messianic optimism can appear only cynical or self-
deceptive, given their common view of material history. One can find similar
tensions in a long history of Marxist critics struggling to reconcile their materialism with a desire for less constrained agency.[62] This is the sort of desire
shared by critics such as Frederic Jameson who champion Hardt's and Negri's
promises of liberation as a remedy for the "relativism" of postmodern thinkers.
In a short piece on Empire, Jon Beasely-Murray has even commended Hardt
and Negri for inverting Gramsci's famous slogan: "Their slogan is optimism
of the intellect, pessimism of the will."[63]

Beasely-Murray equates "optimism of the will" with a passive faith in destiny rather than collective action taken in the absence of utopian expectations.
His rejection of such optimism—and of the disciplines with which he associates such an attitude—is thus understandable. In turn, he argues: "Pessimism
of the intellect . . . condemns in advance the project of revolutionary analysis
as an exercise in bad faith."[64] We should by all means praise Hardt and Negri
for articulating a materialism that refuses both of these alternatives. In their
critical analysis of global sovereignty, Hardt and Negri contribute much to an
appreciation of contemporary possibilities and challenges facing collective
action and imagination without a corresponding forfeit of revolutionary aspirations. Their "ethico-political" polemic, however, evinces its own bad faith.
Given the manifold contingencies within which contemporary forms of political imagination operate, what speaks for such optimism? Are we not at present caught between perfectionist utopias and catastrophic myths, both of
which are linked to terrible violence?

Given the fate of the movements Sorel described, Hardt's and Negri's pessimism of the will might be understandable. But this has not prevented their
optimism of the intellect from evoking deadly serious fears in some quarters.
One of the intriguing aspects of critical reviews of Empire—following the
attacks on the World Trade Center—is their conflation of political threats to

community, nationality, and security with academic threats to discursive for-malism and autonomy. As one author asserts: "Hardt and Negri make a dan-gerously opportunistic move: they simply reinterpret the tradition out of which they write to accommodate the new radicalism, as if Marxism can be moved this way or that way depending upon who happens to be protesting what on any particular day."[65] The danger of such opportunism, clearly, is that the key terms of Marxism, like any other discourse, can indeed be "moved this way or that," and their power harnessed to diverse practical ends. As another critic laments: "Unfortunately, preposterousness has never been a barrier to effec-tiveness. There are plenty of ideas that are fatuous, wrongheaded, or simply ridiculous that nevertheless have a great and baneful influence on the world. Books like *Empire* are a veritable repository of such ideas."[66]

While they rightly assign political import to discursive practice, these crit-ics give *Empire* both too little and too much credit. Hardt's and Negri's rein-terpretation of the Marxist tradition, while creative, is hardly arbitrary. Moreover, their conflation of multiple rhetorics is hardly unique. The left holds no patent on contradictory rhetoric and effective absurdities, as Rumsfeld has demonstrated.[67] As Sorel reminds us, institutional authorities are themselves nourished by mythological abstractions. Might we detect in these hyperbolic attacks on Hardt's and Negri's opportunism a general anxiety surrounding the discursive and political dislocations the Hardt's and Negri attribute to Empire, that is, an anxiety concerning the collapse of discursive, economic, and politi-cal forces as well as that of plural discursive categories? What terms could not be conflated and co-opted today? As we see in the election and subsequent acts of the current U.S. regime, the rhetoric of democratic rule is flexible indeed.

Given the dynamic contingencies in which human action and imagination are involved, might it not make more sense to adopt a tragic rather than mytho-logical view of political action? In opposing tragedy to myth, I follow J. P. Vernant's distinction, according to which tragedy is an "imitation" of myth that invites a critical perspective. For a reading of Gramsci's slogan along tragic lines, we might turn to Walter Benjamin. Benjamin, like Sorel, explicitly dis-tinguished a "pessimistic" approach to creative imagination from the "opti-mistic" utopias of bourgeois politicians:

> "To win the energies of intoxication for the revolution"—in other words, poetic politics? "We have tried that beverage. Anything, rather than that!" Well, it will interest you all the more how much an excursion into poetry clarifies things. For what is the program of the bourgeois parties? A bad poem on springtime, filled to bursting with metaphors. . . . These are mere images. And the stock of imagery of these poets of the social democratic associations? . . . Optimism.[68]

Hardt and Negri include Benjamin among those theorists whose ontology of the possible, along with their own, pales before the material transformations they anticipate. Like them, he was committed to posthumanist notions of collective liberation and endorsed disruptive techniques rather than a direct seizure of sovereign power. The General Strike was an exemplary form of politics for him as well.[69] However, he also sought to democratize the experimental, active pessimism that thinkers such as Sorel and Hardt and Negri reserve for the critic. Following the methods of the surrealists, he combined reflexive criticism, technical innovation, and conceptual complexity: "For to organize pessimism means nothing other than to expel moral metaphor from politics and to discover in political action a sphere reserved one hundred percent for images."[70]

If Hardt's and Negri's contribution to contemporary struggles was restricted to a critique of hegemonic discourse, that would surely be enough to commend them. In practical terms, furthermore, their text has proved tremendously productive, stimulating critical engagements across an unusually broad spectrum of writers and activists. Their situation of theoretical discourse in dynamic global networks, however, highlights the need for further attention to the complex links between critical discourse and current struggles. As Arjun Appadurai has argued, the field of global imagination is "neither purely emancipatory nor entirely disciplined."[71]

According to Hardt, he and Negri are already working on a theory of the multitude that will mirror the practical detail and sophistication of their critique of Empire. This theory, he suggests, will combine two elements: "First, the various theorizations of the body particularly among feminist theorists and, second, the innovative forms of political organization that are emerging in the new social struggles around the world. . . . It may involve finding a way to set up a dialogue between these theoretical problematics on the one axis and the practical experiments on the other."[72] As they draw these links, Hardt and Negri would do well to take more rather than less from Sorel and Benjamin. In short, they should be less moral and more pessimistic. As we have seen, this does not preclude a scientific approach to abstraction, myth, or enthusiasm, by the terms of their own materialism. Like any working hypothesis caught up in the forces it purports to describe, a utopian science is itself to be understood as experimental, tactical, and provisional.

## Notes

1. Michael Hardt, and Antonio Negri, *Empire* (Cambridge, MA: Harvard University Press, 2000), 47. References to *Empire* are inserted parenthetically throughout the text.

2. Cf. Antonio Negri. *The Savage Anomaly* (Minneapolis: University of Minnesota Press, 1991). For further elaboration on their use of the term in relation to political history, see Hardt's and Negri's earlier work, *Labor of Dionysus: A Critique of the State Form. Theory out of Bounds*, vol. 4. (Minneapolis: University of Minnesota Press, 1994).

3. Hence, affective labor, once a constitutive "outside" for the patriarchal wage earner, is brought under the logic of commercial exploitation in the service economy.

4. While they criticize postcolonial nationalisms for miming the logic of European sovereignty, for example, they acknowledge the provisional value of these appropriations in particular instances.

5. Cf. *Empire*, 369; "The *res gestae*, the singular virtualities that operate the connection between the possible and the real, are in the first passage outside measure and in the second beyond measure. . . . The virtual and the possible are wedded as irreducible innovation and as a revolutionary machine."

6. "We have reached the moment when the relationship of power that had dominated the hybridizations and machinic metamorphoses can now be overturned. . . . This new terrain of production and life opens for labor a future of metamorphoses that subjective cooperation can and must control ethically, politically, and productively." *Empire*, 367.

7. *Empire*, 206–207. Local struggles, they explain, have become "incommunicable," insofar as the site of power they confront is not one of many similar centers but a moment in a larger, decentered network.

8. Cf. *Empire*, 61; "The deterritorializing power of the multitude is the productive force that sustains Empire and at the same time the force that calls for and makes necessary its destruction."

9. *Empire*, 142. As Hardt puts it in his interview with Tom Dumm: "Empire rules precisely through a kind of politics of difference, managing hybrid identities in flexible hierarchies. From this perspective, then, a politics of hybridity may have been effective against the now-defunct modern form of sovereignty but it is powerless against the current imperial form." Cf. "Sovereignty, Multitudes, Absolute Democracy: A discussion between Michael Hardt and Thomas Dumm about Hardt's and Negri's Empire." *Theory and Event* 4: 3 (2000), par. 23 and this volume.

10. Cf. Jean-François Lyotard. *The Postmodern Condition* (Minneapolis: University of Minnesota Press, 1984). Lyotard's conception of agonistics—the struggle of multiple discourses not mediated by an Overriding "metalanguage"—emphasizes indefinite contest rather than liberation. It is based on Wittgenstein's theory of language "games."

11. Hardt and Negri describe their positive alternative to Empire as, among other things, a "postmodern republicanism" (*Empire*, 208). Given such claims as "The means to get beyond the crisis is the ontological displacement of the subject" (*Empire*, 384), it is not surprising that, despite their disavowals of "postmodern" politics, they have been taken to task as examples of its worst excesses.

12. Gilles Deleuze and Féix Guattari, *A Thousand Plateaus*, trans. Brian Massumi (Minneapolis, University of Minnesota Press, 1987), 215. Deleuze describes fascism in terms of a "resonance" among various "cells," such as the gang, the neighborhood, etc. Arjun Appadurai uses similar concepts, describing the "focalization and transvaluation" of affective-discursive scripts. Cf. Arjun Appadurai. *Modernity at Large* (Minneapolis: University of Minnesota Press, 1996).

13. Gilles Deleuze. "Postscript on the Societies of Control," *October* 59; 4 (1992).

14. For a more serious consideration of the policing of urban space and multifarious controls over access to various services, see Mike Davis, *City of Quartz* (New York: Vintage, 1992).

15. The BET or Black Entertainment Television network, of course, is itself a response to the predominance of what might be called "white entertainment television." A particularly extreme racial segmentarity is evident, for example, in the award-winning sitcom "Friends," a show with an all-white cast set in an imaginary Manhattan almost entirely evacuated of people of color.

16. For a discussion of this function of television, see Samuel Weber, *Mass Mediaurus* (Stanford, CA: Stanford University Press, 1996). For a discussion of the Internet along similar lines, see Alex Galloway, "Protocol, or, How Control Exists after Decentralization," *Rethinking Marxism* 13; 3/4 (2001).

17. Cf. Empire, 361; "Circulation must become freedom."

18. Deleuze and Guattari, *A Thousand Plateaus*, 9–10.

19. See *Empire*, 211.

20. Donald Rumsfeld "in his own words," Excerpts from September 3, 2002, interview on the events following the September 11, 2001, attacks, *New York Times*, 4 September, 2002, A10.

21. Ibid.

22. On interruption and affective capture, see Brian Massumi's analysis of Ronald Reagan's successful incoherence in his rewarding essay, "The Autonomy of Affect," in *Parables for the Virtual*. (Durham, NC: Duke University Press, 2002).

23. "Nato Strikes Deal To Accept Russia in a Partnership," *New York Times*, May 15, 2002, A1.

24. *New York Times*, May 15, 2002, A1.

25. "The NATO secretary general, Lord Robertson, similarly urged allies to 'think carefully about the

role of this alliance in the future, not least in protecting our citizens from criminal terrorists and criminal states.'" "Rumsfeld Urges NATO to Set up Strike Force," *New York Times*. September 25, 2002, A6.

26. This is the approach outlined by Laclau and Mouffe, who describe a counterhegemonic hegemony. Cf. Ernesto Laclau and Chantal Mouffe, *Hegemony and Socialist Strategy* (New York: Verso, 1990).

27. See *Empire*, 214–215 on the "Barbarian." The poor, they claim, have "digested" the proletariat (a term also generalized by them to signify everyone caught up in the capitalist economy). See also 52–53.

28. *Empire*, 36; see also 314–315.

29. Specifically, Hardt describes their failure to give a "sociological" account of the multitude and promises this will be the basis of the next project. Cf. Michael Hardt, "Sovereignty, Multitudes, Absolute Democracy," paragraph 39.

30. Cf. Michael Hardt, and Antonio Negri, "Adventures of the Multitude," *Rethinking Marxism* 13; 3/4 (2001): 238.

31. Georges Sorel, *Reflections on Violence*, trans. T. E. Hulme (New York: Peter Smith, 1941), 31.

32. We might in this context connect Bergson's theory of virtual freedom with Judith Butler's account of the role played by the "imaginary" in structuring and sustaining symbolic and institutional structures. Cf. Judith Butler, *Bodies that Matter* (New York: Routledge, 1993).

33. *On Violence*, 32–33.

34. *On Violence*, 36.

35. *On Violence*, 54–55. See also 87, where he explains that there can be no "rule" for class compromise, insofar as it dissolves the economic objectivity of struggle. See also 128, on vague slogans.

36. *On Violence*, 87.

37. *On Violence*, 90; see also 98, 82–83, and 88, on replying "by blows to the advances of the propagators of social peace."

38. *On Violence*, 125.

39. *On Violence*, 137.

40. *On Violence*, 22.

41. *On Violence*, 148.

42. Indeed, *logical* consistency and discursive coherence are not ideals to which Sorel pretends. On the contrary, he equates these goals with the pretense of thinkers who would subsume politics and human experience to the laws of the physical sciences and mocks their strained attempts to imitate the latter's deductive argumentation.

43. *On Violence*, 133; emphasis added.

44. *On Violence*, 164.

45. See *On Violence*, 152–153.

46. Cf. *On Violence*, 148.

47. It might be noted that the General Strike in Italy on April 16, 2002 (the first in twenty years) involved just such an abstraction from local or discrete interests and grievances.

48. See *On Violence*, 152.

49. See *On Violence*, 133–134.

50. See *On Violence*, 38; "We may play a useful part if we limit ourselves to attacking middle-class thought in such a way as to put the proletariat on its guard against an invasion of ideas and customs from the hostile class."

51. *On Violence* 85.

52. *On Violence*, 130–131.

53. *On Violence* 166–167.

54. In his now widely read critique of parliamentary democracy, Carl Schmitt sketches a trajectory from Sorel's anarchism to authoritarian nationalism, grounding sovereignty in just the sort of capture of mythological energies Sorel was so concerned to avoid. Cf. Carl Schmitt, *The Crisis of Parliamentary Democracy*, trans. Ellen Kennedy (Cambridge, MA: MIT Press, (1988). I discuss Schmitt's appropriation of Sorel and his emphasis on affective capture in my *Sovereign Nations, Carnal States* (Ithaca, NY: Cornell University Press: 2003).

55. *On Violence*, 195.

56. "Adventures," 238

57. Remarkably, at least some of these protesters have taken up the terms of Empire for their own struggles.

58. Michael Hardt and Antonio Negri, "What the Protesters in Genoa Want," *New York Times*, July 20, 2001. One may safely presume they would similarly endorse the general strike that took place in Italy the following year.

59. Protests, for example, can give the "insider" critics of the Washington consensus a stronger bargaining position, just as the direct actions of the Civil Rights Movement spurred legislative reforms.

60. Francis Fukuyama, for example, draws a specious parallel between the military nationalism of Jesse Helms and what he presumes to be the protesters' territorial demands for democratic control over economic processes. Cf. Francis Fukuyama, "The West May Be Cracking," *International Herald Tribune*, August 9. 2002, A4.

61. *On Violence*, 10.

62. In his fascinating book on Walter Benjamin, for example, Terry Eagleton—like Hardt and Negri—severs the link between critical and ideological Marxism, explicitly reserving "deconstructive" criticism for bourgeois ideology. Hence, while taking "the point" of Gramsci's slogan (taken up by Benjamin), "'Pessimism of the intellect, optimism of the will,'" he prefers "'given the strength of the masses, how can we be defeated?'" Cf. Terry Eagleton, *Walter Benjamin, Towards a Revolutionary Criticism* (London: Verso, 1981), 172.

63. Jon Beasley-Murray, "Lenin in America," *Rethinking Marxism*; 13, 3/4 (2001): 150.

64. Ibid.

65. Alan Wolfe, "The Snake," *New Republic*, October 1, 2001.

66. Roger Kimball, "The New Anti-Americanism," *New Criterion* 20; 1 (2001).

67. The point of drawing parallels to Donald Rumsfeld, it should be clear, is not to conflate Hardt's and Negri's "radical republicanism" with the aims and strategies of al-Qaeda. However, if their own rhetoric were not equally fulminating, one could almost forgive conservative critics for drawing facile connections between Hardt's and Negri's references to "explosive" solutions and those literally explosive subjects that some have taken to calling "homicide" bombers (attempting to erase all tragic connotations of "suicide" from the violent struggles of overmatched antagonists and consigning the latter to the category of criminal rather than political foe). Kimball actually accuses Hardt and Negri of complicity with terror, a heavily freighted charge to say the least in today's political climate, and all the more so in light of Negri's incarceration on such charges. It is not unthinkable that foolish and/or destructive behavior could find justification in their text (though there is little sign that "terrorists" have taken up *Empire* as a new handbook). Is it not possible, as Sorel acknowledged regarding the General Strike, that contemporary struggles could give rise to new forms of slavery?

68. Walter Benjamin, "Surrealism," in *Reflections*, trans. Edmund Jephcott (New York: Schocken Books, 1978), 190

69. See Benjamin, "Critique of Violence," in *Reflections*.

70. Benjamin, "Surrealism," 191. Sorel himself speaks suggestively of revolutionary impulses acquired through educative processes of criticism. Cf. *On Violence*, 85–86. I will have to reserve for another time an extended discussion of Benjamin's techniques and the difference implied between "images" and "mere images" in these two passages. I examine the former notion in my *Sovereign Nations, Carnal States*.

71. Appadurai, *Modernity at Large*, 4

72. Hardt, "Sovereignty, Multitudes, Absolute Democracy," paragraph 39.

# 15

Event

# Representation and the Event
## Paul A. Passavant and Jodi Dean

## Hegemony and Identity

In *Being Singular Plural*, Jean-Luc Nancy states, "The surprise—the event—does not belong to the order of representation."[1] Although not unthinkable, the event shocks, exceeding everyday patterns of thinking and acting, opening up a space beyond itself. It breaks up the preceding constellation, enabling its elements to be seen not as already given components of an inevitable formation, but as figures that can be recombined, rejected, reimagined. If anything, September 11, 2001, marks the displacement effected by an event. Yet all too rapidly the "eventness" is becoming subsumed within various projects of hegemonization. William Bennett has drawn upon the event to support his critique of "theorists" in "our own institutions of higher learning" and his particular vision of superior moral clarity.[2] Russia has exploited the event in support of its actions in Chechnya. Israel has invoked the event to justify its violence against Palestinians. Italy has used the event to defend its excessive mobilization against antiglobal capital protesters in Genoa. And the Bush administration is treating the event as foundational to a new order of meaning, identity, and permanent war.

With this response, the Bush administration equates the defense of freedom with the defense of global capitalism. The administration reduces justice to retribution. It establishes the time frame for the assignment and assumption of responsibility. As Bush said at a memorial service in the National

Cathedral in Washington, D.C.: "This conflict was begun on the time and terms of others. It will end in a way and at an hour of our choosing."[3] With an inspired sense of mission, the Bush administration employs the event in a new articulation of what it means to be us.

The primary mechanism governing the process of hegemonization within the United States has been Bush's "line in the sand," his positing of an "us" and a "them," and his demand that *everyone* must choose a side. This line suggests a clarity, but it is a clarity produced in part through the discourse of civilization versus barbarism—a discourse with a long and ignominious genealogy.[4] Bush's speech of September 20, 2001, makes this clear: the "us" is constituted in the racial tradition and image of the "civilized" West: "This is the world's fight. This is civilization's fight." The "them" appearing in the position of "civilization's" barbarous Other are those who believe the world might be otherwise than what it is within the global capitalist imaginary. They are denounced as "terrorists" and for their "radical" beliefs.

The elision between "terrorist" and "radical" is significant, especially as it informs the increasing condemnations levelled against activists critical of global capital. Consider the words of Peter Beinart, editor of the *New Republic*, "The anti-globalization movement is, in part, a movement motivated by hatred of the global inequities between rich and poor. And it is, in part, a movement motivated by hatred of the United States. Now, after what has happened this week, it must choose."[5] Hence, to dissent from global economic inequities is to consent to terrorism, according to the presently hegemonic view.

To buttress his efforts to eliminate critics of global capital from the sphere of legitimate democratic debate, Beinart turns to the antiglobalization movement's new "bible," Michael Hardt's and Antonio Negri's *Empire*:

> The two academics (one of whom is himself in jail for terrorism) write that "fundamentalism is postmodern insofar as it rejects the tradition of Islamic modernism for which modernity was always overcoded as assimilation or submission to Euro-American hegemony." And what is the anti-globalization movement itself rejecting if not "assimilation or submission to Euro-American hegemony"?[6]

Beinart's odd articulation of disparate elements is clearly not an argument (part of the problem is the weird way he mistakes Hardt's and Negri's description of Islamic fundamentalism as a postmodern development for an endorsement). But it is evidence of a powerful ideological formation. Its ideological claim is announced front and center: "Euro-American hegemony." With America in the position of the nodal point that quilts together the signifying chain (later in the piece Beinart jettisons the Euro component of the hegemonic form), anything or anyone critical of America is easily linked together.[7]

Insofar as antiglobalization protestors reject assimilation or submission to Euro-American hegemony, they are equivalent to Islamic fundamentalists, who are equivalent to those who attacked the World Trade Center and the Pentagon, who are equivalent to Hardt and Negri, who also reject the ideal of assimilation and submission to American hegemony. Beinart's reiteration of the Bush administration's division of the world between "us" and "them" as a division within "us" presents in stark terms the stakes of the current conflict: America's political and economic hegemony. To criticize capitalism is anti-American, radical, and terroristic. Hence, rather than functioning as an argument, Beinart's text acts as evidence of the way a hegemonic field has become formed to exclude critical scholarship, radical politics, challenges to the global capitalist regime, Islamic fundamentalism, and terrorism. Because criticism of global capital and terrorism have been excluded in advance, rhetoric slides easily from one of these exclusions to the other as they have been articulated together as equivalent and as the enemy.

Beinart, like many others in the United States today, enjoys the certainty provided by the chain of significations held together by America. This identity is inspirited by a religious zeal in righteous defense of innocent victims against evil. Put into play through a National Day of Prayer and repeated invocations of God in presidential speeches, this identity formation has generated a moral compass. It tells us who to love and who to hate, issuing a license to hate that some feared was no longer permissible in an America of political correctness, multicultural curricula, and sexual tolerance.[8] At the same time, this articulation of American identity consolidates components of the American experience that became disarticulated during the nineties: religious fundamentalism and capitalist excess. The enjoyments of each reinforce the other in the new formation.[9]

Beinart is not completely wrong. One of the key issues at stake and at risk of being covered over in the move to respond to the events of September 11 is the tumultuous global political and economic crisis of which "globalization" and "terrorism" are both symptoms. But, to misuse a phrase, Beinart seems to enjoy his symptoms too much, relishing the new identity for its clarity and ferocity.

Beinart is also right to suggest that Hardt's and Negri's work speaks to the current crisis. Hardt and Negri argue that the era of the territorial nation-state is now over. As they set out in *Empire*, capital is presently organized on a transnational basis, with branch offices, dispersed yet coordinated production and marketing capacities, and interests all over the world.[10] It makes use of global migratory patterns, profiting from a globalized labor market and globalized consumptive patterns. With the global organization of capital, a new form of sovereignty is called into existence to meet the challenges posed by those who trouble capital's global operations. This form of sovereignty is without a specific territorial location, although various institutions of military, police, and other governing bodies act in its name. Hardt and Negri call this new form of sovereignty Empire. From the attacks on the World Trade Center as a signifier of global financial markets, to the emergence of a transnational military coalition in response to the attacks outside of UN governance, the event of September 11 seems to resonate in profound ways with Hardt's and Negri's theorization of the new world order.

Beinart's elements, then, are right. In light of our democratic commitments, however, we find his enchainment to be clearly, profoundly, wrong—precisely because it is quilted together via the wrong nodal point. Beinart's enchainment presumes in advance the signifying power of Euro-American hegemony when precisely that power is what is being challenged, contested, attacked.

Rather than understanding the current formation of global capital and the rise of various forms of fundamentalism and ethnic hatred as *both* being responses to changes in structures of sovereignty, patterns of migration and immigration, and the global integration of commodity production, distribution, and speculation, the hegemonic field and Beinart's reproduction of it purifies and privileges Americanized capitalism as that which is civilized and immunized from its own pathologies and excesses. With religious devotion to Euro-American hegemony and global capital, Beinart reiterates the terms of Osama bin Laden's own religious discourse. This field illustrates how fundamentalism persists as a kind of obscene supplement to global capital, *confirming* the analysis of Hardt and Negri in its attempt to castigate them.[11] (News reports in the weeks following September 11 accented this obscene supplement with their emphases on drug trafficking, arms deals, and money laundering, practices which integrate al-Qaeda into global networks heavily inscribed in the United States and Britain.)

In the next section of this essay, we will examine the novel form of the Bush administration's response. As a symptom of the changed geopolitical field that Hardt and Negri find emerging, the administration uses antiterrorism to structure its militarized reaction, in contrast to responses structured via a notion of war anchored in national sovereignty or a notion of policing crime anchored in an international juridical principle.[12] This form of response installs a practice organized around the civilized subject that polices terrorism and the barbaric subject that is the terrorist. Since the civilized and the barbaric can only be identified in relation to each other, a totalistic logic is put into play whereby counterterrorism and the potential of barbarism hungrily consume the social space wherein this logic operates.

In the remaining sections of this essay, we wish to preserve September 11 as an event insofar as this will allow us to resist the manner in which it has already become hegemonized. That is to say, we wish to preserve its *political* character, where the political signifies that the very organization of society is in question.[13] We focus on the relationship between representation and response. If the ideological formation that informs the current response to September 11 relies on a representation constructed primarily in terms of a split between civility and barbarism (a split that disavows the excesses of American fundamentalisms—Christian and capitalist—even as it enjoys their excesses), what sort of representations might be invoked to politicize the current response and inform more ethical, democratic alternatives? Or is representation itself the problem?

By posing this question of representation, we return again to Hardt and Negri, who argue that radical politics today must of necessity be unrepresentable. Accordingly, we engage their account of representation. We find that while Hardt's and Negri's *Empire* is important as an intervention seeking to specify the changed terrain of human life that we might expect to unfold, September 11 allows us to see that what democratic politics needs now more than ever, Hardt and Negri do not offer. Because they avoid the terrain of representation, the ways in which the global might be represented, or the question of what represents an act or the interests of the multitude, Hardt and Negri have not provided tools that resist the present hegemonic project of militarized response in the name of global capital, the manner in which critical voices have been discounted, how we might distinguish terrible violence from resistance to global capitalism, and how to represent or put into discourse a response that does not reiterate the injustices of the discourses enabling the current response. Strikingly, *Empire* inverts the problem of representation and the event. In their representation of September 11, Bush and Blair occlude the excesses marking the event, to say nothing of their ongoing assault on the mechanisms of representative democracy. In their embrace of the singular excesses beyond representation, Hardt and Negri occlude the significance of representation for politics, in effect redoubling the present attack on representative democracy.

Finally, we consider the various subject positions from which an ethico-political response to this event might emerge. We argue that neither the nation nor Empire or multitude is adequate to the task. Indeed, insofar as the current hegemony inspirits or substantializes Empire with its articulation of capitalism, race, and religious zeal, Hardt's and Negri's empty, fluid Empire of hybridity seems conceptually out of place. Politics and ideology have not been swept away by a multitude of productive singularities. Hardt and Negri write: "The binaries that defined modern conflict have become blurred. The Other that might delimit a modern sovereign Self has become fractured and indistinct. . . . Today it is increasingly difficult for the ideologues of the United

States to name a single, unified, enemy" (189). The hegemonization of September 11 has established new binaries, a new self, a new enemy. And precisely because of the power and the enjoyment that these certainties provide, democratic responses must turn to politics, ideology, and representation, lest we concede the field to its presently dominant formation.

## Response: Object

If the event can be expanded to include the responses to it, what sort of an event do we have? Clearly, we do not have a war, although warlike terminology has been used, though qualified in the next breath as a *new* war. The subjects of war are the sovereign powers of national states. Each exercises its sovereign right of self-defense. Here, as has been pointed out repeatedly, the situation is new and different in that there is no sovereign state subject to which the attacks can be attributed. Indeed, the rhetoric of war serves to mask a misfire— the misfire of a discourse of national sovereignty when confronted with an event that clearly exceeds its terms.

We also are not facing a police action, although this term has also been widely used—and criticized—in the context of the responsive dimension of this event. *Police*, as the term has evolved within modern political discourse, implies a force that punishes lawbreakers. Criminals, of course, must be defined in relation to a legal standard.[14] Within the hegemonic response to the event, the absence of a discourse of international law, international human rights, or international courts of justice has been notable. The Bush administration refused initially to produce evidence for its accusations against Osama bin Laden, and has continued to insist on the nonnegotiability of bin Laden's being "handed over" to the United States "dead or alive." In Europe and by Jesse Jackson in the United States, this rejection of international legality has been criticized and forms of response that would recognize established and emerging forms of international legality have been suggested.[15] These alternative proposals, however, have been excluded from the present hegemonization of the event.

What, then, do we make of terrorism and the production of the American and the "world" response in and through a discourse of counterterrorism? The proliferating discourse of terrorism and counterterrorism seems to be a return of a second side of "police," but a return that is in itself novel. Historically, the term "police," as Michel Foucault and others have taught us, involves more than just a repressive function. The police state seeks a more thoroughgoing control of society and social effects more in line with the contemporary notion of policy; that is, it is both repressive and productive. As the repressive sense continues to be linked to the concept of "police," the productive sense of police has withered and has been lost in modern political discourse. It has returned, however, in contemporary discourse, but the form of its return has been in the manner of a policy of counterterrorism.

Who or what is the object of this counterterrorism? Of course, the actual perpetrators cannot be punished—they are already dead. Responsibility, however, has been attributed to Osama bin Laden. Yet here too, the objective of counterterrorism is not limited merely to rounding him up; indeed, were that the case, it is hard to see why a full social mobilization is the best or even a coherent response. Hence, accompanying the emphasis on bin Laden as the singular object of counterterrorism is an expansion of the notion of terror to include terrorist networks modeled along the lines of global corporations. These multinational networks are well funded and well integrated via the new technologies of finance and communication.[16] At the same time, not unlike the silent partners and hidden shareholders of contemporary corporations, the terrorist networks also rely on hidden or silent members, members so hidden and silent that they are not yet terrorists. They are the "sleeper" or "dormant" terrorists who live among us, adopting "Western" practices of life, working, going to school, and generally disguising themselves as good neighbors.[17]

Yet some visual characteristics signify a racial otherness that enables the imposition of the terroristic telos upon those who live among "us." This is enabled by the identity of the barbarian—an identity that is produced by the discourse of the West versus the Rest. The articulation of the attacks with barbarism makes all those perceived to be barbarians suspect. Hence, those identified as Arab or as Muslim are presumed guilty, as we have seen in the mobilized actions of airline passengers who have refused to allow planes with Muslim passengers to take off and in media pundit John Leo's columns in *U.S. News and World Report*. Therefore Bush's policy targeting terrorism and those who harbor terrorists inevitably turns inward. This produces a constant scrutiny of those who bear the sign of "dormant" terrorist and activates a policing of points of vulnerability against an enemy who inheres within the space of the United States. Moreover, this constant and pervasive surveillance and eradication of an enemy that is potentially ever present reciprocally produces a subject counter to the barbaric terrorist—the civilized. Bush's line in the sand is not territorial in the sense of two national sovereigns involved in a boundary dispute. It is a line invoking a constant and mutual production of the civilized and the savage throughout the social circuitry. Put somewhat differently, if it is U.S. policy to attack nations that harbor terrorists, then the United States would of course have to attack itself. Indeed, this is not a paradox; rather, it is the logical extension of the signifying economy at work in the discourse and practice of counterterrorism.

## Representation

How might we contest this hegemonization of the field? The American Congress has ceded to, indeed, fully participated in, the Bush administration's representational project. This is hardly surprising. Electoral politics have been in the death grip of neoliberals and conservatives (and the latter have managed to negate those outcomes inconvenient to their interests on those rare occasions when they do arise). The media have also forfeited opportunities for critical investigation and interrogation, again unsurprisingly, given their position in a monopolized entertainment industry. Nevertheless, what is clearly necessary is a response to the current ideological formation that can criticize global capital for its neglect of human interests as well as reject the violent taking of human life. Might Hardt and Negri be helpful in this regard?

In *Empire*, Hardt and Negri suggest that the world may be witnessing the birth to presence of a force for liberation, a force they call the "multitude." Following Deleuze, they argue that disciplinary society has morphed into a society of control. Rather than being institutionally centered, domination is now widely spread throughout the social body.[18] They argue as well that processes of production have changed such that labor is communicative, linked through informational networks to engage in symbolic analyses and the manipulation of affect (30). Although these changes are part of the rise of Empire, the networks of sociality comprising contemporary society also constitute the germs of a new movement, an alternative community of social practices.[19] This is the multitude—a desiring, producing biopolitical subject that resists containment within national boundaries (205). Its revolutionary force will push through Empire and come out on the other side (394).

Hardt and Negri emphasize that the actions of the multitude are constituent rather than representational. The significance of its acts is immediately given, relying on nothing external to it (413). A "self-organized" "bio-political unity," the multitude is "absolute democracy in action" (410–411). As Hardt and Negri put it in an earlier work, the multitude is an "unrepresentable community."[20]

Discovering a manner of politics outside the order of representation is important to Hardt and Negri; they criticize the notion of sovereignty for its alienation of the multitude of singularities as it represents them in a single sovereign will (83–87). Representation disciplines multiplicity. It works in an alienating, counterrevolutionary manner to buttress modern forms of sovereignty. To escape this relation of discipline and alienation, Hardt and Negri call the multitude a community outside sovereignty.[21]

Can the multitude simply "express itself" without relying on something different from, other than, or external to itself to signify its interests?

Linguistically oriented philosophy and psychoanalytic theory have long criticized the notion that there is any such signified, self, or social entity that achieves its meaning merely through self-identity rather than through a process of differentiation, lack, and spacing.[22] Meaning is established not in identity but through relation, and the latter presumes that a space establishing differentiation is a precondition for meaning.[23] On this account, significance cannot do without the processes of representation. Indeed, representation is *constitutive* of meaning. Entities do not have preexisting primary meanings which representation either reflects or, more likely, corrupts. For Hardt and Negri, however, representation corrupts as it represses some possibilities within a plane of immanent singularities in order to present the will of the multitude as *this* rather than *that*.

In a way, then, Hardt and Negri double the death of representational politics that we see crystallized in the hegemonization of the event. This reproduces an important deficiency in left politics today. That is, while the old left pooh-poohed poststructuralist interrogations of the significance of race or gender or sexuality as meaningless for theoretical reasons or for indifference, the new right attacked poststructuralism out of fear. It *knew* that hybridity or multiculturalism, for instance, was out to get Eurocentrism, and it wanted to preserve Eurocentrism. The right, like the poststructuralist left but unlike the old left, understands full well the power of culture.[24] And to this end, the new right has outfoxed the old left, as it seems to have learned from the poststructuralist analyses in order to produce cultural values in support of its position of dominance. Countering the dominant response with a representation of the event is therefore the project to which we now turn. How can we represent the event such that a more adequate response might be implied?

## Response: Subject

These problems that encounter the representation of the response proper to the event appear at another level as well: the representation of the subject of the response, the political and ethical subject who is posited as the agent of the response. That is to say, if the form of the response suggests a shift in logic as indicated by the targeting of its practical address with its object, so too do we encounter problems at the level of the representation of an ethico-political subject position from which to launch a more adequate reply. How is an ethical response possible in the absence of a proper representational form through which it might issue?

The nation no longer provides a tenable subject position—indeed, this is part of the current dilemma of representation. Not only do the corresponding militarized responses—the attack on the Pentagon and World Trade Center, on one hand, and the Bush-Blair-led rejoinder, on the other—clearly exceed the boundaries of the national state, but so too do some of our life-enriching relations. For instance, families and friends who lost loved ones on September 11 reached out across national boundaries to find comfort and to celebrate life. Indeed, to value our families, as we are enjoined to do by the Republicans in the United States, means valuing traditions, languages, and people that exceed a single nation. Hence, to seek national enclosure for most of us would mean cutting ourselves off from that which we find most valuable.

What would a response from the standpoint of Empire entail? On the one hand, Hardt's and Negri's juridical theory of Empire posits a growing abstraction such that Empire itself is unable to mediate social conflict—on their own grounds, Empire cannot provide an ethical or political response. They write: "Empire finds it impossible to construct a system of right adequate to the new reality" (394). But on the other hand, they also discuss how "values" and "humanitarianism" facilitate extending the power and reach of Empire. In this regard, the Blair-Bush tag team of community values and military might seems exemplary of Empire. If this is the case, however, those committed to democracy and the critique of global capitalism would surely want to find another locus of ethical-political response, one that would inform the contestation and politicization of the kinds of values that produce willing subjects and active citizens, one that takes seriously the place of ideological struggle rather than sweeping it aside via the productive desire of the multitude.[25]

Was the attack on the World Trade Center and the Pentagon an act of the multitude? One might read September 11 as a strike at the virtual heart of Empire, insofar as various global industries have been substantially and detrimentally affected, various institutions have been forced to shore up the global capitalist economy financially, and some media organs have stepped up to offer renewed justifications for globalization qua global capitalization.[26] But, is this enough to consider the attacks acts of the *multitude*? And if it is, does this indicate an insufficiency on the part of the "multitude" as a position from which an ethico-political response might issue?

In their earlier work, *The Labor of Dionysus*, Hardt and Negri describe the withering of civil society in terms of the delegitimation of political power; forms of force and violence can no longer be exercised under suppositions of rightness or validity. This presumption against institutionalized forms of political power would seem to leave only nonviolent and terroristic actions as remaining modes of response. Yet they reject both of these options as well— the former because of its staged victimizations and false claims to moral purity. With these rejections, they wish to move debate beyond the question of the acceptability of violence and to investigate instead the different forms and instances of violence in order to differentiate among them.

To this end, Hardt and Negri follow Walter Benjamin's assessment that all violence is either a means of lawmaking or law-preserving. In both instances, there is "an external relation between the action (violence) and its representation (law)." The problem, then, is "how to conceive of a nonrepresentational or unrepresentable violence?" Accordingly, Hardt and Negri borrow Benjamin's invocation of "divine violence," a "revolutionary" form of violence that is "immediate" in the sense that "it does not look to anything external to itself, to any representations, for its effects." Appropriating this conceptualization, Hardt and Negri rename this divine violence "constituent power," that is to say, the "constitutive practice of the multitude."[27]

Certainly, there are effects of the event of September 11 that are beyond representation, that make it an act of "unrepresentable violence." And if the attributions of ultimate responsibility to Osama bin Laden are to be believed, we can also imagine that those who carried out the acts might claim that they were acts of "divine violence." Indeed, we hear a whisper of this justification on the part of Bush or other leaders as they rationalize the West's response. Hardt and Negri reject both terrorism and nonviolent protests because they are performances that rely on representation for their effects. But to determine whether this is an act of the multitude, the event will have to be represented. How to represent the event, what it means in terms of this or that (in other words, exploring the multiple significances of the event), and why the dominant representation is dangerous are exactly the questions that have to be asked right now. These contestations are generally understood as *politics*. But on these questions of how to differentiate (to re-present) the acts of force and violence in play around this event, *Empire* remains unresponsive.

Therefore, if we assess September 11 as an immediately subversive direct action of the multitude that has sought to evade the logic of representation, then we must say that the multitude can neither do justice to this event nor provide a position from which an ethico-political response to global capital might come. There is a pathos in the world today when two or three thousand lives identified as American (hundreds of non-Americans also lost their lives) produce global mourning but tens upon tens of thousands of deaths elsewhere due to a lack of infrastructure, medicine, health care, or armed violence fail to cause even a blink of an eye. Without taking anything away from this truth, however, there is an absolute value to human life such that the violent and unnecessary taking of it, no matter where, is a tragedy, and so we find the loss of life on September 11 to be a tragic injustice. In saying that this violent act does not represent a position from which we might better appreciate the value of human life, we must leave the terrain of the multitude. Hardt's and Negri's evasion of the problematic of representation does not give us the tools we need to do justice to the event.

## Conclusion

In this essay we consider the logic of violence at work in the totalizing mobilization to counter terrorism. It is a logic of power different from the logic of national state sovereignty. While the militarized response put into play by this logic is as dangerous as it is totalizing, we lack a position from which this event can be put into discourse for less dangerous and more adequate ends. Although it is a call to resist global capital, Hardt's and Negri's *Empire* doubles the death of representative democracy that we find in the hegemonization of the event.[28] Perhaps these parallel couplets—global capital and a globally networked violent attack; the attack on representative democracy in the presently dominant ideological formation and Hardt and Negri burying it with their advocacy of direct, nonperformative, and unrepresentable action—are indicative of a new logic of domination, the Other of which is easily construed as terrorism due to the foreclosure of representation and democracy.

In some ways, the event of September 11 can be seen as having interrupted the logic of Empire. Starbucks closed all its shops. Railroads honored air tickets. Numerous companies expressed sympathy in full-page ads. Others suspended advertising. Commercialism, now of all times, seemed crass, pointing toward something other than Empire that made its presence felt. An ethical response seems to inhere in the way that agents of Empire pressed pause on the hungry, consumptive logic that animates imperial practices.

Perhaps, then, we can recommence our response to this event and recognize it through the different light it has cast on our previously accepted practices. If some of us have found value in a manner of mourning or celebrating that crosses national lines, we might ask why this is of value, because perhaps here is a place to begin building a response. Did we help someone on September the eleventh without first investigating their home life or sexual habits? Are some of us are less enchanted with the magic of global capital's shopping malls and more enchanted with other aspects of our lives now? How did we spend our time when a promotional event was cancelled? If we are going out less or maybe in a different way from before, is there something of value in our new mode of socializing? If a capital gains tax cut in the United States has been shelved, we might ask what values this tax cut would have affronted, since the affront has been made more obvious in the wake of September 11.

And if we cheer when a firefighter or emergency medical technician passes by, is it because we recognize the gross misvaluation of them and the acts they are called upon to perform in comparison to the way that our socioeconomic system has valued the lives they were called upon to save on September 11? If so, let us use the presence of this feeling, recognizing a gift given that cannot be repaid, to inspire a more positive response, to give another gift. In other words, there are small ways in which we can commence a response, but we must also figure out if there is something that links these various responses, if there is a way to represent them coherently. Of course, making the microresponses cohere in one way will exclude other possible representations. This division is inherent to representation. It is called politics, and politics occurs in the space created by partisanship, the latter a divisive act. In such acts of divisive representation, perhaps we can construct a more adequate response.

## Notes

1. Jean-Luc Nancy, *Being Singular Plural* (Stanford, CA: Stanford University Press, 2000), 173.

2. In an editorial in the *Los Angeles Times*, October 1, 2001.

3. Quoted in "A Global Outpouring of Grief and Solidarity," *International Herald Tribune*, September 15–16, 2001, 1.

4. Paul A. Passavant, *No Escape: Freedom of Speech and the Paradox of Rights* (New York: New York University Press, 2002), chaps. 2 and 3.

5. Peter Beinart, "Sidelines," *New Republic*, September 24, 2001, 8.

6. Beinart relies on a review by Alan Wolfe, "The Snake," *The New Republic*, October 1, 2001, 31–37. Wolfe finds nothing laudable or even coherent in *Empire*. Indeed, his review is such a blanket rejection that it is impossible to take seriously. A more informed treatment comes from Malcolm Bull, "You Can't Build a New Society with a Stanley Knife," *London Review of Books*, October 4, 2001, 3–7. Both reviews link *Empire* to September 11.

7. For a discussion of the quilting together of an ideological field, see Slavoj Žižek, *The Sublime Object of Ideology* (London: Verso, 1989); and Ernesto Laclau and Chantal Mouffe, *Hegemony and Socialist Strategy* (London: Verso, 1985).

8. For a detailed genealogical analysis of the invocations of political correctness in the consolidation of an American identity, see Passavant, *No Escape*, chap. 5.

9. Žižek emphasizes the role of enjoyment in the production of an ideological formation. See *Sublime Object*, esp. chap. 3.

10. Michael Hardt and Antonio Negri, *Empire* (Cambridge, MA: Harvard University Press, 2000).

11. For a discussion of power's obscene supplement, see Slavoj Žižek, *The Plague of Fantasies* (London: Verso, 1997), esp. 26–27.

12. Hardt and Negri write:

> Today military intervention is progressively less a product of decisions that arise out of the old international order or even U.N. structures. More often it is dictated unilaterally by the United States, which charges itself with the primary task and then subsequently asks its allies to set in motion a process of armed containment and/or repression of the current enemy of Empire. These enemies are most often called terrorist, a crude conceptual and terminological reduction that is rooted in a police mentality. (37)

13. Drawing from Claude Lefort and Ernesto Laclau, Slavoj Žižek conceives the political "as the moment of opennes, of undecidability, when the very structuring principle of society, the fundamental form of the social pact, is called into question"; Žižek, *For They Know Not What They Do* (London: Verso, 1991), 193. See also Yannis Stavrakakis's insightful discussion of politics and the political in *Lacan and the Political* (New York: Routledge, 1999), 71–75.

14. Or, conversely, as Žižek has argued, the very legal standard itself stems from crime's reflexive self-relation; see *For They Know Not What They Do*, 33–42.

15. Geoffrey Robertson, "Lynch Mob Justice or a Proper Trial," *The Guardian*, October 5, 2001, 22.

16. See the account of the Bush administration's "list" of prominent financial backers of al-Qaeda as well as discussion of the role of international financial institutions in providing support to Osama bin

Laden; Joseph Kahn and Judith Miller, "Saudi and Pakastani Assets Cited for Ties to bin Laden," *New York Times*, October 13, 2001, 1ff.

17. On "sleeper terrorists," see John Schmid and Barry James, "French Hold 7 on Terror Suspicions," *International Herald Tribune*, September 22–23, 2001, 1ff.

18. Gilles Deleuze, "Control and Becoming," and "Postscript on Control Societies," *Negotiations 1972–1990*, trans. Martin Joughin, (New York: Columbia University Press, 1995); Michael Hardt, "The Withering of Civil Society," in Eleanor Kaufman and Kevin Jon Heller, eds., *Deleuze & Guattari: New Mappings in Politics, Philosophy, and Culture* (Minneapolis: University of Minnesota Press, 1998); *Empire*, 22–25.

19. Hardt, "Withering," 37.

20. Michael Hardt and Antonio Negri, *The Labor of Dionysus: A Critique of the State Form* (Minneapolis: University of Minnesota Press, 1994), 295.

21. *Labor of Dionysus*, 308.

22. Jacques Derrida, *Of Grammatology*, trans. Gayatri Spivak (Baltimore, MD: Johns Hopkins University Press, 1976).

23. See Nancy, *Being Singular Plural*.

24. For discussions emphasizing the interconnections between political theory and cultural representations, with particular attention to ways that these interconnections have been put to use for conservative ends, see the contributions to *Cultural Studies and Political Theory*, ed. Jodi Dean (Ithaca, NY: Cornell University Press, 2000).

25. Indeed, one might even say that insofar as Hardt and Negri see "every limit of liberty" as an "obstacle to be overcome, a threshold to pass through" in the very emergence of the American Constitution as a constitutive network of powers and counterpowers, it seems clear that antipathy toward Islamic fundamentalism would accompany the further intensification of Empire; *Empire*, 167.

26. "Global Media Concerns Deepen: Companies Warn of Sharp Drop in Advertising after Terrorist Attacks," *Financial Times*, October 3, 2001, 17; "The Case for Globalisation," and "The Hubris of the West: Is Globalisation Doomed?" *The Economist*, September 29–October 5, 2001, cover and 14.

27. *Labor of Dionysus*, 290–295. Walter Benjamin had called this "Sovereign Violence." See Walter Benjamin, "Critique of Violence," in *One-Way Street and Other Writings*, trans. Edmund Jephcott and Kingsley Shorter (London: New Left Books, 1979), 154. This renaming disturbs the absolute separation between constituent and constituted power that Hardt and Negri advocate.

28. Jacques Derrida, "Force of Law: The 'Mystical Foundation of Authority,'" in Drucilla Cornell, Michel Rosenfeld, and David Gray Carlson, eds. *Deconstruction and the Possibility of Justice* (New York: Routledge, 1992), contextualizes Benjamin's piece, which Hardt and Negri appropriate, as a "critique of representation not only as a perversion and fall of language, but as a political system of formal and parliamentary democracy. From that point of view, this revolutionary essay . . . belongs, in 1921, to the great anti-parliamentary and anti-'*Aufklärung*' wave on which Nazism so to speak surfaced and even surfed in the 1920s and the beginning of the 1930s" (64, n. 6).

# Contributors

**Ruth Buchanan** is an Associate Professor at the Faculty of Law, University of British Columbia. She is currently engaged in a research project on "global civil society," antiglobalization protest, and international economic institutions. Recent publications include "Collaboration, Cosmopolitanism and Complicity," *Nordic Journal of International Law* (part of an ongoing collaboration with Sundhya Pahuja); "Feminized Work, New Technologies and Hope," *University of New Brunswick Law Journal*; and "Lives on the Line: Low Wage Work in the Teleservice Economy," in *Laboring below the Line: The New Ethnography of Poverty, Low Wage Work and Survival in the Global Economy*, edited by F. Munger (2002).

**Malcolm Bull** is a Fellow of St. Edmund Hall, Oxford, and, during 2003–2004, a Getty Scholar. The author of *Seeing Things Hidden* (2000), he is currently writing a book against Nietzsche.

**William Chaloupka** is Chair and Professor of Political Science at Colorado State University. His books include *Everybody Knows: Cynicism in America* and, coedited with Jane Bennett, *In the Nature of Things: Language, Politics, and the Environment*. Chaloupka helped found and is currently coeditor of *Theory & Event*, an international journal of political and cultural theory published online by Project Muse and the Johns Hopkins University Press.

**Jodi Dean** teaches political theory at Hobart and William Smith Colleges, where she is Chair of the Department of Political Science. She is the author of *Solidarity of Strangers: Feminism after Identity Politics* (1996), *Aliens in America: From Outerspace to Cyberspace* (1998), and *Publicity's Secret: How Technoculture Capitalizes on Democracy* (2002). She has edited *Feminism and the New Democracy* (1997) and *Cultural Studies and Political Theory* (2000). She serves on the *Theory & Event* editorial board.

**Thomas L. Dumm** is the author of several books, including, most recently, *A Politics of the Ordinary*. He served as founding coeditor of *Theory & Event*. He is currently writing a book about loneliness.

**Kevin C. Dunn** is author of *Imagining the Congo: The International Relations of Identity* (2003) and coeditor of *Africa's Challenge to International Relations Theory* (with Timothy M. Shaw, 2001) and *Identity and Global Politics: Theoretical and Empirical Elaborations* (with Patricia Goff, forthcoming in 2004). He is currently Assistant Professor of Political Science at Hobart and William Smith Colleges and Visiting Professor in the Faculty of Development Studies at Mbarara University of Science and Technology, Uganda.

**Peter Fitzpatrick** is Anniversary Professor of Law at Birkbeck, University of London and has taught at universities in Europe, North America, and Papua New Guinea. He has published works on law and social theory, law and racism, and imperialism, the most recent one being *Modernism and the Grounds of Law*. Outside the academy, he has been in an international legal practice and also worked in the Prime Minister's Office in Papua New Guinea for several years.

**Michael Hardt** is Associate Professor of Literature at Duke University. He is author of *Gilles Deleuze* and co-author with Antonio Negri of *Labor of Dionysus* and *Empire*.

**Ernesto Laclau** is Professor of Politics at the University of Essex and Professor in the Department of Comparative Literature at the University at Buffalo. His many publications include *Hegemony and Socialist Strategy* (with Chantal Mouffe), *New Reflections on the Revolution of our Time*, *Emancipation(s)*, *The Making of Political Identities* (editor and contributor), and *Contingency, Hegemony, Universality* (with Judith Butler and Slavoj Žižek).

**Mark Laffey** is Lecturer in International Politics, Department of Political Studies, School of Oriental and African Studies, University of London and an Associate Fellow of the Royal Institute of International Affairs. He has published in the European Journal of International Relations, *Millennium: Journal of International Studies*, and *Review of International Studies*, among others. He is coeditor of *Democracy, Liberalism and War: Rethinking the Democratic Peace Debate* (2001).

**Bill Maurer** is Associate Professor of Anthropology at the University of California, Irvine. He is the author of *Recharting the Caribbean: Land, Law and Citizenship in the British Virgin Islands* and coeditor of *Gender Matters: Re-Reading Michelle Z. Rosaldo.* He is also coeditor of *Globalization under Construction: Governmentality, Law, and Identity* (forthcoming).

**Paul A. Passavant** is the author of *No Escape: Freedom of Speech and the Paradox of Rights* (2002) and numerous essays on law and social identities. He teaches in the Department of Political Science at Hobart and William Smith Colleges.

**Sundhya Pahuja** is a Senior Lecturer in the Law School at the University of Melbourne and a Ph.D. candidate at Birkbeck College, University of London. Recent publications include "Collaboration, Cosmopolitanism and Complicity," *Nordic Journal of International Law* (part of an ongoing collaborative project with Ruth Buchanan), "Globalization and International Economic Law," in *Jurisprudence for an Interconnected Globe*, edited by Catherine Dauvergne, and "Global Formations: IMF Conditionality and the South as Legal Subject," in *Critical Beings: Race, Nation and the Global Legal Subject*, edited by Peter Fitzpatrick and Patricia Tuitt.

**Lee Quinby** holds the Donald R. Harter '39 Chair for Distinguished Teaching in Humanities at Hobart and William Smith Colleges. From 1999 to 2001, she held the Visiting Distinguished Chair on the Millennium at the Rochester Institute of Technology. She is the author of three books: *Millennial Seduction* (1999), *Anti-Apocalypse* (1994), and *Freedom, Foucault, and the Subject of America* (1991). She is editor of *Genealogy and Literature* (1995) and coeditor of *Feminism and Foucault* (1987).

**Saskia Sassen** is the Ralph Lewis Professor of Sociology at the University of Chicago and Centennial Visiting Professor at the London School of Economics. She is currently completing *Denationalization: Territory, Authority and Rights in a Global Digital Age* (forthcoming) based on her five-year project on governance and accountability in a global economy. Her most recent books are *Guests and Aliens* (1999) and the edited *Global Networks, Linked Cities* (Routledge, 2002). She is a Member of the National Academy of Sciences Panel on Cities, a Member of the Council on Foreign Relations, and Chair of the new Information Technology, International Cooperation and Global Security Committee of the Social Science Research Council (USA).

**Kam Shapiro** received his doctorate in political science from Johns Hopkins University. He is an Assistant Professor in the Department of Politics and Government at Illinois State University. He is the author of *Sovereign Nations, Carnal States* (2003).

**Jutta Weldes** is a Senior Lecturer in International Relations at the University of Bristol. She is the author of *Constructing National Interests: The United States and the Cuban Missile Crisis* (1999), coeditor of *Cultures of Insecurity: States, Communities, and the Production of Danger* (1999), and editor of *To Seek Out New Worlds: Science Fiction and World Politics* (2003).

**Slavoj Žižek** is Senior Researcher at the Institute for Social Studies, Ljubljana, Slovenia. His many books include *The Ticklish Subject* (1999), *The Fragile Absolute* (2000), *Did Somebody Say Totalitarianism* (2001), and, most recently, *Revolution at the Gates* and *Welcome to the Desert of the Real* (both 2002).

# Index